DATE DUE

DEMCO 128-5046

SOMETHING ABOUT THE AUTHOR®

Something about
the Author *was named
an "**Outstanding
Reference Source**,"
the highest honor given
by the American
Library Association
Reference and User
Services Association.*

ISSN 0276-816X

SOMETHING ABOUT THE AUTHOR®

Facts and Pictures about Authors
and Illustrators of Books for Young People

EDITED BY
ALAN HEDBLAD

VOLUME 105

The Gale Group

STAFF

Editor: Alan Hedblad

...aphy Features Coordinator: Motoko Fujishiro Huthwaite
...ociate Editors: Sara L. Constantakis, Melissa Hill

Contributing Editors: Sheryl Ciccarelli, Catherine Goldstein, Maria Job, Arlene M. Johnson

Editorial Technical Specialist: Karen Uchic

Managing Editor: Joyce Nakamura
Publisher: Hal May

Research Manager: Victoria B. Cariappa
Project Coordinator: Cheryl L. Warnock
Research Associates: Patricia Tsune Ballard, Tamara C. Nott, Tracie A. Richardson
Research Assistants: Phyllis Blackman, Tim Lehnerer

Permissions Manager: Maria L. Franklin
Permissions Associates: Sarah Chesney, Edna Hedblad, Michele Lonoconus

Production Director: Mary Beth Trimper
Production Assistant: Deborah Milliken

Graphic Artist: Gary Leach
Image Database Supervisor: Randy Bassett
Imaging Specialists: Robert Duncan, Michael Logusz
Imaging Coordinator: Pamela A. Reed

Library of Congress Catalog Card Number 72-27107

ISBN 0-7876-2126-9
ISSN 0276-816X

Printed in the United States of America

10 9 8 7 6 5 4 3 2 1

Contents

Authors in Forthcoming Volumes

Below are some of the authors and illustrators that will be featured in upcoming volumes of *SATA*. These include new entries on the swiftly rising stars of the field, as well as completely revised and updated entries (indicated with *) on some of the most notable and best-loved creators of books for children.

*David A. Adler: A prolific, award-winning author, Adler is best known for his picture-book biographies and the popular "Cam Jansen" mystery series, as well as books on Holocaust and Jewish studies.

*Natalie Babbitt: Babbitt is the author and illustrator of the celebrated *Tuck Everlasting* and the Newbery Honor Book *Kneeknock Rise*. Her recent efforts include the self-illustrated *Bub, or, The Very Best Thing*, and *Ouch!*, her retelling of a Grimm Brothers fairy tale.

Henrietta Branford: Branford's novel *Fire, Bed and Bone*, critically acclaimed in both her native England and the United States, was shortlisted for the Carnegie Medal in 1997 and received a *Guardian* Award in 1998.

Nick Butterworth: Best known for his "Percy the Park Keeper" series, Butterworth has also collaborated with fellow English author and illustrator Mick Inkpen on the popular "Mice of Upney Junction" comic strip, as well as the picture books *Just Like Jasper* and *Jasper's Beanstalk*.

John R. Horner: A celebrated paleontologist, Horner has published several books for children on the ever-popular subject of dinosaurs, including *Maia: A Dinosaur Grows Up* and *Digging Up Tyrannosaurus Rex*.

*Mollie Hunter: Often considered Scotland's most distinguished writer for children and young adults, Hunter is celebrated as the author of powerful, memorable novels and stories which profile Scotland in both historical and contemporary times. A Carnegie Medal-winner for *The Stronghold*, Hunter's most recent efforts include *Gilly Martin the Fox* and *The King's Swift Rider*.

Marisabina Russo: Author and illustrator Russo has won praise for her simple, direct storylines and colorful gouache paintings. In addition to her self-illustrated texts, including *A Visit to Oma* and *When Mama Gets Home*, she has also provided the artwork for such books as Nancy Van Laan's *The Big Fat Worm* and *Good-Bye, Curtis*, by Kevin Henkes.

*Uri Shulevitz: Celebrated Polish-born author and illustrator Shulevitz, winner of the 1969 Caldecott Medal for *The Fool of the World and the Flying Ship*, has garnered a host of honors for his most recent effort, the picture book *Snow*. Praised for the thoughtful and illuminating detail of its illustrations, *Snow* earned Shulevitz the Charlotte Zolotow Award in 1999.

Herma Silverstein: With a number of nonfiction titles to her credit, Silverstein focuses in particular on topics of vital interest to today's teens, including date rape, teen pregnancy, and depression.

*Peter Sis: Two of Sis's latest efforts, *Starry Messenger: Galileo Galilei* and *Tibet: Through the Red Box*, have been named Caldecott Honor Books.

*Thomas Ungerer: A prolific author and illustrator as well as a painter, cartoonist, sculptor, poster artist, and publisher, Ungerer uses his works to present sharp, unsentimental views of humanity. His most recent efforts for children include *Flix* and *Tortoni Tremolo the Cursed Musician*.

Tatjana Wassiljewa: Wassiljewa grew up in Nazi-occupied Leningrad, and was sent to a German work camp as a young girl. Her memoir, *Hostage to War*, describes vividly the terrible plight she and other Soviet prisoners endured during the war years.

Valerie Wilson Wesley: Wesley is the author of the popular "Tamara Hayle" mystery novels featuring black private investigator Hayle, a single parent and ex-cop from the tough streets of Newark, New Jersey.

Introduction

Something about the Author (*SATA*) is an ongoing reference series that examines the lives and works of authors and illustrators of books for children. *SATA* includes not only well-known writers and artists but also less prominent individuals whose works are just coming to be recognized. This series is often the only readily available information source on emerging authors and illustrators. You'll find *SATA* informative and entertaining, whether you are a student, a librarian, an English teacher, a parent, or simply an adult who enjoys children's literature.

What's Inside SATA

SATA provides detailed information about authors and illustrators who span the full time range of children's literature, from early figures like John Newbery and L. Frank Baum to contemporary figures like Judy Blume and Richard Peck. Authors in the series represent primarily English-speaking countries, particularly the United States, Canada, and the United Kingdom. Also included, however, are authors from around the world whose works are available in English translation. The writings represented in *SATA* include those created intentionally for children and young adults as well as those written for a general audience and known to interest younger readers. These writings cover the entire spectrum of children's literature, including picture books, humor, folk and fairy tales, animal stories, mystery and adventure, science fiction and fantasy, historical fiction, poetry and nonsense verse, drama, biography, and nonfiction.

Obituaries are also included in *SATA* and are intended not only as death notices but also as concise overviews of people's lives and work. Additionally, each edition features newly revised and updated entries for a selection of *SATA* listees who remain of interest to today's readers and who have been active enough to require extensive revisions of their earlier biographies.

New Autobiography Feature

Beginning with Volume 103, *Something about the Author* will feature three or more specially commissioned autobiographical essays in each volume. These unique essays, averaging about ten thousand words in length and illustrated with an abundance of personal photos, present an entertaining and informative first-person perspective on the lives and careers of prominent authors and illustrators profiled in *SATA*.

Two Convenient Indexes

In response to suggestions from librarians, *SATA* indexes no longer appear in every volume but are included in alternate (odd-numbered) volumes of the series, beginning with Volume 57.

SATA continues to include two indexes that cumulate with each alternate volume: the Illustrations Index, arranged by the name of the illustrator, gives the number of the volume and page where the illustrator's work appears in the current volume as well as all preceding volumes in the series; the Author Index gives the number of the volume in which a person's biographical sketch, autobiographical essay, or obituary appears in the current volume as well as all preceding volumes in the series.

These indexes also include references to authors and illustrators who appear in Gale's *Yesterday's Authors of Books for Children, Children's Literature Review,* and *Something about the Author Autobiography Series.*

Easy-to-Use Entry Format

Whether you're already familiar with the *SATA* series or just getting acquainted, you will want to be aware of the kind of information that an entry provides. In every *SATA* entry the editors attempt to give as complete a picture of the person's life and work as possible. A typical entry in *SATA* includes the following clearly labeled information sections:

- *PERSONAL:* date and place of birth and death, parents' names and occupations, name of spouse, date of marriage, names of children, educational institutions attended, degrees received, religious and political affiliations, hobbies and other interests.

- *ADDRESSES:* complete home, office, electronic mail, and agent addresses, whenever available.

- *CAREER:* name of employer, position, and dates for each career post; art exhibitions; military service; memberships and offices held in professional and civic organizations.

- *AWARDS, HONORS:* literary and professional awards received.

- *WRITINGS:* title-by-title chronological bibliography of books written and/or illustrated, listed by genre when known; lists of other notable publications, such as plays, screenplays, and periodical contributions.

- *ADAPTATIONS:* a list of films, television programs, plays, CD-ROMs, recordings, and other media presentations that have been adapted from the author's work.

- *WORK IN PROGRESS:* description of projects in progress.

- *SIDELIGHTS:* a biographical portrait of the author or illustrator's development, either directly from the biographee—and often written specifically for the *SATA* entry—or gathered from diaries, letters, interviews, or other published sources.

- *FOR MORE INFORMATION SEE:* references for further reading.

- *EXTENSIVE ILLUSTRATIONS:* photographs, movie stills, book illustrations, and other interesting visual materials supplement the text.

How a SATA Entry Is Compiled

A *SATA* entry progresses through a series of steps. If the biographee is living, the *SATA* editors try to secure information directly from him or her through a questionnaire. From the information that the biographee supplies, the editors prepare an entry, filling in any essential missing details with research and/or telephone interviews. If possible, the author or illustrator is sent a copy of the entry to check for accuracy and completeness.

If the biographee is deceased or cannot be reached by questionnaire, the *SATA* editors examine a wide variety of published sources to gather information for an entry. Biographical and bibliographic sources are consulted, as are book reviews, feature articles, published interviews, and material sometimes obtained from the biographee's family, publishers, agent, or other associates.

Entries that have not been verified by the biographees or their representatives are marked with an asterisk (*).

Contact the Editor

We encourage our readers to examine the entire *SATA* series. Please write and tell us if we can make *SATA* even more helpful to you. Give your comments and suggestions to the editor:

BY MAIL: Editor, *Something about the Author,* The Gale Group, 27500 Drake Rd., Farmington Hills, MI 48331-3535.

BY TELEPHONE: (800) 347-GALE

BY FAX: (248) 699-8065

Acknowledgments

Grateful acknowledgment is made to the following publishers, authors, and artists whose works appear in this volume.

BEAR, GREG. Barlowe, Wayne, illustrator. From a cover of *Moving Mars,* by Greg Bear. Tor Books, 1993. Reproduced by permission. / Eggleton, Bob, illustrator. From a cover of *Legacy,* by Greg Bear. Tor Books, 1995. Reproduced by permission. / DiTerlizzi, Tony, illustrator. From an illustration in *Dinosaur Summer,* by Greg Bear. Warner Books, 1998. Illustrations © 1998 by Tony DiTerlizzi. Reproduced by permission.

BLAISDELL, ROBERT E. Blaisdell, Robert E., illustration by Robert E. Blaisdell. Reproduced by permission of Robert E. Blaisdell.

BOWMAN, CRYSTAL. Bowman, Crystal, photograph by Glamour Shots. © Glamour Shots. Reproduced by permission.

BROOME, ERROL. Patrick, Pamela, illustrator. From a jacket of *Tangles,* by Errol Broome. Knopf, 1994. Jacket art © 1994 by Pamela Patrick. Reproduced by permission of Alfred A. Knopf, Inc. / Cover of *Splashback: A Great Greasy Journey,* by Errol Broome. Allen & Unwin, 1996. Reproduced by permission. / Broome, Errol, photograph. Reproduced by permission of Errol Broome.

BROWN, RUTH. Brown, Ruth, illustrator. From an illustration in *Tale of the Monstrous Toad,* by Ruth Brown. Andersen Press, Ltd., 1996. © 1996 by Ruth Brown. Reproduced by permission. / Brown, Ruth, illustrator. From an illustration in *Baba,* by Ruth Brown. Andersen Press, Ltd., 1997. © 1997 by Ruth Brown. Reproduced by permission. / Brown, Ruth, illustrator. From an illustration in *The Wise Doll,* retold by Hiawyn Oram. Andersen Press, Ltd., 1997. Text © 1997 by Hiawyn Oram. Illustrations © 1997 by Ruth Brown. Reproduced by permission. / Brown, Ruth, photograph. Reproduced by permission of Ruth Brown.

BROWNE, ANTHONY. Browne, Anthony, illustrator. From an illustration in *Gorilla,* by Anthony Browne. Knopf, 1983. Copyright © 1983 by Anthony Browne. Reproduced by permission of Alfred A. Knopf, Inc. / Browne, Anthony, illustrator. From an illustration in *The Daydreamer,* by Ian McEwan. HarperCollins, 1994. Illustrations © 1994 by Anthony Browne. Reproduced by permission of HarperCollins Publishers. / Browne, Anthony, illustrator. From an illustration in *Voices in the Park,* by Anthony Browne. DK Ink Books, 1998. © 1998 A.E.T. Browne and Partners. Reproduced by permission. / Browne, Anthony, illustrator. From an illustration in *Willy the Dreamer,* by Anthony Browne. Walker Books Ltd., 1997, Candlewick Press, 1998. © 1997 by Anthony Browne. Reproduced by permission of Walker Books Ltd. In the U.S. by Candlewick Press Inc., Cambridge, MA. / Browne, Anthony, photograph by Ellen Browne. Reproduced by permission of Anthony Browne.

CALDER, DAVID. Calder, David, photograph. Reproduced by permission of Wanganui Newspapers.

CARAHER, KIM. Caraher, Kim, photograph. Reproduced by permission of Kim Caraher.

CARRIER, ROCH. Cohen, Sheldon, illustrator. From an illustration in *The Hockey Sweater,* by Roch Carrier. Tundra Books, 1984. Illustrations © 1984 Sheldon Cohen. Reproduced by permission. / Cohen, Sheldon, illustrator. From an illustration in *Un Champion,* by Roch Carrier. Livres Toundra/GRANDIR, 1991. Illustrations © 1991 by Sheldon Cohen. Reproduced by permission. / Carrier, Roch, 1991, photograph by Randy Velocci. *The Globe and Mail,* Toronto. Reproduced by permission of *The Globe and Mail.*

CATO, HEATHER. Cato, Heather, photograph. Reproduced by permission of Heather Cato.

CHAMBERLIN, KATHRYN. Chamberlin, Kathryn, photograph. Reproduced by permission of Kathryn Chamberlin.

CONNOLLY, PETER. Cover of *Pompeii,* by Peter Connolly. Oxford University Press, 1990. Reproduced by permission of Werner Forman Archive. / City of Troy, illustration by Peter Connolly. Reproduced by permission of Peter Connolly.

DILLON, EILIS. All images reproduced by permission of the Literary Estate of Eilis Dillon.

HARPER, PIERS. Harper, Piers, illustrator. From an illustration in *If You Love a Bear,* by Piers Harper. Walker Books Ltd., 1998, Candlewick Press, 1998. © 1998 by Piers Harper. Reproduced by permission of Walker Books Ltd. In the U.S. by Candlewick Press Inc., Cambridge, MA. / Harper, Piers, photograph. Reproduced by permission of Piers Harper.

HARRIS, CHRISTINE. Scannell, Reece, photographer. From a jacket of *Fortune Cookies,* by Christine Harris. Mark Macleod Books, 1998. Reproduced by permission of Random House Australia. / Harris, Christine, photograph by Steve Kadis. Reproduced by permission of Christine Harris.

HASELEY, DENNIS. Jacket of *Shadows,* by Dennis Haseley. Farrar, 1991. Reproduced by permission of Farrar, Straus & Giroux, Inc. / Elliot, Mark, illustrator. From a jacket of *Getting Him,* by Dennis Haseley. Farrar, 1994. Jacket art © 1994 by Mark Elliot. Reproduced by permission of Farrar, Straus & Giroux, Inc. / Green, Jonathan, illustrator. From an illustration in *Crosby,* by Dennis Haseley. Harcourt, 1996. Illustrations © 1996 by Jonathan Green. Reproduced by permission of Harcourt Brace & Company. / Haseley, Dennis, photograph. Reproduced by permission of Dennis Haseley.

HASKINS, JAMES S. Karp, Cindy, photographer. From a cover of *Colin Powell: A Biography,* by Jim Haskins. Scholastic Inc., 1995. Cover photograph © 1995 Cindy Karp, Black Star. Reproduced by permission of Scholastic Inc. and Black Star Publishing Company, Inc. / Cover of *Count Your Way through Brazil,* by Jim Haskins and Kathleen Benson. Carolrhoda Books, Inc., 1996. Reproduced by permission. / Lewis, Reginald, painting by John C. Ward. Spike, Lee, photograph. AP/Wide World Photos. Johnson, John H., photograph. AP/Wide World Photos. Bragg, Janet Harmon, photograph. National Air and Space Museum, Smithsonian Institute. From a jacket of *Black Stars: African American Entrepreneurs,* by Jim Haskins. John Wiley & Sons, 1998. Reproduced by permission. / Haskins, James S., photograph by George Buchanan. Reproduced by permission of James S. Haskins.

HIGGINS, SIMON. Higgins, Simon, photograph by Annie E. Studios. Reproduced by permission of Simon Higgins.

HILTON, NETTE. Aldridge, George, illustrator. From an illustration in *The Friday Card,* by Nette Hilton. William Collins Pty. Ltd., 1989. Illustrations © George Aldridge 1989. Reproduced by permission. / Power, Margaret, illustrator. From an illustration in *The Long Red Scarf,* by Nette Hilton. Omnibus Books, 1987. Illustrations © 1987 by Margaret Power. Reproduced by permission of Scholastic Australia Pty. Ltd. / Wilcox, Cathy, illustrator. From an illustration in *Andrew Jessup,* by Nette Hilton. Walter McVitty Books, 1992. Illustrations © 1992 by Cathy Wilcox. Reproduced by permission. / Millard, Kerry, illustrator. From an illustration in *The Web,* by Nette Hilton. Angus & Robertson, 1992. Illustrations © 1992 by Kerry Millard. Reproduced by permission. / Hilton, Nette, photograph. Reproduced by permission of Nette Hilton.

HOGG, GARY. Hogg, Gary, photograph. Reproduced by permission of Gary Hogg.

HOOK, BRENDAN. Hook, Brendan, photograph. Reproduced by permission of Brendan Hook.

ISLE, SUE. Isle, Sue, photograph by Michelle Stanley. © Post Newspapers Pty. Ltd. Reproduced by permission.

KING, JEANETTE. King, Jeanette, photograph. Photographic Services, University of Canterbury. Reproduced by permission of Jeanette King.

KOPPER, LISA. Kopper, Lisa, illustrator. Illustration from *I'm a Baby, You're a Baby,* by Lisa Kopper. Hamish Hamilton Ltd., 1994. © Lisa Kopper, 1994. Reproduced by permission of Penguin Books, Ltd. / Kopper, Lisa, illustrator. Illustration from *Daisy Is a Mummy,* by Lisa Kopper. Hamish Hamilton, 1996. Published in the United States as *Daisy Is a Mommy.* Dutton Children's Books, 1997. © 1996 by Lisa Kopper. Reproduced by permission of Penguin Books, Ltd. / Kopper, Lisa, photograph by Caroline Mardon. Reproduced by permission of Penguin Books, Ltd.

LaFAYE, ALEXANDRIA R. T. Ascensios, Natalie, illustrator. From a jacket of *The Year of the Sawdust Man,* by A. LaFaye. Simon & Schuster Books for Young Readers, 1998. Jacket illustration © 1998 by Natalie Ascensios. Reproduced by permission of the illustrator. / LaFaye, Alexandria R. T., photograph by Charles Edward Taylor III. Reproduced by permission of A. LaFaye.

LANE, DAKOTA. Joern, James, and Michel Legrou, illustrators. From a cover of *Johnny Voodoo,* by Dakota Lane. Laurel-Leaf Books, 1996. Reproduced by permission of Random House Children's Books, a division of Random House, Inc. / Lane, Dakota, photograph by Alex Kamin. Reproduced by permission of Dakota Lane.

MAZER, ANNE. Harston, Jerry, illustrator. From an illustration in *Goldfish Charlie and the Case of the Missing Planet,* by Anne Mazer. Troll, 1996. Cover and interior illustrations © 1996 by Troll Communications L.L.C. Reproduced by permission. / Mazer, Anne, photograph by Robert Stark. Reproduced by permission of Anne Mazer.

MAZER, HARRY. Cover of *Who Is Eddie Leonard?* by Harry Mazer. Laurel-Leaf Books, 1995. Reproduced by permission of Random House Children's Books, a division of Random House, Inc. / Buzelli, Christopher, illustrator. From a cover of *The Dog in the Freezer,* by Harry Mazer. Simon & Schuster Books for Young Readers, 1997. Cover illustration © 1997 by Christopher Buzelli. Reproduced by permission of the illustrator. / Lanino, Deborah, illustrator. From a jacket of *The Wild Kid,* by Harry Mazer. Simon & Schuster Books for Young Readers, 1998. Jacket illustration © 1998 by Deborah Lanino. Reproduced by permission of the illustrator. / Mazer, Harry, photograph by Ruth Putter. Reproduced by permission.

MAZER, NORMA FOX. Cover of *Out of Control,* by Norma Fox Mazer. Avon Flare Books, 1994. Reproduced by permission of Avon Books, Inc. / Gallagher, S. Saelig, illustrator. From a jacket of *When She Was Good,* by Norma Fox Mazer. Arthur A. Levine Books, 1997. Jacket art © 1997 by S. Saelig Gallagher. Reproduced by permission of Scholastic Inc. / Sayles, Elizabeth, illustrator. From a jacket of *Crazy Fish,* by Norma Fox Mazer. Morrow Junior Books, 1998. Jacket illustration © 1998 by Elizabeth Sayles. Reproduced by permission of Morrow Junior Books, a division of William Morrow and Company, Inc. / Mazer, Norma Fox, photograph by Darkroom on Wheels. Reproduced by permission of Norma Fox Mazer.

McLAREN, CLEMENCE. Harrison, Mark, illustrator. From a cover of *Inside the Walls of Troy: A Novel of the Women Who Lived the Trojan War,* by Clemence McLaren. Laurel-Leaf Books, 1996. Reproduced by permission of Random House Children's Books, a division of Random House, Inc.

NOLEN, JERDINE. Buehner, Mark, illustrator. From an illustration in *Harvey Potter's Balloon Farm,* by Jerdine Nolen. Mulberry Books, 1994. Illustrations © 1994 by Mark Buehner. Reproduced by permission of Lothrop, Lee & Shepard Books, a division of William Morrow & Company, Inc. / Primavera, Elise, illustrator. From an illustration in *Raising Dragons,* by Jerdine Nolen. Silver Whistle, 1998. Text © 1998 by Jerdine Nolen. Illustrations © 1998 by Elise Primavera. Reproduced by permission of Harcourt Brace & Company. / Nolen, Jerdine, photograph. Reproduced by permission of Jerdine Nolen.

PERERA, HILDA. Lartitegui, Ana G., illustrator. From an illustration in *Javi,* by Hilda Perera. Editorial Everest, S.A., 1997. © Editorial Everest, S. A. Reproduced by permission. / Perera, Hilda, photograph. Reproduced by permission of Hilda Perera.

REES, LESLIE. Rees, Leslie, photograph. Reproduced by permission of Leslie Rees.

ROBINSON, SUSAN MARIA. Robinson, Susan Maria, photograph. Reproduced by permission of Susan Maria Robinson.

ROCHMAN, HAZEL. Rodin, Christine, photographer. From a cover of *Who Do You Think You Are? Stories of Friends and Enemies,* compiled by Hazel Rochman and Darlene Z. McCampbell. Little, Brown and Company, 1993. Reproduced by permission. / Reese, Donovan, photographer. From a cover of *Leaving Home: 15 Distinguished Authors Explore Personal Journeys,* stories selected by Hazel Rochman and Darlene Z. McCampbell. Cover photograph © 1998 by Tony Stone Images/Donovan Reese. Cover © 1988 by HarperCollins Publishers. Reproduced by permission of HarperCollins Publishers. / Rochman, Hazel, photograph by Henrietta Smith. Reproduced by permission of Hazel Rochman.

RUBINSTEIN, GILLIAN. Weiman, Jon, illustrator. From a jacket of *Skymaze,* by Gillian Rubinstein. Orchard Books, 1991. Jacket illustration copyright © 1991 by Jon Weiman. Reproduced by permission of the illustrator. / Pendola, Joanne, illustrator. From a cover of *Galax-Arena,* by Gillian Rubinstein. Aladdin Paperbacks, 1997. Cover illustration © 1995 by Joanne Pendola. Reproduced by permission of the illustrator. / Lee, Victor, illustrator. From a jacket of *Under the Cat's Eye: A Tale of Morph and Mystery,* by Gillian Rubinstein. Simon & Schuster Books for Young Readers, 1998. Jacket illustration © 1998 by Victor Lee. Reproduced by permission of the illustrator. / Rubinstein, Gillian, photograph. Doug Nicholas Photography. Reproduced by permission of Gillian Rubinstein.

RUBY, LOIS. All images reproduced by permission of Lois Ruby.

SCHOTTER, RONI. Hawkes, Kevin, illustrator. From an illustration in *Dreamland,* by Roni Schotter. Orchard Books, 1996. Illustrations © 1996 by Kevin Hawkes. Reproduced by permission of Orchard Books, New York. / Hafner, Marylin, illustrator. From an illustration in *Purim Play,* by Roni Schotter. Little, Brown and Company, 1998. Illustrations © 1998 by Marylin Hafner. Reproduced by permission.

SCHULMAN, ARLENE. "The Prizefighter," photograph by Arlene Schulman. © Arlene Schulman. Reproduced by Arlene Schulman.

SOMETHING ABOUT THE AUTHOR

ALKIVIADES, Alkis 1953-
(Luke Sharp, a joint pseudonym)

Personal

Born January 13, 1953, in Nicosia, Cyprus; son of Andreas and Anastasia Alkiviades; married Ariane Isabelle Bishop, June 6, 1987. *Education:* University of London School of Oriental and African Studies, London, B.A. (with honors), 1975; University of Exeter, Postgraduate Certificate in Education, 1976.

Addresses

Home—Anchor Cottage, Brownshill, Stroud, Gloucestershire GL6 8AG, England. *Electronic mail*—aalkivia @microprose.ltd.uk.

Career

Civil Service Commission, executive officer, 1977-79; Kilburn Skills College, lecturer, 1979-85; London Software Studio, London, England, graphic designer, 1985-87; freelance writer, 1987-91; MicroProse Software Ltd., copywriter, 1991-92, communications manager, 1992-95, product information manager, 1995—.

Writings

The Sports Game, Penguin, 1985.
Star Strider, Penguin, 1986.
(Under joint pseudonym Luke Sharp; with Steve Jackson, Ian Livingstone, and Russ Nicholson) *Steve Jackson and Ian Livingstone Present Chasms of Malice,* Penguin, 1987.
Daggers of Darkness, Penguin, 1988.
(Under joint pseudonym Luke Sharp; with Jackson, Livingstone, and David Gallagher) *Steve Jackson and Ian Livingstone Present Fangs of Fury,* Penguin, 1989.
Dotto and the Pharoah's Mask: An Interactive Connect-the-Dots Adventure, illustrated by Giovanni Caselli, Abrams (New York City), 1997.
Dotto and the Minotaur's Maze: An Interactive Connect-the-Dots Adventure, Abrams, 1998.

Work in Progress

Dotto and the Temple of the Sun, a puzzle book; *The Football Manager,* a football game book; *The Mews,* a novel; *Passatempo,* a novel; *The Game,* a novel about the computer software industry.*

ALLEN, Roger MacBride 1957-

Personal

Born September 26, 1957, in Bridgeport, CT; raised in Washington, DC; son of Thomas B. Allen (an author); married Eleanore Fox (a member of the United States Foreign Service and former literary agent), July 10, 1994; children: Matthew Thomas Allen. *Education:* Boston University, B.S. (journalism), 1979.

Addresses

Home—Washington, DC.

Career

Science fiction writer. Worked variously as a waiter, clerk, temp, salesperson, and a telephone operator.

Awards, Honors

Best short story, *Analog* magazine reader's poll, 1986; Philip K. Dick Award nomination, 1988, for *Orphans of Creation; Isaac Asimov's Utopia* named main selection of *Science Fiction Book Club,* 1997.

Writings

SCIENCE FICTION NOVELS; "TORCH" SERIES

The Torch of Honor, Baen Books (New York City), 1985.
Rogue Powers, Baen Books, 1986.
Allies and Aliens (composed of *The Torch of Honor* and *Rogue Powers*), revised and updated, Baen, 1995.

SCIENCE FICTION NOVELS; "HUNTED EARTH" SERIES

The Ring of Charon, Tor Books (New York City), 1990.
The Shattered Sphere, Tor Books, 1994.

SCIENCE FICTION NOVELS; "CALIBAN" TRILOGY

(With Isaac Asimov) *Caliban,* Ace Books (New York City), 1993.
Isaac Asimov's Inferno, Ace Books, 1994.
Isaac Asimov's Utopia, Ace/Berkley, 1996.

STAR WARS NOVELS; THE "CORELLIAN" TRILOGY

Ambush at Corellia, Bantam (New York City), 1995.
Assault at Selonia, Bantam, 1995.
Showdown at Centerpoint, Bantam, 1995.

OTHER

Orphan of Creation, Baen Books, 1988.
Farside Cannon, Baen Books, 1989.
(With David Drake) *The War Machine,* Baen Books, 1989.
(With Eric Kotani) *Supernova,* Avon (New York City), 1991.
The Modular Man, Bantam, 1992.

Contributor of short stories to *Analog* and other science fiction periodicals.

Work in Progress

The Ocean of Years, a science fiction novel, for Bantam; *The Lost Colony* (working title), a young adult novel, for Avon.

Sidelights

Born just eight days before the 1957 launching of the Sputnik satellite by the former Soviet Union, Roger MacBride Allen is, according to Jay Kay Klein in *Analog,* perhaps the youngest science fiction author who predates the space age. The son of a published writer, Allen "never let classes interfere with getting an education," in Klein's words. A journalism major at Boston University, he absorbed enough knowledge in a variety of scientific fields to write about and extrapolate

from them persuasively. In 1994 he married a member of the United States Foreign Service, Eleanore Fox. The couple lived in Brazil from 1994 to 1997, as Allen followed his wife on her assignment. Since beginning his career as a fiction writer, Allen has become known both for his understanding of "hard science" and for his love of old-fashioned narrative, neither of which have prevented him from creating recognizably human characters and situations. Klein stated: "[Allen's] science fiction certainly shows he gets the facts straight, while the human relationships and individual actions are also handled with rigorous precision."

Allen's first novel, *Torch of Honor,* is "excellent conventional space opera" in the view of *Analog* columnist Tom Easton. The story follows a newlywed couple sent to a moon of planet New Finland in order to construct a special matter transmitter to receive thousands of troops. The troops will be lost forever if the two do not construct the transmitter in time. Easton noted that Allen "has a fine technological imagination ... and a gift for pace." *Booklist* cited *Torch of Honor* as "highly recommended, particularly for collections where Heinlein, Anderson, Dickson, or Drake have an audience." *Voice of Youth Advocates* contributor Jeffrey French opined, "Allen's readable narrative grabs the reader's attention and won't let go." A sequel, *Rogue Powers,* is, in the eyes of a *Booklist* reviewer, "cut from the same cloth—fast-moving, action-laden, technically detailed," and evidence of "a natural storyteller of considerable talents."

In *The Orphan of Creation,* Allen focuses on a paleoanthropologist's discovery in the United States of prehistoric human bones that curiously date from the time of the Civil War. The questions raised by the discovery prompt a search for a form of human that was previously thought extinct. Reviewer Maureen Ritter, writing in *Voice of Youth Advocates,* "thoroughly enjoyed" the work, appreciating the "mixture of science fiction, archaeology, and paleontology." *Farside Cannon,* a novel based on the near future, involves lasers on the moon along with political and social upheaval. *The War Machine,* co-written with David A. Drake as the third volume in the latter's "Crisis of Empire" series, involves a corrupt political system, the Pact, which has managed to hold together all the worlds and star systems in some form of order. The hero of *The War Machine,* a young officer who realizes that chaos and upheaval will result if the Pact is overthrown, defends the system against an unseen enemy.

Another co-authored novel, *Supernova,* written by Allen with Eric Kotani, involves the irradiation of the Earth after the explosion of a nearby star. Dan Chow, writing in *Locus,* called *Supernova* a "hard science fiction novel" that "makes the central idea real enough so that the implied skepticism of 'What if?' is brushed aside by the acceptance of, 'When?'" Kotani and Allen present an examination of the physical effects of the catastrophe on humans and on the earth. As the story was described on Allen's World Wide Web homepage, "At first, the explosion seems just a scientific curiosity, but even from a distance of many light years, a supernova ... can have strange—and disastrous—consequences."

Shortly after the publication of *Supernova*, Allen began his "Hunted Earth" series with *The Ring of Charon*. The premise of the novel is that, after a cosmic disturbance caused by human invention and the use of beams of phased gravity waves, the Earth is stolen by a long dormant alien power and sent through a wormhole in space—a shortcut to another part of the universe—where the human survivors must deal with a new solar system dominated by a strange nonhuman culture. A *Kliatt* reviewer commented that to fully appreciate *The Ring of Charon* "one must both know and like physics," while *Voice of Youth Advocates* contributor David Snider confessed to being confused by switches among settings and characters. However, in *Analog*, Easton applauded the novel—and the potential series—as "grand stuff in a grand tradition."

The second volume in the "Hunted Earth" epic achieved promotion into hardcover publishing (its predecessor had been a paperback original). This sequel, *The Shattered Sphere*, describes the invasion of Earth's new solar system by an age-old enemy of this new world's native inhabitants. The story also continues the human survivors' attempts to find their ancestral solar system. A critic for *Publishers Weekly*, calling the novel "exciting," maintained that Allen's attention to detail allows readers to better understand the story's "technical and emotional imbroglios, while the solutions to these complex situations—in the best thriller tradition—are sure to catch the reader unaware." The critic also implied that a knowledge of physics, although helpful, is not necessary to an enjoyment of *The Shattered Sphere*. *Booklist* reviewer Roland Green maintained that the book's plenitude of "action and ingenious puzzles and more than respectable aliens" rendered it "well up to Allen's normal high standard."

Between the two "Hunted Earth" novels, Allen also published *The Modular Man*, a tale of robotics in which a dying robot scientist has his mind transmitted into the body of one of his robots. Admiringly calling Allen "a throwback to the 50s" for writing "interesting hard science stories" that deal with convincing characters, *Locus* contributor Tom Whitmore dubbed *The Modular Man* a "fine job." Don D'Ammassa, a reviewer for *Science Fiction Chronicle*, called the book "a highly thought provoking, convincing, and entertaining examination of what it means to be human."

Robotics is also the subject of a trilogy of novels that Allen wrote as extrapolations of noted science fiction writer Isaac Asimov's work on that subject. The first volume, *Caliban*, which was co-written with Asimov, explores the further ramifications of Asimov's laws of robotics by considering their effects on a planet named Inferno that has been settled by humans who are excessively dependent on their robots. *Caliban* and its sequel, *Isaac Asimov's Inferno*, were dubbed "worthy, and authorized, successors" to Asimov's novels *The Naked Sun* and *The Caves of Steel* by *Voice of Youth Advocates* contributor Tom Pearson. D'Ammassa, reviewing *Inferno*, observed that "Allen never fails to deliver a good story, this one wrapped around a clever mystery."

After *Inferno*, Allen's next four published efforts were based on the creations of others: a "Star Wars" trilogy (based on the films from George Lucas), published in 1995, and the third volume of the "Caliban" trilogy, *Utopia: Isaac Asimov's Caliban,* in 1996. The "Star Wars" trilogy presents the familiar movie characters Han Solo and Princess Leia (as a married couple) and Luke Skywalker in a series of adventures involving an attempt to re-establish the evil Empire. Observing that the Jedi skills of the Solos' three children are crucial to the resolution of the adventure, *Kliatt* reviewer Hugh M. Flick Jr. called the series as a whole "entertaining and exciting." In a similar vein, the novel *Utopia* was termed a "satisfying conclusion" to its robotics trilogy by a reviewer in *Library Journal.*

Works Cited

Allen, Roger MacBride, homepage, http://www.sff.net/people/roger.allen/, December, 1998.

Chow, Dan, review of *Supernova, Locus,* November, 1991, p. 25.

D'Ammassa, Don, review of *The Modular Man, Science Fiction Chronicle,* April, 1992, p. 29.

D'Ammassa, Don, review of *Inferno, Science Fiction Chronicle,* December, 1994, p. 52.

Easton, Tom, review of *Torch of Honor, Analog,* July, 1985, pp. 183-84.

Easton, Tom, review of *The Ring of Charon, Analog,* October, 1991, pp. 162-63.

Flick, Hugh M., Jr., review of *Showdown at Centerpoint, Kliatt,* January, 1996, pp. 11-12.

French, Jeffrey, review of *Torch of Honor, Voice of Youth Advocates,* August, 1985, p. 191.

Green, Roland, review of *The Shattered Sphere, Booklist,* June 1 & 15, 1994, p. 1780.

Klein, Jay Kay, "Biolog: Roger Allen MacBride," *Analog,* March, 1989, pp. 172.

Pearson, Tom, review of *Caliban* and *Inferno, Voice of Youth Advocates,* April, 1995, pp. 30-31.

Review of *The Ring of Charon, Kliatt,* April, 1991, p. 16.

Ritter, Maureen, review of *The Orphan of Creation, Voice of Youth Advocates,* August, 1988, p. 137.

Review of *Rogue Powers, Booklist,* July, 1985, pp. 1586-87.

Review of *The Shattered Sphere, Publishers Weekly,* July 18, 1994, p. 239.

Snider, David, review of *The Ring of Charon, Voice of Youth Advocates,* August, 1991, p. 176.

Review of *Torch of Honor, Booklist,* April 15, 1985, p. 1158.

Review of *Utopia, Library Journal,* November 15, 1996, p. 92.

Whitmore, Tom, review of *The Modular Man, Locus,* March, 1992, p. 35.*

B

BAXTER, Virginia
See HILTON, Margaret Lynette

*   *   *

BEAR, Greg 1951-

Personal

Born August 20, 1951, in San Diego, CA; son of Dale Franklin (a naval officer) and Wilma (a secretary and homemaker; maiden name, Merriman) Bear; married Christina Nielsen, January 12, 1975 (divorced, August, 1981); married Astrid Anderson, June 18, 1983; children (second marriage): Erik William Anderson Bear, Alexandra Astrid Bear. *Education:* San Diego State College (now University), A.B., 1969.

Addresses

Home—506 Lakeview Rd., Alderwood Manor, WA 98037. *Agent*—Richard Curtis, 171 East 74th St., New York, NY 10021.

Career

Writer. Has also worked as a bookseller, a freelance journalist, and a teacher in San Diego, CA. Member of the Citizen's Advisory Council on National Space Policy, 1983-90. Consultant to businesses, including Microsoft, and to WNET-13 in New York. Science and speculations advisor for pilot episode of *Earth 2,* NBC, 1995. *Member:* Science Fiction Writers of America (former chairman of Grievance Committee and vice-president; president, 1988-90).

Awards, Honors

Nebula Awards, Science Fiction Writers of America, both 1984, for best novelette "Blood Music" and for best novella "Hardfought"; Hugo Award, 1984, for best novelette "Blood Music"; Prix Apollo, 1986, for *Blood Music;* Nebula and Hugo Awards, 1987, for short story "Tangents"; Nebula Award, 1994, for best novel *Moving Mars.*

Writings

NOVELS

Hegira, Dell, 1979.
Psychlone, Ace, 1979, published as *Lost Souls,* Charter, 1982.
Beyond Heaven's River, Dell, 1980, revised edition, Severn House, 1989.
Strength of Stones, Ace, 1981, revised edition, Gollancz, 1988.
Corona: A Star Trek Novel, Pocket Books, 1984.
The Infinity Concerto, Berkeley, 1984.
Eon, Bluejay, 1985.
Blood Music, Arbor House, 1985.
The Serpent Mage, Berkeley, 1986.
The Forge of God, Tor, 1987.
Eternity, Warner, 1988.
Hardfought (bound with *Cascade Point* by Timothy Zahn), Tor, 1988.
Queen of Angels, Easton Press, 1990.
Heads, Legend (London), 1990, St. Martin's Press, 1991.
Anvil of Stars, Warner, 1992.
Songs of Earth and Power (includes *The Infinity Concerto* and *The Serpent Mage*), Legend, 1992, Tor, 1994.
Moving Mars, Tor, 1993.
Legacy, Tor, 1995.
(Editor with Martin Greenberg) *New Legends,* Tor, 1995.
/ [pronounced "slant"], Tor, 1997.
Dinosaur Summer, Warner Aspect, 1998.
Foundation and Chaos, HarperCollins, 1998.

SHORT STORY COLLECTIONS

The Wind From a Burning Woman, Arkham, 1983.
Sleepside Story, Cheap Street, 1988.
Early Harvest, NESFA Press, 1988.
Tangents, Warner, 1989.
Sisters, Pulphouse, 1992.
The Venging, Legend, 1992.
Bear's Fantasies: Six Stories in Old Paradigms, Wildside Press, 1992.

OTHER

Contributor to science fiction periodicals, including *Omni, Analog,* and *Isaac Asimov's Science Fiction Magazine.* Editor, with wife Astrid, of *Science Fiction Writers Association Forum.* Book reviewer for *San Diego Union Book Review* supplement, 1979-82. Bear's work has been translated into a dozen languages.

Adaptations

"Dead Run" was adapted for *The Twilight Zone* television series, 1986; *Blood Music* was broadcast as a radio play by the Canadian Broadcasting Company; "The White Horse Child" was adapted for a CD-ROM multimedia presentation from Ebook, 1993.

Work in Progress

Darwin's Radio, a novel, for Del Ray.

Sidelights

Greg Bear is one of the most important writers in science fiction today. He has won the prestigious Nebula Award three times, and he also has two Hugo Awards to his credit. In the *St. James Guide to Science Fiction Writers,* David Brin stated that few SF authors "have been as influential in transforming the genre as Greg Bear, a prolific leader in exploring the concept of *change* as it affects civilization, science, and even human nature. Perhaps no other writer so well typifies one of the hallmarks of science fiction—the belief that ideas are among the most precious things."

Bear was a precocious youngster. His father was an officer in the U.S. Navy, stationed at posts around the world. By the time Bear was twelve years old, he had traveled with his parents throughout the continental United States, Alaska, Japan, and the Philippines. In Alaska, at the age of nine, Bear wrote his first short story. By the time he was fourteen, he had begun submitting his stories to magazines, and by the age of fifteen he made his first sale, to Robert Lowndes' *Famous Science Fiction.*

It took Bear five years to sell his next short story, and then his work began to appear in science fiction magazines with some regularity. He published a novel, *Hegira,* in 1979. (Bear had finished his first novel, entitled *The Infinity Concerto,* when he was nineteen. The book wasn't published until some twelve years later, after Bear had rewritten it.) *Hegira* is the story of a civilization that is trapped in an artificial world. In this world, the only relief from cultural amnesia is found in inscriptions on the walls of mammoth towers, which stretch above the earth, beyond the sky. Like many of Bear's novels and short stories, *Hegira* combines powerful dreamlike images and imaginative concepts to give the reader a new perspective on science and society.

Bear has strong interests in science, particularly astronomy and physics, and history. He has worked as a bookseller and a freelance journalist. On one assign-

ment, he covered the Voyager missions to Jupiter and Saturn for the *San Diego Union.* He has written many articles on film for the *Los Angeles Times* and lectured for San Diego City Schools, acting as a roving teacher and conducting classes on ancient history, the history of science, and science fiction and fantasy.

Bear is also a talented illustrator, and a founding member of the Association for Science Fiction Artists (ASFA). His illustrations have appeared in *Galaxy, Fantasy and Science Fiction,* and *Vertex,* as well as on bookcovers. As he remarked on his website, however, "My last professional work of art was the cover of my own novel, *Psycholone,* in reprint from Tor. I do very little artwork now, devoting myself almost exclusively to writing."

One of Bear's first novels to become a science fiction best-seller, *Eon,* was published in 1985. In this work, a huge, hollowed-out asteroid appears in the solar system and begins to orbit the earth. Investigators, led by

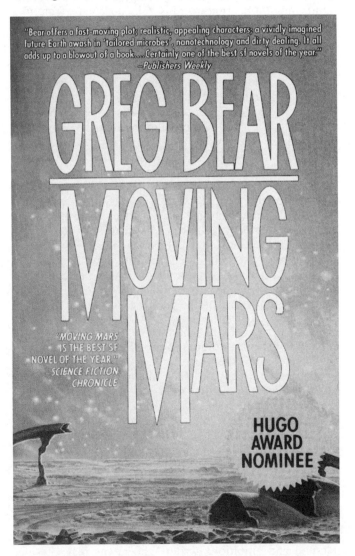

Faced with an escalating technological war between Earth and Mars, Greg Bear's two protagonists must make tough decisions. (Cover illustration by Wayne Barlowe.)

scientist Patricia Vasquez, discover that this asteroid is actually a spaceship, and that deserted chambers inside the ship, which are filled with forests, lakes, rivers, and hanging cities, are endpoints to "hyperspace tunnels" that reach throughout time and paratime. The asteroid has come from the future of a parallel earth, and as such it holds documents that forecast that nuclear war is only months away. Armed with this information, part of the Earth's population escapes by traveling along a path called the Way. Writing in *Science Fiction Chronicle,* Don D'Ammassa described *Eon* as "thoroughly readable, with lots of adventure, a complex plot, an interesting mystery, and well resolved characters." Alex Raskin, writing in the *Los Angeles Times Book Review,* declared that "this attempt to venture beyond the stylistic frontiers of science fiction isn't wholly successful.... Each part, however, is entertaining in itself." In the *Washington Post Book World,* John Clute maintained: "The Way has come to represent so complex an image of Future History that it is impossible to grasp it whole. But Bear's own grasp is unfaltering, his control over the ramifying implications of his tale nearly perfect. *Eon* may be the best-constructed hard SF epic yet."

Eternity, which was published in 1988, is a sequel to *Eon.* As the novel begins, Earth has survived a nuclear war, an encounter with a supercivilization, and an alien invasion. The designer of the Way, Pavel Mirsky, appears to warn Earth's inhabitants that the Way, now sealed, must be reopened and then destroyed. In *Science Fiction Chronicle,* Don D'Ammassa commented favorably on *Eternity's* "strongly realized characters" and "marvelously inventive setting." A *Publishers Weekly* critic called the novel a "slow visionary tale" and noted that Bear's presentation "of the different responses of intricate, interlocking cultures is striking." Reviewing *Eternity* in *Analog,* Tom Easton remarked, "If you enjoyed the first volume of the duo, you'll enjoy the second. If you didn't, you may still enjoy this one, for it does neatly wrap up the whole ball of string, and the characters do seem better realized."

Legacy is the third volume in the "Eon" series. Twenty-five years after the opening of the Way, Olmy Ap Sennon is sent to spy on 4000 "divaricates" who fled the starship *Thistledown* in order to live in the land of Lamarckia, where they believe they could lead a utopian existence. When he gets there, Olmy finds the inhabitants engaged in a full-blown civil war. Lamarckia is a planet whose ecosystem adapts readily to change; it is populated by organisms that sample and share each other's features and incorporate what they find useful. A *Publishers Weekly* reviewer asserted: "This is a stunning SF novel that extrapolates a scientifically complex future from the basic stuff of human nature." In the *New York Times Book Review,* Gerald Jonas wrote: "Greg Bear, a talented and ambitious writer who never plays it safe, has had his share of successes and failures. *Legacy* ... is one of his triumphs." In *Booklist,* Roland Green maintained that the work "will not disappoint *Eon's* fans and ... stands well enough to be read on its own."

A prequel to **Eon,** *Bear's novel follows his protagonist to a biologically complex world engaged in a civil war. (Cover illustration by Bob Eggleton.)*

Blood Music is considered Bear's most influential work. (The novel was based on Bear's short story of the same name, which won both the Hugo and Nebula awards.) Vergil Ulam, a scientist in California, is attempting to design a new form of life. He is determined to tailor a common virus into a computer biochip, but instead he creates an independent microscopic intelligence that breeds, spreads, and mutates. When he is fired from his job because he is caught doing unauthorized experiments, Vergil injects himself with the disease culture in order to smuggle it out of the company. Vergil's cells acquire first the gift of intelligence and then the power to create. Algis Budrys, writing in *Magazine of Fantasy and Science Fiction,* noted that *Blood Music* "is an as yet unaccountably important book; half really real, half painted real, wholly striking." He added that what Bear has written "may be read as a horror novel by some; by dedicated SF readers, it will be read with fascination as we see the classic evolution of the story from its simple initial premise to its fully deployed panoply of eventual consequences."

The Forge of God is the first novel in another series by Bear. This complicated end-of-the-world tale is set in 1996, when the Earth is invaded by alien planet eaters. One alien who is found in Death Valley predicts the Earth's destruction, while aliens who arrive in Australia want to welcome the Earth into their galactic community. This creates confusion for scientists and politicians alike, who do not know how to deal with the aliens. Meanwhile, amidst the confusion, the aliens release a device into the Earth's core that will destroy the planet. A network of humans band together to save themselves. In *Voice of Youth Advocates,* Judy Kowalski described the novel as "An interesting speculation on how humans will react to the knowledge of alien invasion . . . ." John G. Cramer, writing in the *Los Angeles Times Book Review,* noted that Bear's "protagonists are swept along by forces beyond their control, behaving with admirable rationality and doing reasonable and human things in the face of an impossible situation."

In the final pages of *The Forge of God,* young Marty Gordon, who saw the Earth destroyed, begins searching

In Bear's imaginative adventure story, Peter Belzoni and his photojournalist father join the owners of a dinosaur attraction on a treacherous journey to remove the giant beasts from the plateau in Venezuela where they have been kept. (Illustrated by Tony DiTerlizzi.)

for the aliens who are responsible. Bear's sequel, *Anvil of Stars,* features several children who have been rescued from Earth by a group of alien benefactors and are sent on a mission of vengeance to find the planet killers and to destroy their worlds. The children, who live on the spaceship *Dawntreader* and are led by Gordon, grow into young adults who face a moral dilemma—Is it right to eliminate an entire species for revenge? Faren Miller, writing in *Locus,* contended that "next to *Anvil of Stars,* most novels of space war look like garish cartoons. Despite Bear's obvious philosophical/moral agenda, the story feels immensely real." Russell Letson, also writing in *Locus,* maintained: "The book's narrative drive is genuinely impressive: I was involved with the characters, I was eager to see the outcome of their engagements with the traps and tricks of the Enemy, and I turned the pages just as fast as I could." In *Booklist,* Roland Green wrote that Bear is "a master of both technical wizardry and powerful scenes."

Another of Bear's novels, *Queen of Angels,* is set in Los Angeles in 2147. By this time, psychotherapy has become an exact science, creating a rift between the "therapied" and the "untherapied" in society. Many writers and artists choose to remain untherapied because they are afraid that receiving therapy will cause them to become passionless and ruin their creativity. Emanual Goldsmith is a celebrated untherapied poet who has just killed eight of his young disciples, and Mary Choy from the Los Angeles Police Department is assigned to the murder case. As Choy searches for Goldsmith, a team of scientific genius hired by the father of one of the victims is probing Goldsmith's mind to find out why he killed his friends. Laura Staley, reviewing *Queen of Angels* in *Voice of Youth Advocates,* noted that the novel "will provide much entertainment—and food for thought." In *Locus,* reviewer Faren Miller asserted: "*Queen of Angels* is an ambitious literary novel which forms complex material into a meaningful pattern . . . . It is also science fiction of a high order, filled with the excitement of extraordinary technologies and ideas."

/ ("Slant"), a sequel to *Queen of Angels,* concerns artificial intelligence and nanotechnology in the twenty-first century. The action revolves around Omphalos, which is reputed to be a cryogenic repository but is actually a huge survival fortress run by Roddy, an artificial intelligence created by a bizarre genius named Seefa Schnee. Omphalos is owned by the Aristos, a secret group of wealthy and powerful individuals who want to destroy society, and Schnee has already distributed a virus designed to break down the genetic, physical, and mental therapy that holds society together.

The novel *Moving Mars* is set in the same fictional universe as *Queen of Angels.* The novel opens in the year 2171, or Mars Year 53, as the Martian colonists are under pressure to centralize their society of Binding Multiples, or leagues of families. The story is written as a memoir by Casseia Majumbar, a college student who gets caught up in the political conflicts and eventually rises to a diplomatic position. Casseia travels to Earth, where she experiences firsthand the deep social and cultural divisions that exist between the two planets. When Casseia's former lover, Charles Franklin, and his colleagues introduce revolutionary theories in physics that make Mars a threat to Earth, the Earth government disrupts Mars' workings by attacking with computer viruses. Faced with the escalating technological war, Casseia, now vice-president of a newly elected Martian government, and a few others must decide whether to move their planet—literally.

Writing in _School Library Journal,_ Christine C. Menefee noted that _Moving Mars_ "is evocative of the _Martian Chronicles_ in some winning ways, but its scientific and political content is also rich in contemporary questions." In _Analog,_ Tom Easton claimed that Bear does "a grand job of establishing credibility for a Mars with fossils, a society built on Binding Multiples ..., realistic politics, and sympathetic characters." In _Locus,_ Gary K. Wolfe praised "the richness of texture with which [Bear] brings all this off," calling _Moving Mars_ "far more than just another entry in the new Mars sweepstakes.... Bear's depiction of Martian life and landscapes stands up to the best of them." _Moving Mars_ was the winner of the 1994 Nebula Award for best novel.

Works Cited

Bear, Greg, website located at http://www.kaiaghok.com/gregbear.

Brin, David, essay on Bear in _St. James Guide to Science Fiction Writers,_ 4th edition, St. James Press, 1996, pp. 58-59.

Budrys, Algis, review of _Blood Music, Magazine of Fantasy and Science Fiction,_ September, 1985, pp. 26-27.

Clute, John, "Asimov's Old-Fashioned Future," _Washington Post Book World,_ August 25, 1985.

Cramer, John G., "Self-Reproducing Machines From Another Planet," _Los Angeles Times Book Review,_ September 20, 1987.

D'Ammassa, Don, review of _Eon, Science Fiction Chronicle,_ December, 1985, p. 42.

D'Ammassa, Don, review of _Eternity, Science Fiction Chronicle,_ January, 1989, p. 44.

Easton, Tom, review of _Eternity, Analog,_ March, 1989, pp. 181-82.

Easton, Tom, "The Reference Library," _Analog,_ April, 1994, pp. 162-63.

Review of _Eternity, Publishers Weekly,_ September 2, 1988, p. 90.

Green, Roland, review of _Anvil of Stars, Booklist,_ April 15, 1992, p. 1483.

Green, Roland, review of _Legacy, Booklist,_ July, 1995, p. 1865.

Jonas, Gerald, "Science Fiction," _New York Times Book Review,_ September 10, 1995, p. 44.

Kowalski, Judy, review of _The Forge of God, Voice of Youth Advocates,_ February, 1988, p. 285.

Review of _Legacy, Publishers Weekly,_ May 15, 1995, pp. 58-59.

Letson, Russell, review of _Anvil of Stars, Locus,_ March, 1992, p. 63.

Menefee, Christine C., "Up for Discussion," _School Library Journal,_ December, 1994, pp. 38-39.

Miller, Faren, review of _Anvil of Stars, Locus,_ March, 1992, p. 19.

Miller, Faren, review of _Queen of Angels, Locus,_ June, 1990, p. 15.

Raskin, Alex, review of _Eon, Los Angeles Times Book Review,_ July 27, 1986, pp. 8-9.

Staley, Laura, review of _Queen of Angels, Voice of Youth Advocates,_ December, 1990, p. 293.

Wolfe, Gary K., review of _Moving Mars, Locus,_ November, 1993, p. 28.

For More Information See

PERIODICALS

Booklist, June 15, 1989, p. 1783.
Kirkus Reviews, July 1, 1989, p. 958; June 1, 1997, p. 840; January 1, 1998, p. 27.
Library Journal, March 5, 1997, p. 50.
Locus, November, 1993, pp. 17-18.
New York Times Book Review, September 2, 1990, p. 18; November 14, 1993, p. 74.
Publishers Weekly, March 10, 1997, p. 23; November 24, 1997, p. 23; December 8, 1997, p. 59.

*　　*　　*

BLAISDELL, Bob
See BLAISDELL, Robert

*　　*　　*

BLAISDELL, Robert 1959-
(Bob Blaisdell)

Personal

Born November 19, 1959, in Houston, TX.

Addresses

Home—401 West 118th St., No. 33, New York, NY 10027. _Electronic mail_—rblaisdell@kbcc.cuny.edu.

Career

Kingsborough Community College of the City University of New York, Brooklyn, NY, assistant professor.

Writings

RETELLINGS; UNDER NAME BOB BLAISDELL

Robin Hood, illustrated by Thea Kliros, Dover, 1994.
Favorite Greek Myths, illustrated by John Green, Dover, 1995.
The Story of Hercules, illustrated by Thea Kliros, Dover, 1997.

Robert Blaisdell (self-portrait)

*ADAPTOR; ABRIDGED EDITIONS; UNDER NAME BOB
BLAISDELL*

Frances Hodgson Burnett, *The Secret Garden,* illustrated
by Thea Kliros, Dover, 1994.

L. Frank Baum, *The Wizard of Oz,* illustrated by W. W.
Denslow, Dover, 1995.

Carlo Collodi, *The Adventures of Pinocchio,* illustrated by
Thea Kliros, Dover, 1995.

Lucy Maud Montgomery, *Anne of Green Gables,* illustrated by Barbara Steadman, Dover, 1995.

Kenneth Grahame, *The Wind in the Willows,* illustrated by
Thea Kliros, Dover, 1995.

Victor Hugo, *The Hunchback of Notre Dame,* illustrated by
Thea Kliros, 1995.

Daniel Defoe, *Robinson Crusoe,* illustrated by John Green,
Dover, 1995.

Frances Hodgson Burnett, *A Little Princess,* illustrated by
Thea Kliros, Dover, 1996.

E. T. A. Hoffmann, *The Story of the Nutcracker,* illustrated
by Thea Kliros, Dover, 1996.

Robert Louis Stevenson, *Kidnapped,* illustrated by Thea
Kliros, Dover, 1996.

Mark Twain, *The Adventures of Tom Sawyer,* illustrated by
John Green, Dover, 1996.

Twain, *The Prince and the Pauper,* illustrated by Thea
Kliros, Dover, 1997.

Louisa May Alcott, *Little Women,* illustrated by Kliros,
Dover, 1997.

Alcott, *Little Men,* illustrated by Kliros, Dover, 1997.

Mary Wollstonecraft Shelley, *Frankenstein,* illustrated by
Kliros, Dover, 1997.

Edgar Rice Burroughs, *Tarzan,* illustrated by John Green,
Dover, 1997.

Bram Stoker, *Dracula,* Dover, 1997.

Lewis Carroll, *Alice in Wonderland,* illustrated by Marty
Noble, Dover, 1998.

Johanna Spyri, *Heidi,* illustrated by Thea Kliros, Dover,
1998.

Mark Twain, *The Adventures of Huckleberry Finn,* illustrated by John Green, Dover, 1998.

Walter Scott, *Ivanhoe,* illustrated by John Green, Dover,
1999.

OTHER

(Editor) Thomas Hardy, *Hardy's Selected Poems,* Dover
(Mineola, NY), 1995.

(Editor) D. H. Lawrence, *Snake and Other Poems,* Dover,
1999.

(Editor) Leo Tolstoy, *Tolstoy as Teacher: Leo Tolstoy's
Writings on Education,* Teachers & Writers, 1999.

Contributor to periodicals, including *Teaching and
Learning Literature* and *Classical World.*

* * *

BOWMAN, Crystal 1951-

Personal

Born May 9, 1951, in Holland, MI; daughter of Harold
(a contractor) and Gerene (Hulst) Langejans; married
Robert Bowman (a dentist), July 28, 1973; children:
Robert, Scott, Teri. *Education:* Calvin College, B.A.;
University of Michigan, graduate study. *Religion:* Prot-

Crystal Bowman

estant. *Hobbies and other interests:* Sports, travel, family activities.

Addresses

Home—45 Lakeside Dr. S.E., Grand Rapids, MI 49506. *Office*—c/o Cygnet Publishing, 2153 Wealthy S.E., No. 238, Grand Rapids, MI 49506. *Electronic mail*—bowman@grgig.net.

Career

Early childhood educator in Ann Arbor, MI, and (also director) Grand Rapids, MI; mathematics tutor for public schools in Holland, MI. FJH Music Co., children's lyricist, 1990—. Conducts poetry workshops. *Member:* Society of Children's Book Writers and Illustrators, Michigan Reading Association.

Writings

FOR CHILDREN

Cracks in the Sidewalk (poems), Cygnet Publishing (Grand Rapids, MI), 1993.
Jonathan James Says, "I Can Be Brave," illustrated by Karen Maizel, Zondervan (Grand Rapids, MI), 1995.
Jonathan James Says, "Let's Be Friends," illustrated by Maizel, Zondervan, 1995.
Jonathan James Says, "I Can Help," illustrated by Maizel, Zondervan, 1995.
Jonathan James Says, "Let's Play Ball," illustrated by Maizel, Zondervan, 1995.
Jonathan James Says, "School's Out," illustrated by Maizel, Zondervan, 1997.
Jonathan James Says, "I Can Hardly Wait," illustrated by Maizel, Zondervan, 1997.
Jonathan James Says, "Happy Birthday to Me," illustrated by Maizel, Zondervan, 1997.
Jonathan James Says, "Christmas Is Coming," illustrated by Maizel, Zondervan, 1997.
Ivan and the Dynamos, Eerdmans (Grand Rapids), 1997.
If Peas Could Taste like Candy, and Other Funny Poems for Kids, illustrated by Lynn Jeffery, Zondervan, 1998.

Author of lyrics for about a hundred children's songs.

Sidelights

Crystal Bowman comments: "I have spent all of my adult years working with children. This has allowed me to observe the innocence and humor with which children view their world. It is this perspective that I attempt to capture in my writing. Most of my ideas come from real-life events. Behind my stories and poems are true stories of children in everyday life situations. My work is influenced by my children, students, and my own childhood memories."

For More Information See

PERIODICALS

Kirkus Reviews, March 1, 1997, p. 378.
School Library Journal, September, 1997, p. 213.

BROOME, Errol 1937-

Personal

Born August 3, 1937, in Perth, Australia; daughter of Edmund Carew Moss (a solicitor) and Hazel Joy Hill; married Michael Broome (a business executive), September 24, 1960; children: Nicholas, Jonathon, Benjamin. *Education:* University of West Australia, B.A., 1957. *Hobbies and other interests:* Gardening.

Addresses

Home and office—33 Seymour Grove, Brighton Beach, Victoria 3186, Australia. *Agent*—(for speaking engagements only) Albert Ullin, Show & Tell/Books for All Reasons, 708 Burke Rd., Camberwell 3124, Australia.

Career

The West Australian, Perth, Western Australia, journalist, 1958-60; Herald-Sun Television, Melbourne, Victoria, Australia, journalist, 1961; writer, 1978—. *Member:* Australian Society of Authors, Fellowship of Australian Writers, Society of Women Writers, National Book Council, Children's Book Council of Australia.

Awards, Honors

Mary Grant Bruce Award (Australia), 1990, for a children's short story; West Australian Premier's Children's Book Award, 1992, for *Dear Mr. Sprouts.*

Errol Broome

Writings

Wrinkles, illustrated by Terry Dyer, Collins, 1978.

The Smallest Koala, illustrated by Gwen Mason, Buttercup, 1987.

Dear Mr. Sprouts, Allen & Unwin (Sydney, Australia), 1991, Knopf (New York), 1991.

Garry Keeble's Kitchen: How One Boy Left Home and Survived with 28 Recipes That Anyone Can Cook and Everyone Will Eat, illustrated by Maya, Random House (Australia), 1992.

Tangles, illustrated by Ann James, Allen & Unwin, 1993, Knopf, 1994.

Rockhopper, illustrated by Ann James, Allen & Unwin, 1995.

Nightwatch, illustrated by Helen Brooshooft, Fremantle Arts Centre Press (South Fremantle, Western Australia), 1995.

Splashback: A Great Greasy Journey, illustrated by Gregory Rogers, Allen & Unwin, 1996.

Fly with Me, illustrated by Jane Walker, Fremantle Arts Centre Press, 1996.

Pets (series of eight), Macmillan Educational, 1996.

What a Goat!, illustrated by Sharon Thompson, Fremantle Arts Centre Press, 1997.

Quicksilver, illustrated by Anna Pignataro, Allen & Unwin, 1997.

Tough Luck, illustrated by Sharon Thompson, Fremantle Arts Centre Press, 1998.

Magnus maybe, illustrated by Ann James, Allen & Unwin, 1998.

Also author of *Bird Boy* and *Town and Country Ducks,* both 1986, and *A Year of Pink Pieces* and *Have a Go!,* both 1988.

Work in Progress

Magnus mostly, a sequel to *Magnus maybe.*

Sidelights

Australian author Errol Broome has written more than a dozen books for children that usually tackle difficult themes with humor and grace. Often, her characters must deal with situations that resonate with readers—the loss of a parent, a classroom trauma, or a dilemma that tests their morals. Some of Broome's works are aimed at early elementary children, but most appeal to readers above the age of nine or so who are often struggling with some of the same issues. Many are set in Western Australia, where Broome, the mother of three and onetime journalist, spent her early life.

Broome told *SATA:* "People ask me if I was called after Errol Flynn. No. But my name, spelled as it is, helped to turn me into a writer. When I was born Errol Carew Moss, the doctor said, 'With a name like that, she should write a book.' I grew up hearing my mother tell this story—and I (nearly) always did as I was told.

"At school I liked writing stories. I won my first award for writing when I was nine. We lived near the Swan River in Perth, West Australia, and I learned to swim there among the great brown jellyfish. We caught fish from the jetty and crabs and prawns in the shallows. As soon as we were old enough, we rode our bicycles across the highway to swim in the clear, deep water of the Indian Ocean. When the shark alarm rang, it was *everybody out!* (But I never once saw a shark.)

"I majored in English at the University of West Australia, and joined the *West Australian* as a cadet journalist. Journalism took away some of my imagination. On a newspaper, you get into trouble if you make things up! But it taught me to write clearly and never to use a long word when a short one would do.

"Marriage took me across Australia to Melbourne. We have lived since in Sydney and in Papua New Guinea, and now in Melbourne again, for good. We have three grown-up sons, so at home today it's just my husband and me and Ben's three-legged dog, Bondi. When I'm not writing, I spend time in the garden. Before I began writing books, I combined these two loves in lifestyle articles set in our garden. I believe this stirred my imagination, and helped me step into the world of fiction writing. The garden and growing things form a background to many of my books, especially *Dear Mr. Sprouts* and *Tangles,* and so does the sea *(Rockhopper* and *Splashback).*"

Broome's first book for children was published in 1978, and only ten years after *Wrinkles* appeared did she write her second. This was *The Smallest Koala,* for early elementary readers, and it set the tone of much of her fiction with its deft handling of a personal predicament—in this case, a disobedience situation with which young readers could certainly empathize—combined with a fantastical, almost surreal episode. Its protagonist, Kinta, is a curious little koala who eats an acorn leaf against her mother's orders. As a result, she is magically miniaturized and then chased by acorn people. She finds a eucalyptus tree (the only food koalas can eat), eats a leaf from it, and returns to her normal stature.

Broome's next book, *Dear Mr. Sprouts,* targeted a readership from nine to thirteen years of age. Anke, newly arrived in Australia from Holland, lets a balloon go as part of a school project. Inside are mountain ash seeds and a note with her name and address. A farm boy finds it, and she and the boy, named Freddie, become pen pals. *Dear Mr. Sprouts* is told through their nine-year correspondence. Anke is a loner who also suffers from a stutter; Freddie struggles with issues particular to growing up on an isolated farm. Broome gives special weight to conservation issues, beginning with the symbolism of tree seeds sparking a friendship between two dissimilar people. Freddie knows that his family's land will need to be re-forested, and the planting of Anke's seeds becomes the first step in that direction. When Anke and Freddie finally meet after seven years, only then does he learn of her speech impediment and encourages her to seek therapy. At the end of the book is a glossary of Australian terms. Reviewers especially praised Broome for her characterization. The author, noted *Horn Book's* Maeve Visser Knoth, was successful "in giving each a distinctive voice and honest adolescent emotional swings and insecurities."

Broome next wrote *Garry Keeble's Kitchen: How One Boy Left Home and Survived with 28 Recipes That Anyone Can Cook and Everyone Will Eat.* Garry, the title character, is a twelve-year-old boy who loves food after he begins to excel in concocting the one family meal a week his mother has decreed he and his brother must cook. But over the course of the story, he encounters problems with his girlfriend and then at home, and runs away from it all. This tale is told in the first person, and when Garry mentions a dish, a recipe for it appears on the next page—sometimes appearing to be scribbled down on the back of a scrap of paper, like a train ticket, from wherever he is. "The story is told in a lively manner appropriate to the thinking of a disgruntled and misunderstood teenager," wrote Anne Hanzl in *Magpies.*

Tangles, Broome's 1994 novel for young readers, begins with a terrible incident: the death of Sophie's cat Ginger

After Sophie steals the money from her neighbor's lost wallet to purchase a kitten, her initial exhilaration turns into unbearable guilt. (Cover illustration by Pamela Patrick.)

by a car. Though Sophie initially does not want a replacement, she attends a church fair and spots a cute black kitten for sale. Sophie has already wasted her money that day and is heartbroken about walking away from the cat. Then she spies a dropped wallet. It belongs to her elderly neighbor, but she takes the money to buy Tangles, whose name is appropriate for the inner turmoil she feels every time she looks at her new kitty with a mixture of love and guilt. Finally she confesses to her neighbor, but the discomfort she had been feeling also had a physical basis, and she is rushed off for an appendectomy. Stephen Matthews, writing in the *Australian Book Review,* called *Tangles* "a marvelously understated gem of a book," while a *Kirkus Reviews* contributor declared that "Sophie is a strong, endearing character who invites reader identification."

The theme of how one deals with permanent physical disability runs through the story of *Nightwatch,* Broome's 1995 novel for young readers. The story of Georgia "Chippy" Chipman, who is blind, begins with her disappointment when she is told her family does not have the funds to send her to music camp that summer. Instead they plan to visit her grandparents' farm, and Chippy's sadness abates somewhat when she makes a new friend in her neighborhood, Areti, newly arrived in Australia from Greece. It is initially agreed that Areti can come with them to the farm, but circumstances change at the eleventh hour when Chippy's cousin Monty comes along and there is not enough room for the disappointed Areti. Chippy dislikes Monty, but while staying at the farm one night they hear crying and decide to investigate. She then discovers that her egotistical, self-assured cousin is afraid of the dark. In turn, Monty gains a new respect for Chippy, who goes through life in complete darkness. *Nightwatch* includes guidelines at the end from the Royal Australian Institute for the Blind about helping blind people, and Broome won praise for portraying Chippy's day-to-day life in a sensitive and realistic manner. Writing in *Magpies,* John Murray called it "an engaging and optimistic story," and a heroine "whose need for love, friendship, responsibility, and respect ... are the same as anybody's."

Broome had a second title published in 1995, *Rockhopper,* that stars Quentin, a diminutive boy whose father has died. Quentin is the target of harassment at school, but must also suffer the dilemma of a worried, overprotective mother. He runs away, meets a helpful mentor, and has an adventure on the high seas complete with an exciting rescue. Hazel Rochman, reviewing the work for *Booklist,* found "too much plot" in *Rockhopper,* but praised Broome's characterizations. *Fly with Me,* published in 1996, chronicles the friendship between an Australian boy and a Japanese youth. Ben meets Yoshito when he visits Australia with his family, and upon parting each holds the end of streamer that breaks apart when the ship sails off. Ben sends the pieces to Yoshito, who makes a kite from the paper and sends it to Ben, who then travels to Japan with it. Hanzl, again writing in *Magpies,* found the story too fantastical—"there is an awkward crossing over of genres from realism to

Splashback
a great greasy journey

Errol Broome

Ned travels back in time and acquires confidence and self-respect when he helps a whaling family with their arduous work.

fantasy," she noted, but appreciated Broome's portrayal of both learning from one another's culture.

Broome penned another fantasy novel in 1996, but this one featured time-travel in a coming-of-age story. *Splashback: A Great Greasy Journey* chronicles the tale of Ned, whose father is a championship swimmer. Ned dislikes the water intensely, but one day he accidentally falls in the water and lands in 1836 at the height of the whaling era. A piece of scrimshaw with a young girl's image connects him with a whaling family from Cornwall, and he overcomes his fear of the sea when he is forced to participate in their difficult job, which includes harpooning a whale and slaughtering the massive animal at sea—hence the "grease" of the title. In the end, Ned returns to his real family with a newfound self-respect. "The plot is tightly structured and the characters both engaging and believable," opined Joan Zahnleiter in *Magpies,* who deemed Broome's work "an absorbing read."

In her 1997 book *What a Goat!,* Broome centers the action around Gerda, the beloved pet goat of Eliza's family. Gerda, however, is now old and has become somewhat of a bother to the family because of the trouble she inadvertently causes. When Eliza's father loses his job, they can no longer afford to keep her, and the parents hope to conceal the plan to euthanize Gerda from Eliza. She learns of it and runs away with Gerda to save her, but in the end a new home for the goat is found nearby. Margaret Philips, reviewing *What a Goat!* for *Magpies,* termed it "a pleasant story." Moreover, Philips noted, the tale is one with which young readers might especially sympathize—Eliza thinks "at times that her parents are too hard—what child doesn't?"—but Broome, the reviewer pointed out, presents the adults fairly.

Another book from Broome published in 1997 was *Quicksilver,* which again uses a fantasy-driven plot. Luisa misses her father greatly and becomes quite attached to the charm bracelet he sends her from Paris for her eleventh birthday. The piece of jewelry and its small tokens become links between far-apart people and places over the course of the narrative. Ricki Blackhall, reviewing the book for *Magpies,* noted that Broome fails to provide an easy conclusion for Luisa and her problems, but instead "leaves the reader with room for hope that the family relations may improve."

Broome continues to write about children and the issues they must face from her hometown of Brighton Beach. In 1998, another two novels were published, *Tough Luck* and *Magnus maybe,* the latter chronicling the lives of some unusual new characters whom Broome hopes to re-visit in later fiction. "Most of my books portray children and their daily dramas," Broome told *SATA.* "I try to weave in some adventure or underlying mystery. *Magnus maybe* is different. People are not important in the story, but I want my readers to feel for the family of mice the way they'd feel for any human character." The mouse family made an impression on a *Reading Time* contributor, who praised Broome's "well-drawn" characters, calling *Magnus maybe* "a credible and moving tale."

Of the future of her writing career, Broome told *SATA:* "At a school recently, a boy asked me when I was going to write my last book. It was a good question. And I'm glad I don't know the answer."

Works Cited

Blackhall, Ricki, review of *Quicksilver, Magpies,* July, 1997, p. 32.

Hanzl, Anne, review of *Fly with Me, Magpies,* September, 1996, p. 29.

Hanzl, review of *Garry Keeble's Kitchen: How One Boy Left Home and Survived with 28 Recipes That Anyone Can Cook and Everyone Will Eat, Magpies,* July, 1993, p. 33.

Knoth, Maeve Visser, review of *Dear Mr. Sprouts, Horn Book,* July, 1993, pp. 464-465.

Review of *Magnus maybe, Reading Time,* November, 1998, p. 20.

Matthews, Stephen, "From the Word Go," *Australian Book Review,* June, 1993, pp. 59-60.

Murray, John, review of *Nightwatch, Magpies,* July, 1995, pp. 23-24.

Philips, Margaret, review of *What a Goat!, Magpies,* March, 1997, p. 31.

Rochman, Hazel, review of *Rockhopper, Booklist,* January 1, 1996, p. 832.

Review of *Tangles, Kirkus Reviews,* April 15, 1994, p. 552.

Zahnleiter, Joan, review of *Splashback: A Great Greasy Journey,* July, 1996, p. 29.

For More Information See

PERIODICALS

Booklist, June 1 & 15, 1993, p. 1808; March 15, 1994, p. 1347.

Cranbourne Sun (Victoria, Australia), October 28, 1991.

Reading Time, November 1996, pp. 9-11.

School Library Journal, April, 1988, p. 78.

*   *   *

BROWN, Ruth 1941-

Personal

Born May 20, 1941, in Tiverton, England; daughter of Hughbert Niels (a company executive) and Dorothy Alice (Wicks) Antonsen; married Kenneth James Brown (an illustrator), August 29, 1964; children: Hogan, James. *Education:* Bournemouth College of Art, 1957-59; Birmingham College of Art, 1959-61, first class honors; Royal College of Art, M.A., 1964. *Politics:* Liberal. *Hobbies and other interests:* Gardening, walking the dog in the countryside, reading, travelling, visiting antique shops, cooking.

Addresses

Office—Andersen Press Ltd, Random House, 20 Vauxhall Bridge Road, London SW1V 2SA, England.

Career

Author and illustrator, 1979—.

Awards, Honors

Shortlisted for Greenaway Medal, British Library Association, 1988 and 1996, for *Ladybird, Ladybird* and *The Tale of the Monstrous Toad; Redbook* Children's Book Award, 1988, for *Blossom Comes Home.*

Writings

FOR CHILDREN; SELF-ILLUSTRATED

Crazy Charlie, Andersen (London, England), 1979.

A Dark, Dark Tale, Andersen, Dial, 1981.

If at First You Do Not See, Andersen, 1982, Holt, 1983.

The Grizzly Revenge, Andersen, 1983.

The Big Sneeze, Andersen, 1985, Lothrop, 1985.

Our Cat Flossie, Andersen, Dutton, 1986.

Our Puppy's Holiday, Andersen, 1987, published in the U.S. as *Our Puppy's Vacation,* Dutton, 1987.

Ladybird, Ladybird, Andersen, 1988, published in the U.S. as *Ladybug, Ladybug,* Dutton, 1988.

I Don't Like It!, Andersen, 1989, Dutton, 1990.

The World That Jack Built, Andersen, 1990, Dutton, 1991.

The Four-Tongued Alphabet: An Alphabet Book in Four Languages, Andersen, 1991, published in the U.S. as *Alphabet Times Four: An International ABC,* Dutton, 1991.

The Picnic, Andersen, Dutton, 1992.

One Stormy Night, Andersen, 1992, Dutton, 1993.

Copycat, Andersen, Dutton, 1994.

(Reteller) *Greyfriars Bobby,* Andersen, 1995, published in the U.S. as *The Ghost of Greyfriar's Bobby,* Dutton, 1996.

The Tale of the Monstrous Toad, Andersen, 1996, published in the U.S. as *Toad,* Dutton, 1997.

Baba, Andersen, 1997, published in the U.S. as *Cry Baby,* Dutton, 1997.

Ruth Brown's Mad Summer Night's Dream, Andersen, 1998, Dutton, 1999.

The Shy Little Angel, Andersen, Dutton, 1998.

Ruth Brown

ILLUSTRATOR; "YOU AND ME" STORYBOOK SERIES

Judith Miles, *The Three Little Pigs,* Longman (Harlow, England), 1979.
Barbara Parker, *The Three Bears,* Longman, 1979.
Mary Harris, *The Black and White Cat,* Longman, 1979.
Judith Miles, *The Ugly Duckling,* Longman, 1979.
Francesca Zeissl, *King Gargantua,* Longman, 1981.
Barbara Parker, *Town Mouse, Country Mouse,* Longman, 1981.

ILLUSTRATOR; ALL WRITTEN BY JAMES HERRIOT

The Christmas Day Kitten, Michael Joseph (London, England), St. Martin's, 1986.
Bonny's Big Day, Michael Joseph, St. Martin's, 1987.
Blossom Comes Home, Michael Joseph, St. Martin's, 1988.
The Market Square Dog, Michael Joseph, St. Martin's, 1989.
Oscar, Cat-About-Town, Michael Joseph, St. Martin's, 1990.
Smudge's Day Out, Michael Joseph, 1991, published in the U.S. as *Smudge, the Little Lost Lamb,* St. Martin's, 1991.
(With Peter Barrett) *James Herriot's Animal Storybook,* Michael Joseph, 1992, published in the U.S. as *James Herriot's Treasury for Children,* St. Martin's, 1992.

OTHER

Jeanne Willis, *In Search of the Hidden Giant,* Andersen, 1993, published in the U.S. as *In Search of the Giant,* Dutton, 1994.
Frances Thomas, *Mr. Bear & the Bear,* Andersen, 1994, Dutton, 1995.
Toby Forward, *The Christmas Mouse,* Andersen, 1996, published in the U.S. as *Ben's Christmas Carol,* Dutton, 1996.
Hiawyn Oram, *The Wise Doll: A Traditional Tale,* Andersen, 1997, published as *Baba Yaga and the Wise Doll: A Traditional Russian Folktale,* Dutton, 1998.

Adaptations

Several of Brown's books have been adapted for audiocassette.

Sidelights

English author Ruth Brown has written and illustrated numerous children's books, which have been published both in England and the United States. "I'm very lucky to earn my living by writing and illustrating books," Brown told *SATA.* "It means I can work at my own pace in my own time and in my own house. Sometimes I work very hard—seven days a week—and then when I've finished a book I can take a little time off before I start the next one."

Born in England in 1941, Brown grew up in Germany and in Bournemouth, England. After five years of arts studies, Brown married an illustrator and fellow author of children's books and began a family. In 1979, she published her first children's book, *Crazy Charlie.* The story of a voracious crocodile who becomes less intimidating when his teeth fall out, the book was well received in England, and its 1983 publication in the U.S. introduced the author to American audiences. Christine C. Seibold, writing in *School Library Journal,* noted that "Children will identify with Charlie's longing for attention, and will cheer when he finally learns it's better to smile than growl." Seibold also commented on the "bold double-spread watercolor illustrations ... rich in jungle colors and detail."

A *Kirkus Reviews* commentator noted of Brown's second book, *A Dark, Dark Tale,* that "this ... teeny tiny scare story [is] tailor-made for a picture book." A black cat finds its way across a dark moor to a gloomy castle and then to a darkened corner of a mysterious room. "Brown's rich acrylic paintings are all shadows and cobwebs," noted *Booklist's* Ilene Cooper. "This will work well as a read-aloud with young listeners sure to be chanting the words 'dark, dark' as the cat pads along," Cooper concluded.

As well received as these early titles were, Brown's third book, *If at First You Do Not See,* won over larger numbers of critics and readers alike. A reviewer in *Publishers Weekly* noted that Brown's early books had been praised as "beautiful and original," but that her "new and astonishing feat overshadows the most eminent among them." A caterpillar wanders off looking for something to eat, but soon discovers that everything it chooses to munch on turns out—with a turn of the book sideways or upside down—to be something else. Grass, for example, becomes the head of an angry giant. "Brown's radiantly hued paintings have been executed with an artfulness that one must marvel at and admire," the *Publishers Weekly* critic concluded. "Is it a book?" wondered a reviewer for *Junior Bookshelf.* "Is it a toy? One thing is certain. Young children will get many hours of delight discovering and re-discovering the hidden faces. A book to possess rather than borrow."

"The very hardest part of my job is thinking of good ideas," Brown told *SATA.* "The writing is the next most difficult thing and doing the illustrations is the most fun." Fun is certainly something that Brown's illustrations display. Known for her delicate use of watercolors and her realistic and atmospheric representations of animals and rural life, Brown has been highly praised for her richly textured and colored artwork. She takes inspiration from the most commonplace of events. A fly lands on the nose of a sleeping farmer in *The Big Sneeze,* and sets off a chain reaction of accidents when it causes the dozing agrarian to sneeze. A *Junior Bookshelf* contributor called Brown's artwork in this book "delightfully evocative," while Moira Small noted in *Books for Keeps* that Brown "has produced a visual treat in this wonderful picture book ... and a lesson in logic for small people!"

Animals of all sorts provide further inspiration. In *Our Cat Flossie,* Brown follows a house cat through a typical day, from her favorite haunts to her favorite pastimes. "Brown is, quite obviously, gone on cats," Christina Olson remarked in a *School Library Journal* review of the book. Olson was right, for Brown's household is

Toad's covered in warts and lumps and bumps, with stains and spots and speckled humps.

***Toad's grotesqueness saves his life when he wanders into the jaws of a large predator and is spit back out again.** (From* Toad, *written and illustrated by Brown.)*

home to three cats and a Labrador retriever. The real Flossie died in 1985, the year before publication of *Our Cat Flossie.* "The paintings," Olson concluded in her review, "softly colored portraits of Flossie, are charming.... A book that is simple—fulfillingly so." Chris Powling, writing in *Books for Keeps,* called the book a "straightforward charmer." The adventures of a Labrador puppy are served up in *Our Puppy's Vacation,* which Kristi Thomas Beavin called "visually appealing" in *School Library Journal,* and Betsy Hearne declared was "Well worth the trip!" in *Bulletin of the Center for Children's Books.*

Other popular animal and nature titles from Brown include *Ladybird, Ladybird* (published in the U.S as *Ladybug, Ladybug), The Picnic,* and *One Stormy Night.* The ladybird or ladybug of the first book is the subject of a Mother Goose rhyme which Brown adapts into something of an environmental message, expanding the rhyme to include the animals and plants of the countryside. "It is Brown's lush, dramatically staged illustrations that add real weight to the poem," averred Phyllis Wilson in *Booklist.* Margery Fisher of *Growing Point* noted that "there is an unobtrusive lesson in natural history implied in the pages of this expressive picture-book." Humans in the countryside almost unwittingly cause disaster for the rabbits, mice, and moles who inhabit an underground burrow near a picnic site in *The Picnic.* "Brown's talent for illustrating nature is admirably displayed here," commented Judy Constantinides in *School Library Journal,* while Kristina Lindsay remarked in *Magpies* that "Brown's illustrations are superb, with her delicate watercolours highlighting the stark difference between the bright daylight outside and dark burrow underground." In *One Stormy Night,* the reader is presented with a dog's-eye view of a stormy night as the animal goes through the gates of a scary manor to find shelter from the weather. But as the storm clears in the morning, the white dog is seen as a carved figure on a tomb at the nearby church. A *Junior Bookshelf* critic concluded a review of the book by stating that "Brown knows her animals and her architecture, and she captures the muted tones of night with great skill."

A nursery rhyme, the alphabet, and a Russian folktale served as inspirations for three other books from Brown. *The World That Jack Built* employs "the old cumulative Jack verse for a picture book about the environment," according to *Booklist's* Hazel Rochman. Two contrasting valleys—one verdant and pristine, the other industrial and polluted—depict the conservation message in this "powerful book," according to *Magpie's* Cynthia Anthony. *Alphabet Times Four* (originally published in England as *The Four-Tongued Alphabet*) goes beyond the bounds of traditional alphabet books by portraying words in four languages—English, Spanish, French, and German—that happen to begin with the same letter. Hearne, writing in *Bulletin of the Center for Children's Books,* noted that "Teachers, librarians, and parents will find this a long-term, broad-based aesthetic investment." Reviewing the British edition, *Junior Bookshelf* called the book "beautifully pictured, in richly coloured and mysterious, imaginative paintings of such subjects as the ark, flowers in a window ... a Chinese dragon design...." *Baba Yaga and the Wise Doll* uses the traditional fairy tale witch Baba Yaga to create a book with "luscious watercolors" that "wallow in the grotesque and the slimy," according to *Booklist's* Rochman.

Returning to the animal kingdom, Brown tells the story of the imitative cat, Buddy, in *Copycat;* retells the tale of a loyal dog in *The Ghost of Greyfriar's Bobby;* tips the hat to Dickens in a mousey version of Scrooge in *Ben's Christmas Carol;* and gets to the heart of a very ugly amphibian in *Toad.* Buddy lives with two other cats and a dog—just as Brown's cat of the same name does—and thus always has a companion to imitate. Buddy will snuggle up to any sleeping cat, or perch like a squirrel on the garden wall. However, when he bites into a dog bone, he realizes that there are some things he can not imitate. Ellen Mandel, reviewing *Copycat* in *Booklist,* noted that "Brown's lush paintings convey humor and affection as well as the animals' personalities," while a

Brown's lively illustrations reflect the distasteful details in the traditional Russian fairy tale of a child-eating witch and the girl who meets her challenges. (From *Baba Yaga and the Wise Doll,* retold by Hiawyn Oram and illustrated by Brown.)

A surprise ending distinguishes Brown's picture-book tale of a very sensitive child and her exasperated older siblings. (*From* Cry Baby, *written and illustrated by Brown.*)

reviewer for *Publishers Weekly* concluded that the book was "as comfortable and familiar as a beloved pet."

Two modern-day children, tourists in Edinburgh, Scotland, take the reader back in time in *The Ghost of Greyfriar's Bobby* when they happen upon a fountain commemorating a dog named Bobby who is buried in a nearby churchyard. They—and the reader—learn, through a bit of magical flashback, of the loyalty of the dog that followed its master to his grave and then lingered nearby for fourteen years until it died as well. "Atmospheric prose and beguiling full-spread watercolors unfold Bobby's life with his master, Old Jock," commented a reviewer in *Publishers Weekly.* Lisa S. Murphy, writing in *School Library Journal,* noted how "Brown's masterful watercolors paint an inviting picture of both the town of Edinburgh and the gorgeous Scottish countryside," and concluded that this was a "beautiful retelling of a hard-to-find legend." From loyal dog to stingy mouse—*Ben's Christmas Carol* puts a mouse

named Ben into the role of Ebeneezer Scrooge. With text by Toby Forward, *Ben's Christmas Carol* was heralded by critics, such as Susan Dove Lempke of *Booklist,* for its "sumptuous" paintings displaying London "in all its moods—from spooky and grimy to celebratory."

With *Toad,* Brown pulled out the stops on the grotesque. As the book says, *Toad* is the tale of a "toad odorous, foul and filthy, and dripping with venomous fluid." But Toad's very ugliness is his defense: when he wanders into the jaws of a large predator, he is spit back out again. Deborah Stevenson, reviewing the book in *Bulletin of the Center for Children's Books* thought that it "seems a bit unfair to turn the toad's natural defenses into such a condemnatory judgment ... about his personal charms, but the story trips along rhythmically nonetheless." Focusing on the artwork, Caroline Ward commented in *School Library Journal* that, "from the wart-encrusted end paper to the browns and greens of the slimy mire, the fluid watercolor illustrations aptly depict the setting."

Brown has also taken paintbrush in hand to illustrate six stories from James Herriot, doing for the Yorkshire veterinarian what she has for her own texts: providing atmospheric and lovingly detailed artwork that enhances and often transcends the usual bounds of book illustration. Reviewing her illustrations for *The Market Square Dog* for example, a *Publishers Weekly* reviewer remarked that "Brown's softly shaded watercolors recall an England of an earlier era, a place of cozy stone cottages and country gardens." Brown's evocative brushwork and meaningful texts have captured young readers on both sides of the Atlantic. In a review of Brown's 1997 title, *Baba* (U.S. edition, *Cry Baby*), about a pesky baby sister, Angela Redfern wrote in *School Librarian* that "you come to Ruth Brown's books with high expectations. You know she will write about something that matters." It is a comment that may be applied to each of Brown's works.

Works Cited

Anthony, Cynthia, review of *The World That Jack Built, Magpies,* March, 1991, p. 26.

Beavin, Kristi Thomas, review of *Our Puppy's Vacation, School Library Journal,* January, 1988, p. 63.

Review of *The Big Sneeze, The Junior Bookshelf,* August, 1985, p. 172.

Brown, Ruth, *Toad,* Dutton, 1997.

Constantinides, Judy, review of *The Picnic, School Library Journal,* March, 1993, p. 171.

Cooper, Ilene, review of *A Dark, Dark Tale, Booklist,* December 1, 1981, p. 494.

Review of *Copycat, Publishers Weekly,* August 22, 1994, p. 54.

Review of *A Dark, Dark Tale, Kirkus Reviews,* November 15, 1981, p. 1403.

Fisher, Margery, review of *Ladybird, Ladybird, Growing Point,* July, 1988, p. 5013.

Review of *The Four-Tongued Alphabet: An Alphabet Book in Four Languages, The Junior Bookshelf,* December, 1991, p. 238.

Review of *The Ghost of Greyfriar's Bobby, Publishers Weekly,* March 11, 1996, p. 63.

Hearne, Betsy, review of *Alphabet Times Four: An International ABC, Bulletin of the Center for Children's Books,* November, 1991, pp. 57-58.

Hearne, Betsy, review of *Our Puppy's Vacation, Bulletin of the Center for Children's Books,* October, 1987, p. 23.

Review of *If At First You Do Not See, The Junior Bookshelf,* December, 1982, p. 218.

Review of *If At First You Do Not See, Publishers Weekly,* May 13, 1983, p. 57.

Lempke, Susan Dove, review of *Ben's Christmas Carol, Booklist,* September 1, 1996, p. 1.

Lindsay, Kristina, *The Picnic, Magpies,* July, 1993, p. 27.

Mandel, Ellen, review of *Copycat, Booklist,* October 1, 1994, p. 331.

Review of *The Market Square Dog, Publishers Weekly,* October 13, 1989, p. 51.

Murphy, Lisa S., review of *The Ghost of Greyfriar's Bobby, School Library Journal,* August, 1996, p. 133.

Olson, Christina, review of *Our Cat Flossie, School Library Journal,* November, 1986, pp. 72-73.

Review of *One Stormy Night, The Junior Bookshelf,* February, 1993, p. 11.

Powling, Chris, review of *Our Cat Flossie, Books for Keeps,* May, 1986, p. 27.

Redfern, Angela, review of *Baba, School Librarian,* August, 1997, pp. 129-30.

Rochman, Hazel, review of *Baba Yaga and the Wise Doll: A Traditional Russian Folktale, Booklist,* January 1, 1998, p. 818.

Rochman, Hazel, review of *The World That Jack Built, Booklist,* March 1, 1991, p. 1397.

Seibold, Christine C., review of *Crazy Charlie, School Library Journal,* September, 1983, p. 102.

Small, Moira, review of *The Big Sneeze, Books for Keeps,* May, 1993, p. 7.

Stevenson, Deborah, review of *Toad, Bulletin of the Center for Children's Books,* March, 1997, p. 2442.

Ward, Caroline, review of *Toad, School Library Journal,* March, 1997, p. 149.

Wilson, Phyllis, review of *Ladybug, Ladybug, Booklist,* November 1, 1998, p. 479.

For More Information See

PERIODICALS

Booklist, July, 1997, p. 1822.

Books for Keeps, May, 1992, p. 27; May, 1993, p. 36; May, 1996, p. 28; September, 1997, p. 20.

Bulletin of the Center for Children's Books, March, 1991, pp. 159-60; September, 1996, p. 6.

Horn Book, January-February, 1986, p. 54; January-February, 1987, p 46.

Kirkus Reviews, September 15, 1991, p. 1230.

New York Times Book Review, March 14, 1993, p. 18.

Publishers Weekly, July 5, 1993, p. 70; December 12, 1994, p. 62; September 30, 1996, p. 89.

School Library Journal, March, 1995, p. 187; February, 1998, p. 79.

Times Educational Supplement, July 18, 1997, p. 35.

—*Sketch by J. Sydney Jones*

*   *   *

BROWNE, Anthony (Edward Tudor) 1946-

Personal

Born September 11, 1946, in Sheffield, England; son of Jack Holgate (a teacher) and Doris May (Sugden) Browne; married Jane Franklin (a violin teacher), July 26, 1980; children: Joseph, Ellen. *Education:* Leeds College of Art, B.A. (with honors), 1967. *Hobbies and other interests:* Reading, music, theater, films, swimming, tennis, squash, cricket.

Anthony Browne

Addresses

Home and office—The Chalk Garden, The Length, St. Nicholas-at-Wade, Birchington, Kent CT7 0PJ, England.

Career

Victoria University of Manchester, Manchester, England, medical artist at Royal Infirmary, 1968-70; Gordon Fraser Greeting Cards, London, England, designer, 1971-88; author and illustrator of children's books, 1975—. Browne has also held two teaching positions. *Exhibitions:* Browne's illustrations from *Alice's Adventures in Wonderland* were exhibited in Barbicon, London, England, 1988, and an exhibition of his work was presented in Mexico and opened by the wife of the Mexican president, 1994.

Awards, Honors

Kate Greenaway Medal commendation, British Library Association, 1982, and International Board on Books for Young People (IBBY) Award for Illustration in Great Britain, 1984, both for *Hansel and Gretel;* Kate Greenaway Medal and Kurt Maschler/"Emil" Award, Book Trust (England), 1983, *New York Times* best illustrated children's books of the year citation, 1985, *Boston Globe-Horn Book* Honor Book for illustration, 1986, Child Study Association of America Children's Books of the Year citation, 1986, *Horn Book* Honor List, 1986,

and 1989, and Silver Pencil Award (Netherlands), 1989, all for *Gorilla;* Deutscher Jugendliteratur Preis (German Youth Literature Prize; with Annalena McAfee), and Notable Children's Trade Book in the Field of Social Studies, National Council for Social Studies and Children's Book Council, both 1985, both for *The Visitors Who Came to Stay;* Parents' Choice Award, Parents' Choice Foundation, for *Piggybook*, 1987, and 1988, for *Look What I've Got!;* Kate Greenaway Medal, highly commended, 1988, Kurt Maschler/"Emil" Award, Book Trust (England), and Parents' Choice Award, both 1989, all for *Alice's Adventures in Wonderland;* Silver Pencil Award, 1989, for *The Tunnel;* Kate Greenaway Medal, 1992, for *Zoo;* silver medal, Society of Illustrators, 1995, for *King Kong;* Kurt Maschler Award, Book Trust (England), Best Books, *Publishers Weekly,* and Best Books, *School Library Journal,* all 1998, Fanfare list, *Horn Book,* and Notable Books for Children, American Library Association, both 1999, all for *Voices in the Park.*

Writings

"BEAR" SERIES; SELF-ILLUSTRATED

Bear Hunt, Hamish Hamilton (London), 1979, Atheneum, 1980.
Bear Goes to Town, Hamish Hamilton, 1982, Doubleday (New York), 1989.
The Little Bear Book, Hamish Hamilton, 1988, Doubleday, 1989.
A Bear-y Tale, Hamish Hamilton, 1989.

"WILLY" SERIES; SELF-ILLUSTRATED

Willy the Wimp, Knopf, 1984, MacRae (London), 1984.
Willy the Champ, Knopf, 1985, MacRae, 1985.
Willy and Hugh, Knopf, 1991, MacRae, 1991.
Willy the Wizard, Knopf, 1995, MacRae, 1995.
Willy the Dreamer, Walker (London), 1997, Candlewick (Cambridge, MA), 1998.

RETELLINGS

(Adaptor) Jacob Grimm and Wilhelm Grimm, *Hansel and Gretel,* MacRae, 1981, Watts, 1982.
(Story conceived by Edgar Wallace and Merian C. Cooper) *King Kong,* Turner Publishing (Atlanta), 1994, published in England as *Anthony Browne's King Kong,* MacRae, 1994.

PICTURE BOOKS

Through the Magic Mirror, Hamish Hamilton, 1976, Greenwillow, 1977.
A Walk in the Park, Hamish Hamilton, 1977, revised edition, Doubleday (London), 1990, U.S. edition as *Voices in the Park,* DK Ink (New York), 1998.
Look What I've Got!, MacRae, 1980, Knopf, 1988.
Gorilla, Knopf, 1983, MacRae, 1983, revised edition, 1991.
Piggybook, Knopf, 1986, MacRae, 1986.
I Like Books, Knopf, 1989, MacRae, 1989.
Things I Like, Knopf, 1989, MacRae, 1989.
The Tunnel, Knopf, 1989, MacRae, 1989.
Changes, Knopf, 1990, MacRae, 1990.
Zoo, Knopf, 1992, MacRae, 1992.
The Big Baby: A Little Joke, MacRae, 1993, Knopf, 1994.

ILLUSTRATOR; FICTION, EXCEPT AS NOTED

Annalena McAfee, *The Visitors Who Came to Stay,* Hamish Hamilton, 1984, Viking, 1985.

Sally Grindley, *Knock, Knock! Who's There?,* Hamish Hamilton, 1985, Knopf, 1986.

Annalena McAfee, *Kirsty Knows Best,* Knopf, 1987.

Lewis Carroll, *Alice's Adventures in Wonderland,* Knopf, 1988, MacRae, 1988.

Gwen Strauss, *Trail of Stones* (young adult poems), Knopf, 1990.

Gwen Strauss, *The Night Shimmy,* Knopf, 1992.

Ian McEwan, *The Daydreamers,* HarperCollins, 1994.

Janni Howker, *The Topiary Garden,* Orchard, 1995.

OTHER

Browne's works have been translated into several languages, including Spanish, Welsh, French, Italian, German, Hebrew, Japanese, Chinese, Dutch, Finnish, Swedish, and Danish.

Adaptations

Bear Hunt was adapted as a filmstrip by Weston Woods, 1981.

Sidelights

Called "one of the most original and accomplished of our picture book artists" by Chris Powling in *Books for Keeps* and "one of the most highly original creators of picture books to arrive on the scene in recent years" by Amy J. Meeker in *Children's Books and Their Creators,* Anthony Browne is an English author, illustrator, and reteller who is acclaimed as a gifted artist and incisive social critic whose works have helped to define the modern picture book. Celebrated for creating unconventional, often provocative works that challenge and delight both young readers and adults, Browne uses spare texts and symbolic pictures filled with surrealistic details and humorous visual puns to address serious themes about personal relationships, social conventions, human behavior, and the thin line between perception and reality. His artistic style is a highly individualistic, intensely personal approach that combines fantastic and representational imagery in a precise, meticulous technique. It is noted for its bold, rich colors; use of animals to represent humans, especially gorillas and chimpanzees; and references to popular culture, to literary characters, to his own work, and to artists such as Rene Magritte, Salvador Dali, Leonardo da Vinci, and Edvard Munch.

Browne is perhaps best known as the creator of *Gorilla,* a picture book that features a lonely girl infatuated with apes who, after receiving a toy gorilla from her often absent father, dreams that it turns into a real animal. Browne has also written and illustrated two popular series of picture books—the first about Willy, an ingenuous chimp, and the second about Bear, a jaunty teddy who averts danger with the aid of his magic pencil. In addition, he has retold the fairy tale *Hansel and Gretel* and the story of the film *King Kong* and has illustrated the works of such authors as Lewis Carroll,

Janni Howker, Ian McEwan, Annalena McAfee, and Gwen Strauss in a style that features his familiar motifs.

As a writer, Browne often uses the formats of the folktale, fairy tale, and cautionary tale as the framework for stories that depict humans and anthropomorphic animals who use their imaginations and interior strength to effect their personal situations. Browne's characters face loneliness, neglect, boredom, jealousy, ridicule, and social differences with spirit and resourcefulness, and the author presents his readers with subtle messages about being true to oneself and reaching out to others. Praised for his sensitivity to the needs and concerns of children, Browne has also developed a reputation as a sharp social observer; several of his books skewer contemporary adult behavior—especially that of males—by showing how foolishness, cruelty, and self-absorption bring out the baseness of our animal natures. As an artist, Browne uses color and pattern to define the symbolism of his pictures, detailed, hyper-realistic paintings often set against white backgrounds. His art is

Browne's illustrations, with their blend of realism and fantasy, suit Ian McEwan's story of a young boy's imaginative adventures. (From The Daydreamer.*)*

often credited with helping readers to view the world in a new way. In his depiction of the inner nature of things, Browne includes some details that are considered disturbing, a factor for which he has been criticized. In addition, his books are sometimes considered too clever and sophisticated, especially for children. However, most reviewers view Browne as a writer and artist of great talent and singular vision whose works contain emotional depth and foster powerful responses. A critic in *Kirkus Reviews* noted that Browne's picture books "comment on the human condition with perception and originality," while Jane Doonan of *Twentieth Century Children's Writers* claimed that he "has given a large audience (of all ages) consistently interesting work that, at every level, contains something to be enjoyed, discovered, and considered." Writing in *Magpies,* Browne's longtime editor Julia MacRae said that he "is truly an artist who opens our minds—and our hearts."

Browne was born in Sheffield, Yorkshire, in the north of England, to pub owners Jack and Doris May Browne. A teacher and salesman who worked in a variety of professions before settling down, Jack Browne was described by his son in *Sixth Book of Junior Authors and Illustrators* as "an unusual man—he had a strong,

outwardly confident manner, but also a shy, sensitive nature." Jack Browne, his son wrote, "would spend hours drawing for my brother and me, he wrote poetry for us and made beautiful delicate models of castles and boats and houses. Yet he also encouraged us to play rugby and soccer and cricket, to box and wrestle, to lift weights and to run." In an interview in *Something about the Author (SATA),* Browne recalled, "Books were a huge part of our lives. We had annuals, *The Beano Annual* or *The Dandy Annual,* that sort of thing. And fairy stories, particularly *Hansel and Gretel.* I do remember *Alice in Wonderland,* which must have been read to me. Perhaps I have better recall of the Tenniel pictures than the story." When he was a child, Browne wanted to be a boxer like his father had been, and then a newspaper reporter. "I suppose what I really wanted was to be like my dad—a big, powerfully built man, and I was always a small boy," he mused.

Both Browne's father and brother Michael had artistic talent. The author recalled in *SATA* that they would draw "a British and a German soldier, for instance, with all the details of uniforms and guns. I, on the other hand, would draw battle scenes with jokes thrown in—a decapitated head speaking or a picture of an invisible

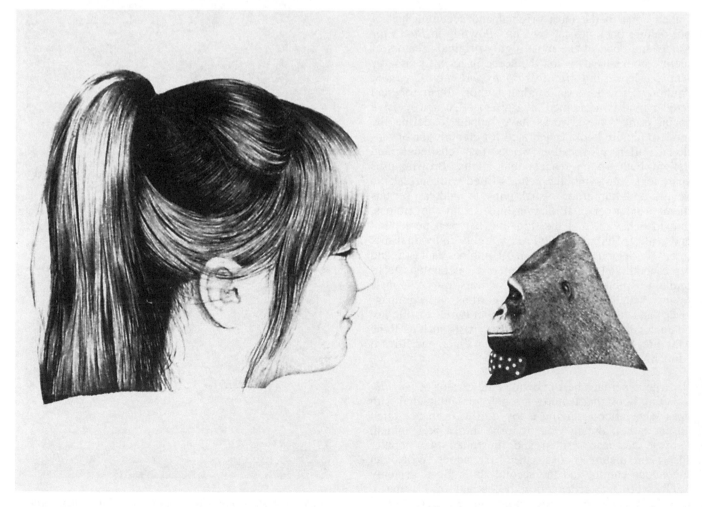

A lonely girl, infatuated with apes, receives a toy gorilla from her often-absent father and dreams that it turns into a real animal in Browne's award-winning book. (From Gorilla, *written and illustrated by Browne.)*

Mild-mannered Willy, protagonist of several Browne picture books, fantasizes about heroic deeds and exciting professions. (*From* Willy the Dreamer, *written and illustrated by Browne.*)

man. Knights on horseback and cowboys and Indians shared the same battle. Looking back I see that my pictures took on a narrative form." On occasion, Browne would stand on a table in the tap room of his parents' pub and tell stories to the patrons. One of these tales featured a Superman-like hero called Big Dumb Tackle. Browne recalled in *SATA,* "My mother told me that in one of my stories Big Dumb Tackle went to heaven and knocked on the door of heaven and said, 'Can Jesus come out to play?' I shudder to think what the answer might have been!"

In his interview in *SATA,* Browne called himself "a kid with terrors—people coming after me, things under the bed, in the wardrobe . . . . Looking back, I was quite the wimp" (In 1984, Browne published *Willy the Wimp,* the story of a skinny, refined young chimp who triumphs over his gorilla tormentors.) By the age of five, Browne was learning Latin at a local private school. When he was seven, Browne and his family moved to Wyke, near Bradford, a tough industrial area. The author noted in *Junior Authors and Illustrators,* "[I]t could have been quite difficult for a boy who was small, didn't speak with the broad local dialect, and who liked drawing and writing poetry. Being good at sport saved me from being bullied, the hours of playing games and fighting with my brother had paid off." Throughout his school years, Browne continued drawing, mostly detailed sketches of battles "strongly influenced by the comics I was reading at the time, and with macabre little jokes and speech bubbles in the background," he noted in *Junior Authors and Illustrators.* He was also learning to appreciate literature. His most memorable teacher, Browne recalled in *SATA,* "introduced me to the work of Beckett and Pinter. Encountering Beckett was a bit like discovering surrealism in painting—something at once totally unexpected and yet deeply familiar. It struck a chord, because I seemed to recognize something in it."

At sixteen, Browne announced that he wanted to go straight from high school to art college; his family agreed. During Browne's first year as a graphic design major at Leeds College of Art, his father passed away. The author recalled in *SATA,* "It was terrible. His two previous massive heart attacks should have prepared me, but I didn't take in the significance of that." When asked by Chris Powling in *Books for Keeps* if he is, to some extent, fulfilling his father's ambition to become an artist, Browne replied, "It's not something I think about but I suppose in a way, yes. If he'd been given the opportunities I had, I'm pretty sure he'd have done something very similar."

Browne recalled that his work during his three years of art school was "morbid, no doubt in response to my father's death. I spent a lot of time in life-drawing classes, because I enjoyed painting women with no clothes on, and later making grotesque images based on the insides as well as the outside of the human body." Although Browne noted in *Junior Authors and Illustrators* that the most useful thing he learned in art school "was to keep my drawings free from thumb prints and smudges," he was excited by his introduction to complementary colors and also began going to galleries. Then, Browne recalled in *SATA,* "I came across Francis Bacon's work and was totally bowled over." In 1967, Browne left Leeds with, he noted in *Junior Authors and Illustrators,* "a hatred of the commercial art world, a morbid fascination with the inside of people's bodies, and an ambition to be the next Francis Bacon." Realizing that he didn't belong in graphic arts, he decided to go to London and become a painter. After returning home disappointed, he applied for a course in medical art. Although he was denied admission, Browne's interviewer informed him of a job opening as an assistant medical artist at the Royal Infirmary in Manchester; he got the job. From this experience, Browne recalled in *Junior Authors and Illustrators,* "I learned to tell stories in pictures.... To decide what to show and what to leave out [in an operation], what can be explained in pictures and what to explain in words. Just like a picture book." He added in *SATA,* "the job did exorcise my morbidness forever."

After two years as a medical artist, Browne felt that he needed to stretch his imagination, so he began creating a collection of greeting cards while working in an ad agency. He sent his cards to Gordon Fraser, a large greeting card company in London, and shortly thereafter began a long career there as a card artist. Through his company's founder, Browne was introduced to the world of children's books. He recalled in *SATA,* "I began thinking about books, because cards weren't a proper living, really." Hamish Hamilton published Browne's first book, *Through the Magic Mirror,* in 1976. A picture book in which young Toby—bored in the house—enters a fantastic world through a looking glass before returning home, *Through the Magic Mirror* is noted for introducing the stylistic touches that would later become the hallmarks of Browne's work. Writing in *Horn Book,* Aidan Chambers noted that the book "firmly announces in an uncompromising way that Browne intends to bring into children's books some of the twentieth-century art which has often been thought too difficult for children to understand."

His next work, *A Walk in the Park,* was published in 1977 in England and reprinted in the United States with different illustrations as *Voices in the Park* in 1998. In this picture book, working-class Smudge and her father take their dog to the park, where they meet middle-class Charles, his mother, and their dog. The children and the dogs play together happily while the parents ignore each other. Writing in *Twentieth Century Children's Writers,* Jane Doonan wrote, "Smudge and Charles are accompanied by a yob and a snob, but win for themselves a spell of perfect happiness," while a reviewer in *Publishers Weekly,* assessing the American edition, noted, "Browne again proves himself an artist of inventive voice and vision as he creates perhaps his most psychologically complex work to date."

In 1980, Browne married violin teacher Jane Franklin; the couple have two children, Joseph and Ellen. In 1981, Browne published his retelling of the Grimm Brothers' fairy tale *Hansel and Gretel,* a work that is often considered a creative breakthrough as well as one of the artist's most controversial titles. Rather than presenting the tale as a period piece, Browne sets his illustrations in the present day and uses them to reflect the subconscious of young children. Writing in the *Times Literary Supplement,* Tanya Harrod wrote, "What ... do we make of this contemporary stepmother's squalid dressing table with lipsticks, talcum powder and cigarette ends lovingly depicted by Anthony Browne? Is her taste for fake furs and stiletto heels the cause of the family's poverty? Why have the Social Services let them slip through the net? I really cannot envision buying any child this book." Writing in *Signal,* Jane Doonan claimed, "Without question, Anthony Browne's pictures supply a piece of visual storytelling, a psychological commentary, which interprets the folktale in a positive way.... Browne's visual interpretation of *Hansel and Gretel* offers children a chance to recognize the nature of their deeper and truer feelings." In his *SATA* interview, Browne said that he did *Hansel and Gretel* "in fifties dress, a style of my own childhood, I suppose. I felt very vulnerable with this book, because so many fine illustrators have had their crack at it. I wanted each

Four characters offer four different perspectives on their walk in the park in Browne's humorous and thought-provoking story. (From Voices in the Park, *written and illustrated by Browne.)*

picture to be a painting in its own right. And I wanted to illustrate what was between the lines, so to speak."

Two years after the publication of *Hansel and Gretel*, Browne created *Gorilla*. In this work, small Hannah longs both for a gorilla and for the attention of her father. After she dreams that her stuffed toy is transformed into a huge ape that dons her father's hat and coat and takes her to the zoo and to the movies, her father takes her to the zoo. A reviewer in the *Junior Bookshelf* commented that the book's detail "will yield more each time to the reader—it is brilliantly worked out," while Kenneth Marantz of *Horn Book* commented, "Despite the fantasy, Browne has created a picture book that explores real emotions with a beautifully realized child protagonist. Using his artistic skills, he's fashioned the visual metaphors that help to transcend superficial meanings and feel the power of the more archetypal emotions that bind children to parents and people to the other animals." In her article in *Magpies*, Julia MacRae wrote, "*Gorilla* speaks individually to each reader and always will." In 1984, Browne won his first Greenaway Medal for *Gorilla*, which also won the Kurt Maschler Award from Germany in 1983 and the Silver Pencil Award from the Netherlands in 1989. The author has noted that *Gorilla* had its origin in a greeting card that he did for Gordon Fraser; the card depicted a big male gorilla holding a teddy bear. In his interview in *SATA*, Browne said, "I think the image goes back to my father, who in some ways was like a gorilla, big and potentially aggressive during his pub days." The author added, "I must confess that [*Gorilla*] has changed my life."

Following the success of *Gorilla*, Browne continued his fascination with simian characters with his series about Willy, a chimp who lives in a world dominated by gorillas. A critic in *Publishers Weekly* described Willy, who has prompted more letters from children than any of Browne's other characters, as "an earnest and endearing youngster, often lonely and sometimes bullied, but who wins out thanks to perseverance and pluck." In 1986, Browne also wrote and illustrated *Piggybook*, a picture book that is often considered among his best works. *Piggybook* features Mrs. Piggott, a harried wife and mother in a male-dominated family who is tired of doing all of the housework in addition to her other job. Her husband and sons, sloppy and demanding, infuriate Mrs. Piggott to the point that she shouts "You are pigs!" before storming out of the house. In her absence, the men become pink pigs. Before Mrs. Piggott returns and order is restored, they discover the joys of a clean home. Challenging male chauvinism and sexual stereotyping, *Piggybook* is acknowledged for its humorous but pointed examination of male and female roles. Kathleen Brachmann of *School Library Journal* called it a "wickedly feminist tale if ever there was one" and added that in "terms of cleverness and style, this one brings home the bacon," while Jane Doonan of the *Times Literary Supplement* noted that, "Both funny and disturbing, Browne achieves a fine balance between the humour of the fantastic imagery and the seriousness of his message."

In the mid-1980s, editor Julia MacRae made the suggestion, the author once told *SATA*, "that I should break away and make a big change. She suggested a number of classics, among them *Alice's Adventures in Wonderland*. 'After Tenniel,' I thought, 'who am I to even attempt.' But the story seeped into my consciousness...." Browne published his illustrated version of Lewis Carroll's book in 1988, and his pictures are noted for their imagination, detail, and humor as well as for reflecting the surreal quality of the text. However, as with *Hansel and Gretel*, *Alice's Adventures in Wonderland* received a mixed critical reception. Marcus Crouch of *Junior Bookshelf* called the artist's pictures "intellectually rather than emotionally satisfying" while Frances Spaulding of the *Times Literary Supplement* noted that Browne's illustrations "are freshly imagined but overloaded. In trying to dislodge Tenniel he offers intensely detailed renderings of scenes that far exceed the text." In contrast, Ann A. Flowers of *Horn Book* stated, "Anthony Browne's illustrations certainly add a new and suggestive dimension to *Alice's Adventures in Wonderland* and even extend the story," while Bernard Ashley of *Books for Keeps* called Browne's version of *Alice* "a marvelous way for Juniors to drink from the labelled bottle.... The Junior mind may not understand Browne's allusions all the time any more than it will understand Carroll's, but it will be somehow aware of being in the presence of an artist it will never forget." In his interview in *SATA*, Browne noted that *Alice*, which won the Kurt Maschler Award and was named a highly commended title by the Greenaway Award committee, is "one of the very few books I'm pleased with...."

Browne won his second Greenaway Medal for *Zoo*, a picture book in which the doltish behavior of a family of zoo visitors is juxtaposed against the dignity of the caged animals. At the end of the family's visit—in which boorish dad and his impatient sons behave insensitively—the mother, who alone feels some sympathy for the animals, says, "I don't think the zoo's really for animals. I think it's for people." Browne's illustrations reflect this sentiment—paintings on opposite pages balance the family's actions with the zoo's animals and settings. Other visitors to the zoo are pictured sporting flippers and tails beneath their clothes. Writing in *Booklist*, Stephanie Zvirin noted, "Browne is just as sly as ever. Here ... he brings the surreal and the real together to give us a world transformed. This time, however, he challenges us to examine not only the things we take for granted, but also the way we are." Writing in *School Librarian*, Griselda Greaves stated, "Browne's propaganda is unsubtle. The suitability of much of his work for the young is questionable, because it seems to express such distaste for humanity that no redemption is possible. Those who like Browne's work will find all they have come to expect in this book, but there is nothing new here." A reviewer in *Publishers Weekly* concluded, "Browne's effectively stark, magnificently realistic illustrations of the zoo animals offer a distinct contrast to his clever renditions of the supposedly human visitors to the zoo...."

Among the most personal of Browne's recent works is his illustrated retelling of the classic 1930s film *King Kong*. In his version, Browne bases many of his illustrations on the movie while adding several twists of his own. For example, the female lead now bears a striking resemblance to Marilyn Monroe. His dramatic, dreamlike illustrations have been noted for their new mastery of crowd scenes and group movement, while his text—considered both a love story and a tragedy by critics—is described by a reviewer in *Publishers Weekly* as "appropriately cinematic." Writing in *Junior Bookshelf*, Marcus Crouch—noting the "fine production and superb art-work"—stated that whether Browne's version of *King Kong* "adds anything to the interpretation to justify his efforts is open to doubt. This is not to say that the book is anything other than a remarkable achievement." A reviewer in *Publishers Weekly* commented, "[I]f ever a couple seemed made for each other artistically, it's the multitalented Browne and King Kong.... Browne's imagery reaches new heights—think *Gorilla* on steroids—with his powerful renderings of the fabled beast...." Julia MacRae of *Magpies* concluded that Browne's "dramatic pictures complemented to perfection this classic of the cinema." Writing in *Books for Keeps*, Browne acknowledged that *King Kong* pays homage to his father: "I have in the past tried to explain my fascination with gorillas by comparing them to my father. He was a big man and I was a small boy. He was strong and physical.... Yet he was also artistic and sensitive.... It's the dual nature of Kong which attracts me—the terrifying beast who is, in reality, a gentle beautiful creature. Memories of my father's death have, for me, terrible echoes of Kong's fall from the Empire State Building." Browne called *King Kong* "the most exhausting book I've ever worked on." However, the author wrote, "I'm just beginning to consider the possibilities of *Dr. Jekyll and Mr. Hyde*, or *Tarzan*, or *Frankenstein* or ... any suggestions?"

Writing in *Twentieth Century Children's Writers*, Browne stated, "I have now produced a body of picture books which are unified by style and themes, and which offer a very particular view of the world of my characters. I try to make my books work on different levels—so what seems a very simple story, appreciated on one level—can also stimulate reflection upon the nature of society and its complex values. While my style is often concerned with the materiality of objects and figures, I assemble them then to refuse the possibility of material reality—in this way revealing the interior states of the protagonists. I also try to make them funny!" Asked by a critic in *Publishers Weekly*, "What's with all the gorillas?," Browne replied, "For one, it's the fact that they are so close to us. To look at one of them is to look at ourselves. But they are not quite like us—there's just that slight odd difference. Also they're great creatures to draw and to look at. And I feel so sympathetic toward them; they're so powerful and so strong and so kind." Now that he has published more than thirty books, Browne noted in *Publishers Weekly* that his job has gotten harder, not easier. "You're much more aware of what people expect from you. Twenty years ago I just had an idea and I did it. Now I'm a bit more conscious of

what I'm doing and the effect of what I'm doing." Asked if he is still having fun at his chosen occupation, Browne replied, "Yes, absolutely. Every bit as much as when I started."

Works Cited

"About Our Cover Artist," *Publishers Weekly,* July 20, 1998, p. 121.

Ashley, Bernard, review of *Alice's Adventures in Wonderland, Books for Keeps,* November, 1988, p. 28.

Brachmann, Kathleen, review of *Piggybook, School Library Journal,* October, 1986, p. 157.

Browne, Anthony, essay in *Sixth Book of Junior Authors and Illustrators,* edited by Sally Holmes Holtze, Wilson, 1989, pp. 44-45.

Browne, Anthony, "Capturing Kong," *Books for Keeps,* November, 1994, pp. 24-25.

Browne, Anthony, comments in *Twentieth Century Children's Writers,* edited by Laura Standley Berger, 4th edition, St. James Press, 1995, p. 160.

Browne, Anthony, comments in *Publishers Weekly,* July 20, 1998, p. 121.

Browne, Anthony, and Chris Powling, in an interview in *Books for Keeps,* May, 1987, pp. 16-17.

Chambers, Aidan, "Hughes in Flight," *Horn Book,* April, 1980, pp. 211-14.

Crouch, Marcus, review of *Alice's Adventures in Wonderland, Junior Bookshelf,* February, 1989, p. 19.

Crouch, Marcus, review of *King Kong, Junior Bookshelf,* August, 1995, pp. 125-26.

Doonan, Jane, review of *Piggybook, Times Literary Supplement,* November 28, 1986, p. 1345.

Doonan, Jane, "Talking Pictures: A New Look at 'Hansel and Gretel,'" *Signal,* September, 1983, pp. 123-31.

Doonan, Jane, entry in *Twentieth Century Children's Writers,* edited by Laura Standley Berger, 4th edition, St. James Press, 1995, pp. 159-61.

Flowers, Ann A., review of *Alice's Adventures in Wonderland, Horn Book,* March-April, 1989, p. 208.

Review of *Gorilla, Junior Bookshelf,* August, 1983, p. 152-53.

Greaves, Griselda, review of *Zoo, School Librarian,* February, 1993, p. 20.

Harrod, Tanya, "Illustrating Atmosphere," *Times Literary Supplement,* November 20, 1981, p. 1360.

Review of *King Kong, Publishers Weekly,* November 7, 1994, p. 76.

Meeker, Amy J., entry in *Children's Books and Their Creators,* edited by Anita Silvey, Houghton Mifflin, 1995, pp. 98-99.

MacRae, Julia, "Anthony Browne," *Magpies,* May, 1996, pp. 8-10.

Marantz, Kenneth, review of *Gorilla, Horn Book,* January-February, 1986, p. 46.

Review of *Piggybook, Kirkus Reviews,* August 15, 1986, p. 1288.

Spaulding, Frances, "Up-to-date embellishments," *Times Literary Supplement,* November 25, 1988, p. 1320.

Review of *Voices in the Park, Publishers Weekly,* June 1, 1998, p. 48.

Review of *Zoo, Publishers Weekly,* February 15, 1993, p. 236.

Zvirin, Stephanie, review of *Zoo, Booklist,* December 15, 1992, p. 730.

For More Information See

BOOKS

Children's Literature Review, Volume 19, Gale, 1990.

PERIODICALS

Bulletin of the Center for Children's Books, March, 1993, p. 206; October, 1998, p. 53.

Five Owls, September-October, 1998, pp. 12-13.
Horn Book, November-December, 1998, p. 713.
The Lion and the Unicorn, January, 1999, pp. 30-56.
Magpies, May, 1993, p. 30.
Reading Time, May, 1996, p 11.
School Library Journal, September, 1998, p. 164.

—Sketch by Gerard J. Senick

C

CALDER, David 1932-1997

Personal

Born August 26, 1932, in Wellington, New Zealand; died March 1, 1997, in Wanganui, New Zealand; son of Albert (an automotive mechanic) and Marjorie (a schoolteacher; maiden name, Lazarus) Calder; married Barbara Gronn, November, 1957 (divorced February 16, 1984); married Valerie Barnes (a dental nurse), March 17, 1984; children: Graeme, Susan Calder Foster.

Career

Worked as a journalist and sub-editor in Hawera, New Plymouth, Masterton, Gisborne, and Wanganui, New Zealand. Ward Observatory, member of board of directors; Wanganui Museum Board, chairperson; justice of the peace for Wanganui.

Awards, Honors

Elected Fellow, Royal Astronomical Society, London, 1973; A.M.P. Financial journalism prize, 1978; Honour Award, junior section, *New Zealand Post* Children's Book Awards, 1998.

Writings

Seeing the Southern Sky, Whitcoulls (London, England), 1977.
The Dragonslayer's Apprentice, Scholastic New Zealand (Auckland, New Zealand), 1997.

Contributor to periodicals, including *Cricket* and New Zealand *School Journal.* Author of the unpublished works *The Mind-Wars* and *The Wonderful World of Wendy Warmer,* two books for teenagers, and of several humorous poems.

Sidelights

The late David Calder's widow, Valerie, notes that the author became aware of language at an early age. When he was seven, a teacher complimented him on a description in an essay. "I was committed to trying to be clever with words from that moment," Calder once commented. He was also greatly influenced by a great-aunt who loved literature and language. "[She] taught me from early childhood that language was a precision instrument, and should be used as such. Directly and indirectly, she was responsible for my interest in poetry, Shakespeare, astronomy and museums."

David Calder

Following his graduation from high school, Calder enjoyed a career in journalism that spanned more than four decades. "I always thought that when I retired it would be nice to write for children," Calder commented, "that after 45 years of writing for the people who read newspapers, it would be nice to have an intelligent readership.... I finally got round to it."

Calder brought a broad perspective to his new occupation as an author of fiction. An avid reader, he had considerable knowledge of many subjects, especially naval history, the history of World War II, and poetry. He was also an enthusiastic and noted amateur astronomer and potter and had a good understanding of law and the Justice system. After a long career in journalism, Calder found that what he most enjoyed about writing fiction was "feeling a piece, and individual characters, come alive and develop a life of their own." "I don't plan," Calder asserted. "I know broadly what I want to say, or where I want to end, and the detail suggests itself en route." The author acknowledged that his book, *The Dragonslayer's Apprentice,* "grew out of the thought: Dragons are invariably associated with fantasy and magic—could the theme be treated realistically?"

Once asked whether he had any advice for would-be writers, Calder said: "All writing, for any purpose, must be practised and improved endlessly. Learn to recognize bad work—which is easy. Then learn to recognise good work which could be better—which is very difficult. Think about the meaning and impact of every word and phrase used. Above all, learn to read your work as if you were seeing it for the first time. This is *very* difficult. And it takes a long time."

*　　*　　*

CARAHER, Kim(berley Elizabeth) 1961-

Personal

Born December 7, 1961, in Belfast, Northern Ireland; daughter of Samuel James (an industrial chemist) and Elizabeth Park (an intellectual disability services officer; maiden name, McAllister) Thompson; married Michael George Caraher (a teacher), January 10, 1987; children: Stephen Michael, Marion Elizabeth, Kieran James. *Education:* University of the Witwatersrand, B.A. (with honors), 1982; La Trobe University, Diploma in Education, 1984; Edith Cowan University, Diploma in Applied Sciences, 1991. *Politics:* "Left."

Addresses

Home—Darwin, Australia. *Electronic mail*—caraher@dove.net.au. *Agent*—Debbie Golvan, Golvan Arts Management, P.O. Box 766, Kew, Victoria 3101, Australia.

Kim Caraher

Career

Writer. Northern Territory Department of Education, Darwin, Australia, teacher, 1985—. Northern Territory University, lecturer in gifted education, 1993—. *Member:* Children's Book Council, Northern Territory Association for Education of the Gifted and Talented, Northern Territory Writers Centre.

Writings

There's a Bat on the Balcony, illustrated by Mark Sofilas, McGraw, 1993, SRA School Group (Santa Rosa, CA), 1994.
My Teacher Turns into a Tyrannosaurus, illustrated by Robert Dickins, Addison-Wesley Longman (South Melbourne, Australia), 1996, Sundance Publishing (Littleton, MA), 1997.
Up a Gum Tree, Addison-Wesley Longman, 1997.
The Cockroach Cup, illustrated by Craig Smith, Random House (Milsons Point, Australia), 1998.
Yucky Poo, Macmillan, 1998.

Work in Progress

The Darkening, a young adult fantasy set in northern Australia; a picture book; textbooks; a junior novel.

Sidelights

Kim Caraher told *SATA:* "Reading, writing, and living are all aspects of the same thing to me. As a child, I resented anything that disturbed my reading, and most of my play with other children was an imaginative adaptation of what I had been reading.

"I had moved from Belfast to Cape Town, from Cape Town to Harare, from Harare to Johannesburg, all before I turned fourteen. Books gave me a consistency of friendship and culture while the world outside was always changing. However, that constant change helped me to develop ways of seeing behind things that other people took for granted and to develop a writer's perspective.

"I enjoy being with children. When I talk to children, sometimes I feel like I understand their point of view so strongly that I could forget my own experience and see the world afresh through their eyes. That is what I want to put in my writing.

"I greatly admire the Australian author, Morris Gleitzman, for his ability to write about profoundly serious subjects with a sardonic humor that is very appealing to children. That is something I would love to be able to do one day, perhaps incorporating the political upheavals I experienced in my childhood.

"For now, I write every day when my third child, aged fifteen months, takes his (short) nap. I have a queue of ideas waiting to be sculpted into stories."

*   *   *

CARRIER, Roch 1937-

Personal

Born May 13, 1937, in Sainte-Justine-de-Dorchester, Quebec, Canada; son of Georges (in sales) and Marie-Anna (Tanguay) Carrier; married Diane Gosselin, 1959; children: two daughters. *Education:* Attended College Saint-Louis; received B.A. from L'Universite de Montreal, M.A., 1961; further study at the Sorbonne, University of Paris, 1961-64.

Addresses

Home—Montreal, Quebec, Canada.

Career

Novelist, poet, dramatist, screenwriter, and author of short fiction. Has held teaching positions at College Militaire Royal de Saint-Jean, Quebec, and at L'Universite de Montreal, Montreal, Quebec; lecturer. Theatre du Nouveau Monde, Quebec, secretary-general, 1970—; chair, Salon du Livre, Montreal; Canada Council, Ottawa, director, 1994—.

Awards, Honors

Prix Litteraire de la Province de Quebec, 1964, for *Jolis deuils: Petites tragedies pour adultes;* Grand Prix Litteraire de la Ville de Montreal, 1981.

Writings

TRANSLATED WORKS; FOR CHILDREN

Les Enfants du bonhomme dans la lune, Stanke, 1979, translation by Sheila Fischman published as *The Hockey Sweater, and Other Stories,* Anansi, 1979.

Un Champion, translation by Fischman published as *The Boxing Champion,* illustrated by Sheldon Cohen, Tundra Books, 1991.

Un Bonne et heureuse annee, published as *A Happy New Year's Day,* illustrated by Gilles Pelletier, Tundra Books, 1991.

Canada je t'aime-I Love You, illustrated by Miyuki Tanobe, Tundra Books, 1991.

Le Plus Long Circuit, Tundra Books, 1993, translation by Fischman published as *The Longest Home Run,* illustrated by Sheldon Cohen, Tundra Books, 1993.

Joueur de basket-ball, Tundra Books, 1996, translation by Fischman published as *The Basketball Player,* illustrated by Cohen, Tundra Books, 1996.

Roch Carrier

UNTRANSLATED WORKS; FOR CHILDREN

Ne faites pas mal a l'avenin, Les Editions Paulinas, 1984.

OTHER TRANSLATED WORKS

La Guerre, Yes Sir!, Editions du Jour, 1968, translation by Sheila Fischman published under the same title, Anansi, 1970.

Floralie, ou es-tu?, Editions du Jour, 1969, translation by Fischman published as *Floralie, Where Are You?,* Anansi, 1971.

Il est par la, le soleil, Editions du Jour, 1970, translation by Fischman published as *Is It the Sun, Philibert?,* Anansi, 1972.

Le Deux-millieme etage, Editions du Jour, 1973, translation by Fischman published as *They Won't Demolish Me!,* Anansi, 1974.

Le Jardin des delices, Editions la Press, 1975, translation by Fischman published as *The Garden of Delights,* Anansi, 1978.

Il n'y a pas de pays sans grand-pere, Stanke, 1979, translation by Fischman published as *No Country without Grandfathers,* Anansi, 1981.

La Dame qui avait des chaines aux chevilles, Stanke, 1981, translation by Fischman published as *Lady with Chains,* Anansi, 1984.

De l'amour dans la ferraille, Stanke, 1984, translation by Fischman published as *Heartbreaks along the Road,* Anansi, 1987.

Prieres d'un enfant tres tres sage, Stanke, 1988, translation by Fischman published as *Prayers of a Very Wise Child,* Penguin, 1991.

L'Homme dans le placard (mystery), Stanke, 1991, translation by Fischman published as *The Man in the Closet,* Viking, 1993.

Fin, Stanke (Montreal), 1992, translation by Fischman published as *The End,* Viking, 1994.

Petit homme tornade, Stanke, 1996, translation by Fischman published as *The Lament of Charlie Longsong,* Viking, 1998.

OTHER UNTRANSLATED WORKS

Les Jeux incompris (poems), Editions Nocturne, 1956.

Cherche tes mots, cherche tes pas, Editions Nocturne, 1958.

Jolis deuils: Petites tragedies pour adultes (stories), Editions du Jour, 1964.

L'Aube d'acier (poem), illustrated by Maurice Savoie, Les Auteurs Reunis, 1971.

Les Fleurs vivent-elles ailleurs que sur la terre, Stanke, 1980.

Les Voyageurs de l'arc-en-ciel, illustrations by Francois Olivier, Stanke, 1980.

Le Cirque noir, Stanke, 1982.

L'Ours et le kangourou, Stanke, 1986.

Un Chameau en jordanie, Stanke, 1988.

Enfants de la planete, Paulines, 1989.

Prieres d'un adolescent tres tres sage, Stanke, 1998.

Contributor of short stories to periodicals, including *Etudes francaises* and *Ellipse.* Contributor of articles to periodicals, including *Ecrits du Canada francais.*

PLAYS

La Guerre, Yes Sir! (four-act; adapted from Carrier's novel of the same title; produced in Montreal, 1970; English-language version produced in Stratford, Ontario, 1972), Editions du Jour, 1970, revised edition, 1973.

Floralie (adapted from Carrier's novel *Floralie, ou es-tu?;* produced in Montreal, 1974), Editions du Jour, 1974.

Il n'y a pas de pays sans grand-pere (adapted from Carrier's novel of the same title), produced in Montreal, 1978.

La Celeste bicyclette (produced in Montreal, 1979; translation produced in Toronto as *The Celestial Bicycle,* 1982), Stanke, 1980.

SCREENPLAYS

Le Martien de Noel, National Film Board of Canada, 1970.

The Ungrateful Land, National Film Board of Canada, 1972.

The Hockey Sweater (short subject), animated by Cohen, National Film Board of Canada, 1980.

Sidelights

Quebec writer Roch Carrier is considered one of French Canada's most important novelists. With the translation of many of his works into English, he has also become one of the most widely read Quebecois writers in North America and England. Carrier first earned recognition with a trilogy of adult novels—*La Guerre, Yes Sir!; Floralie, Where Are You?;* and *Is It the Sun, Philibert?*—that together span about fifty years of Quebec's history. He has established a reputation for his sensitive portrayal of the often-turbulent misunderstandings that exist between French- and English-speaking Canadians. A multitalented writer, Carrier has also adapted several of his novels for the stage. In addition, he is the author of a selection of works about and for children, including *The Hockey Sweater, A Happy New Year's Day, The Basketball Player,* and *The Longest Home Run.*

The Hockey Sweater, an illustrated story for primary graders, exhibits Carrier's characteristic political overtones on such topics as French Canadian nationalism and the English-French language barrier. In the story, "a disastrous boyhood episode is fondly recreated," according to *Horn Book* reviewer Ethel L. Heins. Growing up in rural Quebec, young Roch and all of his friends idolize the beloved Montreal Canadiens. Roch is understandably mortified when his mother presents him with a new jersey—that of the hated rival Toronto Maple Leafs. To make matters worse, Roch is expected to wear the dreaded blue-and-white in public. "*The Hockey Sweater* is a funny story," asserted *School Library Journal* contributor Joan McGrath, "but it is the fun of an adult looking indulgently back to remember a horrible childhood humiliation from the tranquil plateau of adulthood."

As a companion to *The Hockey Sweater,* Carrier published *The Boxing Champion,* featuring the same young protagonist as he strives to become a winning boxer. Young Roch also appears in *A Happy New Year's Day.* Like the two earlier books, *A Happy New Year's*

A young fan of the Montreal Canadiens hockey team agonizes over having to wear a Toronto Maple Leafs sweater in Carrier's humorous story. (From The Hockey Sweater, *illustrated by Sheldon Cohen.)*

Day is also a picture-book reminiscence. The work features Carrier's recollections of New Year's Day 1941, including numerous details about his large extended family. "Carrier has filled his story with humour and an eye for the sort of clever details that many think children miss," remarked Linda Granfield in *Quill & Quire.* Patricia L. M. Butler, writing in *Canadian Materials,* called *A Happy New Year's Day* "a story full of wonder, hope, joy and promise that should be felt by all each New Year's Day."

In *The Longest Home Run,* Carrier infuses a seemingly simple story with complex, adult-oriented themes. Set in 1940s Quebec, the story features a boys' baseball game that is interrupted by a girl named Adeline, who asks to play. She promptly hits the longest home run that any of the boys have ever witnessed; when asked who she is, Adeline gives her name and divulges that she is a magician associated with a traveling theater act visiting the area. The boys later attend the magic show, view Adeline's father make her "disappear," and then are not allowed to see her anymore. Jetske Sybesma, writing in *Canadian Children's Literature,* offered a favorable assessment of the story's wry commentary on the "older generation's stereotypical opinion about a girl's abilities which results in denying a talented child ... the opportunity to develop her potential." A *Kirkus Reviews* critic, who called *The Longest Home Run* "another offbeat sports story" from Roch and illustrator Sheila Fischman, concluded: "There's no real plot here, but the incidents are lively and amusing, while the near-surreal illustrations glow with energetic perspectives and intriguing comical details."

Prayers of a Very Wise Child, while not written explicitly for children, nevertheless features a seven-year-old narrator whose brief prayers form the basis of the book. Once again set in the author's home terrain of rural Quebec, this autobiographical work portrays a child's pious simplicity, his puzzlement at the presence of evil—the child wonders why God "kills" little children and allows wars to happen—and his growing awareness of the differences between boys and girls. "The simplicity of [a] child's prayers belies the complexities of life and one's ability to grasp them," maintained Theo Hersh in *Canadian Materials.* Hersh added that "one of the beauties of Carrier's writing" is that the author "softens the blow of growing up with tender and poignant—and funny—remembrances of childhood." *Quill & Quire* commentator Daniel Jones asserted that "*Prayers of a Very Wise Child* succeeds by its richly comic invention." *Canadian Literature* reviewer John Lennox asserted: "Carrier is skilled at underlining the characteristics of human community and in using the child to illustrate the potential and limitations of human understanding."

The Basketball Player is another of Carrier's sports-related children's stories. In this work, familiar protagonist Roch is on his way to a seminary boarding school.

Although he does not really want to go, Roch tries to make the best of it—but runs away after he is dealt with harshly by one of the school's priests and is forced to play basketball, a sport he despises. Outside of school and on his own at night, Roch experiences some fearsome realities that prompt his hasty return. After encouragement and practice on the basketball court, he finally makes his first basket. However, as *Quill & Quire* contributor Barbara Greenwood observed, "the story ends on a wry note with one of Carrier's trademark subversive twists." Welwyn Wilton Katz, reviewing *The Basketball Player* in *Books in Canada,* described the work as "a book about fear, and cold, and loneliness, about saying goodbye, about death. Roch Carrier looks back on his past with the eyes of one who has seen too much, and loses the basketball player of the title in

visions of weeping boys, freezing rain, gunshots in the dark, blood and death.... All these memories matter much more to Carrier than the solitary page of text that takes him from failure at basketball to a team championship."

Once a recipient of grants from Canada's art agency Canada Council, Carrier became director of the agency in 1994. "It was time to give back to the system," Carrier told Diane Turbide in a *Maclean's* interview. Carrier further explained to Turbide that things have changed since he was an aspiring writer. "I received $15,000 over eight different grants. That money helped me do a lot of things that I would not have done otherwise. And now when I see how difficult it is to provide financial support to emerging artists, I feel very sad." However, in the

Carrier's young protagonist strives to become a winning boxer. (*From* Un Champion, *illustrated by Sheldon Cohen.*)

same interview, Carrier expressed optimism about the future of Canada's arts. "[T]here would be no planes today if there hadn't been somebody, somewhere, who was dreaming of flying. It always starts with a dream. And artists are the ones who are dreaming. We need dreams.... Because dreams are vision, and people need vision."

Works Cited

Butler, Patricia L. M., review of *A Happy New Year's Day, Canadian Materials,* March, 1992, p. 78.

Carrier, Roch, *Prayers of a Very Wise Child,* Penguin, 1991.

Granfield, Linda, review of *A Happy New Year's Day, Quill & Quire,* November, 1991, p. 26.

Greenwood, Barbara, review of *The Basketball Player, Quill & Quire,* December, 1996, p. 36.

Heins, Ethel L., review of *The Hockey Sweater, Horn Book,* May, 1992, p. 371.

Hersh, Theo, review of *Prayers of a Very Wise Child, Canadian Materials,* March, 1992, p. 100.

Jones, Daniel, review of *Prayers of a Very Wise Child, Quill & Quire,* October, 1991, pp. 27, 30.

Katz, Welwyn Wilton, review of *The Basketball Player, Books in Canada,* April, 1997, p. 34.

Lennox, John, review of *Prayers of a Very Wise Child, Canadian Literature,* autumn, 1992, pp. 174-76.

Review of *The Longest Home Run, Kirkus Reviews,* June 1, 1993, p. 716.

McGrath, Joan, review of *The Hockey Sweater, School Library Journal,* March, 1985, p. 164.

Sybesma, Jetske, review of *The Longest Home Run, Canadian Children's Literature,* winter, 1995, pp. 90-91.

Turbide, Diane, "People Need a Vision," *Maclean's,* April 22, 1996, pp. 81-82.

For More Information See

BOOKS

Cameron, Donald, *Conversations with Canadian Novelists,* Macmillan of Canada, 1973, pp. 13-29.

Dictionary of Literary Biography, Volume 53: *Canadian Writers since 1960, First Series,* Gale, 1986.

PERIODICALS

Bulletin of the Center for Children's Books, February, 1985, p. 102.

Canadian Children's Literature, vol. 69, 1993, p. 74; fall, 1994, pp. 77-79.

Canadian Literature, autumn-winter, 1989, pp. 209-11.

Horn Book, March, 1985, p. 174.

Quill & Quire, March, 1991, p. 20; March, 1993, p. 46; June, 1994, p. 45.

School Library Journal, July, 1991, pp. 54-55; February, 1992, pp. 71-72.*

CATO, Heather

Personal

Born in Auckland, New Zealand; daughter of Maxwell (a journalist) and Olga (an interior decorator) Bunker; married Alan Stuart Cato (a company director), December 5, 1973; children: Daniel, Kristin, Simon. *Education:* Attended University of Auckland and Auckland Law School. *Religion:* Anglican.

Addresses

Home and office—5 Arney Cres., Remuera, Auckland 5, New Zealand.

Career

Writer. Operator of a horseback riding school. *Member:* Pakuranga Hunt Club.

Awards, Honors

Tom Fitzgibbon award, best children's fiction by a previously unpublished author, 1997, for *Dark Horses.*

Writings

Dark Horses (novel), Ashton Scholastic (Auckland, New Zealand), 1997.

Heather Cato

Work in Progress

In Full Cry, a novel.

Sidelights

Heather Cato told *SATA:* "When I first sat down to write *Dark Horses,* I did not envisage a published book. My writing comes from a place I found and buried myself in to escape my grief for my daughter. My legal studies at Auckland Law School came to an abrupt end when Kristin had a riding accident. Her pony flipped over a fence, landed on her, and broke her back in four places. Kristin stopped breathing for three minutes, needed cardio-pulmonary resuscitation, and was very lucky to survive. Her accident happened on the same day that [actor] Christopher Reeve had his fall. News of him somehow made what I was going through much worse, but it had the opposite effect on Kristin. She followed Christopher Reeve's progress, gaining courage from his courage, and feeling relieved that her injuries were not as bad as his were. Because so many good things have come out of Kristin's accident, she says that, knowing what she knows now, if she found herself placed in front of that jump again, she would jump the jump. She is now studying law herself, perhaps taking over where I left off, and I have found my passion in writing children's books. I have almost completed my second novel, *In Full Cry,* and have plans for a third."

For More Information See

PERIODICALS

Magpies, New Zealand Supplement, May, 1998, p. 7.
New Zealand Horse and Pony, August, 1998, p. 43.

*　*　*

CHAMBERLIN, Kate 1945-

Personal

Born July 20, 1945, in Northampton, MA; married David W. Chamberlin, August 15, 1970; children: William, Paul, Marion. *Education:* Attended Universidad de Valladolid, Spain; West Chester College, B.S.; University of Rochester, M.A.

Addresses

Home—3901 Orchard St., Walworth, NY 14568-9548. *Electronic mail*—kathryngc@juno.com.

Career

Elementary schoolteacher in Newburgh, NY, 1967-69; Rochester Institute of Technology, Rochester, NY, departmental secretary for National Technical Institute for the Deaf, 1971-73; Wayne Central School District, Walworth, NY, substitute teacher and tutor, 1973-97. Rochester Museum and Science Center, instructor in youth program, 1976-82; Teddy Bear Trail Nursery School, teacher, 1984-86; Community Partners: The

Homework Place, director, 1993-95. *Member:* National Society of the Daughters of the American Revolution, Rochester Area Children's Writers and Illustrators, Wayne Area Low-Vision Support Group, Walworth Garden Club (past president), Palmyra Garden Club (past president).

Writings

The Night Search, illustrated by Dot Yoder, Jason & Nordic (Hollidaysburg, PA), 1997.

Work represented in anthologies, including *Poetic Voices of America,* Sparrowgrass Press, 1996. Author of "Cornucopia," a weekly column in *Wayne County Star,* 1994—, and "School Daze," a column in *Wayne Weekly,* 1997—. Contributor to magazines and newspapers, including *Good Dog!, Threads,* and *Organic Gardening.*

Work in Progress

Research on the ways in which blind children interact with the world.

Sidelights

Kate Chamberlin told *SATA:* "I've known since third grade that I wanted to be a teacher. I just never realized that I would be a blind teacher. I had no choice about

Kate Chamberlin with her guide dog, Finchlee Grace.

going blind, but I do have a choice about how to handle my handicap and the people around me.

"Teaching is still exciting for me. Instead of having a class of twenty-five students for the whole year, I teach hundreds of students through my 'Feely Can and Sniffy Jar' presentations. I tell my audiences that, while we are going to have fun, it in no way mocks or diminishes the trauma and devastation being blind can cause. Through my presentations, students and adults get to really understand what it is like to be blind. The audience participates actively in various problem-solving situations with humor, innovation, and technology. An important part of the presentation is the question-and-answer time slots. Some of the topics I address are the talking computer, my guide dog, the long, white cane, how I became blind, the independent living aids I use, and freelance writing.

"Now I can reach even more students through my twin-vision book *The Night Search*."

*   *   *

CONNOLLY, Peter 1935-

Personal

Born May 8, 1935, in Surrey, England; son of Harold (an artist) and Mollie (Naw) Connolly; married Maureen Jennings, July 4, 1959 (divorced, 1969); married Barbara Carpenter (a company secretary), August 2, 1973; children: Sarah Anna, Matthew. *Education:* Attended Brighton College of Arts and Crafts, 1951-53. *Politics:* "Pragmatist; believe in democracy but opposed to party politics." *Religion:* Agnostic. *Hobbies and other interests:* Model making, photography, and building topographical models of battlefields.

Addresses

Home and office—22 Spring St., Spalding, Lincolnshire PE11 2XW, England.

Career

Writer and illustrator. Worked as a commercial artist in various studios and advertising agencies, 1956-61; Institute of Archaeology, University College, London, research associate, 1986-89. Painter for museums, including Romische Germanische Zentralmuseum, Mainz, Germany. *Military service:* Royal Air Force, 1953-56. *Member:* Society for the Promotion of Roman Studies, Society for the Promotion of Helenic Studies, Society of Antiquaries (fellow).

Awards, Honors

Senior Information Award, *Times Literary Supplement*, 1986, for *The Legend of Odysseus*.

Writings

FOR CHILDREN; SELF-ILLUSTRATED

The Roman Army, Macdonald, 1975, Silver Burdett, 1979.
The Greek Armies, Macdonald, 1977, Silver Burdett, 1979.
Hannibal and the Enemies of Rome, Macdonald, 1978.
Pompeii, Macdonald, 1979.
Greece and Rome at War, Macdonald, 1981, Prentice-Hall, 1981.
Living in the Time of Jesus of Nazareth, Oxford University Press, 1983, also published as *A History of the Jewish People in the Time of Jesus: From Herod the Great to Masada,* P. Bedrick, 1987, as *The Jews in the Time of Jesus: A History,* 1995, and as *The Holy Land,* 1998.
The Legend of Odysseus, Oxford University Press, 1986, published as *The Ancient Greece of Odysseus,* 1998.
Tiberius Claudius Maximus, Volume 1: *The Cavalryman,* Volume 2: *The Legionary* (two volumes), Oxford University Press, 1988.
The Roman Fort, Oxford University Press, 1991.
Greek Legends: The Stories, The Evidence, Simon & Schuster, 1993.
(With Hazel Dodge) *The Ancient City: Life in Classical Athens and Rome,* Oxford University Press, 1998.

Author's works have been translated into French.

ILLUSTRATOR

Sampson and the Philistines, Macdonald, 1971.
Moses and Pharaoh, Macdonald, 1972.
Mountains, Macdonald, 1972.
Sandie Oram, *Roman Soldiers,* Macdonald, 1972.
Ruth Thompson, *Columbus,* Macdonald, 1973.
Thompson, *Cousteau the Diver,* Macdonald, 1973.
Thompson, *Vanishing Animals,* Macdonald, 1973.
Thompson, *Hannibal,* Macdonald, 1974.
H. Russell Robinson, *The Armour of Imperial Rome,* Arms & Armour Press, 1975.
R. Tomlin and B. Dobson, *Greece and Rome at War,* Macdonald, 1981.
Roy E. C. Burrell, *The Greeks,* Oxford University Press, 1989.
Burrell, *The Romans,* Oxford University Press, 1991.
Burrell, *Oxford Children's Ancient History,* Oxford University Press, 1994.

Contributor of illustrations to books, including Judith Crosher, *The Greeks,* Silver Burdett, 1974; Tim Healey, *The Life of Monkeys and Apes,* Macdonald, 1974; Joan Forman, *The Romans,* 1975; and Anne Millard, *The Egyptians,* Silver Burdett, 1975. Also author/presenter of five-part television series, *Background to the Gospels,* BBC-TV, 1984. Contributor to *Cambridge Ancient History.*

Work in Progress

An adult book on the military campaigns of Julius Caesar; ongoing research on the Roman Colosseum.

Sidelights

Since beginning his career as an author and illustrator, Peter Connolly has always had a clear goal: to create a well-researched library of Greek and Roman history for young people. For nearly three decades, he has inspired the interest of boys and girls in historical subjects with the detailed illustrations and fluid writing that characterize his books, among the better-known of which are *The Greek Armies, Hannibal and the Enemies of Rome,* and *The Legend of Odysseus.* Describing *The Ancient City: Life in Classical Athens and Rome,* which Connolly wrote with co-author Hazel Dodge, *School Library Journal* contributor David N. Pauli praised Connolly's artwork and maintained that, "For anyone assigned a report on the design, construction, and use of the Parthenon or the Roman Colosseum, it would be hard to find a better source than this one."

Born in Surrey, England in 1935, Connolly first became interested in Greek and Roman history in the 1950s, while serving in the Royal Air Force. As he once admitted to *SATA,* the subject became his "consuming interest, particularly military history and architecture," and he combined it with the artistic skills he had been inspired to develop from his artist father. Connolly soon focused on a specialty within the broad field of military history, becoming an expert on ancient armor. "I believe it is wrong to write about things one has not seen," Connolly told *SATA.* For this reason, as part of his continuing studies he will sometimes construct reproductions of ancient shields and cuirasses in order to better understand how such weapons were used in battle. Connolly's need to see the subject of his books has taken him to museums throughout Europe and North Africa, as well as on an eight-thousand-mile trip to the many Roman battlefields marking the conquests of Julius Caesar throughout Western Europe.

Connolly's greatest hero is Hannibal, a Carthaginian soldier born in the middle of the third century BC who led his North African troops through the treacherous passage over the Alps to conquer the Roman Army. "Over a period of fifteen years I have visited the sites of all his battles and crossed every possible route that he could have taken over the Alps—several of them on foot as there is no road," he explained. Connolly put all this research to good use in his book *Hannibal and the Enemies of Rome.*

In *The Legend of Odysseus,* Connolly tells the tale of another ancient hero, this time the subject of Homer's *Iliad* and one of the heros of the mythic Trojan War. Combining Homer's tale with actual facts about costume, weapons, ships, chariots, burial rights, and other information gleaned from the archeological investigations at Troy and other sites, *The Legend of Odysseus* is "a well-rounded attempt to explain the lives of men and women of the ancient cities" of Greece and Rome, according to a *Publishers Weekly* reviewer. Not only mortals such as the beautiful Helen of Troy and the brave Achilles feature in Connolly's narrative, but also the gods and goddesses, the sea monster Scylla, and the

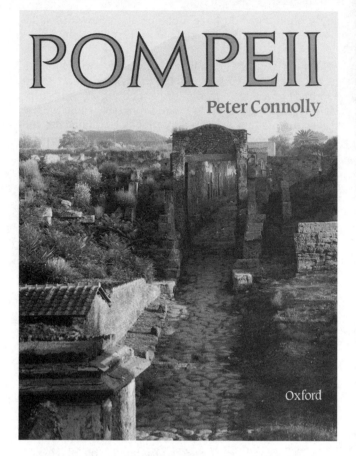

Peter Connolly relates the story of the Roman city of Pompeii, from its burial under volcanic ash and pumice during the eruption of Mount Vesuvius in 79 AD to its discovery by nineteenth-century archaeologists.

treacherous ocean whirlpools of Charybdis, making Connolly's work "quite satisfactory to history and mythology buffs," in the opinion of *School Library Journal* contributor Sally T. Margolis. Margolis also noted that "the text is accessible to curious ten year olds while remaining interesting enough for older readers."

The fascinating story of the Roman city of Pompeii—its burial under volcanic ash and pumice during the eruption of Mount Vesuvius in August of the year 79 AD, and its later discovery by nineteenth-century archaeologists—is related by Connolly in his 1979 work, *Pompeii.* Connolly begins by describing the daily habits of the citizens of that city, then captures the attention of budding scientists by describing the way archeologist Guiseppe Fiorelli used the hardened pumice to cast the bodies of the volcano's victims, and by recreating, through illustrations, the way the city would have looked on the eve of its destruction. With attention given to even the most minute detail of life in ancient Rome, *Pompeii* was praised by *School Library Journal* contributor David M. Pauli for being "as complete and thorough a documentation of the story of Pompeii as any that can currently be found in children's collections." A *Junior Bookshelf* reviewer called the book "quite substantial" and it's story "well told."

Continuing his efforts to provide young readers with books that answer questions about life in ancient times, Connolly published a series of books called "The Roman World." In *The Roman Fort,* he explores the ruins of an army fort near Hadrian's Wall—the stone barrier stretching across northern Britain that was constructed by the Emperor Hadrian in an effort to keep the Picts and Scots from attacking Roman settlements in England. The two-volume set entitled *Tiberius Claudius Maximus* was inspired by the mid-1960s discovery of the tombstone of a Roman soldier who died in Northern Greece nearly two thousand years ago. In his characteristic manner, Connolly recreates the life of Maximus by compiling details of the life of a Roman soldier, tracing Maximus's accomplishments as a military leader under the emperor Trajan. Praising the illustrations in each of these works as "quite superb," reviewer Steve Rosson noted in *Books for Keeps* that Connolly's pictures "should provide much to talk about with [children of] all ages and abilities."

Works Cited

Review of *The Legend of Odysseus, Publishers Weekly,* March 18, 1988, p. 88.

Margolis, Sally T., review of *The Legend of Odysseus, School Library Journal,* June-July, 1988, p. 110.

Pauli, David N., review of *Pompeii, School Library Journal,* February, 1991, p. 94.

Pauli, David N., review of *The Ancient City: Life in Classical Athens and Rome, School Library Journal,* July, 1998, p. 104.

Review of *Pompeii, Junior Bookshelf,* June, 1991, pp. 107-08.

Rosson, Steve, review of *Pompeii, The Roman Fort,* [and] *Tiberius Claudius Maximus, Books for Keeps,* November, 1997, p. 107.

For More Information See

PERIODICALS

Books for Keeps, March, 1987, p. 8; September, 1991, p. 20.

Kirkus Reviews, March 15, 1988, p. 453; May 15, 1989, p. 762.

School Librarian, February, 1987, pp. 70-71.

School Library Journal, December, 1991, p. 139.

D

Eilis Dillon

1920-1994

Long before I knew it was real, I carried a picture in my mind of something so extraordinary that I could not believe I had imagined it in such detail. The scene is an upstairs room without a carpet. Three children, of whom I am the smallest, are standing by the open door, watching two thin men dressed in British army uniforms. The men are wearing puttees and the broad-topped caps of the time. One is standing, leaning on his rifle, the other is kneeling and prising up the floorboards with something shiny attached to the barrel of his gun—a bayonet, of course. I never saw a British army uniform nor indeed a bayonet in my conscious life, but years later my mother told me that this scene actually occurred on the day that she was arrested and taken away to prison. I was exactly one year old, March 1921. No guns were found under the floorboards. Other damage was done as well, and the soldiers made a lot of noise. There was a general policy of creating disturbance and destruction during an arrest, to frighten the onlookers.

I don't remember being frightened at the time, though I went through a long period when my nights were full of horrors. Nor do I remember the noise that day. Gradually I began to discover that we had had an unusual childhood. The games that my two older sisters played were about hiding from soldiers, but there was never any shooting. My parents could not have tolerated that. Too many of their friends were dead, including my mother's eldest brother, the poet Joseph Plunkett, who was executed by firing squad in 1916.

My memories then became related to sounds: a squeaking pram which I knew contained my baby brother, in Herbert Park in Dublin, under the rose arbour, the breeze rustling the leaves and making changing shadows on the path. Then voices, friendly or angry, meaningless but expecting a response which I could not give. The two older sisters played a game of despising me, though my brother

seemed to be immune. If I revealed my thoughts, they were foolish and provided ammunition for further attacks. If I concealed my thoughts, I was deceitful or stupid. With five children, including a second baby brother who was delicate, my parents had no time for protecting me. Besides, in those days one didn't over-protect children. One toughened them.

Eilis Dillon

My father was Professor of Chemistry at the University in Galway, on the west coast of Ireland. He had a doctorate from the National University in Dublin, but at the time when he might have been given a chair there, one was required to take an oath of allegiance to the King of England. This he could not do, and it was while he was a political prisoner in England in 1919 that he was appointed to Galway. At that time there was only one professor, who was also head of the department for life. Times were changing. The oath was no longer required. My godfather was Professor of French—he had been a member of the garrison of the College of Surgeons in Dublin during the initial stage of the war of independence. The godfather of one of my sisters was executed during the civil war that followed independence. I soon became aware that almost every one of my parents' circle had been a political prisoner at one time or another.

After the Civil War of 1922-23, political arguments between my parents and their friends whistled and whirled above our heads. We detested the anger but found the knowledge we acquired very interesting. They made sure we were informed about politics and never attempted to conceal the facts from us, as some parents did. It took time to get it all into focus. There was no feeling of triumph when the new Irish Free State was established because, as everyone repeatedly said, the partition of Ireland into two states would be a source of trouble as long as it lasted. My mother's family, the Plunketts, had fought on the Republican side because they believed that the treaty ending the war of independence should not have included partition. All of them remained doggedly of this opinion to the day of their deaths. My father's family had been associated with the old Irish Parliamentary Party and were more inclined towards using constitutional methods. They innocently believed that Irish unity would be restored some day without bloodshed.

When my father was appointed professor he bought a big country house outside Galway. My mother had lived until her marriage in big houses with walled gardens and fruit trees and all the amenities of the country, even though they were close to Dublin. She knew all the things that made such a life possible: taking care of animals, gardening, making butter, bread, jam, black puddings, garlands of flowers for Christmas decorations, even breeding donkeys for us to ride. And there was the river, two fields away, where we had a boat whose oars were kept hidden in a thorn bush until our next visit.

Sounds: dried reeds crackling underfoot at the river's edge; brown water lapping on the shining boat; water running off the oars, dropping into the river; swans talking to each other in low grunts; water hens rising suddenly, squawking; the strange long cry of a grey heron taking off from the reeds; the roar of the wind in the tops of the pines; the swish of the boat through the rushes in the shallows; the crunch of the boat on soft gravel at the landing. And voices—not ours but of the people in other boats—words without meaning, echoing hollowly. Then, at home in bed on warm summer nights, the rattling song of the corncrake came through the open window and mixed with another element, the scent of the wistaria that grew against the house wall.

But I was not a happy child. I was born with a love for order, and order is impossible for small children. I had a

sense of inadequacy because I couldn't do the things that the older children did. Reading was one of these, and I was almost five years old before I could read a Hans Andersen story comfortably. I remember the occasion well—another picture. It was a sunny day and I had gone alone into my father's study where the good books were kept. I took down the precious volume, with illustrations by Harry Clarke, and opened it at the right place—"The Tinder Box." I read it all, sitting on the floor by the bookcase, enjoying everything around me, including the beautiful black curtains with white cranes embroidered on them that hung at the two tall windows.

I think that was when I became a writer, a weigher of words, a builder with words, and especially a listener to them, though I rarely heard them spoken as they sounded in my inner ear. My father sometimes read Shakespeare for us, and I elbowed my way into the party somehow. He had small volumes of the plays, and my older sisters and he would pass these from hand to hand while they read the different parts. They were music—the vowel sounds especially. My father knew large sections of the plays from memory and would sometimes begin to recite them when the books were absent. One such occasion was when we were swimming together and I was sitting on his shoulders having a ride. He began:

> I was born as free as Caesar, so were you.
> We both have fed as well, and we can both
> Endure the winter's cold as well as he,
> For once, upon a raw and gusty day,
> The troubled Tiber chafing with her shores,
> Caesar said to me: "Darest thou, Cassius, now,
> Leap with me into this angry flood
> And swim to yonder point?"

So he went on until he came to the place where Caesar says:

> "Help me, Cassius, or I sink!"

With that he sank, so that I clung to his back for dear life. A moment later he came up and continued:

> And I, as Aeneas our great ancestor did
> From the flames of Troy the old Anchises bear,
> So from the waves of Tiber did I the tired Caesar.

In the same way I became acquainted with *Macbeth* and *The Tempest* and *The Merchant of Venice*. When the family in general was accused of some destruction, one of us would be likely to say:

> Thou canst not say I did it—never shake
> Thy gory locks at me.

When we played tag, the one who had been elected pursuer would stand aside and say:

> I am Sir Oracle, and when I ope my lips let no dog
>   bark.

The others would yell:

"Bow-wow! Bow-wow!"

And the game was on. While this was a great preparation for the literary life, it meant that when we went to children's parties we found "Musical Chairs" and "Here We Go Gathering Nuts in May" rather dull.

Isolated in the country, for the most part we were able to be as odd as we pleased. When it became time to go to school, we were sent to the local National School. It was about a mile away as the crow flies, but when our long avenue was counted in, it was more like two. Sometimes we were driven in the donkey trap by our nurse, Charlotte, but usually we walked.

My mother had rarely been to school, though she had put up a fight to get there when she was young. Governesses and tutors were supposed to be more than adequate but she always felt that she had missed something vital. I would have been very glad to miss it too. The school was a miserably poor one with three teachers, a man and two women. The woman who taught the small children was a delightful old body, who wore a long skirt and a plaid shawl crossed in front and tied firmly at the back. She taught us how to read and write in Irish and English and, now that there was no law against it, she taught us to sing lots of patriotic songs in both languages. That part of County Galway was Irish-speaking, and we absorbed the language without the smallest difficulty.

But the cold, the evil-smelling lavatories, the screams of the boys and girls from the next room, being belaboured by the man and wife who taught them, all added up to a thoroughly unpleasant experience. At home there was Shakespeare and Hans Andersen, and recordings of Kreisler playing Dvorák, and John MacCormack singing Mozart and German lieder and Moore's Irish melodies. My mother and Charlotte sang for us, dozens of patriotic ballads as well as other Irish songs. I loved Yeats's "Down by the Salley Gardens" and Padraic Colum's "She Moved through the Fair." Padraic was a friend of my parents and sometimes came to visit.

I learned to separate experiences. My father observed that we spoke three languages: English as spoken at home, English as spoken at school, and Irish, which he was very anxious that we should know well. Irish political prisoners always start up language classes, and he had learned enough Irish in Gloucester jail to be able to speak it to his children. Until I was an adult he never addressed a word to me in English. That was my mother's province, and we learned good Victorian English from her. She never mastered Irish, though she made a good try, but her French was excellent.

The post-war period was unstable everywhere but especially in Ireland, since the cost of the civil war had to be met by the new Free State. University professors' salaries were not paid for six months. Everyone was in debt. My parents' bank manager compelled them to sell their beautiful house, without giving them time to appeal to my grandparents for help. The bank manager wanted the house for a friend of his, and got it. The friend died within a year. I learned that in the midst of security we are on the

Mother, Geraldine Dillon, age seventy-five.

move. I think my childish heart was broken then. Another stage of the writer's development was reached, silently.

My parents faced this new difficulty with their usual fortitude. They took two cottages to the west of Galway, in a village named Barna, which is now an outer suburb of Galway city. There we found ourselves again surrounded by Irish-speaking country people, some of whom worked as maids for us. In many ways this was a most important part of my life. There was much more freedom, more people lived near us; I began to learn about character and how people behave under stress. I began to make up stories.

The Barna interlude lasted only a year but its impact is still enormous. We went to the local school, a much cleaner one. There was no cow, no donkeys, no walled garden, no river—but the sea was only a few yards away. A little bubbling stream ran into it. Water was drawn from a well in the middle of an overgrown field five minutes' walk away. One had to climb a low wall and follow a vague path through brambles to reach it. Juicy dark-blue sloes appeared on the thorn bushes in the autumn. In spring they were covered with white flowers.

Our maid, Sarah, sang a love song about the whitethorn tree. It had a haunting melody. She sang a great many songs for us, in Irish and in English. One of them was "Barbara Allen," which I thought the most beautiful song I had ever heard.

At seven years old I couldn't conceal the fact that my head was full of stories. I learned to keep quiet about it until I had written them down, but I soon noticed that even then, after a casual compliment, they were quickly dismissed. It seemed dangerous to call attention to myself in any way. I stopped writing.

After a year we moved back into Galway city, to an old cut-stone house that had been bought by the university. It had once been a model school; my father's laboratories were now housed at one end of it. There were vacant rooms where the schoolrooms had been, and a good-sized house that had been used by the headmaster. Here one could escape, to read or just to be alone. There was time to think, especially when the older children and my younger brother were sent away to boarding school.

The cut-stone house was full of mice and rats. Two working cats were brought in and they did their best, but the mice were too smart for them. I became interested in the secret lives of mice that lived in fear behind the wainscot and under the floor-boards, in daily terror of our cats. But I had an idea that they took the danger in their stride and went on with the business of living as well as they could.

About that time, when I was eight or nine years old, I read a book by Edgar Wallace called *The Square Emerald.* It gave me horrible dreams. It concerned a gang of thieves, some of them Chinese, in the London underworld. They hid on the tops of wardrobes. They slid down drainpipes. They lowered themselves and their victims into the Thames by means of trapdoors. They drove fast cars along the Edgeware Road, hotly pursued by the police of Scotland Yard. I wrote quite a long story about a mouse named Harry, who led an evil life and was caught and hanged in the end.

My parents were delighted with my story. My mother had read every available book in her father's vast library, as soon as she was able to read at all. It never occurred to her to prevent someone from reading anything that he or she could understand. My father was particularly amused by

Father, Thomas Dillon, about 1950.

the moral tone. From that day onwards I knew where I was going.

At about this time both of my parents became directors of a newly established theatre in Galway, whose purpose was to produce plays in the Irish language. The dream of an entirely Irish-speaking nation still existed. It was soon found that there were not enough original plays to keep a theatre going. Translations of Abbey Theatre plays into Irish filled the gap for a while, and then the directors decided to make translations of plays from all over the world. Thus I saw the works of Molière, Ibsen, Lorca, Shaw, Granville Barker and various other playwrights for the first time, in the Irish language. Some of the directors wrote plays themselves, including my father, whose play *The Commissioner* was performed a number of times by the Abbey Theatre.

It was then that I found out how a theatre worked. My mother had been associated with the Theatre of Ireland before it merged with the Abbey Theatre. Her brother had been one of the founders and her family leased the Hardwicke Hall, which they owned, to the original company. She loved stage design and costume, and she designed and made costumes for a great many of the Galway productions. My godfather, the professor of French, translated Moliere and Gheon into Irish, and even acted parts in some of the plays. I remember him playing Conor MacNessa in Synge's *Deirdre,* and the father in T.C. Murray's *Autumn Fire.*

At home, in the empty rooms at the far end of the house, we acted the plays all over again, pressing our friends into service and composing new plays of our own. Our parents were a polite audience. In the same rooms my mother undertook to rehearse a production by an amateur group of O'Casey's *Juno and the Paycock,* in English. I thought it powerful stuff but decided that I would never choose to write like that.

My first year at the boarding school in Sligo, where my sisters had gone, was not a success. I was an outsider, eleven years old in a class of children who were all aged thirteen and over. They were studying *Julius Caesar,* which I knew by heart, elementary French, which I had learned already, and the Irish language, which I spoke like a native. These classes were a deadly bore but the lessons in mathematics were far beyond me. In a state of total confusion I was rescued by a kindly young nun who needed a cellist for the school orchestra. She began to give me lessons and life took on some meaning again. However, at the end of the year it was decided that I should not go back there.

I was overjoyed. The plan was revealed to me gradually. I was sent to stay with my grandparents in Dublin and an Irish-speaking school was found for me. My grandfather, Count Plunkett, was a bibliophile and owned a notable library. He had been Curator of the National Museum at one time and was the author of a book on Botticelli. He had collected some remarkable paintings in his youth, among them a Rubens and a Barry. My grandmother and my mother disliked each other heartily but they kept a distant civility. My grandmother had been a good amateur musician, in the manner of Victorian ladies, and when she found that I had begun to play the cello she engaged the leader of the cello section of the symphony orchestra to come to the house and give me lessons three times a week.

Best of all, I was alone. One bachelor uncle lived in the house. Otherwise there were only my grandparents, the housekeeper, and a maid or two. Time to think: I began to write poetry.

My grandfather fed me with books of all kinds, old German romances, translations of the *Odyssey* and of Virgil and Ovid, Shakespeare of course, and a great many books about Spanish and Italian painting. Through these and the necessity of being able to discuss them with him, I learned how to study difficult subjects. My grandmother and I became fast friends and remained so to the end of her life. It was she who bought me a cello and paid for my lessons when I went back to the same boarding school in Sligo at the end of the year. She was a non-literary person and made no demands on me.

The Ursuline nuns were all university graduates, each teaching her own subject. They were an enclosed order, which meant that they never went outside the precincts of the convent except on some necessary occasion such as visiting a doctor. At the university they had lived in an isolated group. They saw no reason why anyone should feel cramped or claustrophobic in those conditions, and we accepted our circumstances. They were learned and kindly and orderly, and they devoted themselves to their school, an Italian foundation. Their ideal was the educated wife and mother.

With all the time in the world, one could ask to be taught a great many things in the certainty of finding a willing teacher. Within a few years I knew enough to begin translating Yeats's poetry into French. Yeats was fond of being thought a Sligo man, since some of his relatives lived there, and his early poetry had its background in Sligo. It was beautiful country, what we could see of it from the windows of our high building. By the time I was sixteen my poetry had improved, so that I had the courage to submit some of it to a small magazine. This was my first publication. I used a pseudonym, because I had discovered that poetry is useless unless it is personal. I got paid for it, half a guinea, which was a respectable sum in those days.

At about the same time a friendly teacher told me that she thought I had a future as a writer of fiction, and she described how a friend of hers had taught himself the craft, so successfully that he had published several novels. I was by no means ready to write a novel but the idea took hold and I began to read whatever I could find on the theory of literature. This was not much, though prefaces—which I had hitherto passed over—were a great source of information.

I had a new reason for wanting to educate myself to a profession. My sisters had both gone on to the university, one to study medicine and the other law. I had had the same successes as they—scholarships and prizes as well as successes in music—but since my failure at the age of eleven a tradition had grown up that I was incapable of profiting from extensive education. My mother, somewhat overwhelmed by her responsibilities, was becoming anxious about the two boys, who were younger than I. My father, in midcareer, had little time for planning his children's education.

I realised that I was destined for something called "Domestic Science," which led to teaching sewing and cooking and related subjects in a school, or else taking charge of the domestic arrangements in an institution. The most exciting prospect was hotel management. Always ahead of her time, my mother had foreseen the tourist boom that was about to hit the whole world. And she said: "Time some of the family got back into business." One source of her family's wealth was a leather and handmade shoes business which they had owned and operated in the nineteenth century. They had sold it when they felt they had made enough money, and she regarded this as a backward step.

Nothing about the plan was to my taste, but it had been noticed that I was good at domestic things and this was regarded as a talent to be developed. I put up a resistance for a while, pointing out that I was a national first-prize winner in French in the state examinations and that I wanted above all things to study French literature and language. My mother said impatiently that one doesn't need to go to the university to study that kind of thing. Every educated person speaks French, and the books were all in the house. What more did one need? And with the kind of intuition that mothers sometimes have, she commented in passing that a university education would probably destroy my confidence as a writer.

So, to the astonishment of my former teachers and classmates, I applied myself to learning the hotel business.

Maternal grandmother, Countess Plunkett, with her eldest child.

Maternal grandfather, Count Plunkett, about 1942.

No hotel school existed at the time but there was a system of apprenticeship. However, in matters of this kind my mother was anything but conventional. I can safely say that she had the most original mind of anyone I have ever known. This was splendid when it came to creating theatre costumes, or constructing pup tents for us to camp in, or demanding reasonable treatment for us when we were children. But when it came to using the ordinary tried-and-true machinery of contemporary living, her imagination failed her.

In January 1939, under her supervision, I found myself dressed in a housemaid's uniform, masquerading as a real housemaid in a small Dublin hotel. It was a converted Georgian house of the kind that my mother's family had had as a town house when she was young. The maids slept in the basement, which was partly underground and unheated. They were issued old cotton blankets. Washing, if any, was done in an enamel basin. The lavatory was outside in the tiny yard. Black rats, of a breed that, as I learned later, only occurs in Dublin and the Far East, came down the chimney to inspect us when we lay in bed. My roommate sang herself to sleep, with a song called "The Red River Valley."

I couldn't possibly conceal my origins for long. Everyone was curious and naturally assumed that I was a runaway of some kind. Then the niece of the owners appeared and turned out to have been a classmate of mine at school. Small world, I thought, but it didn't make my lot any easier.

The blow to my personality was almost fatal. At that period it was unheard of for a girl from my background to do menial work, though it's accepted everywhere now. I tried to live that life for six months, drawing my family's attention to my plight from time to time, but without any good result. I moved from one Dublin hotel to another, four or five in all, in an attempt each time to improve my position. With no source of income except the then very meagre pay of a hotel servant, I was glad when I could manage a small increase in wages. I couldn't throw myself on my grandmother's mercy without ratting on my mother, and this was unthinkable. No other member of the family was interested. My friends in Dublin were aghast but there was nothing they could do. And the war was looming. Everyone said it would happen when the harvest was in, just like last time. That prospect was what finished one of my most ingenious plans for escape—to find an *au pair* job in France or Switzerland, where I could get back to learning French. No one would take in a foreigner then.

The odd thing about that interlude is that so far I have never made the smallest use of it as background material for a novel. It was utterly dreary and unproductive, and left my intellectual development at the exact point where it had been before. Music, poetry, all the things that had preoccupied me, simply came to a standstill.

I rescued myself at last, by offering myself as a manager to an old friend of my father's who ran a summer colony where Irish was taught. Fortunately he needed me. On an unforgettable day in late June 1939, I left Dublin by bus for Ardmore, a little village in County Waterford, on the south coast. It is one of the most beautiful coastlines in the world, and the sleepy village looked like paradise to me. I was responsible for the management of a big country house where about a hundred children of all ages, and some adults, lived and had daily classes in the Irish language. Every evening there was a *ceili*—Irish dancing rather like square dancing—in a hall in the grounds. The dancing was interspersed with Irish songs, sung by teachers or students or casual visitors who were known to be able to sing.

When the children had gone to bed, I and the teachers sat around a long table in the deserted dining room drinking tea and chatting. Not a word of English was spoken. My Connacht Irish was a source of great amusement. There were long conversations about derivations of words, versions of songs, and other scholarly topics. It was all very soothing and delightful. No one talked about the impending war.

When I had been there a week or two, one evening at the *ceili* someone pointed out a man to me, tall, dark, very quiet, with humorous brown eyes. I had spoken to him for a moment when I was introduced to him, and I had noticed that he was treated with great respect. Now I was told that he had announced his intention of marrying me. Nothing could have been farther from my mind than marriage. After all, I had barely put myself together again.

And so I met my companion of thirty years, Cormac O Cuilleanain, named like the old Kings of Cashel, a freedom fighter during the war of independence and at this time an assistant professor of Irish at the university in Cork. He was in his thirties then, and already had a lifetime of dedicated work behind him. He had studied Irish at first for patriotic reasons and had come to love the literature of all the different eras. Most of the scholars were more interested in the language than in its literature. One of my ancestors had been that kind of Irish scholar, and when he died his widow burned all his books because, she said: "The study of the Irish language arouses all the native ferocity of the Celt." Cormac was a peaceful scholar.

We were married the following spring, March 28, 1940, three weeks after my twentieth birthday, and I went to live in the beautiful city of Cork. It is the third largest

Dillon at boarding school, age eighteen.

city in Ireland, which doesn't mean that it's very big—about 100,000 when I went there first. The war had indeed started when the harvest was in. Germany was overrunning Europe. Ireland had declared neutrality and all political parties were united in what might have been a last stand to save what had been achieved less than twenty years before. No one complained about Spain and Switzerland being neutral but the British were never done saying that the Irish had let them down by not joining with them. They simply could not understand that Ireland was independent and a mother country in her own right. Some still think of her as an inevitable appendage of England. Yet they never tried to enforce conscription in Northern Ireland, because it would have been impossible.

In our part of Ireland, an army of 250,000 was mobilised for defence against any invader, German or British. The regular army drilled the recruits, and so did the old Irish Republican Army men who had thought they would never have to campaign again. Among them was Cormac, wearing a cinnamon-coloured battle-dress made of heavy cotton and, as an officer, carrying an immense Colt .45 in a holster in his belt. I joined the Air Raid Precautions Unit and had a gas mask bigger than those that I fitted on civilians. I learned how to extinguish firebombs with shovelfuls of sand. No one had the least idea what was going to happen. My father, then in his fifties, also joined the volunteer army but was soon set to take charge of a telephone exchange. My mother organized women volunteers to feed the army on maneuvres.

After a while, though the country remained on the alert, we all relaxed somewhat and prepared to sit it out. It was clear from the start that Germany would not be able to hold its positions, especially when America began to pour in its enormous resources. In Ireland, electricity, gasoline, soap, and some items of food were rationed, but we were never hungry, so long as we could pay for what we needed. Money was in short supply. Salaries were frozen while the

cost of living doubled. We learned to look twice at every penny and not to waste anything.

While Cormac taught evening classes I went to the School of Art, where there were life classes twice a week under the direction of a good painter. I joined the university symphony orchestra which met for rehearsals once a week, and carried my cello swinging from one hand as I rode my bicycle. Together we laid the foundations of our personal library, going to book auctions and secondhand bookstores where one could still get all kinds of treasures cheap. Cormac's life had been as chaotic as my own but he had managed to accumulate a few French and Irish books, as well as some English classics.

Before the war was over we had two little girls. It was easy to get maids and nurses but, with no gasoline at all, I was immobilised anyway. A bicycle was not practical, though we had basket-chairs for the children that we could use in summertime. In my long hours of leisure, I began to write seriously, first unconsciously imitating the writers I most admired. I was appalled when I saw the results. If this meant that I had no originality, the sooner I gave up the idea the better.

Then I decided that I would have to work a long apprenticeship, going back to basic principles and practicing every day as I would on a musical instrument. I soon discovered that a style was emerging but one not like anyone else's that I could see. Models were useless now. I felt ignorant, wishing, as I have often done since, that I had a quiet Ph.D. in some obscure subject, where I could dodder away my life in decent privacy.

I began to write in Irish, a children's book—not about mice behind the walls but rabbits underground. I used the beautiful old script that was still standard in Ireland. It was all handwritten, of course, since typewriters with that script were rare. The story ran to about 30,000 words and was well plotted. I sent it to the Government Publications Sale Office, which had a program of publishing as well as distributing official documents. It was accepted at once. By the time I was notified of this, I was one-third way through the next one.

It was never my intention to write only in Irish but by the time I had changed back to the language I found most congenial, Irish had served its purpose. I discovered, as I think many other people have done, that the use of a second language clears away cliches and forces one to be clear and precise. Hitherto I had regarded my distaste for complication as a disadvantage. I even aimed at obscurity for its own sake before I discovered that if there is any distinguishing mark of Irish writers in general, it is this liking for clarity of expression. One must except James Joyce, but even he was marked by the same characteristic in his early work.

Cork had produced several writers just before I went to live there—Frank O'Connor and Sean O'Faolain, and their mentor Daniel Corkery. O'Faolain had delivered a series of lectures over the radio on the art of writing, and these were a revelation to me. He was now the editor of a Dublin literary magazine, *The Bell,* in which he educated a whole generation of budding writers. He was a ruthless editor—a born meddler, he told me himself later. I should perhaps have submitted material to him but I had already decided that I didn't want to write short pieces. Irish short stories are justly renowned but the medium seemed too narrow for me.

What then would I do? Continuing to work my apprenticeship, I finished a third children's book in Irish, and then changed languages. Back with English, I found that I had made progress, though there was still a crippling lack of confidence. The time I was spending at my desk seemed hardly justified by the results. Cormac insisted that I must have leisure for it. The war was over, but nothing was yet back to normal. Having escaped the devastation suffered by Europe, no one in Ireland was complaining. Still, times were hard and I felt that my continuing to learn to write might prove to be a foolish waste of time.

Publishing was almost an unknown business in Ireland at that time. One or two houses existed, mainly for producing school texts, and occasionally they published a novel of guaranteed respectability. But England, always a great publishing country, was frantically looking for material after the long years of the war when no one had the time or inclination to write. I decided to make one attempt and to stand or fall by that. I don't know whether or not I would have stuck to writing anyway—rather suspect that I would. I had written a very old-fashioned children's book about a magic loaf of bread that gave animals the power of speech. The river figured in it, and the burned-out castle on the opposite bank, and the lovely house that we had left so long ago. Macmillan in London accepted it and published it with black and white drawings by an artist who knew how to give character to animals. Then Macmillan decided against publishing children's books and handed me on to Faber and Faber, who had always had Irish writers on their list.

By this time I had become that nebulous creature, a professional writer. I began to discover that all writers who intend to produce a considerable body of work must sooner or later set up an organisation that will allow them to work regularly. Whether they work by night or by day is immaterial—the most important thing is to be present in a certain place at a certain time, ready to begin. Ireland was full of talented writers, their heads bursting with unwritten books, their critical faculties on the alert to assess the achievements of their friends and acquaintances, their wit devastating. Only a few of them worked regularly, however, often because they had to support life by some other means. I had the greatest respect for their talents but none for their industry.

Industry seemed to me to be the mark of the Renaissance artists, the painters and musicians who produced unbelievable quantities of work during relatively short lives. It was a quality that was often despised, the suggestion being that it denoted a pedestrian mind. Inspiration was the sign of the true artist—but I had discovered that inspiration must be invited, and that it descends on the same spot where it found its host the day before. I began to work regularly every morning for two or three hours, a habit I have kept for thirty-five years.

Faber and Faber, which had the distinction of having T. S. Eliot on its board of directors, published what I considered my first real children's book, in 1951. This was *The Lost Island,* about a boy's search for his father, who has gone off on a wild-goose chase to a mysterious island in the Atlantic, in search of a vague treasure. The Barna experience was the source of the background, and I found

that a distinctive voice had taken over the style. I knew exactly how it was done: when in doubt as to how the people of the Galway seacoast spoke, I thought first in Irish and then in the careful, classical English that those people use.

In 1950 I had a small boy of my own, named Cormac like his father. My older daughter, Eilean, had learned to read well by the time she was four years old and was a fascinated audience for everything I wrote. My second daughter, Maire, spent most of her waking hours playing the violin which she had been given when she was six years old: Irish jigs and reels and hornpipes, of which she appeared to know hundreds. She also read my stories, always with an incisive comment that I took to heart. I had played the cello almost until the day she was born, and music remained for her the whole of life.

In 1949 we went to live in the Warden's House at the university. A forty-room hall of residence had been built about 1875, at the time when my great-grandfather William Kirby Sullivan was President of the College. It was intended to house Protestant students under the eagle eye of the Reverend Mr. Webster, the first warden. He had also thoughtfully built a house for himself, very large and comfortable, with beautiful gardens adjoining the main campus. From the windows of the thirty-five-foot drawing room we could look across at the cut-stone quadrangle which Lord Macaulay said was fit to stand in the main street of Oxford. A branch of the river Lee ran through the lower grounds and a grey heron nested down there, in the tall trees. It was our domain for two days at every weekend and it hummed with glorious life for the other five.

Protestant students had never wished to inhabit the hostel, and after lying idle for some time it had been bought by a trust fund in 1915, to house Catholics. The charter said that the warden was to be a Catholic professor, and that his wife should be "able and willing to assist him" in his function, which indeed I was. The house was a joy to live

Author's husband Cormac O Cuilleanain (foreground right) with other officers on maneuvers, 1940. A sentry stands guard at the back during a rest period.

in, especially with three such individualistic children. To my amazement, my grisly hotel experience paid off, as I had more or less to supervise a large staff of servants both in our own house and in the students' quarters. Even more useful was my grandmother's training in the proper conduct of the lady of the house, what she might and might not do to hold the respect and attention of her servants. My mother made the connection at once when she came to visit, saying that we were living the kind of delightful life that she had had in her youth, and which she had thought was departed from the face of the earth.

Far from interfering with my writing, as I had feared it might, the fifteen years' stay in the Warden's House was very productive for me. Life had to be orderly or everything would have collapsed. Every morning at eleven o'clock found me at my desk. By that time I had made a grand tour of my responsibilities and dealt with all the troubles that were presented to me. I learned to concentrate fiercely on what I was writing, not even to turn my head when the postman came to the door. I learned to use every moment profitably, in the certainty that at one o'clock, come hell or high water, I must go downstairs and join Cormac and the university chaplain at our high table.

Meals were served formally. In my first week I had decreed that we should eat the same food as the hungry students, so that I could judge its quality. I was the only woman present apart from the waitresses. The chaplain was a former classmate of Cormac's, who had studied at the Irish College in Rome and had a doctorate in theology. His company was entertaining and instructive. This routine was only observed during the thirty weeks of the three terms. For the other twenty-two, the hostel remained firmly closed and the staff, except our own, went home. They were all old and tired, so as not to be a temptation to the young men, and they liked the system.

When I had finished *The Lost Island* I decided that the time had come at last to write a novel. Though I had learned the importance of constructing a compelling plot for children, I knew that something different would be necessary now. It seemed to me that Irish writers were weak on plots, perhaps imagining that a good plot was a compromise with the commercial world. Of all forms, the mystery is the one that demands perfect plotting. The opening must excite interest and doubt, the development must reveal and conceal carefully planned data, the finale must make all clear.

I wrote three mysteries over the next few years, alternating them with full-length children's books and occasional shorter ones. The mysteries were very literary, as I had intended them to be, and they were read by the people whose judgement I valued. My father enjoyed them immensely and delighted in suggesting methods of poisoning that couldn't be easily detected. I knew there was—and still is—a large public of tired intellectuals who read mysteries in order to relax and forget their troubles. The editor of the *Irish Times,* Bertie Smyllie, inaugurated his new literary section with a serial of my first mystery, *Death at Crane's Court.* I could no longer stay in hiding. The second mystery, *Sent to His Account,* fell into the hands of Jacques Barzun, who had just written his delightful book on the mystery novel. In an interview in *Time* magazine he described it firmly as "an out-of-the-way classic" and my agent began to get enquiries from Hollywood. Nothing came of these—too old-fashioned, they said, too literary. The third mystery, which I knew would be my last, was placed in an imaginary university which I called the King's University of Dublin. It was titled *Death in the Quadrangle.* In this I synthesised a lifetime of close contact with academics, so well that my father was constantly asked by colleagues from Oxford, Cambridge, Queen's University in Belfast, and Trinity College, Dublin, if my book was located in their territory. The Cork people firmly believed it was about them, and I made some lifelong enemies. The time had come to move to higher things. All of these mysteries, however, are being republished in 1986.

My first novel—I have always thought of it in this way—was *The Bitter Glass.* It was a story about some young people cut off in Connemara by the blowing up of a railway bridge, during the Irish Civil War. Stress is provided by the fact that they have twin babies with them, the children of their aunt, and before help can come one of the babies dies of dysentery. It was quite different from writing a mystery. I could pause and turn aside from the main plot now and then, to deepen the atmosphere or increase the tension. I could take time to broaden the characterisation or describe the landscape, though my training in writing mysteries made me ensure that there was a clear sequence of ideas whenever I did this.

The book got excellent reviews in the big London papers as well as in the literary magazines. At its American publication the *New York Times* reproduced Augustus John's painting *Galway Girls* alongside a very favorable

Eilis Dillon, 1948.

Husband, Cormac O Cuilleanain, about 1954.

review. Eudora Welty wrote of it: "An excellent piece of work, full of reality, full of poetry, written with a very sure and sensitive hand. I was completely won by it. I was never more at home in a book." In Ireland some of the reviews expressed shock, as if I had blasphemed in writing a novel about that period at all. One reviewer came up with a proverb that I had never heard before: "It's a bad ass that eats his own straddlemat." I had arrived. Short of being banned by the still rampant Irish Censorship Board, I could hardly have hoped for better. *The Bitter Glass* has stood the test of time: when it was republished in 1981 it made the paperback best-seller list in Ireland. The reviewers had changed—now it was welcomed politely on all sides.

My next novel was *The Head of the Family*. It was a story about a famous writer and his bloodsucking, useless family. I felt very much at home with this book, though I always doubt if writers should write about other writers. It also was successful when it was reprinted in 1982, for a different generation. Then I reached a new turning point, by no means my last.

About 1960 it became obvious that Cormac's rheumatoid arthritis, a relic of his soldiering days, would have to be taken seriously. It had flared up after the Asian flu and refused to die down again. Cortisone, the new wonder drug, was administered in large doses, a miracle for a short while and then a disaster. He began to see that he couldn't continue as warden unless things improved, which they showed no signs of doing. I had already begun to make

preparations for a lecture tour at American universities and colleges. I knew American literature well, but the point had been reached where I had to see that country if I were ever to understand it properly. My American publishers were enthusiastic. Friends gave me advice and help. I sensed that my profession, which had hitherto been almost a lady's hobby, was about to become a vital part of our lives.

I landed in New York from the *Mauretania* in September 1961 and took a taxi at once to Funk and Wagnalls' office downtown. The ship was a day late because of a hurricane at sea, but the welcome I got made it all worthwhile. I had to set out at once for Poughkeepsie, where I was scheduled to give a lecture on Frederick "Baron Corvo" Rolfe that same evening. The train journey up the Hudson was a good opener for my trip—everything bigger than life-size. Back in New York I lectured in Columbia and then set out for Kentucky, Ohio, Illinois, Massachusetts, Connecticut and Maine.

My old Dublin friend Vivian Mercier was living in Great Neck with his beautiful Italian-American wife Gina, and on my return I spent an evening with them. Vivian was teaching at City College, having gone to America in 1996, and we had met again once or twice on his brief visits home to Ireland. He was able to unravel some of the mysteries of the country.

I came home with a firm conviction that Americans are the most hospitable, healthy, cheerful, confident, curious people in the world. I received so much kindness and hospitality on that first trip that I instructed my entire family to treat like a king every American who visits Ireland. I also learned to put my goods in the shop window, never to minimise my own achievements, and to put up a fight for what I wanted. If I had done any of those things in Ireland, I would have been shot down at once.

The most startling thing I encountered was the reaction to my accent, which was commented on by anyone and everyone throughout my journey. Everyone had an Irish grandmother, or was taught by an Irish nun who spoke as I did. Since I had the accent of my mother, I doubted this, but some overtone was apparently instantly recognisable. I had to explain that not every Irish person who comes to America lives in a thatched cottage at home. One thing was certain: I was determined to come back. Irish literature was much better known in America than I had realized, and I felt that any contribution I could make would be thoroughly appreciated. I was specially interested in the way in which American students listened to the sounds of Irish poetry, even when they couldn't understand a word of it.

By the time my next trip came round, we had had to leave the Warden's House. Our older daughter, Eilean, had already graduated from the university and had had some poetry published. She was a brilliant student, obviously headed for the academic life like so many of her forebears. Maire, our second daughter, had become a first-class violinist and was battling with decisions about how to use her art. Our son, also a promising violinist, was away at boarding school in Dublin. The doctors said a sojourn in a warm climate was indicated for Cormac. Out of the depths of her ancient wisdom my mother said: "Algiers for tuberculosis, Rome for arthritis." To Rome we went.

We had always loved Rome and had passed through it many times on our way to the Bay of Naples for summer holidays. Our children welcomed the idea of our living in

Italy too and seemed resigned to being deserted. In theory it was to be a year but in fact we settled there for six years, not coming back to live in Ireland until 1969. It was there I learned that the only reality is inside the human brain, and that everywhere one goes, memory and experience remain constant.

In September 1963, we rented an apartment in Frascati, south of Rome, in a house that had been built inside the park of the Villa Grazioli. A forbidding mansion just across the lane from us was the Villa itself. The Grazioli are an ancient Italian family, with property all over the country, including Sardinia. They hadn't occupied the villa for years—in fact the last occupant had been Field-Marshal Kesselring, who had his headquarters there during the German occupation of Italy. The American Air Force had bombed the town of Frascati several times in the hope of hitting him but they were about a mile short of their target.

Cormac stayed in a *pensione* in Rome while I went off to America again, for a six-week tour that took me this time to more distant places. Colorado was the farthest west. At Fort Collins, where the University of Colorado had its veterinary school, thousands of unexpected students were pouring in. Most of them were more interested in subjects other than agriculture. The liberal arts departments found themselves overwhelmed, with an empty library and unprecedented sums of money for books. The librarian asked me to donate a manuscript to the new library, and later I sent him *The Bitter Glass*. There was an air of optimism everywhere.

I went to the Writers' Workshop in Iowa City and gave some talks on Irish poetry. It was an international group, difficult to assess, all enjoying themselves and producing a great deal. The fact that they were always snowed up for part of the year may have had something to do with the claustrophobic feel of it. Later I found that a good many Irish writers learned professionalism—that great virtue—in Iowa.

Back in New York, I was having a farewell lunch with my publishers in the President restaurant in Manhattan when I heard a waiter say: "Il Presidente e morto." Then the same waiter came to our table, tears rolling down his cheeks, saying: "You are the only people who are not watching the television. Someone has shot Mr. Kennedy."

I went back to Rome by way of Ireland, where the whole country was in mourning. John F. Kennedy had captured the hearts of everyone that very summer, with his simple good manners and his obvious pleasure in life. Later there was gossip about him but the picture that has remained in Ireland is of a man full of vitality, with a sense of humor, an intellectual who managed to bridge the gap between that mental type and the political one. On my next trip to America, two years later, I saw that his loss there was irreparable. The excitement of creation had dimmed, though the Peace Corps satisfied a need for the ideal in the young.

We stayed in Frascati for a year, trying to live a dull country life. It was not possible. In Rome we had friends at both embassies, the Quirinale and the Vatican, who were constantly inviting us to receptions and dinners. The Opera House had an artistic director of genius, Massimo Bogianchino, now the Mayor of Florence, who was putting on an extraordinary season of opera and who had reformed the ballet so that it was unrecognisable. Rudolf Nureyev and

Erik de Bruhn were dancing there. The Conservatorio di Santa Cecilia had a season of recitals as well as chamber music concerts. The Radio Orchestra had symphony concerts with avant-garde music and young, lively conductors. Zubin Mehta was one. There was a cinema with English-language films. Vittorio Gassman and Eduardo de Filippo were putting on exciting plays.

In Frascati our house was surrounded by olive trees in which owls roosted, making a curious snoring sound after dark. At night the quiet was intense. A Sardinian woman, whose husband worked on the estate for the absent Princess Grazioli, came daily to clean the house. We knew enough Italian to communicate with her. As in every Italian house, we were not the only occupants. A whole family, who owned the house, lived upstairs. It never occurred to them that their shouts of joy or anger could possibly disturb anyone. Workmen came to dig the garden at four in the morning, taking advantage of the coolness, and yelled to each other outside our bedroom window. From the point of view of time, the whole world was upside down. We learned the truth of Cyril Connolly's statement that the essence of living in the country is waiting for the post to arrive.

Still, every morning I set to work to cover some sheets of paper. I was writing a play, something I had always wanted to do, plotting it as carefully as I had done with the mysteries. I had finished a novel called *Bold John Henebry*, which surveyed the life of a countryman who comes to town, makes a fortune, and brings up a family whose

Eldest daughter, Eilean, a poet and scholar.

standards differ drastically from his own. The background had created difficulties, in that it was necessary to get dates right, and I was not sure how well I had succeeded in creating the atmosphere I wanted. I was anxiously waiting to see what reception the book would get. Our telephone was on a party line and was not altogether reliable. We began to feel totally cut off.

The last straw was when our son arrived for the summer vacation. He was not enjoying boarding school and complained that he had never before spent all his time exclusively with *boys.* He was accustomed to adult company and felt that he had been siphoned off into a backwater. We asked him if he would like to stay with us and go to school in Rome. He fell on the suggestion with delight. This experience was what eventually turned him into an Italian scholar.

It became essential to move to Rome, since he wanted to continue studying the violin. I began to find out about Italian bureaucracy, the convolutions of which can scarcely be believed. In the end we invoked the Irish Ambassador, and young Cormac was placed both at a state school and in the Conservatorio di Santa Cecilia. He learned more Italian in one month than we had learned in a year. He brought friends to the house. He found out about concerts and exhibitions and museums. He escorted me to cocktail parties and receptions. He revolutionized our lives—there was no more talk of living in retirement in the backwoods.

For all of us, one of the great experiences of living in Rome was friendship with Ignazio Silone. He had been a courageous opponent of fascism and had had to leave the country, living first in Paris and then in Zurich. He spoke no English, but we communicated in French or Italian. His wife was Irish, so we had met at the Embassy. Silone had represented the Italian Communist Party in the late twenties, had visited Russia, and quickly saw where Communism was going. His pamphlet concerning his reasons for leaving the Communist Party is a classic in Italy still. He had only one theme—and he believed that writers never have more than one, which keeps recurring in various forms. His was the freedom of the individual and the individual's right to oppose oppression in all forms. *Bread and Wine* and *Fontamara* were his best-known novels outside of Italy, but I found and read the others one by one. In general very serious, he had a quiet humor which showed at its best in talking and writing about the peasants of the Abruzzi, where he had lived as a child.

Among the books I had brought out from Ireland was a definitive edition of *Caoine Airt Uí Laoire (The Lament for Arthur O'Leary),* a 400-line poem written in 1773 to lament the death of the poet's husband. She was Eileen O'Connell of Derrynane in Kerry, the great-aunt of Daniel O'Connell, the man who achieved civil rights for Catholics in Ireland in 1829 and one of the great names in Irish history. I began to translate the *Lament,* and continued it off and on over the next six years. A number of translations had been published but none of them seemed to me successful, mainly because they all failed to follow the rhythms of the original. These rhythms seemed to me an essential part of the poem and I laboured long and hard to get them right. I doubt if I had intended to translate the whole poem but at last it was finished, and was published

Second daughter, Maire, violinist.

in the *Irish University Review.* Peter Levi saw it there and was fired with great enthusiasm both for the poem and the translation. It was very interesting and gratifying to know that a poem which means so much to us in Ireland could cross the barriers of nationality. The poem has been anthologised, wholly or in part, many times since then. Peter Levi read the entire translation at his inaugural lecture as Professor of Poetry at Oxford in 1984, after his talk on classic lamentations for the dead.

My play *A Page of History* was produced in the Abbey Theatre in Dublin in November 1966. I was reluctant to leave Cormac, whose health was deteriorating, but I went to Ireland to watch rehearsals and see the first performances. It was a pleasant surprise to find that the director was a man I had known in the Irish Theatre in Galway when I was a child. He was Frank Dermody, an inspired director but a very lonely man. He received me as an old friend and put endless work into the production; the cast included some of the big names of the Abbey. They were delightful to work with and gave everything they had to the play, which received excellent reviews.

But it was never produced again. The reason was a simple one: the old Abbey Theatre had burned down, and the National Theatre was temporarily housed at the Queen's Theatre. The company moved into their new theatre early the following year, and while they were feeling their way towards a new lease of life, my play got lost somewhere. I never tried to get it revived. Though I love the theatre and have various plans for more plays eventually, at the time I was not capable of the kind of single-minded determination that would have been necessary. I had it years later, when I adapted one of my old children's books, *The Cats' Opera,* for the theatre. It was produced at the Abbey as their Christmas show in 1981. It's a story about some cats rehearsing an opera after midnight, when all cats can talk. The last act consists entirely of the opera, for which I composed the music myself.

By 1968, life in Rome had become impossible for us. Cormac was almost helpless and, with no family members near, it was an unending strain just to keep things limping along. We decided to go back to Ireland, to Dublin, where Eilean was teaching in the English department at Trinity College and our son was a student at the National University. We rented a house and moved in early in March 1969. Before nightfall on the day of our arrival, Maire was home from Belfast, where she had been playing in the Ulster Orchestra. She stayed for six months, savouring family life, until she departed for London and eventually to the London Philharmonic Orchestra, where she plays in the first violin section still.

Now we had a student in the house again, which meant friends dropping in for talk and meals, music day and night, frantic studying for examinations—all the things that make life interesting. Our son was a tower of strength as Cormac's health failed more and more. Less than a year after our return he had to move to a nursing home. In October 1970 he died.

Just before we left Rome my agent had written to suggest that I might write a long novel, covering a hundred years or so, with a background in Irish history. *Bold John Henebry* had seemed to him to be a sort of first run, and he thought I might go much more deeply into characters and events, with more scope than I had had thus far. He had both an American and an English publisher interested. Glad of any suggestion for my future work, I had accepted the commission and had written about one third of the novel when Cormac died. How I finished it I don't know. My other personality took over somehow and worked independently. Cormac's old classmate, Sean O'Faolain, was endlessly helpful, full of praise rather than criticism. The details of daily life had become so complicated that my desk was an oasis.

The book was eventually named *Across the Bitter Sea*, a quotation from a Yeats poem, as the title *The Bitter Glass* was. Yeats liked the word "bitter," probably for the short vowel and the throwaway second syllable. It was another turning point, a dangerous one, I thought. I took a true story that I had once heard, of a nineteenth-century landlord in the west of Ireland who married a poor girl with just enough education to handle life in a higher station. In the novel, the landlord is sickened by the behaviour of his own class and tries to improve the lot of the miserable people around him. For the background I included Irish songs, some of which I translated since no translations existed. The main characters were fictional but some real people were used, as several of the critics recommend. It was intensely painful to write. When my landlord character was murdered I was desolate for a month—but I knew that my own strong emotion was no guarantee of the book's success.

Across the Bitter Sea has been steadily in print since 1973 and was an instant success both in Ireland and abroad. On the day before its publication, the London *Sunday Times* reviewer gave it an ecstatic notice, saying that it was "a novel of which Zola might have been proud." Conor Cruise O'Brien spoke at the launching in Dublin, saying

Son, Cormac, age sixteen, Rome, 1966.

that Ireland needed books like this to promote understanding between us and England. I was quite surprised at all this praise, though I knew I had put a lifetime of experience into the book. I had researched it very carefully from the historical point of view, and it is used by history departments in Ireland, and perhaps elsewhere, to bring history to life.

While I was working on the book, I went to Rome to visit old friends and take a holiday. There I met an Irish friend of mine, Tom Murphy the playwright, who was a member of the International Commission on English in the Liturgy. The Commission was set up to translate the Latin liturgy into English. Hurried translations of some texts had been made and now these were being revised and more worked on. The Commission was frantically looking for poets and writers of literary prose to continue the program. Tom introduced me to the members, and I soon found myself elected a committee member. I worked with the Commission for seven years, and still do occasional consulting work for it. My translating experience was very useful, and my knowledge of Latin proved adequate, though I only knew enough of it to read what interested me greatly. The meetings took place either in Washington or in some other big center around the world. These dedicated clerics and scholars were excellent company.

Back in Dublin I was nominated by the Irish government to be a member of the newly-constituted Arts Council of Ireland. We had great support from the Prime Minister, and *carte blanche* so far as planning was concerned. The members were mostly working artists—a poet, an actor, one or two musicians, writers, and painters. We made full use of our opportunities, setting up grant schemes, a course for writers at the university in Galway—my invention—a retreat for artists in Tyrone Guthrie's old country house, which he had left to the nation, and a great many other projects that are still in operation. I began to wonder if this was where my future lay.

J ust as I was finishing *Across the Bitter Sea,* Vivian Mercier arrived in Dublin from Boulder, Colorado, where he had moved some years before. He had a Guggenheim Fellowship and a plan to write a book about Samuel Beckett, on whom he was something of an expert. It was Vivian who made the celebrated remark about *Waiting for Godot*: it's a play where nothing happens, twice. Gina had died a year after Cormac, having battled for a long time with multiple sclerosis. We were both raw from our experiences. Soon it became obvious that we needed each other desperately. We were married in April 1974, and life moved out of limbo and began again. My children became deeply attached to Vivian and he was soon one of the family.

While he was on leave, the University of California at Santa Barbara invited Vivian to join the faculty. We had both been to Santa Barbara and remembered it as a paradise, the most perfect climate in America and on the seacoast, which is very important to island people, far from all the troubles that we hoped to forget in time. We moved there at the end of 1974 and have since divided our time between California and Ireland. Our working arrangements in our house in Ireland are a constant source of astonishment to visitors: we have two desks, face to face, in the same room, and we work comfortably without disturbing each other. There are some advantages in the kind of existence we have both led: all neuroses about conditions of work have had to be abandoned.

In 1981, Maire and I rented an apartment in a huge stone house in Italy, not far from Perugia. It was an old dream of hers to get away sometimes from the stresses of a London musician's life, and she and her husband spend six weeks there in late spring every year. Since we always write wherever we are, Vivian and I use it for working holidays, for a few weeks in the summer or fall. *The Cats' Opera* was written there. Eilean and Cormac, with their families, began to use it too. Gradually it has become a family retreat where one can work or relax at any time. Strange books fill the shelves. There is no telephone.

Back and forth across the North Pole or the Atlantic Ocean, I still continue to produce an amazing quantity. There is always more and more to do, but as most of my relatives have lived close on a hundred years I have no great sense of urgency. Since living in America I have written three children's books; two about ancient Rome and one about the wicked bank manager who deprived us of our lovely house so long ago. One of the ancient Rome books was a Junior Literary Guild choice. I have also written three long novels, several short pieces of one kind or another, a one-act play which is awaiting a production in Galway, and a play for one actor about Jonathan Swift which may never get a production at all, but may well find a publisher. My favorites among my recent books are

Inside Ireland, a travel book, and *Citizen Burke,* a psychological novel, which may prove to be another turning point.

Though I love America deeply and have a great many friends here, Ireland is still my spiritual home. There is an involvement with writers there that I have never experienced anywhere else. The Irish make sure that no one will become conceited and they slap down any tendency in that direction unhesitatingly. I have a great many admirers there, but I have never been honored in any way. When I was invited to become a Fellow of the Royal Society of Literature, founded in England by George III, I had no difficulty in deciding to accept, since the letters F.R.S.L. are the only ones I am entitled to place after my name. Still, the Irish do love their writers, though one has an impression that they feel, as Chekhov said, that a country which nurtures writers is like a farmer who owns a granary and breeds rats.

[Editor's note: It is with great sadness that we learned from Dillon's son, Cormac O Cuilleanain, of the death of Eilis Dillon on 19 July 1994. Cormac O Cuilleanain is now Dillon's literary executor. A new Irish children's book prize was named in her honour, and her children's books continue to be reissued. There is a web site for Eilis Dillon's books at http://homepage.tinet.ie/~writing.

Dillon's daughter Eilean Ni Chuilleanain became an academic and currently heads the Department of English at Trinity College Dublin, Ireland's oldest university; she has published several books of poetry in Ireland and in the United States. Daughter Maire Ni Chuilleanain remained a professional violinist in the London Philharmonic Orchestra until her early death in 1990. Son Cormac O Cuilleanain

Dillon and her second husband, Vivian Mercier, California, 1978.

teaches Italian, also at Trinity College Dublin, and is a prize-winning translator. Vivian Mercier died in 1989. His last work of scholarship, *Modern Irish Literature: Sources and Founders,* was published in Oxford by the Clarendon Press in 1994. Dillon had interrupted her own last novel to complete the editing of this book; her novel remains unfinished. In 1992, she received an honorary D.Litt. from the National University of Ireland.]

Writings

FOR CHILDREN; FICTION

Midsummer Magic, illustrated by Stuart Tresilian, Macmillan, 1949.

The Lost Island, Faber & Faber, 1952; Funk & Wagnalls, 1954.

The Island of Horses, Faber & Faber, 1956; Funk & Wagnalls, 1957.

The Singing Cave, Faber & Faber, 1959; Funk & Wagnalls, 1960.

The Cats' Opera (also see below), illustrated by Vanecek, Faber & Faber, 1962; Bobbs-Merrill, 1963.

A Family of Foxes, Faber & Faber, 1964; Funk & Wagnalls, 1965.

The Sea Wall, Faber & Faber, 1965; Farrar, Straus, 1965.

The Seals, Faber & Faber, 1968; Funk & Wagnalls, 1969.

A Herd of Deer, Faber & Faber, 1969; Funk & Wagnalls, 1970.

Living in Imperial Rome, Faber & Faber, 1974; published as *Rome under the Emperors,* Thomas Nelson, 1975.

The Shadow of Vesuvius, Thomas Nelson, 1977; Faber & Faber, 1978.

Down in the World, Hodder & Stoughton, 1983.
The Island of Ghosts, Macmillan, 1989.
Children of Bach, Macmillan, 1992.

FOR ADULTS; FICTION

Death at Crane's Court, Faber & Faber, 1953; Walker, 1963.

Sent to His Account, Faber & Faber, 1954; Walker, 1969.

Death in the Quadrangle, Faber & Faber, 1956; Walker, 1968.

The Bitter Glass, Faber & Faber, 1958; Appleton-Century, 1959.

The Head of the Family, Faber & Faber, 1960; Ward River Press, 1980.

Bold John Henebry, Faber & Faber, 1965.

Across the Bitter Sea, Simon & Schuster, 1973; Hodder & Stoughton, 1974.

Blood Relations, Simon & Schuster, 1977; Hodder & Stoughton, 1978.

Wild Geese, Simon & Schuster, 1980; Hodder & Stoughton, 1981.

Citizen Burke, Hodder & Stoughton, 1984.

The Interloper, Hodder & Stoughton, 1987.

PLAYS

Manna, produced on Radio Eireann, Dublin, 1962.
A Page of History, first produced in Dublin, 1966.
The Cats' Opera (with music; for children), first produced in Dublin, 1981.

OTHER

Inside Ireland (travel), Hodder & Stoughton, 1982; Beaufort Books, 1984.

Dillon is also the translator of poetry from the French and the Irish, published in anthologies and periodicals.

DOOLING, Michael 1958-

Personal

Born July 13, 1958, in Philadelphia, PA; married; wife's name, Jane; children: Rachel, Lisa. *Education:* Syracuse University, M.F.A., 1988.

Addresses

Home—161 Wyoming Ave., Audubon, NJ 08106.

Career

Illustrator of children's books. *Exhibitions:* Norman Rockwell Museum, Delaware Art Museum, Society of Illustrators. *Member:* Society of Illustrators.

Awards, Honors

Pick of the Lists, American Booksellers Association, for *Mary McLean and the St. Patrick's Day Parade* and *The Gift of the Magi and Other Stories;* Notable Trade Book in the Field of Social Studies, National Council for the Social Studies-Children's Book Council, for *George Washington: A Picture Book Biography;* Editor's Choice award, *Booklist,* for *Thomas Jefferson: A Picture Book Biography.*

Illustrator

Johanna Hurwitz, *Astrid Lindgren: Storyteller to the World,* Viking, 1989.

Zibby Oneal, *A Long Way to Go,* Viking, 1990.

Freya Littledale (adaptor of the story by Washington Irving), *Rip Van Winkle,* Scholastic, 1991.

Tom Paxton's story of how woodsman Claus leaves the forest to establish his shop at the North Pole is illustrated with detailed paintings by Dooling. (From The Story of Santa Claus.)

Steven Kroll, *Mary McLean and the St. Patrick's Day Parade,* Scholastic, 1991.

James Cross Giblin, *George Washington: A Picture Book Biography,* Scholastic, 1992.

Mark Harshman, *Uncle James,* Cobblehill Books, 1993.

Rona Rupert, *Straw Sense,* Simon & Schuster, 1993.

Judith Logan Lehne, *When the Ragman Sings,* HarperCollins, 1993.

Jane Resh Thomas, *Lights on the River,* Hyperion, 1994.

James Cross Giblin, *Thomas Jefferson: A Picture Book Biography,* Scholastic, 1994.

Tom Paxton, *The Story of Santa Claus,* Morrow, 1995.

Johanna Hurwitz, *Even Stephen,* Morrow, 1996.

O. Henry, *The Gift of the Magi and Other Stories,* Morrow, 1997.

Elvira Woodruff, *The Memory Coat,* Scholastic, 1999.

James Cross Giblin, *The Amazing Life of Ben Franklin,* Scholastic, 1999.

Jeannine Atkins, *Mary Anning and the Sea Dragon,* Farrar, Straus & Giroux, 1999.

Sidelights

Michael Dooling is the illustrator of a number of books for young readers, many of them focused on historical figures or epochs in American life. A graduate of Syracuse University and a resident of New Jersey, Dooling is married and has two stepdaughters, who

Michael Dooling

sometimes serve as models for characters in his work. Many of the books he has illustrated have been singled out for praise by the American Booksellers' Association and the American Library Association. Among these are the titles *George Washington: A Picture Book Biography* and *Thomas Jefferson: A Picture Book Biography,* both written by James Cross Giblin. The first book won praise from *School Library Journal* reviewer Jean H. Zimmerman, who noted that "Dooling's full-page oil paintings effectively evoke both the legendary aspects" of Washington's life, as well as his quieter, more human moments. *Thomas Jefferson: A Picture Book Biography* was named an Editor's Choice pick by *Booklist,* the magazine of the American Library Association, in 1994. Like many of the titles Dooling has illustrated, it is aimed at primary graders. Dot Minzer, writing for *School Library Journal,* called Dooling's striking two-page spreads "richly executed, making Jefferson ... come alive."

Another work bearing Dooling's name that won an industry citation was the 1997 edition of *The Gift of the Magi and Other Stories.* The title story, a perennial Christmas favorite from the American short-story writer O. Henry, is a heartbreaking tale about an impoverished newlywed couple who have no money to buy one another a gift. Hazel Rochman, writing in *Booklist,* praised the color plates Dooling drew for each O. Henry story, calling them "both low-key and warm, with a realistic style that captures the wry characterization" of the writer and his work. Dooling also drew behind-the-scenes glimpses for *The Story of Santa Claus,* written by Tom Paxton. Dooling's oils for this tale of how Santa found his elves and devised his method of reindeer transportation were consistently deemed "rich" by reviewers; a *School Library Journal* assessment termed them "highly textured and filled with homey details." Many reviewers have compared Dooling's style to that of renowned American illustrator Norman Rockwell, and fittingly, Dooling has exhibited his work in the Norman Rockwell Museum. He also makes school visits with the theme "History through Picture Books," a behind-the-scenes look at creating a picture book.

Works Cited

Minzer, Dot, review of *Thomas Jefferson: A Picture Book Biography, School Library Journal,* September, 1994, p. 228.

Rochman, Hazel, review of *The Gift of the Magi and Other Stories, Booklist,* October 15, 1997, p. 397.

Review of *The Story of Santa Claus, School Library Journal,* October, 1995, p. 40.

Zimmerman, Jean H., review of *George Washington: A Picture Book Biography, School Library Journal,* September, 1992, p. 216.

For More Information See

PERIODICALS

Booklist, October 15, 1992, pp. 433-34; September 15, 1993, p. 157; August, 1994, p. 2053; October 15, 1994,

p. 421; September 15, 1995, p. 172; January 1, 1999, p. 892.
Horn Book, September-October, 1992, pp. 598-99.
Publishers Weekly, October 4, 1993, p. 80; September 19, 1994, p. 30; September 18, 1995, p. 103; January 18, 1999, p. 339.
School Library Journal, October, 1993, p. 100.

* * *

DOYLE, Debra 1952-

Personal

Born in 1952, in Florida; married James D. Macdonald (Doyle's writing collaborator and a former navy officer), August 5, 1978; children: Katherine, Brendan, Peregrine, Alexander. *Education:* University of Pennsylvania, Ph.D. (English literature); also educated in Florida, Texas, and Arkansas.

Addresses

Home—127 Main St., Colebrook, NH 03576. *Agent*—Valerie Smith, 1746 Route 44-55, Modena, NY 12548.

Career

Writer. Computer Assisted Learning Center, teacher of fiction writing.

Awards, Honors

Mythopoeic Society Aslan Award for young adult literature, 1992, and Books for the Teen Age selection, New York Public Library, 1993, both for *Knight's Wyrd.*

Writings

NOVELS; "CIRCLE OF MAGIC" SERIES; WITH JAMES D. MACDONALD

School of Wizardry, Troll Books, 1990.
Tournament and Tower, Troll, 1990.
City by the Sea, Troll, 1990.
The Prince's Players, Troll, 1990.
The Prisoners of Bell Castle, Troll, 1990.
The High King's Daughter, Troll, 1990.

NOVELS; "MAGEWORLDS" SERIES; WITH JAMES D. MACDONALD

The Price of the Stars, Tor Books (New York City), 1992.
Starpilot's Grave, Tor, 1993.
By Honor Betray'd, Tor, 1994.
The Gathering Flame, Tor, 1995.
The Long Hunt, Tor, 1996.

NOVELS; "BAD BLOOD" SERIES; WITH JAMES D. MACDONALD

Bad Blood, Berkley, 1993.
Hunters' Moon, Berkley, 1994.
Judgment Night, Berkley, 1995.

OTHER NOVELS WITH JAMES D. MACDONALD

(Under pseudonym Robyn Tallis) *Night of Ghosts and Lightning* (Planet Builders #2), Ivy, 1989.
(Under pseudonym Robyn Tallis) *Zero-Sum Games* (Planet Builders #5), Ivy, 1989.
(Under pseudonym Nicholas Adams) *Pep Rally* (Horror High #7), Harper, 1991.
(Under pseudonym Victor Appleton) *Monster Machine* (Tom Swift #5), Archway Paperback, Pocket Books, 1991.
(Under pseudonym Victor Appleton) *Aquatech Warriors* (Tom Swift #6), Archway Paperback, Pocket Books, 1991.
Timecrime, Inc. (Robert Silverberg's "Time Tours" #3), Harper, 1991.
Night of the Living Rat (Daniel Pinkwater's "Melvinge of the Megaverse" #2), Ace Books, 1992.
Knight's Wyrd, Harcourt, Brace, 1992.
(Under pseudonym Martin Delrio) *Mortal Kombat* (movie novelizations: adult and young adult versions), Tor, 1995.
Groogleman, Harcourt, Brace, 1996.
(Under pseudonym Martin Delrio) *Spider-Man Super-Thriller: Midnight Justice,* Byron Preiss Multimedia Co. & Pocket Books, 1996.
(Under pseudonym Martin Delrio) *Spider-Man Super-Thriller: Global War,* Byron Preiss Multimedia & Pocket Books, 1996.
(Under pseudonym Martin Delrio) *Prince Valiant* (movie novelization), Avon Books, 1997.

OTHER

Contributor (with James D. Macdonald) of short stories to anthologies, including "Bad Blood" in *Werewolves,* edited by Yolen & Greenberg, Harper Junior Books, 1988; "Nobody Has to Know" in *Vampires,* edited by Yolen & Greenberg, HarperCollins, 1991; "The Last Real New Yorker in the World" in *Newer York,* edited by Lawrence Watt-Evans, Roc, 1991; "Now and in the Hour of Our Death" in *Alternate Kennedys,* edited by Mike Resnick and Martin Greenberg, Tor, 1992; "Uncle Joshua and the Grooglemen" in *Bruce Coville's Book of Monsters,* edited by Bruce Coville, Scholastic, 1993; "Why They Call It That" in *Swashbuckling Editor Stories,* edited by John Betancourt, Wildside Press, 1993; "The Queen's Mirror" in *A Wizard's Dozen,* edited by Michael Stearns, Harcourt, Brace, 1995; "Crossover" in *A Starfarer's Dozen,* edited by Michael Stearns, Harcourt, Brace, 1995; "Witch Garden" in *Witch Fantastic,* edited by Mike Resnick and Martin Greenberg, DAW Books, 1995; "Holly and Ivy" in *Camelot,* edited by Jane Yolen, Philomel, 1995; "Please to See the King" in *The Book of Kings,* edited by Richard Gilliam and Martin Greenberg, Roc, 1995; "Stealing God" in *Tales of the Knights Templar,* edited by Katherine Kurtz, Warner, 1995; "Ecdysis" in *Otherwere,* edited by Laura Anne Gilman and Keith R. A. DeCandido, Berkley/Ace, 1996; "Up the Airy Mountain" in *A Nightmare's Dozen,* edited by Michael Stearns, Harcourt, Brace, 1996; "Jenny Nettles" in *Bruce Coville's Book of Spine Tinglers,* edited by Bruce

Coville, Scholastic, 1996; "Block G-18" in *High-Tech Wars #2,* edited by Pournelle and Carr.

Contributor of "The Last God of Dura Europus," parts I and II, to the comic book *Timewalker #10,* Valiant Comics, April, 1995, and of "We Who Are About to Die" to the comic book *Timewalker #15,* Valiant Comics, June, 1995.

Work in Progress

The novels *City of Dreadful Night,* Tor; *Erassi: The Professor's Story* ("Mageworlds" no. 6), Tor; and untitled "Mageworlds" novels nos. 7 and 8.

Sidelights

Debra Doyle, along with her husband and coauthor James D. Macdonald, issued six fantasy novels for the couple's "Circle of Magic" series in one year's time in 1990. Making the feat more impressive, these were the first novels Doyle and Macdonald published under their own names; previously, they had contributed two books under the pseudonym Robyn Tallis to Ivy's "Planet Builders" series. The pair were relatively new to professional writing at that time but created stories prolifically during the 1990s, combining their individual gifts and experiences to constitute a productive and imaginative team.

Debra Doyle grew up in Florida, then studied in other locales, eventually receiving a doctorate in Old English literature from the University of Pennsylvania. While living and studying in Philadelphia, she met Macdonald, who was then serving with the Navy, where he rose in rank from enlisted man to officer during a fifteen-year career. In the intervening years, the pair traveled to Virginia, California, and Panama, eventually settling to raise their four children in a nineteenth-century Victorian house in New Hampshire.

Doyle's husband, Macdonald, once described for SATA the unique working arrangement of their very effective collaboration. "Years ago, before we started writing together, Doyle and I noticed that we had some characteristic weaknesses," Macdonald stated. "Doyle's prose style is very good, but her plotting is straight-line predictable. I do pretty decent plots, but my prose is deepest purple. So we got together, and now I plot while Doyle proses. My outlines—what anyone else would call 'first drafts'—are about eighty percent of the length of the eventual finished work. They read like someone telling about a movie. Fast, slangy, self-referential, with the characters and backgrounds lightly sketched in. Doyle takes this and fleshes it out, adding additional dialog, fuller descriptions, transition scenes, and so on. Then I take her output, add missing parts, trim and move other scenes, and otherwise mess with the structure. By the time we're done, usually a fourth or fifth draft, we're handing individual sheets of paper back and forth between us, scribbling, drawing arrows, and coming to some kind of consensus. We don't argue about things:

Thirteen-year-old Dan embarks on a dangerous journey to rescue his friend, who has been kidnapped by the mysterious and menacing grooglemen in Debra Doyle's fantasy novel, cowritten with James D. Macdonald. (Cover illustration by Cliff Nielsen.)

Doyle has the final say on words, I have the final say on plot."

Doyle's collaboration with Macdonald has produced dozens of stories and novels for adults, young adults, and children, under their authors' own and pen names. Some works have been entries in fantasy or science fiction series; others have been novelizations of the computer game-based movie *Mortal Kombat* and the comic-book-based movie *Prince Valiant,* as well as Spiderman comic book stories; there have even been a couple of "Tom Swift" adventure novels. The pair have also written novels within series created by other writers, namely Robert Silverberg and Daniel Pinkwater.

Especially worthy of note are two young-adult novels that Doyle and Macdonald wrote as solo projects unconnected to any series. *Knight's Wyrd,* published in 1992, is a knights-in-armor fantasy involving magic. In it, young Will Odosson must find his wyrd—his fate. When he discovers that his destiny is doom, he journeys bravely to meet it, with complex and adventurous results. The New York Public Library listed this novel as one of its Books for the Teen Age in 1993, and the novel won the Mythopoeic Fantasy award the previous year. A *Kirkus Reviews* critic commended *Knight's Wyrd* for "a strong sense of time, place, and code of honor." *Voice of Youth Advocates* contributor Jennifer A. Long asserted: "Strong main characters and a smoothly written plot make this a hard book to put down."

Another important non-series novel for Doyle and Macdonald, *Groogleman,* takes place in a quasi-medieval culture that has developed after an unspecified technological collapse of contemporary civilization. Young hero Dan Henchard possesses weller's blood, a kind of inherited immunity to a plague that has claimed the lives of many. A stranger named Joshua eventually joins Dan at his farm, and the two, along with another "weller," Leezie, travel to a nearby village to help plague victims in need of assistance. Upon arrival they find that the area has been terrorized by the mysterious groogleman, who manage to kidnap Leezie. The stranger, Joshua, claims to know which way the groogleman have traveled, and he leads Dan on a arduous journey to find her. Reviewing the novel for *School Library Journal,* Susan L. Rogers called it a "successful" example of its genre: "Dan and Joshua quickly become sympathetic and interesting characters on a desperate journey through a foreboding landscape." Janice M. Del Negro of the *Bulletin of the Center for Children's Books* admired *Groogleman*'s writing for conveying the sensory qualities of the setting, and called Dan "a believable adolescent in a grimly dangerous situation." Commending the way in which the authors created a vivid, convincing alternate culture in a few pages, Del Negro stated, "This intriguing novel suggests more than it reveals and could provoke some thoughtful group discussion."

Works Cited

Del Negro, Janice M., review of *Groogleman, Bulletin of the Center for Children's Books,* December, 1996, p. 132.

Review of *Knight's Wyrd, Kirkus Reviews,* October 1, 1992, p. 1253.

Long, Jennifer A., review of *Knight's Wyrd, Voice of Youth Advocates,* June, 1993, p. 102.

Rogers, Susan L., review of *Groogleman, School Library Journal,* December, 1996, pp. 120, 122.

For More Information See

PERIODICALS

Booklist, November 15, 1992, pp. 589-90.
Bulletin of the Center for Children's Books, February, 1993, pp. 173-74.
School Library Journal, November, 1992, p. 90.*

DRESCHER, Henrik 1955-

Personal

Born December 15, 1955, in Denmark; immigrated to United States, 1967; married; wife's name, Lauren; children: Uli. *Education:* Studied illustration at Boston Museum School.

Career

Writer and illustrator. Conducts workshops on bookmaking for children.

Awards, Honors

Best Illustrated Books, *New York Times,* 1982, for *The Strange Appearance of Howard Cranebill, Jr.,* 1983, for *Simon's Book,* and 1987, for *The Yellow Umbrella; Simon's Book* received a Parents' Choice Award and was selected for the Graphic Gallery Showcase of Books by *Horn Book* and for the television program *Reading Rainbow.*

Writings

AUTHOR AND ILLUSTRATOR

The Strange Appearance of Howard Cranebill, Jr., Lothrop, 1982.
Simon's Book, Lothrop, 1983.
(With Calvin Zeit) *True Paranoid Facts!,* Quill, 1983.
Looking for Santa Claus, Lothrop, 1984.
Look-alikes, Lothrop, 1985.
Whose Scaly Tail? African Animals You'd Like to Meet (nonfiction), Lippincott, 1987.
Whose Furry Nose? Australian Animals You'd Like to Meet (nonfiction), Lippincott, 1987.
The Yellow Umbrella, Bradbury, 1987.
Pat the Beastie: A Pull-and-Poke Book, paper engineering by Dennis K. Meyer, Hyperion, 1993.
The Boy Who Ate Around, Hyperion, 1994.
Tales From the Crib: True Confessions of a Shameless Procreator, Harcourt Brace, 1994.
Klutz, Hyperion, 1996.

ILLUSTRATOR

Marc Ian Barasch, *The Little Black Book of Atomic War,* Dell, 1983.
Harriet Ziefert, *All Clean!,* Harper, 1986.
Ziefert, *All Gone!,* Harper, 1986.
Ziefert, *Cock-a-Doodle-Doo!,* Harper, 1986.
Ziefert, *Run! Run!,* Harper, 1986.
Mark Dittrick and Diane Kender Dittrick, *Misnomers,* Collier Books, 1986.
Jack Prelutsky, selector, *Poems of A. Nonny Mouse,* Knopf, 1989.
Joel Chandler Harris, collector, and Eric Metaxas, adapter, *Brer Rabbit and the Wonderful Tar Baby,* Picture Book Studio, 1990.
Marc Ian Barasch, *No Plain Pets!,* HarperCollins, 1991.
Eric Metaxas, *The Fool and the Flying Ship,* Rabbit Ears Books (Rowayton, CT), 1992.

Drescher's collages reflect the whimsical nature of Richard Wilbur's poems about antithetical objects. (*From* Runaway Opposites.)

Jonathan Williams, *No-nonse-nse: Limericks (invented in Ireland c. 1765), Meta-fours (invented during the nonsummer of 1985 by Edmund Lower Stodgedale) and Clerihews (invented in 1890 by Edmund Clerihew Bently)*, Perishable Press (Mt. Horeb, WI), 1993.

Richard Wilbur, *Opposites*, Harcourt Brace, 1994.

Wilbur, *Runaway Opposites*, Harcourt Brace, 1995.

Junto a la Bahia (Dejame Leer, Nivel, 3), also illustrated by Len Cabral, Goodyear Publishing, 1995.

Ken Nordine, *Colors*, Harcourt Brace, 1999.

OTHER

Contributor of illustrations to periodicals, including *New York Times Book Review* and *Rolling Stone*.

Adaptations

Simon's Book was adapted as a filmstrip by Random House.

Sidelights

Henrik Drescher is the author and illustrator of *The Strange Appearance of Howard Cranebill, Jr., Simon's Book,* and other award-winning children's books known for their innovative illustrations. Born in Denmark, Drescher came to the United States with his family when he was an adolescent. Though he decided at the age of fifteen to become an artist, he later pursued little formal training, opting instead to travel the world with a drawing notebook in hand. "I travel often," the author told Jim Roginski in *Parents' Choice.* "Notebooks are my way of keeping in touch with bookmaking. I draw in little theme books. This is where a lot of my ideas come from. All the squiggles, the lines, the textures—all graphic and sensual."

Beginning his career as a political illustrator, Drescher contributed editorial drawings to periodicals, including *Rolling Stone* and the *New York Times Book Review.* The author told Roginski that the inspiration for his first book, *The Strange Appearance of Howard Cranebill, Jr.,* came when "a friend who works in children's books as a designer ... encouraged me to do children's books, or to try one anyway. I always put it off. Eventually I got to the point when I thought I had something in me. That was *Howard Cranebill.*"

The story of the destiny of a stork-delivered baby with a unique proboscis, *The Strange Appearance of Howard Cranebill, Jr.* was named a *New York Times* Best Illustrated Book of 1982. Critics praised Drescher's pictures for their characteristic combination of squiggly lines, splotches of paint, and decorative borders. Selma G. Lanes, writing in the *New York Times Book Review,* enthused: "Whether he is simulating an elephant's leathery hide with airy, black-line scribbles or improvising rainbow-hued page borders comprised of sprouting greenery and awesomely inventive comic calligraphy, Mr. Drescher makes every squiggle enhance the visual richness of the story he tells." In creating his singular style, Drescher acknowledges that he was influenced by the artists of Northern Europe. "Drawing is a cultural phenomenon there," he told Roginski, "it's all around you. My line quality, my spontaneity, my sensibility is northern European. I draw very heavily from their traditions and bookmaking."

Lauded for their distinctive illustrations, Drescher's books are also noted for their unique and delightful stories. The author told Roginski: "My purpose with children's books is to open the book up, engage the mind. That's if I have a 'Big Purpose' at all. My personal purpose is to make children's books *fun!*" In *Simon's Book,* an artistic boy named Simon dreams one night that he is being pursued by a fearsome but ultimately friendly monster. Two pens and a bottle of ink come to life in order to draw Simon's way to safety. "Original, fresh, and engaging," commented Mary M. Burns in *Horn Book,* "the book is deliciously thrilling but never terrifying." Writing in the *New York Times Book Review,* Leonard S. Marcus applauded the "engaging elements of the zestful graphics" contained in *Simon's Book.*

In addition to other books that push the envelope of convention, such as *Pat the Beastie,* which lampoons the childhood favorite *Pat the Bunny,* and *Looking for Santa Claus,* an off-the-wall Christmas story, Drescher wrote and illustrated *The Boy Who Ate Around.* Mo is a young lad who objects to his dinner of cheese souffle and string beans, referring to the meal as lizard guts and bullfrog heads. He proceeds to turn himself into a ferocious monster and eat his parents and everything else in the whole world except for the offending dinner, which he sends spinning out into the cosmos. Martha V. Parravano, writing in *Horn Book,* asserted that "Drescher's outrageous fantasy is a child's dream." Parravano also spoke favorably of the book's design, which blends multiple typefaces, bright colors, and collages of stamps, photos, manuscript, and sketches. In a *Booklist* review, Ilene Cooper referred to Drescher's artwork as "tumultuous as always," commenting on the visual asides and day-glo colors that are hallmarks of Drescher's work.

Klutz, another self-illustrated book by Drescher, is the story of a very ungraceful family. Wearing oafish black work boots, Momma, Poppa, and Louise Klutz stumble and bumble their way through life until they literally bump into a circus caravan and become premiere clowns and highwire artists. Incorporating collage, rich colors, and a text that weaves in and out of the images, Drescher creates his "most appealing characters yet," according to Virginia Golodetz, a contributor to *School Library Journal.* While commenting that the family's antics may be a little scary for younger readers, a *Kirkus Reviews* contributor stated that "those old enough to put the goofiness in context will eat up this cacophony of collage." Among Drescher's other self-illustrated titles are *Whose Furry Nose? Australian Animals You'd Like to Meet* and *Whose Scaly Tail? African Animals You'd Like to Meet,* two nonfiction books that teach children to identify some lesser known animals.

Throughout his career, Drescher has also provided pictures for stories by other authors. Among the titles he

They were *magnificent* clowns.
No one had *ever* seen such hayseed shenanigans before.
People had to be carried out on stretchers from laughing *too* much.

The Klutz family finds their calling in Drescher's zany picture book. (From Klutz, *written and illustrated by Drescher.)*

has illustrated are two books of verse, *Poems of A. Nonny Mouse,* selected by Jack Prelutsky, and *Runaway Opposites* by Richard Wilbur. The former is based on the premise that, due to a fateful typographical error, the works of poet A. Nonny Mouse have been attributed to the ubiquitous "Anonymous." The mistake has been cleared up in this collection of seventy nonsense poems that includes limericks, chants, and quips. *Horn Book* reviewer Elizabeth S. Watson opined, "it is difficult to decide whether the poems or the illustrations are the more hilarious, but easy to see that they are perfect for each other." "Fluid and exuberant, the crazy cast of characters gaily prance across double-page spreads," stated *School Library Journal* contributor Luann Toth, referring to the dancing sausages, talking shoes and other assorted phantasmagorical creatures that populate the *Poems of A. Nonny Mouse.* A *Publishers Weekly* reviewer found "equal parts silliness and wit" in Drescher's images that accompany Pulitzer-Prize winner Richard Wilbur's zany verses in *Runaway Opposites.* In a selection of poems culled from *Opposites* and *More Opposites,* Drescher once again uses multiple typefaces, collage and other media to create an effect that Mary Harris Veeder of *Booklist* said "young artist-rebels will love the look of ... and want to try to imitate."

Works Cited

Burns, Mary M., review of *Simon's Book, Horn Book,* December, 1983, p. 699.

Cooper, Ilene, review of *The Boy Who Ate Around, Booklist,* November 1, 1994, p. 506.

Golodetz, Virginia, review of *Klutz, School Library Journal,* December, 1996, p. 92.

Review of *Klutz, Kirkus Reviews,* August 1, 1996, p. 1151.

Lanes, Selma G., review of *The Strange Appearance of Howard Cranebill, Jr., New York Times Book Review,* October 10, 1982, p. 25.

Marcus, Leonard S., review of *Simon's Book, New York Times Book Review,* November 20, 1983, p. 39.

Parravano, Martha V., review of *The Boy Who Ate Around, Horn Book,* September-October, 1994, p. 574.

Roginski, Jim, interview with Henrik Drescher, *Parents' Choice,* autumn, 1985, pp. 11, 26.

Review of *Runaway Opposites, Publishers Weekly,* March 13, 1995, p. 68.

Toth, Luann, review of *Poems of A. Nonny Mouse, School Library Journal,* April, 1990, p. 110.

SUDDENLY, IT JUMPED AT SIMON!

When Simon dreams he is being pursued by a monster, two pens and a bottle of ink come to life and sketch Simon's way to safety. (From Simon's Book, *written and illustrated by Henrik Drescher.)*

Veeder, Mary Harris, review of *Runaway Opposites, Booklist,* April 15, 1995, p. 1497.

Watson, Elizabeth S., review of *Poems of A. Nonny Mouse, Horn Book,* January-February, 1990, p. 82.

For More Information See

BOOKS

Children's Literature Review, Volume 20, Gale, 1990.

PERIODICALS

Horn Book, September-October, 1991, p. 556.

Kirkus Reviews, October 15, 1994, p. 1407.

New York Times Book Review, November 8, 1987, p. 42.

Publishers Weekly, July 29, 1996, p. 87.*

F

FARMER, Penelope (Jane) 1939-

Personal

Born June 14, 1939, in Westerham, Kent, England; daughter of Hugh Robert MacDonald (a civil servant at the House of Commons) and Penelope (a homemaker; maiden name, Boothby) Farmer; married Michael John Mockridge (an attorney), August 16, 1962 (divorced, 1977); married Simon Shorvon (a neurologist), January 20, 1984 (divorced, 1999); children: (first marriage) Clare Penelope, Thomas. *Education:* St. Anne's College, Oxford, Degree in History (with second-class honors), 1960; Bedford College, London, Diploma in Social Studies, 1962; has also done doctoral studies at Keele University. *Politics:* "Centre left." *Hobbies and other interests:* "Reading, walking, travelling, cinema, listening to music, opera."

Addresses

Home—12 Dalling Rd., London W6 0JB, England. *Agent*—Deborah Owen, 78 Narrow St., London E14 8BP, England.

Career

Writer, educator, social worker. Teacher for London County Council Education Department, 1961-63, sociological researcher, 1985-90. *Member:* Society of Authors, PEN.

Awards, Honors

Carnegie Medal commendation and American Library Association notable book, both 1963, both for *The Summer Birds.*

Writings

"CHARLOTTE" SERIES; MIDDLE-GRADE FANTASIES

The Summer Birds, illustrated by James J. Spanfeller, Harcourt, 1962, Chatto and Windus (London), 1962, revised editions, Dell, 1985, Bodley Head (London), 1985.

Emma in Winter, illustrated by James J. Spanfeller, Harcourt, 1966, illustrated by Laszlo Acs, Chatto and Windus, 1966.

Charlotte Sometimes, illustrated by Chris Connor, Harcourt, 1969, Chatto and Windus, 1969, revised edition, Dell, 1985.

Penelope Farmer

"STEPHEN" BOOKS; PRIMARY GRADE FICTION

The Seagull, illustrated by Ian Ribbons, Hamish Hamilton (London), 1965, republished as *The Sea Gull,* Harcourt, 1966.

Dragonfly Summer, illustrated by Tessa Jordan, Hamish Hamilton, 1971, Scholastic, 1974.

"TRAIN" BOOKS; HISTORICAL FICTION

The Coal Train, illustrated by William Bird, Heinemann, 1977.

The Runaway Train, illustrated by William Bird, Heinemann, 1980.

JUVENILE FICTION

The China People (short stories), illustrated by Pearl Falconer, Hutchinson (London), 1960.

The Magic Stone, illustrated by John Kaufmann, Harcourt, 1964, Chatto and Windus, 1965.

The Saturday Shillings, illustrated by Prudence Seward, Hamish Hamilton, 1965, published as *Saturday by Seven,* Penguin (London), 1978, illustrated by Janet Duchesne, Walker, 1990, revised edition, Dell, 1986.

William and Mary: A Story, Chatto and Windus, 1974, Atheneum, 1974.

August the Fourth, illustrated by Jael Jordon, Heinemann, 1975, Parnassus (Berkeley, CA), 1976, republished as *Long Ago Children's Omnibus,* Heinemann, 1976.

(Translator from the Hebrew, with Amos Oz) Oz, *Soumchi,* illustrated by William Papas, Harper, 1980.

Thicker than Water, Walker (London), 1989, Candlewick, 1995.

Stone Croc, illustrated by Robert Bartlett, Walker, 1991.

Penelope: A Novel, Bodley Head, 1993, Simon and Schuster, 1996.

Twin Trouble: Stories for Five Year Olds, illustrated by Liz Roberts, Walker, 1996.

Granny and Me, Walker, 1998.

YOUNG ADULT NOVELS; FANTASIES

A Castle of Bone, Atheneum, 1972, Chatto and Windus, 1972, revised edition, Bodley Head, 1992.

Year King, Chatto and Windus, 1976, Atheneum, 1977.

PICTURE BOOK RETELLINGS

Daedalus and Icarus, illustrated by Chris Connor, Harcourt, 1971, Collins (London), 1971.

The Serpent's Teeth: The Story of Cadmus, illustrated by Chris Connor, Collins, 1971, Harcourt, 1972.

The Story of Persephone, illustrated by Graham McCallum, Collins, 1972, Morrow, 1973.

Heracles, illustrated by Graham McCallum, Collins, 1975.

FICTION FOR ADULTS

Standing in the Shadow, Gollancz (London), 1984.

Eve: Her Story, Gollancz, 1985, Mercury House (San Francisco, CA), 1988.

Away from Home: A Novel in Ten Episodes, Gollancz, 1987.

Glasshouses, Gollancz, 1988, Trafalgar Square (North Pomfret, VT), 1989.

Snakes and Ladders, Little, Brown, 1993, Abacus (London), 1994.

OTHER

(Editor) *Beginnings: Creation Myths of the World,* illustrated by Antonio Frasconi, Chatto and Windus, 1978, Atheneum, 1979.

(Editor and contributor) *Two, or the Book of Twins and Doubles: An Autobiographical Anthology,* Virago, 1996.

Also author of short stories and of television and radio scripts, including the screenplay *The Suburb Cuckoo,* 1961, and the radio play *Jerusalem—Finding the Thread,* BBC Radio Three, 1980. Contributor to anthologies of children's literature criticism such as *The Thorny Paradise: Writers on Writing for Children,* edited by Edward Blishen, Kestrel, 1975, and *Writers, Critics, and Children,* edited by Geoff Fox and others, Agathon, 1976. Contributor to magazines and newspapers such as the *Times Literary Supplement,* the *New York Times,* and *Nova Magazine* and coauthor of papers on epilepsy published in academic journals.

Adaptations

The Summer Birds was released on video by PBS Video in 1987. *Charlotte Sometimes* inspired the song of the same name by English rock group the Cure; an adaptation of the novel was released on audio cassette by Chivers Children's Audio Books in 1993. *Charlotte Sometimes* was serialized on British television. In addition, Farmer has been profiled in two volumes of the "Writers Talk: Ideas of Our Times" video series.

Work in Progress

Back Country, an adult novel.

Sidelights

An English author of fiction for primary and middle graders and young adults as well as novels and scripts for adults, Penelope Farmer is the creator of realistic and historical fiction, fantasies, short stories, and retellings of Greek myths for young people. Although all of her work is highly respected, she is most celebrated as the writer of fantasies that transform her personal concerns into challenging, moving works with universal relevance. Farmer is considered a particularly imaginative and inventive writer whose books have reduced the distinction between literature for children and adults. She is also recognized for her ease in juxtaposing reality and fantasy, for her insight into the thoughts and emotions of children, for her talent in capturing mood and atmosphere, and for her elegant, lyrical prose style.

As a fantasist, Farmer characteristically writes what she calls "introvert" fantasies, works that explore psychological concepts and use the symbols and images of myth, magic, dreams, and the supernatural to address such issues as identity, maturity, the nature of reality, and the facing of mortality. Favorably compared to such writers as E. Nesbit, C. S. Lewis, Alan Garner, William Mayne, L. M. Boston, and Philippa Pearce, Farmer often uses the format of the time-travel fantasy to describe children caught between the worlds of reality and dream. Her young male and female protagonists are often faced with life-altering choices, such as whether or not to remain in a fantasy dimension. These children, usually loners or outsiders, reach within themselves to solve their problems and ultimately forego the temptations of immortality or other fantastic possibilities to embrace humanity and human relationships. Upon their return to familiar surroundings, her characters find that their lives have been illuminated by the insights they received from their experiences. Farmer's works reveal several of her thematic preoccupations, such as sibling rivalry, the division between the worlds of children and adults, discovery of identity through meaningful relationships, and the exploration of loss and grief. The author uses motifs such as twins (of which she herself is one), flying, and dream journeys to help uncover the subconscious, delineate character through fantasy, and explore the nature of reality.

Considered an unconventional writer whose books are both ambitious and original, Farmer is also criticized for the complexity and disturbing quality of her works as well as for the density of some of her writing. However, most critics laud her as a major fantasist whose unusual, thought-provoking titles have helped to break the conventions of children's literature. Writing in the *Dictionary of Literary Biography (DLB)*, David L. Russell called Farmer a "writer of extraordinary range, and her works are the products of a lively imagination and penetrating mind." David Rees, writing in his *The Marble in the Water*, concluded that Farmer "should be more widely known and read than she is. She deserves much greater recognition. She's one of the finest of English authors and the most underrated of them all."

In her entry in *Twentieth-Century Children's Writers*, Peggy Heeks commented that the "feeling of personal involvement in Farmer's novels is particularly strong, the images, landscapes, and characters seemingly spun out of her own life threads." Born in Westerham, Kent, a country village near London, Farmer was the second born of fraternal twin girls. "[A]s for most twins, I suspect," she wrote in her essay in *Something about the Author Autobiography Series (SAAS)*, "my twinship was and is probably the most important fact about me. It explains a lot about what I am, what has happened to me, and what I've done with my life—including writing books." Farmer's twin Judy was expected; Penelope's arrival, half an hour after the birth of her sister, was a complete surprise. She wrote in *SAAS*, "Some people might say—my sister would have agreed with them—that after such a hazardous start, my life has been one long yell for attention." She noted that due to "the way I've always felt obliged to shout about myself so loudly, I sometimes wonder if I've managed to forgive the world for denying my existence in the womb." Both girls were small at birth; Farmer, for example, weighed only three pounds. Farmer stated, "My sister, side by side with me, told me who I was, and who I wasn't. One of the ways we told each other who we were was by fighting." Love, Farmer wrote, "sometimes shows itself in anger and fighting. Ours certainly did."

Flora is perplexed by her inexplicable memories of places, people, and events, until she learns that she is the reincarnation of a young girl named Penelope. (Cover illustration by John Clapp.)

Farmer was born to a civil servant who worked in Parliament and a homemaker whom the author described in *SAAS* as "the storyteller in our family." Both orphans who had survived unhappy childhoods, her parents, Farmer wrote in *SAAS*, "continued to adore each other until my mother died when I was twenty-three. Fond parents as they were, I sometimes think we children were, for them, above all, an extension of their love and that our role was to make up by our happy childhood for the one they never had." Farmer's father Hugh was quiet and conservative, while her mother Penelope was talkative and unconventional. She later served as the inspiration for the character of Emily in one of Farmer's best known books, *Charlotte Sometimes,* while her mother's sister inspired the character of Charlotte. In addition to the twins, the Farmers had two other children, Tim, who was three years older than the girls and Sally, who was seven years younger. However, it was with each other that Penelope and Judy had their most intense family bond.

Minor celebrities in their village, where they were the only twins, the girls dressed alike and were called

"Twin" rather than their given names until they went to school. Farmer noted, "But even if it was school that made us more aware of our twinship, it was also the place that began to bring out, much more clearly, the differences between us." Judy was more outgoing and was better in science and math, while Penelope learned to read first and was better at drawing and painting. Farmer wrote in *SAAS* about the first book that she read to herself, a collection of stories about Jean de Brunhoff's Babar the elephant that were compiled by Enid Blyton. "Even then," Farmer noted, "sitting under the table, I realised what learning to read meant; I sensed a whole new world lying out there, to which I had been given the key. I started to write my own stories not so much later. Since all my favourite books at that point seemed to be about talking animals—the Beatrix Potter books, Little Grey Rabbit, as well as Babar—not surprisingly, my stories, too, were about talking animals."

When she was eight, Farmer developed a tubercular lump on her neck, caught, she wrote in her essay in *Fourth Book of Junior Authors and Illustrators,* "from drinking that supposedly healthy drink, milk." Staying in bed for three months, she read and drew and listened to "The Children's Hour" on the radio as well as to programs on history, literature, and music. "I suppose it was there," Farmer noted in *Junior Authors and Illustrators,* "that I started to read as voraciously as I have always done since. Then it was an Arthur Ransome book a day . . . ." The author wrote in *SAAS* that she read the Ransome books "perhaps because the children in them were so very energetic; their sailing and swimming and walking over fells . . . made up for all the energetic things I could not do." After her period of bed rest ended, Farmer entered a hospital to have her tubercular lump removed and was then sent to a convalescent home in the country. After approximately three months, she was allowed to go home.

"We had a good childhood in most ways," Farmer recalled in *SAAS.* "Our family was a noisy and demanding one, crammed with family phrases, games, stories, family songs. . . . We lived in houses with big gardens. . . . The gardens were perfect for playing in, hiding in. . . . As we grew older we were allowed to play in the fields and woods around, sometimes only coming home for meals." For entertainment, the children read, listened to the radio, and went to the movies—"to *Pinocchio* but not *Snow White,* which my mother thought too frightening," the author noted in *SAAS*—as well as to plays such as *Peter Pan,* which they attended every year in London. At twelve, the girls went to boarding school, which "was a pivotal time for my twin and me," Farmer wrote in *SAAS.* Separated after the first term because their roommates were upset by the girls's constant fighting, the twins gradually began developing their own friendships and interests. However, since Penelope was better at the subjects in which her school specialized such as English, art, and languages, she was dubbed "the clever one." Farmer noted in *SAAS* that Judy "suffered from that, being clever enough in her own way—she went to university in her thirties and got

a degree as good as mine. But the sense of failure she was left with did her no good, nor me." After graduating, Penelope went to St. Anne's College, Oxford, where she received an honours degree in history. Judy was sent to a local secretarial college. "Added to this," Farmer wrote, "I'd found a publisher for my first stories and was going to have a book published. You could hardly expect her not to be jealous, and she was."

Since early childhood, Farmer had been writing stories which she had kept in notebooks. At about fifteen, she finished several of them, which she called "fake fairy stories." After her graduation from high school, she went to Munich to learn German, "where," she recalled, "for the first time since my hospital stay I was bereft of everything and everyone I knew. In particular, I found myself bereft of my twin. To cheer myself up, to fill her place in my life, I wrote more and more stories, most of which I sent home in letters to my small sister." Unknown to Farmer, her father had the stories typed and sent to a publisher friend, who passed them on to a literary agent. The agent demanded a whole book, so, Farmer recalled in *SAAS,* "at Oxford, alongside history essays, I continued to write fairy stories."

At nineteen, she was contracted for a book, and at twenty-one, her first work, the short story collection *The China People,* was published. Taking its name from the first story in the collection, *The China People* is a volume of literary fairy tales for primary graders about such subjects as an impatient princess who is turned into a bee and a silver flower that extinguishes all who admire it. A critic in *Junior Bookshelf* noted that *The China People* "showed great promise. Here, many readers felt, was an artist in words, a writer with a keen and witty imagination whose stories could be read aloud with pleasure and success to most children of about six-to-eight or older." In another *Junior Bookshelf* essay, Marion R. Hewitt commented that Farmer's "portrayal of witches, wizards, and princesses shows a very shrewd appraisal of more mortal beings." After the publication of *The China People,* Farmer waitressed, worked as a teacher for the London County Council Education Department, and tried her hand at writing autobiographical novels, none of which she finished. Asked by the American editor Margaret K. McElderry if she was interested in writing a novel for children, Farmer took a story which had proven too long for *The China People* and turned it into the first chapter of *The Summer Birds.* Thus, she wrote in *SAAS,* "almost by accident, [I] became a children's writer and remained one for the twenty-odd years it took me to get around to finishing an adult book." She added in *Junior Authors and Illustrators* that since *The Summer Birds* "I've gone on from there, the books growing up as I've grown up, painfully." In 1962, Farmer received a diploma in social studies from Bedford College, London. In the same year, she married attorney Michael John Mockridge, with whom she had two children, Clare Penelope and Thomas. Divorced in 1977, she later married and divorced neurologist Simon Shorvon. In 1991, Farmer lost her twin sister Judy, an experience she described in *SAAS* as "probably the worst time of my life—the time I had to begin working out what it was to be a twin in order to learn how to live without one."

Farmer's initial fantasy novel *The Summer Birds* describes how a mysterious boy appears to a group of village schoolchildren during their summer vacation. Over the course of two weeks, he teaches the children to fly. The boy turns out to be a bird—the last of his race—who offers the children the chance to become birds in order to restore his kind. Tempted by the prospect of avoiding adulthood and of being able to fly freely all the time, the children consider the boy's offer. However, at the end of the novel, all but one of them, a neglected girl, have refused to fly away in order to stay with their families and, ultimately, to grow up. In his essay in *Signal,* Hugh Crago called *The Summer Birds* "*Peter Pan* pared down, ... leaving the core of essential wonder," while David L. Russell of *DLB* dubbed it "*Peter Pan* without the sentimentality." A reviewer in the *Junior Bookshelf* noted, "Miss Farmer's book is well done; she is an author to watch." Also in *Junior Bookshelf,* Marion R. Hewitt said that *The Summer Birds* "more than fulfills the promise" of *The China People.* "This is a beautiful book," she added, predicting that Farmer "will take her place among the finest children's authors writing today." May Hill Arbuthnot and Zena Sutherland, writing in *Children and Books,* remarked that *The Summer Birds* has "an almost palpable aura of magic and an ending that has the inevitability of Greek drama."

In *The Summer Birds,* the bird boy appears first to sisters Charlotte and Emma Makepeace, young girls who live with their grandfather at Aviary Hall, a home named for the bird images found in it. Farmer continued the stories of the Makepeace sisters in *Emma in Winter,* a novel published in 1966, and in *Charlotte Sometimes,* a book published three years later that is often considered the author's best and most popular work. In *Emma in Winter,* Emma finds herself dreaming nightly of flying as she did in *The Summer Birds.* She and classmate Bobby Fumpius, a boy whom Emma dislikes who also appeared in the previous book, discover that they are having the same dreams. Eventually, they fly back in time to the beginning of the world, where they find another Emma and Bobby who threaten to swallow them up. After Bobby rejects the doppelgangers and drags Emma away, the two children must decide to choose reality before they can return to the present. As a result of their adventures, Emma and Bobby develop a close friendship. Writing in *Growing Point,* Margery Fisher noted that *Emma in Winter* is "not everyone's book but for some it may become a key to more than just a story." Amy Kellman of *Library Journal* added that "all children should have a chance at it."

Charlotte Sometimes finds the title character at boarding school in 1958. One morning, she wakes up to find that she has changed places with Clare, a girl from 1918 who attended the same school and slept in the same bed forty years before. The girls, who are almost identical in appearance, exchange places on alternate days. Events become complicated when Clare is moved away from the magic bed in the school dorm and Charlotte is unable to return to her own time. For several weeks, Charlotte must play the role of Clare. Fearing that she will be trapped in the wrong time, Charlotte struggles to maintain her identity. Shortly after Charlotte and Clare manage to get back to their own eras, Charlotte learns that Clare has died of influenza. In her review in *Growing Point,* Margery Fisher wrote of *Charlotte Sometimes,* "Like *Emma in Winter,* this is really a study in disintegration, the study of a girl finding an identity by losing it." Fisher concluded that the novel "is well-found in every respect . . . . Above all, here is a dream-allegory which teaches not through statement but through feeling. We sense the meaning of Charlotte's changes of identity in the way that she senses them herself." Calling *Charlotte Sometimes* "a book of quite exceptional distinction" and "a haunting, convincing story which comes close to being a masterpiece of its kind," Neil Millar of the *Christian Science Monitor* said that it "is essentially about humanity caught up in the still trickery of time." Peggy Heeks of *Twentieth-Century Children's Writers* opined that *Charlotte Sometimes* "shows a brilliant handling of the time-switch technique and a sincerity which rejects slick solutions to the dilemmas of the two heroines."

A Castle of Bone, a fantasy for young adults published in 1972, is perhaps Farmer's most recognized work after *Charlotte Sometimes.* When awkward, artistic Hugh buys a cupboard from an old man in a secondhand shop, he discovers that it has the power to reduce whatever is placed inside to its earliest stage of development. Hugh also begins to have strange dreams where he finds himself in a strange land dominated by a large castle made of bone. Hugh, his friend Penn, and their respective sisters Jean and Anna are transported by the cupboard back and forth from this fantastic world. When Penn is transformed into an infant after he is put into the cupboard during a violent quarrel with his sister, the other children attempt to care for him while trying to keep the accident a secret from their parents. During Hugh's third trip to the magical world, he and Jean watch as Anna holds her brother—still an infant—over a basin of fire. After Hugh stops Anna, the dreams end, Penn is returned to normal, and the children resume their everyday lives, with Hugh having gained a deeper understanding of himself from his experience.

Filled with symbols and allusions—such as references to *The Odyssey* and a Celtic tree calendar that assigns a tree to each day of the week and gives it a particular character—*A Castle of Bone* is usually considered an allegoric delineation of Hugh's rite of passage and subsequent self-discovery. As Margery Fisher wrote in *Growing Point,* Hugh "learns that the castle of bone that is his body contains his past, present, and future, and is locked in unity with his thoughts and feelings." The theme of the novel is also viewed as Hugh's first glimpse of his own mortality. Although it ranks high in Farmer's oeuvre, *A Castle of Bone* has received a mixed reception from critics. Some observers find that it is more suitable for adults than children, with its stark theme and intense, even disturbing symbolism. However, other reviewers praise *A Castle of Bone* as an outstanding fantasy, unique and profound. Margery Fisher concluded her review by claiming, "With this book (reality lit with fantasy which is itself lit by myth) Penelope Farmer emphatically claims her place in the front rank of writers for the young," while C. S. Hannabuss of *Children's Book Review* remarked, "In a most original way the story explores the 'shut-offness' of adolescents, their spasmodic panic at being isolately 'themselves,' their reaction to an unforeseeable world. Fantasy rarely probes as deeply as this." Writing in the *New York Times Book Review,* Doris Orgel said that *A Castle of Bone* is "an exhilarating, troubling book, unlike any other, and unforgettable." In *The Marble in the Water,* David Rees stated, "*A Castle of Bone* ought to have been [Farmer's] best book; its central idea is more strikingly original [than *Charlotte Sometimes*], the characters more vivid and varied, its potential, both serious and comic, greater. But it remains a flawed achievement."

A Castle of Bone includes the primitive ritual of the Year King, a custom in which a child was burned to death as an annual surrogate for the king. Through this process, the child was thus given immortality. Farmer used this concept as a motif in her next young adult fantasy, *Year King,* a novel published in 1977 that is considered among her most distinguished works. The story introduces nineteen-year-old identical twins Lewis and Dylan—Lew and Lan—who are students at separate universities, Lew at Cambridge, Lan at a local university. Although the novel focuses on both teens, it is really about Lan's search for identity. Less confident and successful than his twin, Lan retreats to a cottage in Somerset, where he goes through hallucinatory periods where his mind becomes Lew's. At first, Lan is thrilled by his new power, but gradually he becomes terrified that he might lose himself in his brother, whom he feels may be trying to kill him—or kill them both. Lan is aided by Novanna, a visiting American girl who becomes his lover as well as his brother's. Finally, the twins engage in a battle of souls in a labyrinthine underworld. Later, Lan realizes that he has prevented Lew's suicide attempt.

Farmer, who named the brothers after pagan Welsh deities, twin gods of water and sun, was praised for writing a meaningful novel that is close in depth and texture to adult fiction. However, critics also questioned the sophistication and explicit sexuality and language of the book as appropriate for young readers. Margery Fisher of *Growing Point* claimed, "At times turgid and over-elaborate, even repetitive, the book has a brooding, heavily powerful atmosphere which could be disturbing to some teenage readers." However, M. Hobbs of the *Junior Bookshelf* called *Year King* "a close-textured, most imaginative novel," while Ann Evans of the *Times Literary Supplement* commented that it is "a story of exceptional originality and interest and its rewards are as rich as the demands it makes on the reader's intelligence and maturity."

Several of Farmer's fantasies published in the 1980s and 1990s reflect a pronounced emphasis on the supernatural. For example, *Thicker than Water,* a young adult novel published in 1989, includes the ghost of a young boy, killed in a Derbyshire mine a century ago, as a pivotal character. The story is narrated alternately by Becky, a spoiled, overweight teenage girl who is teased at school, and her cousin Will, an abused, fatherless boy of the same age who has come to live with Becky's family after his mother, twin to Becky's mom, has committed suicide. After Will sees a face at his window and hears cries at night, he enlists Becky and his friend Zakky in a desperate plan to discover the source. The children learn that the ghost—like Will, neglected in life—seeks burial for his abandoned bones. At the end of the novel, the remains of the child are safely laid to rest after a perilous adventure at Christmas. Through their experience, Becky and Will grow from mutual dislike to mutual acceptance.

Calling *Thicker than Water* "a subtle exploration of loss, grief, and family ties," a critic in *Kirkus Reviews* stated, "Deftly individualizing even her minor players, Farmer crafts the family dynamics ... with leisurely care, building toward a splendidly dramatic denouement. Unusually rich and involving." A. R. Williams of *Junior Bookshelf* noted that "the real excitement of the book may be found in the bonded impressions of existence in the Matlock countryside, the tensions of the household-family relationship, the concern of adults, the rivalries of school hours and the corporate village life which surfaces in the convincing descriptions of the end-of-term pantomime and carol service. Not many writers do this well."

Penelope, a young adult novel published in 1994, addresses the subject of reincarnation. Flora Penelope, a contemporary teen whose mother has died and father has disappeared, has memories of another Penelope, a girl who lived in the eighteenth century. Flora's aunt, with whom she lives, is convinced that her niece is the reincarnation of the earlier Penelope. As time goes on, Flora begins to answer the call of the past more frequently. After her father returns and Flora visits the tomb where the earlier Penelope, a small girl, is buried, the teen learns that she had a twin sister—also named Penelope—who died at birth. This discovery unites Flora with her past and brings peace to the spirit of the earlier Penelope. Writing in *Bulletin of the Center for Children's Books,* Deborah Stevenson noted, "The reincarnation motif (which recalls *Audrey Rose*) is an inviting one and Farmer handles it well, intriguingly combining it with a story of present-day difficulties to examine the question of identity in the here and now as well as across time." Jessica Yates of *School Librarian* commented that *Penelope* "is a time-slip fantasy, a genre Penelope Farmer excels at, but brought right up to date with circumstantial details of 1990s life....". The reviewer concluded, "all credit to Penelope Farmer ... for updating the genre with contemporary multicultural references and slang."

Farmer has also written several fantasies for adults, including *Eve: Her Story,* a novel that describes the life of the Bible character Eve from her perspective, and *Glasshouses,* a work published three years later that features a seventeenth-century ghost.

In addition to her fantasies, Farmer is the author of well-received realistic fiction for children, including *The Seagull,* a story for middle graders, and its sequel *Dragonfly Summer.* These works, praised for their characterizations, feature Stephen, a young boy who wants to keep a wounded seagull in the first book and learns to get along with his cousin in the second, and his understanding grandmother. In addition, the author is celebrated for her success in writing historical fiction for young children with *August the Fourth,* and the related titles *The Coal Train* and *The Runaway Train.* In *August the Fourth,* Farmer juxtaposes a childhood incident against the day in 1914 on which England declared war on Germany. The "Train" books—narrated by the young daughter of a railway engineer—are companion volumes set in 1947 that describe exciting incidents while providing a realistic view of postwar England.

Farmer is also the reteller of four Greek myths in volumes for children published in the 1970s: *Daedalus and Icarus, The Serpent's Teeth: The Story of Cadmus, The Story of Persephone,* and *Heracles.* These picture book introductions to the myths, written in what is considered spare but lively prose, are noted for under-scoring the relevance of the legends and their themes to modern readers. Farmer is also the compiler of *Beginnings,* a collection of international creation myths that was published in 1977.

The author has also published two books that reflect what is perhaps her most compelling personal concern—twinship. *Twin Trouble* is a story for readers in the early primary grades about how a pair of twin sisters create separate identities for themselves, and *Two, or the Book of Twins and Doubles* is an anthology of writings for adults that Farmer edited and to which she contributed autobiographical introductions.

In addition, she has written plays for film and radio and has contributed to various magazines, journals, and anthologies. In assessing her career, Farmer wrote in *SAAS* that "above all, I've kept on writing; sometimes successfully, sometimes not. I daresay I will be writing till the day I die. Writers don't retire, I think. This one doesn't intend on retiring. She would not know how to."

Works Cited

Arbuthnot, May Hill, and Zena Sutherland, *Children and Books,* 4th edition, Scott, Foresman, 1972, p. 256.

Crago, Hugh, "Penelope Farmer's Novels," *Signal,* May, 1975, pp. 81-90.

Evans, Ann, "Transcendental Meditations," *Times Literary Supplement,* October 21, 1977, p. 1246.

Farmer, Penelope, essay in *Fourth Book of Junior Authors and Illustrators,* edited by Doris De Montreville and Elizabeth D. Crawford, Wilson, 1978, pp. 124-26.

Farmer, Penelope, essay in *Something about the Author Autobiography Series,* Volume 22, Gale, 1996, pp. 67-83.

Fisher, Margery, review of *Emma in Winter, Growing Point,* November, 1966, p. 791.

Fisher, Margery, review of *Charlotte Sometimes, Growing Point,* November, 1969, p. 1408.

Fisher, Margery, review of *A Castle of Bone, Growing Point,* September, 1972, pp. 1983-84.

Fisher, Margery, "Dual Worlds," *Growing Point,* March, 1978, pp. 3277-78.

Hannabuss, C. S., review of *A Castle of Bone, Children's Book Review,* October, 1972, p. 150.

Heeks, Peggy, entry in *Twentieth-Century Children's Writers,* edited by Tracy Chevalier, 3rd edition, St. James Press, 1989, pp. 126-27.

Hewitt, Marion R., "Emergent Authors: Penelope Farmer," *Junior Bookshelf,* January, 1963, pp. 20-22.

Hobbs, M., review of *Year King, Junior Bookshelf,* February, 1978, p. 54.

Kellman, Amy, review of *Emma in Winter, Library Journal,* November 15, 1966, pp. 5747-48.

Millar, Neil, "Tales from School," *Christian Science Monitor,* November 6, 1969, p. B5.

Orgel, Doris, "A Magic Cabinet, Kissing Wolves and a Running Nose: 'A Castle of Bone,'" *New York Times Book Review,* January 21, 1973, p. 8.

Rees, David, *The Marble in the Water: Essays on Contemporary Writers of Fiction for Children and Young Adults,* The Horn Book, Inc., 1980, pp. 1-13.

Russell, David L., essay in *Dictionary of Literary Biography,* Volume 161: *British Children's Writers since 1960,* Gale, 1996.

Stevenson, Deborah, review of *Penelope: A Novel, Bulletin of the Center for Children's Books,* July-August, 1996, pp. 369-70.

Review of *The Summer Birds, Junior Bookshelf,* December, 1962, pp. 318-19.

Review of *Thicker than Water, Kirkus Reviews,* May 15, 1993, p. 659.

Williams, A. R., review of *Thicker than Water, Junior Bookshelf,* February, 1990, p. 40.

Yates, Jessica, review of *Penelope, School Librarian,* November, 1994, p. 164.

For More Information See

BOOKS

Children's Literature Review, Volume 8, Gale, 1985, pp. 63-86.

Stoddard, Jewell, essay in *Children's Books and Their Creators,* edited by Anita Silvey, Houghton Mifflin, 1995, p. 238.

PERIODICALS

Booklist, April 1, 1996, p. 1354.

Growing Point, May, 1990, pp. 5335-40.

Horn Book, May-June, 1996, p. 339.

Junior Bookshelf, February, 1990, p. 40.

—Sketch by Gerard J. Senick

FERRIS, Jean 1939-

Personal ˉ

Born January 24, 1939, in Fort Leavenworth, KS; daughter of Jack W. (an army officer/surgeon) and Jessie (Wickham) Schwartz; married Alfred G. Ferris (an attorney), September 8, 1962 ; children: Kerry Ordway, Gillian Anne. *Education:* Stanford University, B.A., 1961, M.A., 1962. *Hobbies and other interests:* Travel, reading, movies, and theatre.

Addresses

Home—2278 San Juan Rd., San Diego, CA 92103.

Career

Writer, 1977—. Veterans Administration Hospital, San Francisco, clinical audiologist, 1962-63; San Diego Speech and Hearing Association, San Diego, clinical audiologist, 1963-64; clinical audiologist in a doctor's office in San Diego, 1975-76; secretary and office assistant in San Diego, 1979-84. *Member:* Society of Children's Book Writers and Illustrators, Authors Guild, Southern California Council on Literature for Children and Young People, San Diego Zoological Society.

Awards, Honors

Grants from the Society of Children's Book Writers, 1984, for *Invincible Summer,* and 1987, for *Across the Grain;* Outstanding Work of Fiction for Young Adults, Southern California Council on Literature for Children and Young People, Best Books for Young Adults, American Library Association (ALA), Best Books, *School Library Journal,* and Editor's Choice, *Booklist,* all 1987, all for *Invincible Summer;* Young Adults Choice, International Reading Association, 1991, Virginia Young Reader's Award nomination, 1992-93, and Iowa Teen Award nomination, 1992-93, all for *Looking for Home;* Best Books for Young Adults, ALA, 1992, and California Young Reader's Medal nomination, 1992-93, both for *Across the Grain;* Utah Children's Book Award nomination and South Carolina Young Adult Book Award nomination, both 1994-95, both for *Relative Strangers;* Junior Library Guild selection, 1995, for *Signs of Life;* Oklahoma Sequoyah Book Award nomination, Junior Library Guild selection, 1996, Young Adult Reading List selection, Texas Library Association, 1997-98, and Virginia Young Reader's Award nomination, 1998-99, all for *All That Glitters;* National Book Award nomination, National Book Foundation, 1998, Best Books for Young Adults, ALA, 1999, and Quick Pick for Young Adults, ALA, 1999, all for *Love among the Walnuts;* Notable Children's Trade Book in the Field of Social Studies, National Council for the Social Studies-Children's Book Council, and Quick Pick for Young Adults, ALA, both 1999, both for *Bad.*

Jean Ferris

Writings

NOVELS; FOR YOUNG ADULTS

Amen, Moses Gardenia, Farrar, Straus, 1983.
The Stainless Steel Rule, Farrar, Straus, 1986.
Invincible Summer, Farrar, Straus, 1987.
Looking for Home, Farrar, Straus, 1988.
Across the Grain, Farrar, Straus, 1990.
Relative Strangers, Farrar, Straus, 1993.
Signs of Life, Farrar, Straus, 1995.
All That Glitters, Farrar, Straus, 1996.
Bad, Farrar, Straus, 1998.
Love among the Walnuts, Harcourt, 1998.

NOVELS; "AMERICAN DREAMS" SERIES

Into the Wind, Avon, 1996.
Song of the Sea, Avon, 1996.
Weather the Storm, Avon, 1996.

Sidelights

The author of several popular novels for young adult readers, Jean Ferris combines likeable characters, realistic teen problems, and her optimistic outlook to create fiction that has been praised as well-written and engaging. In novels that include *Invincible Summer, Across the Grain,* and *Signs of Life,* Ferris portrays teen feelings "convincingly and movingly," "without providing pat resolutions to problems," according to a *Publishers Weekly* commentator. In addition to her novels featuring modern teens, Ferris has also written several installments in Avon's "American Dreams" series that feature American privateer Raider Lyons and the beautiful

Rosie, their budding nineteenth-century romance set against a series of adventures, including a voyage to the Yucatan.

Ferris's first novel, *Amen, Moses Gardenia,* was inspired by the attempted suicides of two teens who were schoolmates of her own children. "I began to wonder how many other kids were feeling this way," the author recalled, "and why a young person would decide that there would never be anything worth living for in the long future. I became—and remain—deeply concerned about teenage depression, and wrote *Amen, Moses Gardenia* to give some hope and humor to kids who feel depressed and frightened enough to contemplate ending their lives. There is so much time ahead for situations to change; there is so much reason for hope. And *Amen, Moses Gardenia* has a happy ending."

In the novel, the stresses of living with an alcoholic mom and a workaholic dad combine to make tenth-grader Farrell feel like an outsider. The one confidante Farrell has is her housekeeper, the upbeat Earl Mae. Encouraged to join a high school hiking club, Farrell meets and falls for Ted Kittredge, one of the most popular boys in school. Unsure of both herself and her relationship with Ted, Farrell plans to attempt suicide by taking sleeping pills before she is stopped by a school guidance counselor. While some reviewers noted that the plot and characters were of average YA novel standards, *Booklist* contributor Sally Estes commented in her review of *Amen, Moses Gardenia* that Farrell "has vitality and credibility, and the relationship between Farrell and Earl Mae is satisfyingly affecting."

Ferris believes that every young person needs at least one other person who loves them unconditionally, "who is absolutely bonkers about him or her." Such a person isn't always a parent, or even a family member. In *Amen, Moses Gardenia,* for example, Earl Mae is cast as that special person. "My own adolescent years haven't dimmed a bit in my memory," the novelist explained to *SATA.* "I remember all the things that gave me pain and pleasure, all the things that worried and confused me—and how much I wished I had a sympathetic grown-up I could talk to. Through my books I try to be that sympathetic grown-up for today's teenagers who have things to be concerned about that could never even have occurred to my own teenage mind. Times of change can be the most difficult times—yet, in retrospect, often times of great growth and learning, too. And adolescence is nothing if not a time of change. I'm interested in these changes—in the choices we make, the reasons for these choices, and what we can do to recover from the results of bad choices. This is where I find the ideas for my books."

In her second novel, *The Stainless Steel Rule,* Ferris again focuses on teen friendships during the high school years. Mary, Fran, and Kitty are best friends whose relationship is tested after Mary falls for handsome but controlling Nick. Nick's personality and Mary's increasing willingness to give in to him cause Mary to withdraw from Fran and Kitty after she senses her friends' discomfort with her boyfriend. Meanwhile, the couple's romantic relationship ultimately results in tragedy after Nick convinces Mary—an insulin-dependent diabetic—that she does not need to take insulin to control her condition. Only after Mary sinks into a diabetic coma and then recovers does she realize that her friends had good intentions in trying to break her relationship with Nick. Calling the novel "several cuts above" Ferris's first effort, Audrey B. Eaglen noted in *School Library Journal* that "the plot [of *The Stainless Steel Rule*] is strong, the characters well portrayed, and the denouement is completely believable." A *Publishers Weekly* contributor agreed, calling the novel "taut" and "compelling . . . with moments of high humor." *Booklist* reviewer Hazel Rochman maintained that the story, narrated by Kitty, is "told . . . with warmth and humor."

A life-threatening illness also figures in *Invincible Summer,* published in 1987. Living in a Midwest farming community, Rick and his seventeen-year-old girlfriend Robin both have leukemia, and Rick is facing his second series of chemotherapy treatments. Together the two teens attempt to gain as much life experience as

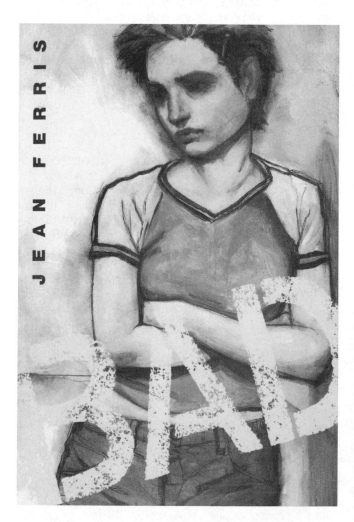

Sixteen-year-old Dallas, arrested as she and her friends try to rob a convenience store, finds herself confined to a Girls' Rehabilitation Center and offered the chance to turn her life around. (Cover illustration by Paul Lee.)

Wealthy Alexander unveils a plot devised by his greedy uncles to poison his family and take their fortune in Ferris's novel of intrigue. (Cover photo by Claudine Guerguerion.)

they can, and provide comfort and support as they confront the fact that Rick has little time left to live. Praising Ferris's dialogue, Zena Sutherland of the *Bulletin of the Center for Children's Books* noted that *Invincible Summer* is "not just a compassionate case history, but a good story." Sutherland's enthusiasm was shared by *School Library Journal* contributor Merilyn S. Burrington, who commented that the novel's ending "affirms life with such intensity that it will leave readers appreciating the present moment more fully."

Several of Ferris's novels feature protagonists travelling overseas. In *Relative Strangers,* seventeen-year-old Berkeley receives a special graduation gift from her father, whom she has rarely seen: a two-week trip to Europe, where she meets his new wife and stepdaughter. The process by which Berkeley copes with her mixed emotions about her father and learns to get along with her new family is woven into "an unusually likable and thought-provoking novel," according to a *Kirkus Reviews* critic. In *Signs of Life,* high school senior Hannah and her parents travel to France in the hopes that fresh surroundings will help the family recover from the tragic

death of Hannah's twin sister. In France, Hannah meets a gypsy juggler who steals her heart and helps her to tap her inner strength. While some reviewers noted that portions of the novel bordered on melodrama, a *Publishers Weekly* contributor maintained that *Signs of Life* "celebrates the regenerating power of love and the resiliency of the spirit."

Across the Grain is Ferris's first novel to feature a male protagonist. In the wake of his father's disappearance and his mother's death, seventeen-year-old Will is forced to move with his older sister, Paige, to California to find work. Obtaining employment as the manager of a small restaurant in the California desert, Paige puts her brother to work, and the two become friendly with a host of regular customers, including an anthropologist and her daughter and Sam, an retired man who becomes Will's surrogate father. Praising Ferris for her well-drawn settings and for developing main characters in a way that is "strong, perceptive yet subtle," *School Library Journal* contributor Libby K. White concluded that "the author makes readers care about likable, earnest Will and his friends." Reviewer Gale Ashe also offered a favorable assessment of *Across the Grain,* noting in *Voice of Youth Advocates* that Ferris's novel "is not just another coming-of-age story, but a story of love and friendship."

All That Glitters is another Ferris novel centering on a young man's emotional growth. In this work, Brian braces himself for a summer with his dad, who lives in the Florida Keys. Now sixteen, Brian has a tense relationship with his father, but when some neighbors invite the pair to join them on a scuba diving expedition to explore the wreckage of a Spanish treasure ship, father and son begin to mend their relationship. Although some reviewers felt that the novel fell below Ferris's usual high standards, Deborah Stevenson of the *Bulletin of the Center for Children's Books* commended the author's "good, solid writ[ing]," and *Voice of Youth Advocates* contributor Penny Blubaugh called *All That Glitters* "a pleasant read with a few moments of excitement and some thought-provoking comments on race and identity." Commending Ferris for addressing issues of race and the importance of strong male role models, *School Library Journal* contributor Bruce Anne Shook concluded that *All That Glitters* "is a good YA problem novel with a nice mix of suspense and adventure thrown in for good measure."

Ferris continues to be concerned about the future of her young readers. "I try, in my work, to give them hope of the future and some guideposts for achieving a satisfying life," she once explained to *SATA,* "even when circumstances seem bleak and/or dismaying!" She is also fascinated by the adolescent years because, as she noted, "There's so much going on then, so many emotional changes, decisions for the future, social problems. I remember my own teenage years vividly and they weren't all beer and skittles."

The mother of two grown daughters, Ferris makes her home in San Diego, California with her husband, an attorney, and a fat orange cat. "I feel certain that I will continue to write for young people because I care so much about them and find them so brave and complex," she once told *SATA*. "My first love will always be writing for kids. They're great."

Works Cited

Review of *Across the Grain, Publishers Weekly,* October 26, 1990, pp. 70-71.
Ashe, Gail, review of *Across the Grain, Voice of Youth Advocates,* February, 1991, p. 350.
Blubaugh, Penny, review of *All That Glitters, Voice of Youth Advocates,* June, 1996, p. 95.
Burrington, Merilyn S., review of *Invincible Summer, School Library Journal,* August, 1987, p. 93.
Eaglen, Audrey B., review of *The Stainless Steel Rule, School Library Journal,* May, 1986, p. 102.
Estes, Sally, review of *Amen, Moses Gardenia, Booklist,* October 1, 1983, p. 233.
Review of *Relative Strangers, Kirkus Reviews,* July 15, 1993, p. 933.
Rochman, Hazel, review of *The Stainless Steel Rule, Booklist,* April 15, 1986, p. 1202.
Shook, Bruce Anne, review of *All That Glitters, School Library Journal,* March, 1996, p. 218.
Review of *Signs of Life, Publishers Weekly,* March 27, 1995, p. 86.
Review of *The Stainless Steel Rule, Publishers Weekly,* April 25, 1986, p. 80.
Stevenson, Deborah, review of *All That Glitters, Bulletin of the Center for Children's Books,* March, 1996, p. 224.
Sutherland, Zena, review of *Invincible Summer, Bulletin of the Center for Children's Books,* July-August, 1987, p. 206.
White, Libby K., review of *Across the Grain, School Library Journal,* December, 1990, p. 121.

For More Information See

PERIODICALS

Booklist, July, 1995, p. 1874; February 15, 1996, p. 1004; October 1, 1998, p. 324.
Bulletin of the Center for Children's Books, July-August, 1989, p. 274; February, 1991, p. 140.
Kirkus Reviews, June 1, 1989, p. 835; September 1, 1998.
Publishers Weekly, July 12, 1993, p. 81; April 1, 1996, p. 77; July 13, 1998, p. 78.
School Library Journal, September, 1993, p. 248; April, 1995, p. 150.
Voice of Youth Advocates, October, 1996, p. 208; April, 1997, p. 21.

*   *   *

FISHER, Suzanne
See STAPLES, Suzanne Fisher

FLETCHER, Ralph 1953-

Personal

Born March 17, 1953; son of Ralph (a textbook publisher) and Jean (Collins) Fletcher; married JoAnn Portalupi (a professor), May, 1989; children: Taylor Curtis, Adam Curtis, Robert Fletcher, Joseph Fletcher. *Education:* Dartmouth College, B.A., 1975; Columbia University, M.F.A., 1983. *Politics:* Democrat.

Addresses

Home—Durham, NH. *Agent*—Marian Reiner, 20 Cedar St., New Rochelle, NY 10801. *Electronic mail*—fletcher17@earthlink.net.

Career

Educational consultant, 1985—; author, 1990—.

Writings

FOR CHILDREN

Fig Pudding, Clarion, 1995.
A Writer's Notebook: Unlocking the Writer Within You, Avon, 1996.
Twilight Comes Twice, illustrated by Kate Kiesler, Clarion, 1997.

Ralph Fletcher

Spider Boy, Clarion, 1997.
Flying Solo, Clarion, 1998.
Live Writing: Breathing Life into Your Words, Avon, 1999.

POETRY

Water Planet: Poems About Water, Arrowhead, 1991.
I Am Wings: Poems About Love, photos by Joe Baker,
    Atheneum, 1994.
Ordinary Things: Poems from a Walk in Early Spring,
    illustrated by Walter Lyon Krudop, Atheneum Books
    for Young Readers, 1996.
Buried Alive: The Elements of Love, photographed by
    Andrew Moore, Atheneum Books for Young Readers,
    1996.
Room Enough for Love, Aladdin, 1998.
Relatively Speaking: Poems About Family, Orchard, 1999.

OTHER

*Walking Trees: Teaching Teachers in the New York City
    Schools,* Heinemann, 1990.
*Walking Trees: Portraits of Teachers and Children in the
    Culture of Schools,* Heinemann, 1995.
What a Writer Needs, Heinemann, 1993.
Breathing In, Breathing Out: Keeping a Writer's Notebook,
    Heinemann, 1996.
(With JoAnn Portalupi) *Craft Lessons: Teaching Writing
    K-8,* Stenhouse, 1998.

Work in Progress

Grandpa Never Lies, illustrated by Harvey Stevenson,
and *The Circus Surprise,* illustrated by Vladimir Vagin,
both for Clarion.

Sidelights

Ralph Fletcher is the author of a number of well-
received volumes of fiction and poetry for young
readers. An educational consultant, he has also written
extensively on the craft of writing. As Fletcher told
SATA: "I have always loved words. As a little boy I used
to ask my mother about the difference between 'read'
and 'red,' 'bear' and 'bare.' It fascinated me that two
words could sound the same but mean completely
different things.

"I've always treasured books, too. Books opened my
eyes. They moved me from the inside out. At some point
I dreamed of becoming a writer. Today, when I write,
I'm trying to put the reader through a powerful
experience. I want to move my readers in the same way
other authors have moved me with their books. My
novel *Fig Pudding* has been translated into Dutch,
German, and French. It gives me a thrill to think that
children in other countries can enter the world of my
books.

"I didn't plan to write books for children. In 1983, I
earned a master's degree in writing at Columbia
University. That year I took a job in New York City,
teaching teachers new ways of teaching writing. I did
lots of demonstration teaching and lugged around a huge
bag of children's books to give children ideas for their

**When their substitute teacher doesn't show up, a group
of bright sixth-graders take over the class and learn
much about themselves, including how to rely upon,
trust, and forgive one another. (Cover illustration by
Ben Caldwell.)**

writing. Surprise: I fell in love with many of these
books! I began trying to write books for children."

Fletcher, when asked about who were some of his
inspirations, was forthcoming about his influences:
"Cynthia Rylant has inspired me with her honesty, and
the stirring beauty of her language," he told *SATA.*
"William Steig writes and illustrates great books with
wonderful word play. And many, many other authors—
Katherine Paterson, Byrd Baylor, Jane Yolen, Gary
Paulsen, Jon Scieszka, Gary Soto, John Steptoe, Bill
Martin Jr., Lois Lowry, Aliki, Richard Margolis to name
a few—have profoundly influenced my work.

Fletcher's first few published titles appeared in the early
1990s: *Walking Trees: Teaching Teachers in the New
York City Schools* was a direct result of his New York
City experiences. *Water Planet: Poems About Water*
was published in 1991, and *What a Writer Needs* the
following year. Yet it was his 1994 volume of poetry for
young adults, *I Am Wings: Poems About Love,* that
garnered him solid reviews and established him as a
popular writer with adolescent readers. *I Am Wings*
consists of several short, unrhymed poems coupled with
black-and-white photographs of teens by Joe Baker. The
poems chronicle a romance, told by a boy named Lee,

from start to finish. Divided into two sections, "Falling In" and "Falling Out," Fletcher's verse attempts to capture the gamut of feelings that many young teens struggle with and find bewildering: the crush, the kiss, the betrayal. It is written in the vernacular of teen speech, and for this Fletcher won recurrent praise from reviewers for creating "accessible" verse for an age group that is usually not expected to gravitate toward poetry. Diane Tuccillo reviewed *I Am Wings* for *Voice of Youth Advocates* and found the verse "romantic and pensive, but not mushy."

Fletcher's next book of poetry, *Ordinary Things: Poems from a Walk in Early Spring,* was also geared toward teen readers and consisted of thirty-three brief poems with pencil drawings by Walter Lyon Krudop. The verses serve as a tutorial for the reader on how to leave the house and become an observer of the magic of nature. "Fletcher reminds young people that such a walk can be mind-clearing and therapeutic," remarked Sharon Korbeck in *School Library Journal.*

His third volume of verse returned once again to the subject of love, but tied in observations of the natural world outside with the inner turmoil of ardor. *Buried Alive: The Elements of Love* was published in 1996 and again interspersed poetry with photographs. Sectioned into four parts—Earth, Water, Fire, and Air—the thirty-one poems with almost as many narrators each recount a tale of love or love's woe: the magic of mutual attraction; a secret crush on the baby-sitter; a gay girl ostracized but still proud, though her yearbook contains no signatures. A *Kirkus Reviews* assessment praised Fletcher for creating "articulate, intense poems that treat the subject of love with dignity and compassion." *School Library Journal* reviewer Marjorie Lewis wrote that *Buried Alive,* as a whole, puts Fletcher "a step above" some of the other poets who write for adolescents. "Plainspeaking but lyrical, Fletcher makes poetry accessible while still keeping it, well, poetry," opined Roger Sutton in a review of the work for *Bulletin of the Center for Children's Books.*

Fletcher has also penned *Twilight Comes Twice,* another volume of verse. Illustrated by Kate Kiesler with drawings of a young girl and her dog out for a walk, the poems are structured around a twenty-four-hour period. Fletcher begins with the coming of night in a somewhat rural, though still populated setting, and picks up again with the arrival of daylight, hence the title. Observations of commuters, children playing, and animals and their activities make up parts of the verse. A *Publishers Weekly* review found it somewhat "cerebral," but granted "both art and text are filled with sumptuous detail." *Kirkus Reviews* termed *Twilight Comes Twice* "a quietly alluring mood piece" that might entice "readers to move beyond the page...." and explore dusk and dawn's special quietness for themselves.

The fifth and sixth volumes of Fletcher's poetry for young readers arrived in 1998 with *Room Enough for Love,* the complete poems from *I Am Wings* and *Buried Alive,* and *Relatively Speaking: Poems About Family,*

A combination of two previous poetry collections, Fletcher's book for adolescents proclaims the exhilaration and disappointments of falling in love. (Cover illustration by Valerie Spain.)

published the following year. Yet the writer has also penned several acclaimed novels for late-elementary readers. The first of these was *Fig Pudding,* published in 1995 to excellent reviews. Its narrator is Cliff Abernathy III, the oldest of six children in a pleasant and close-knit family. Fletcher structures the narrative around a year in the life of the Abernathy family, beginning at Christmas of the previous year and ending with the present holiday season. Each chapter revolves around a family member, and through Cliff's tale that encompasses everything from daily events to the tragic death of a sibling, readers come to know the characters and their very different personalities. "Written with humor, perception, and a clarity of language, the book resonates with laughter and sorrow," declared Alice Casey Smith in a review of *Fig Pudding* for *School Library Journal.* Chris Sherman, assessing the work for *Booklist,* termed the hero of Fletcher's story "a sympathetic and thoughtful narrator." The tragedy and the way in which the family deals with its grief was written about "with remarkable restraint and understatement," opined a *Publishers Weekly* review.

Fletcher created yet another likable kid for the title character of his 1997 novel *Spider Boy.* Seventh-grader Bobby loves his pet tarantulas and is fascinated by spiders in general. This never seemed to be a problem until Bobby's family leaves Illinois and moves halfway across the country. Bobby is suddenly known as the new kid in school with the bizarre hobby. Furthermore, his beloved tarantula Thelma has stopped eating, probably because of the stress of the move. So has Bobby, who still keeps his watch set on Illinois time. Coming to terms with the bully at school, who derisively names

Bobby "Spider Boy" and then is responsible for the death of one of his tarantulas, is the great trial of his life and one that resonates with its intended audience. Candace Smith, writing in *Booklist* called *Spider Boy* an "appealing story" and said that "Fletcher portrays the new-kid-on-the-block syndrome honestly by making Bobby a sympathetic but not perfect character." A *Kirkus Reviews* contributor said of the book, "Creating and guiding a winning cast with a light, sure hand, Fletcher puts a fine, fresh spin on a familiar premise."

Fletcher drew upon his classroom experiences to create a novel that details a fantasy day in the life of any young school-goer in his novel *Flying Solo*. The day the substitute teacher never shows up, a classroom of smart sixth-graders seize the opportunity and take charge of their own education for a day, while struggling to keep others at the school in the dark regarding the situation. Fletcher introduces a host of students as lead characters, each with their own personal travail to resolve: Bastian is moving to Hawaii with his family the next day and must decide whether he will leave his dog with a family here or force it to undergo a long period of quarantine; Rachel has not spoken since a classmate who had a crush on her died several months earlier; Sean, a boy with a troubled family life, has a crush on her now; Karen emerges as a natural leader, while Jessica shows herself as too uptight to learn from the experience of having a bit of responsibility for once. In the end, Rachel finally talks, Bastian's dog finds the right home, and all the students learn more about themselves in one day than they expected—including how to rely upon, trust, and forgive one another. The author, noted Kathleen Squires in *Booklist*, "expertly balances a wide variety of emotions, giving readers a story that is by turns sad, poignant, and funny...." Writing in *Horn Book*, Susan P. Bloom stated: "This kaleidoscopic novel is more thoughtful and poignant than most school stories, while still appropriately leavened with comic moments; it demonstrates an utter respect for its characters and its readers, who will appreciate the honest and uncondescending portrayal."

Fletcher has also written several nonfiction works focused on the writing process, including the 1996 title *Breathing In, Breathing Out: Keeping a Writer's Notebook*. He begins the book by positing that it is not altogether necessary for a writer to keep such a journal, and then moves on to provide guidelines for those who decide they would like to. He explains such a tool can help one learn to write without fear of judgment, and thus develop a clear voice. Such journals are also excellent ways for writers to find their inspiration, and Fletcher provides examples of how insignificant details, rhetorical questions, lists of oddities, and even the conversations of strangers can spark fire to the creative process. Compared to most "how-to" works for aspiring writers, "this one is refreshingly varied and undogmatic in its approach," noted Jeffrey Cooper in *KLIATT*.

Fletcher told *SATA* that he has a passion for nurturing young writers.

In addition to *Breathing In, Breathing Out*, Fletcher has penned writing books geared specifically to budding authors—*A Writer's Notebook* and *Live Writing* among them. *A Writer's Notebook* offers realistic advice on how to keep notes and use them to create stories and poems. *Live Writing* instructs young writers on how to use words, imagination, ideas, and a love of books to create written works that "live and breathe."

Of his own working style, Fletcher said: "My habits are simple. I get up, make school lunches, get my kids off to school, make coffee, and write. I have learned that I need to devote the best hours of the day to my writing. I work about three or four hours daily. Fortunately, I work quickly. Often my editors push me further with their suggestions for revisions. I have been lucky to work with excellent editors—especially Nina Ignatowicz and Ana Cerro—who continue to stretch me as a writer."

To aspiring writers, Fletcher has this to say: "There's no one single way to write. Everyone has to find his or her own way. I think it begins with your uniqueness. Sandra Cisneros says: 'Write about what makes you different.'"

Works Cited

Bloom, Susan P., review of *Flying Solo, Horn Book,* November-December, 1998, pp. 728-29.

Review of *Buried Alive, Kirkus Reviews,* April 15, 1996, p. 601.

Cooper, Jeffrey, review of *Breathing In, Breathing Out, KLIATT,* September, 1997, p. 25.

Review of *Fig Pudding, Publishers Weekly,* April 24, 1995, p. 72.

Korbeck, Sharon, review of *Ordinary Things: Poems from a Walk in Early Spring, School Library Journal,* May, 1997, p. 144.

Lewis, Marjorie, review of *Buried Alive, School Library Journal,* May, 1996, p, 138.

Sherman, Chris, review of *Fig Pudding, Booklist,* May 15, 1995, p. 1645.

Smith, Alice Casey, review of *Fig Pudding, School Library Journal,* July, 1995, p. 78.

Smith, Candace, review of *Spider Boy, Booklist,* June 1, 1997, p. 1702.

Squires, Kathleen, review of *Flying Solo, Booklist,* August, 1998.

Review of *Spider Boy, Kirkus Reviews,* March 15, 1997, p. 460.

Sutton, Roger, review of *Buried Alive, Bulletin of the Center for Children's Books,* July-August, 1996, pp. 370-71.

Tuccillo, Diane, review of *I Am Wings, Voice of Youth Advocates,* June, 1994, pp. 106-07.

Review of *Twilight Comes Twice, Kirkus Reviews,* September 1, 1997, p. 1388.

Review of *Twilight Comes Twice, Publishers Weekly,* October 27, 1997, p. 75.

For More Information See

PERIODICALS

Booklist, March 15, 1994, p. 1345; May 1, 1996, p. 1500; June 1-15, 1997; October 15, 1997, p. 414.
Bulletin of the Center for Children's Books, June, 1994, p. 318.
Horn Book, July-August, 1997, p. 454-455.
Publishers Weekly, February 2, 1998, p. 91.
School Library Journal, October, 1998, p. 135.
Voice of Youth Advocates, October, 1996, p. 228.

*   *   *

FRAZEE, Marla 1958-

Personal

Born January 16, 1958, in Los Angeles, CA; daughter of Gerald W. (in business) and Nancy (a schoolteacher) Frazee; married Tim Bradley (a photographer and college administrator), May 29, 1982; children: Graham, Reed, James. *Education:* Art Center College of Design, B.F.A., 1981.

Addresses

Home—Southern California. *Office*—c/o Harcourt Brace & Co., 6277 Sea Harbor Dr., Orlando, FL 32887.

Career

Freelance illustrator, 1981—; picture book illustrator, 1989—. Commercial work has included team characters for the National Football League made into plush toys and licensed for other sales, Happy Meal boxes for McDonald's, and toy design for Mattel, Milton Bradley, and Parker Brothers. Art Center College of Design, teacher of children's book illustration, 1991—. *Exhibitions:* "Children's Book Illustration Today," Boehm Gallery; "Original Art Show-Children's Book Illustration" (juried exhibition) New York City, 1995, 1997. *Member:* Society of Children's Book Writers and Illustrators.

Awards, Honors

Notable Book, American Library Association, 1995, for *That Kookoory!* by Margaret Walden Froehlich; Pick of the Lists, American Bookseller, 1997 and 1998, respectively, for *The Seven Silly Eaters* by Mary Ann Hoberman and *On the Morn of Mayfest* by Erica Silverman; Excellence in Illustration Award, Southern California Council on Literature for Children and Young People, 1998, for *The Seven Silly Eaters.*

Illustrator

Sue Alexander, *World Famous Muriel and the Magic Mystery,* Crowell, 1990.
Margaret Walden Froehlich, *That Kookoory!,* Browndeer Press, 1995.
Mary Ann Hoberman, *The Seven Silly Eaters,* Browndeer Press, 1997.
Erica Silverman, *On the Morn of Mayfest,* Simon & Schuster Books for Young Readers, 1998.
Hush Little Baby: A Folk Song with Pictures by Marla Frazee, Browndeer Press/Harcourt Brace, 1999.
Mem Fox, *Harriet, You'll Drive Me Wild,* Harcourt Brace, in press.

Sidelights

Marla Frazee has created illustrations for a number of well-received books for children. Frazee told *SATA* that illustrating children's books was a childhood career goal. "I have wanted to be a children's book illustrator for a very long time," she said. "A host of crayoned and stapled childhood efforts attest to that fact. I was first 'published' in the third grade, when my best friend, Lisa Gilden, wrote a story called 'The Friendship Circle' and I illustrated it. It won an award in a state competition, so we were asked to make a duplicate copy for our elementary school library. It was made out of construction paper and held together with brass fasteners, but it sat in the library for years. I remember sneaking peeks at the shelf as our class filed in for library time, and seeing it keeping company with REAL books. I felt as if I'd arrived!

"Speaking of real books, I spent many afternoons at the Tarzana Public Library, wandering through the stacks. I would go from the picture book area, where I then belonged, to the illustrated chapter books, to the Young Adult books—boy, those looked interesting!—and over across the linoleum to the carpeted area of the Grown-Up Books! Of course, I couldn't read many of the titles, much less make sense of them, but I knew that every single book had something interesting in it, something to tell me that I didn't yet know.

Marla Frazee

"*Where the Wild Things Are,* by Maurice Sendak, was published when I was ten and by then a reader of words. Nevertheless, I was floored by the visual impact of Max's bedroom transforming into the forest. Those four simple page turns held within them all the magic I'd ever seen, from the cinematic wonders of Oz to the E ticket rides at Disneyland. This was what I wanted to do when I grew up! I wanted to try and create page turns that opened onto changing worlds. I also pored over Robert McCloskey's illustrations in *Blueberries for Sal,* searching for clues. How did he make Sal so endearing? Was it her messy hair? Her T-strap sandals, which I coveted and begged my mother to please, please, please buy for me? The way her overalls kept falling off her shoulder? I spent countless hours studying those wonderful endpapers of Sal and her mother canning blueberries in their cozy kitchen. I wondered how an illustrator could draw a room that somehow included me, the viewer. I don't remember talking to anyone about these issues, but my fifth-grade teacher, Mrs. Holcomb, made some predictions about what some of her students would grow up to be. She said I would illustrate children's books, painting outdoors in a sunlit meadow. So far, no meadow.

Frazee's illustrations of a topsy-turvy household and seven distinctly individualized children lend humor to Mary Ann Hoberman's fanciful story of a frantic mother and her demanding brood. (From The Seven Silly Eaters.*)*

Frazee's pictures depict the high-spirited May Day parade which results when a sleepwalking girl sets up a chain reaction in Erica Silverman's cumulative-verse story. (From On the Morn of Mayfest.*)*

"It was a long road to becoming a children's book illustrator. It has been much easier to find work as an advertising illustrator, a magazine illustrator, an educational illustrator, and as a toy and game illustrator. While I worked at whatever job was then available, I kept sending my work to publishers. After many, many rejections, I was finally offered the chance to illustrate my first book."

This opportunity came when Frazee illustrated Sue Alexander's *World Famous Muriel and the Magic Mystery,* published in 1990. It was the third in Alexander's series about the clever junior detective, certainly no easy shoes for an illustrator to step into. Yet Bessie

Egan, writing in *School Library Journal,* praised the art as "full of vitality and humorous detail."

Frazee's next picture book was *That Kookoory!,* written by Margaret Walden Froehlich. Her pen-and-ink drawings garnered rave reviews for their vintage feel, which complemented the tale of an indomitable rooster who is so excited by the local fair that he wakens before his barn friends and sets off alone. Kookoory then unwittingly finds himself in danger when he is stalked on the road by a hungry weasel. In the end, his friends rescue him and everybody enjoys the fair—even the weasel. A *Publishers Weekly* contributor lauded the way in which Frazee managed to convey the various shifts of time over the course of Kookoory's long and event-filled day, and mentioned "her bucolic scenes" that evoked "the rural America of a more relaxed era." Ann A. Flowers, writing for *Horn Book,* termed it "a gentle and affectionate story with illustrations to match."

"The most rewarding aspect of my work is telling stories with my pictures. Often the story I'm telling in the illustrations is different from the story that is being told in the words. Of course the word-story and the picture-story should work together to create a seamless whole. That is the unique challenge of the picture book, and the reason it gives me such pleasure to illustrate them. I have been very fortunate to have worked for so many years with my editor, Linda Zuckerman, now the editorial director of Browndeer Press, an imprint of Harcourt Brace Children's Books," Frazee told *SATA.* "She has been my teacher, fair critic, and gentle guide.

"Creating the pictures for my books generally takes me a year. I usually start by visualizing the characters, because once I know who my characters are, I can then imagine where they live and how they act. As I'm defining the characters and the setting, I am trying to visualize the entire book as an object. What size should it be? Is it horizontal or vertical? At what point in the text will the page turns be? Where is the type and where is the image? I work out the answers to these questions by doing tiny thumbnail sketches of the entire book on one piece of paper. Sometimes I work on thumbnail sketches for months."

Frazee, a mother of three herself, tackles every parent's biggest dinnertime nightmare in her illustrations for Mary Ann Hoberman's *The Seven Silly Eaters,* published in 1997. The Peters family demands from their harried, cellist mother a separate dish for each of them; as the family grows larger, she grows more frantic and her days more arduous. Mary Lou will only eat homemade bread. Lucy is partial to lemonade made from scratch. Homemade applesauce is the only thing Jack will eat. "The limber lines and cartoon-like animation . . . handily match the energy and wit of the text's quatrain couplets," noted a *Publishers Weekly* reviewer. Critics also praised the inviting, though cheerily chaotic household Frazee created, which would be most children's dream domicile. Writing for the *New York Times Book Review,* Jon Agee lauded the "busy, animated pictures [that] cleverly elaborate the story's growing disorder."

Frazee recounted the process by which she imagined the Peters family. "In the case of *The Seven Silly Eaters,*" she told *SATA,* "I had nine characters and a house to imagine. The characters were inspired by my own children, nieces, nephews, and neighbors—each one a very specific person, with a very specific set of quirks and endearments. This is how I know how each person would behave in a variety of circumstances. For instance, Peter Peters, the first-born son, tucks in even his pajamas in a quest for fastidiousness in that chaotic household, just as my own first-born son does. Jack Peters, goofball kid, sleeps in a bunk with a rope ladder and has a peg to hang his hat, because I know that my middle son would want to do the same. And Flo and Fran Peters, the twins, were modeled after my youngest son, who was rarely seen without his pacifier. I built the Peters's family home out of foamcore, so that I knew the floor plan as well as I do in the house I live in. Anything I can do to make the book come alive for me, in the most tangible sense, will make it that much more believable to my readers.

"I recently completed the illustrations for *Hush, Little Baby,* the familiar folk song about Papa buying baby a mockingbird, a looking glass, and other goodies. The lullaby's American roots can be traced to Appalachia, so I researched the book in a pioneer village in the hills of West Virginia. The illustrations for *That Kookoory!* were inspired by the beautiful Wisconsin countryside, where my husband grew up, and where we often visit. I spent a great deal of time in chicken coops during the making of that book, and even planted a small cornfield in our backyard. *On the Morn of Mayfest* was loosely set in a Renaissance Italian hill town, and while I would have loved to go to Italy to research the book, I did attend the local Renaissance Faire for costume ideas. Maybe because of that, the characters in my book wear sunglasses and hi-top tennis shoes, as though they are merely in costume, too." Carol Ann Wilson, in *School Library Journal,* also found praise for this fanciful tale of a young girl who becomes queen of the festival that heralds the arrival of spring. Wilson particularly liked Frazee's acrylic color drawings that "jauntily portray an entertaining cast of human and animal characters." A *Publishers Weekly* contributor remarked that Frazee and author Erica Silverman "form a happy, uncomplicated collaboration with a festive hint of history."

"The picture book audience is often pre-literate, so they 'read' the pictures as the words are being read to them," Frazee explained to *SATA.* "Consequently, these young children notice very detail, follow every sequential action, pick up on every clue, and will carefully go back into the book after it has been read and find things they may have missed the first, second, or third time around. There isn't anything I've ever put into a book that a child hasn't, at one time or another, noticed. I can't say the same for adults. It is a rare grown-up that catches anything but the broad action. Also, there isn't any guessing when it comes to how much or if a child likes a given book. If a book bores them, they will get up and find something else to do. And if it's a book they like, they will hold onto it for dear life. When children's book authors and illustrators visit classrooms and bookstores, they are often the recipient of real big hugs. These are hugs of thanks, really, for the gift of a story.

"It is wonderful to work for an audience of children. I hope I am lucky enough to be a children's book illustrator for a very long time."

Works Cited

Agee, Jon, review of *The Seven Silly Eaters, New York Times Book Review,* July 6, 1997, p. 16.

Egan, Bessie, review of *World Famous Muriel and the Magic Mystery, School Library Journal,* July, 1990, p. 55.

Flowers, Ann A., review of *That Kookoory!, Horn Book,* July-August, 1995, p. 449.

Review of *On the Morn of Mayfest, Publishers Weekly,* May 18, 1998, p. 78.

Review of *The Seven Silly Eaters, Publishers Weekly,* February 3, 1997, p. 106.

Review of *That Kookoory!, Publishers Weekly,* April 3, 1995, p. 62.

Wilson, Carol Ann, review of *On the Morn of Mayfest, School Library Journal,* June, 1998, p. 122.

For More Information See

PERIODICALS

Booklist, April 15, 1995, p. 1505; March 1, 1997, p. 1172. *School Library Journal,* May, 1995, p. 84.

* * *

FRIESEN, Bernice (Sarah Anne) 1966-

Personal

Born November 8, 1966, in Rosthern, Saskatchewan, Canada; daughter of James H. and Margaret (Labach) Friesen; married Colin Boyd, July 22, 1995. *Education:* University of Saskatchewan, B.F.A., 1988, B.Ed., 1990. *Hobbies and other interests:* History, archaeology, art, travel, photography.

Addresses

Agent—c/o Thistledown Press, 633 Main St., Saskatoon, Saskatchewan S7H OJ8, Canada.

Career

Department of Art, University of Saskatchewan, lab assistant, 1986-87; A.K.A. Gallery, Saskatoon, Saskatchewan, project coordinator of "26 and Under: Young Saskatoon Artists," 1987; Y.W.C.A., Saskatoon, art class instructor, 1988; Mendel Art Gallery, Saskatoon, instructor of "Clue Into Art", 1989, instructor of children's color class, 1993; Estevan National Exhibition Centre, art educator, 1990-91; Valley Action Industries, Rosthern, Saskatchewan, junior group home operator, 1992-93; freelance writer, 1995—. Saskatoon Correctional Center, art teacher for young offenders, 1985; "Ballet de les Americas" (a folk dance troupe), Montreal, Quebec, costume designer, 1991. *Exhibitions:* B.F.A. Exhibition, Gordon Snelgrove Gallery, University of Saskatchewan, 1988; "Women and Exchange," A.K.A. Artist Run Centre, Saskatoon, 1988; "Saskatchewan Open Exhibition," Mendel Art Gallery, Saskatoon, 1990; "Brownlee and the Aftermath," Station Arts Centre, Saskatchewan, 1991; and "Spirit Matters," O.S.A.C. provincial traveling exhibition, 1992-94. *Member:* Saskatchewan Writers Guild.

Awards, Honors

Major Award for short fiction, Saskatchewan Writers Guild Annual Literary Awards, 1991 and 1994; Major Award for children's literature, Saskatchewan Writers Guild Annual Literary Awards, 1992; Saskatchewan Arts Board C Grant, 1994-95; Tilden Canadian Literary Awards finalist, 1996, for nonfiction manuscript "Beijing in Four Days"; Vicky Metcalf Short Story Award, Canadian Authors Association, 1996, for short story "The Seasons Are Horses"; C.B.C. Radio Canadien Literary Awards finalist, for poetry manuscript "Aviatrix"; runner up, League of Canadian Poets National Poetry Contest, and Sterling Writing Awards, 1997.

Writings

The Seasons Are Horses (juvenile short stories), Thistledown Press (Saskatoon, Saskatchewan, Canada), 1995.
Sex, Death, and Naked Men (poems), Coteau Books (Regina, Saskatchewan, Canada), 1998.

Contributor to anthologies, including *eye wuz here,* edited by Shannon Cooley, Douglas & McIntyre (Victoria, British Columbia), 1996; *The Landmarks,* Nelson Canada (Scarborough, Ontario), 1996; and *Vintage 97,* 1998. Contributor to C.B.C. Radio broadcast *Ambience,* 1993, and *Gallery,* 1998. Contributor to periodicals, including *CV2, Antigonish Review, Capilano Review, Fiddlehead, Paris/Atlantic, New Quarterly, Envoi, Ca-*

Bernice Friesen

nadian Literature, Malahat Review, Event, Global Tapestry Journal, Dalhousie Review, Grain, NeWest Review, Prairie Fire, Prairie Journal, and *Western People.* Commercial and video writer.

OTHER

Illustrator for books and periodicals, including *Hutterite Community Cookbook,* Hofer, 1992; *Grain,* 1992; (cover) *Prism International,* 1994; (cover) *Dig,* Longbottom & MacIntyre/Pachyderm Press, 1994; *Prairie Fire,* 1997; and four book covers for Coteau Books "Open Eye" series.

Work in Progress

The Mutual Charities of Saints and Beasts, a novel; *The Sun,* a novel; *Mary Presley and the Virgin Elvis,* a poetry manuscript.

Sidelights

Bernice Friesen's award-winning *The Seasons Are Horses* is a collection of fifteen short stories for young adults. The stories take place in the fictional small town of Grassbank, Saskatchewan, and are loosely linked together. Told from the first-person viewpoints of female narrators of varying ages, the tales deal with such topics as love, alcohol and drug abuse, racism, and unhealthy relationships.

Reviewing *The Seasons Are Horses* in *Canadian Book Review Annual,* Darleen R. Golke commented, "The narratives reverberate with the tone and flavor of young people's language, which the reader might well hear in the hallways of any junior or senior high." Marie Campbell, writing in *Quill and Quire,* commented: "There are no cheap shots here, no easy observations, nothing that appears in uncrystallized form." *Canadian Children's Literature* critic Lynne McKechnie maintained that "Friesen's realistic and moving work should certainly appeal to adolescent readers who are likely to see themselves reflected in her characters."

Friesen comments: "I am glad to be born in this century."

Works Cited

McKechnie, Lynne, review of *The Seasons Are Horses, Canadian Children's Literature,* No. 86, summer, 1997, p. 87.

Golke, Darleen R., review of *The Seasons Are Horses, Canadian Book Review Annual,* 1995, p. 499.

Campbell, Marie, review of *The Seasons Are Horses, Quill and Quire,* May, 1995, p. 46.

G

GLOVACH, Linda 1947-

Personal

Surname is pronounced *Glo*-vack; born June 24, 1947, in Rockville Centre, NY; daughter of John Maurice (a maintenance engineer) and Elvira (Martone) Glovach. *Education:* Attended Farmingdale University, 1956-66, Art Students League of New York, 1966-68, and California Art Center College of Design, 1969. *Politics:* Liberal. *Hobbies and other interests:* Biking, running, traveling, gardening, and raising cats and Afghan hounds.

Addresses

Home and office—237 8th Ave., Sea Cliff, Long Island, NY 11579.

Career

Freelance artist and writer. Has worked as a secretary and a hostess at Disneyland, CA. Speaker in grade schools in Brentwood, NY, and local Long Island libraries and schools. *Member:* Catholic Society for Welfare of Animals, Society for Animal Rights, Defenders of Wildlife, Library Club of Bayshore.

Awards, Honors

Quick Picks for Reluctant Young Adult Readers, Young Adult Library Services Association of the American Library Association, 1999, for *Beauty Queen.*

Writings

SELF-ILLUSTRATED PICTURE BOOKS

Hey, Wait for Me! I'm Amelia, Prentice-Hall, 1971.
The Cat and the Collector, Prentice-Hall, 1972.
Let's Make a Deal, Prentice-Hall, 1974.
The Rabbit and the Rainmaker, Prentice-Hall, 1974.

"LITTLE WITCH" SERIES; SELF-ILLUSTRATED

The Little Witch's Black Magic Cookbook, Prentice-Hall, 1972.
The Little Witch's Black Magic Book of Disguises, Prentice-Hall, 1973.
The Little Witch's Black Magic Book of Games, Prentice-Hall, 1974.
The Little Witch's Christmas Book, Prentice-Hall, 1974.
The Little Witch's Halloween Book, Prentice-Hall, 1975.
(With Charles Keller) *The Little Witch Presents a Monster Joke Book,* Prentice-Hall, 1976.
The Little Witch's Thanksgiving Book, Prentice-Hall, 1976.
The Little Witch's Book of Yoga, Prentice-Hall, 1979.
The Little Witch's Birthday Book, Prentice-Hall, 1981.
The Little Witch's Carnival Book, Prentice-Hall, 1982.
The Little Witch's Spring Holiday Book, Prentice-Hall, 1983.
The Little Witch's Valentine Book, Prentice-Hall, 1984.
The Little Witch's Dinosaur Book, Prentice-Hall, 1984.
The Little Witch's Cat Book, Prentice-Hall, 1985.
The Little Witch's Summertime Book, Prentice-Hall, 1986.
The Little Witch's Book of Toys, Prentice-Hall, 1986.

OTHER

Potions, Lotions, Tonics, and Teas, Prentice-Hall, 1977.
Beauty Queen (young adult novel), HarperCollins, 1998.

Sidelights

Author and illustrator Linda Glovach has created a number of picture books for young children, many of which feature a little witch who is both helpful and handy around the house. In such works as *The Little Witch's Book of Toys* and *The Little Witch's Book of Halloween,* Glovach's spunky young spook shows her creative talents by crafting everything from toys to holiday decorations, all from objects found around the house. Despite her magical skills, Little Witch works totally without the aid of spells of any sort; young readers unskilled at witchcraft can still be "crafty" in a different sense while working on projects along with her.

Glovach was born in Rockville Centre, New York, in 1947. As the only child of working parents, she spent much of her childhood in the care of babysitters. She recalls one in particular as "an elderly lady who drank beer hidden in the pantry and then fell asleep." Often left to her own devices, Glovach developed a colorful imagination. "Since I can remember I have been writing stories about the simple every day things I see around me," she once told *SATA*. "It starts with an eerie or uncanny or uncommon feeling about a particular person or place and I cannot rest until I have my say either in words, pictures or both."

Glovach sent her first horror story to Twentieth Century-Fox at age eleven, hoping it might be made into a movie. Although she never got a call from a Hollywood producer, she continued to write and draw, attending art school in California and New York City after graduating from high school. "I write early in the morning (4:00 a.m.), or late at night," Glovach once told *SATA*, "draw or illustrate during the day, and worry about it in between. I find storybook characters wherever I go."

In 1971, Glovach published her first picture book, *Hey, Wait for Me! I'm Amelia*. Another of her early books, *Let's Make a Deal*, which Glovach illustrated in watercolor tones of pink and brown, features best friends Tom and Dewey. As a team, the boys decide to adopt a stray puppy whom they name Lucy, but Tom's eventual move out of town presents them with the problem of which boy should take the dog. Praising the book as helping to "instill ideals of honesty and loyalty" in young readers, a *Publishers Weekly* contributor called *Let's Make a Deal* "a tender story of friendship."

Most notable among Glovach's works for children is the "Little Witch" series of books. In *The Little Witch's Book of Toys*, for example, a tin woodsman, "Monster Mitts," and a haunted castle are a sampling of the simple projects that can be assembled from everyday household objects. In Glovach's story, which the author illustrates with black and gold drawings, Little Witch and a few friends decide to host a toy sale, which also provides an excuse to have a party. The story serves as a framework to introduce the craft projects, which include a recipe for "Pinocchio Cookies." *The Little Witch's Christmas Book* finds the young spell-caster in a holiday mood, as she helps around the house and then turns her talents to making gifts for charity giving. With "crisp instructions and amusing pictures" of everything from popcorn rope, taffy, and a pinata, according to a *Publishers Weekly* contributor, Glovach's yuletide picture book also stresses safety first when creating any of the projects. Comparing *The Little Witch's Christmas Book* to similar holiday craft books for children, Zena Sutherland of the *Bulletin of the Center for Children's Books* noted that for younger children, Glovach's work possessed "the double advantages of greater variety and a breezy style."

Along with her many works for primary graders, Glovach has also written the well-received young adult novel *Beauty Queen*. A realistic, cautionary tale about the dangers of drug use, the book consists of the journal of likeable nineteen-year-old Samantha as she leaves her dysfunctional family only to fall into drug use and a demeaning job as a topless dancer. A relationship with a dishonest city cop gives Sam easy access to a wealth of street drugs, and readers witness her relentless downhill spiral. "Reading this diary of a heroin addict is like watching someone fall into an abyss," commented a *Publishers Weekly* contributor, who, in praise of the novel, went on to note that *Beauty Queen* "offers a shocking, thoroughly credible glimpse of addiction, which forces readers to draw their own conclusion about Sam's tragic life." According to a commentator in *Kirkus Reviews, Beauty Queen* "contains a heartfelt anti-drug message in the swift, downward spiral of a likable main character."

Works Cited

Review of *Beauty Queen, Kirkus Reviews,* August 15, 1998, p. 1187.
Review of *Beauty Queen, Publishers Weekly,* July 27, 1998, p. 78.
Review of *Let's Make a Deal, Publishers Weekly,* March 17, 1975, p. 56.
Review of *The Little Witch's Christmas Book, Publishers Weekly,* October 28, 1974, p. 18.
Sutherland, Zena, review of *The Little Witch's Christmas Book, Bulletin of the Center for Children's Books,* December, 1974, p. 62.

For More Information See

PERIODICALS

Booklist, December 1, 1986, p. 577.
Bulletin of the Center for Children's Books, November, 1975, p. 45.
Kirkus Reviews, October 1, 1974, pp. 1057-58; March 15, 1975, p. 304.
School Library Journal, February, 1987, p. 80; September, 1998, p. 203.
Voice of Youth Advocates, December, 1998, p. 354.*

*   *   *

GREENFIELD, Eloise 1929-

Personal

Born May 17, 1929, in Parmele, NC; daughter of Weston W. (a federal government worker and truck driver) and Lessie (a clerk-typist and writer; maiden name, Jones) Little; married Robert J. Greenfield (a procurement specialist), April 29, 1950 (now divorced); children: Steven, Monica. *Education:* Attended Miner Teachers College (now University of the District of Columbia), 1947-49. *Hobbies and other interests:* Listening to music, playing the piano.

Addresses

Office—P.O. Box 29077, Washington, DC 20017. *Agent*—Marie Brown, Marie Brown Associates, 412 West 154th St., New York, NY 10032.

Career

Author and poet. U.S. Patent Office, Washington, DC, clerk-typist, 1949-56, supervisory patent assistant, 1956-60; worked variously as a secretary, case-control technician, and administrative assistant, 1964-68; writer-in-residence, District of Columbia Commission on the Arts and Humanities, 1973 and 1985-87. Participant in numerous school and library programs and workshops for children and adults. *Member:* African American Writer's Guild, Authors Guild, Black Literary Umbrella, District of Columbia Black Writers' Workshop (co-director of adult fiction, 1971-73; director of children's literature, 1973-74).

Awards, Honors

Carter G. Woodson Book Award, National Council for the Social Studies, 1974, for *Rosa Parks;* Woodson Award (outstanding merit), 1980, for *Childtimes: A Three-Generation Memoir;* Irma Simonton Black Award, Bank Street College of Education, 1974, for *She Come Bringing Me That Little Baby Girl;* Jane Addams Children's Book Award, Jane Addams Peace Association, 1976, for *Paul Robeson;* Coretta Scott King Award, American Library Association, 1978, for *Africa Dream,* 1990, for *Nathaniel Talking* (honor book), and 1992, for *Night on Neighborhood Street; Boston Globe-Horn Book* Award, nonfiction honor, 1980, for *Childtimes;* Classroom Choice book citation, International Reading Association and the Children's Book Council, 1978, for *Honey, I Love and Other Love Poems;* Parents' Choice Silver Seal Award, Parents' Choice Foundation, 1988, for *Under the Sunday Tree.* Several of Greenfield's works have been named notable books by the American Library Association and have been named outstanding books of the year, children's books of the year, and notable children's trade books of the year by such organizations as the Child Study Association of America, the New York Public Library, the National Council for Social Studies, the Children's Book Council, the *New York Times,* and *School Library Journal.*

Greenfield has also received several awards for her body of work: a citation from the Council on Interracial Books for Children, 1975; citations from the District of Columbia Association of School Librarians and Celebrations in Learning, both 1977; National Black Child Development Institute Award, 1981; Mills College Award and Washington, DC Mayor's Art Award in literature, both 1983. In addition, she won the Black Women in Sisterhood for Action Award, 1983, and received a grant from the District of Columbia Commission on the Arts and Humanities, 1985. In 1998, Greenfield was given the Hope Dean Award by the Foundation for Children's Literature in Boston.

Writings

PICTURE BOOKS

Bubbles, illustrated by Eric Marlow, Drum and Spear Press (Washington, DC), 1972, published as *Good News,* illustrated by Pat Cummings, Coward, 1977.

She Come Bringing Me That Little Baby Girl, illustrated by John Steptoe, Lippincott, 1974.

Me and Neesie, illustrated by Moneta Barnett, Crowell, 1975.

First Pink Light, illustrated by Moneta Barnett, Crowell, 1976, revised edition, illustrated by Jan Spivey Gilchrist, Black Butterfly, 1991.

Africa Dream, illustrated by Carole Byard, John Day, 1977.

(With mother, Lessie Jones Little) *I Can Do It by Myself,* illustrated by Carole Byard, Harper, 1978.

Darlene, illustrated by George Ford, Methuen, 1980.

Grandmama's Joy, illustrated by Carole Byard, Putnam, 1980.

Daydreamers, illustrated by Tom Feelings, Dial, 1981.

Grandpa's Face, illustrated by Floyd Cooper, Putnam, 1988.

William and the Good Old Days, illustrated by Jan Spivey Gilchrist, HarperCollins, 1993.

Lisa's Daddy and Daughter Day, illustrated by Jan Spivey Gilchrist, Sundance (Littleton, MA), 1993.

Honey, I Love, illustrated by Jan Spivey Gilchrist, Harper/Festival, 1995.

On My Horse, illustrated by Jan Spivey Gilchrist, Harper/Festival, 1995.

For the Love of the Game: Michael Jordan and Me, illustrated by Jan Spivey Gilchrist, HarperCollins, 1997.

Easter Parade, illustrated by Jan Spivey Gilchrist, Hyperion, 1998.

POETRY

Honey, I Love and Other Love Poems, illustrated by Leo and Diane Dillon, Crowell, 1978.

Daydreamers, illustrated by Tom Feelings, Dial, 1981.

Nathaniel Talking, illustrated by Jan Spivey Gilchrist, Black Butterfly, 1988.

Under the Sunday Tree, illustrated by Amos Ferguson, HarperCollins, 1988.

Night on Neighborhood Street, illustrated by Jan Spivey Gilchrist, Dial, 1991.

Angels, illustrated by Jan Spivey Gilchrist, Hyperion, 1998.

NONFICTION; BIOGRAPHIES, EXCEPT AS NOTED

Rosa Parks, illustrated by Eric Marlow, Harper, 1973.

Paul Robeson, illustrated by George Ford, Harper, 1975.

Mary McLeod Bethune, illustrated by Jerry Pinkney, Harper, 1977.

(With Lessie Jones Little; additional material by Patricia Ridley Jones) *Childtimes: A Three-Generation Memoir* (autobiography; for young people), illustrated by Jerry Pinkney and with family photographs, Harper, 1979.

(With Alesia Revis) *Alesia* (for young people), illustrated by George Ford, and with photographs by Sandra Turner Bond), Putnam, 1981.

BOARD BOOKS; ILLUSTRATED BY JAN SPIVEY GILCHRIST

My Doll, Keshia, Black Butterfly, 1991.

I Make Music, Black Butterfly, 1991.
My Daddy and I, Black Butterfly, 1991.
Big Friend, Little Friend, Black Butterfly, 1991.
Aaron and Gayla's Alphabet Book, Black Butterfly, 1992.
Aaron and Gayla's Counting Book, Black Butterfly, 1992.
Sweet Baby Coming, HarperCollins, 1994.
Kia Tanisha, HarperCollins, 1996.
Kia Tanisha Drives Her Car, HarperCollins, 1996.

FICTION

Sister (for young people), illustrated by Moneta Barnett, Harper, 1974.
Talk about a Family, illustrated by James Calvin, Harper, 1978.
Koya DeLaney and the Good Girl Blues, Scholastic, 1992.

OTHER

Also author of bookmark poem for the Children's Book Council, 1979. Contributor to anthologies, including *The Journey: Scholastic Black Literature,* edited by Alma Murray and Robert Thomas, *New Treasury of Children's Poetry,* edited by Joanna Cole, and *Scott, Foresman Anthology of Children's Literature,* edited by Zena Sutherland and Myra Cohn Livingston. Contributor to *Friends Are Like That: Stories to Read to Yourself,* selected by the Child Study Children's Book Committee at Bank Street, Crowell, 1974; *Pass It On: African American Poetry for Children,* selected by Wade Hudson, Scholastic, 1993; *Stick to It,* Open Court, 1995; *Finding Friends,* Open Court, 1995; *African American Poets,* edited by Michael R. Strickland, Enslow, 1996. Contributor to the *World Book Encyclopedia.* Contributor to periodicals, including *Black World, Cricket, Ebony, Jr.!, Horn Book, Negro Digest, Interracial Books for Children Bulletin, Ms., Negro History Bulletin, Scholastic Scope,* and *Washington Post.*

Adaptations

Honey, I Love was recorded for album and audio cassette with music by Byron Morris and released by Honey Productions, 1982. *Daydreamers* was dramatized for the Public Broadcasting System (PBS) series *Reading Rainbow. Lisa's Daddy and Daughter Day* was adapted as an analog audio cassette by Sundance Publishing.

Sidelights

An African American author of fiction, nonfiction, poetry, and picture books, Eloise Greenfield is celebrated as a gifted writer of extensive range and profound sensitivity whose works affirm the positive attributes of the black experience in a manner considered both specific and universal. Characteristically, Greenfield seeks to inspire young readers by providing them with strong role models from both historical and contemporary periods and by stressing such values as the power of love and the importance of family and friends. Several of the author's books are considered groundbreaking titles in their respective genres, and she is often praised for her understanding of the thoughts, feelings, and emotions of the young as well as for her lyrical prose

style. By providing her audience with authentic images of ancestry and solid family relationships, Greenfield is credited with helping to foster confidence and self-esteem in her readers while providing them with balanced overviews of African American life.

Although her works contain death, illness, divorce, disability, and racism as well as poverty and loneliness, Greenfield is consistently hopeful in her message to the young: they can find hope and strength in knowledge of the past, in the closeness of family ties, and within themselves. The author is occasionally criticized for didacticism and for the abrupt conclusions of some of her earlier works; however, most observers regard Greenfield as a major figure in the field of juvenile literature as well as a particularly influential black author. Called "a writer of substance" by Jane Langton in the *New York Times Book Review* and the creator of "good, solid, serious, *soulful* books" by Geraldine L. Wilson in *Interracial Books for Children Bulletin,* Greenfield, according to Sheila McMorrow Geraty of *Children's Books and Their Creators,* "integrates a strong commitment to minority experience with an impassioned love of words to create a wide range of fiction and nonfiction." Writing in *Interracial Books for*

Kevin is disappointed when his new baby sibling is a girl, until his mother helps him to appreciate his important new role as big-brother and protector of his little sister. (From She Come Bringing Me That Little Baby Girl, *written by Eloise Greenfield and illustrated by John Steptoe.)*

Children Bulletin, Beryle Banfield trumpeted, "I hereby declare Eloise Greenfield a national treasure! This extremely gifted and sensitive writer consistently produces exquisitely wrought works which illumine key aspects of the Black experience in ways that underline both its uniqueness and universality."

Born in Parmele, North Carolina, Greenfield moved to Washington, D.C., with her family at the age of four months. Writing in *Childtimes: A Three-Generation Memoir,* a reminiscence that she wrote with her mother, Lessie Jones Little, Greenfield remembered, "I'm three years old, sitting on the floor with Mama. Cutting out a picture for my scrapbook, a picture of a loaf of bread. Cutting it out and pasting it in my book with the flour-and-water paste I had helped to make. As far as I know, that was the day my life began." Greenfield learned to read as a kindergartner by sitting next to her older brother Wilbur in the evenings while their mother, a former teacher, went over his first-grade reading lessons with him. "For the most part," Greenfield wrote in her essay in *Something about the Author Autobiography Series (SAAS),* "I liked school. I enjoyed being with friends and was a very good student through elementary and junior high school." Greenfield attended segregated schools, where often there were not enough materials to go around. Throughout her school years, Greenfield was consistently shy, a quality that sometimes affected her grades. At Cardozo High School, the author wrote in *SAAS,* "some of my grades dropped a little, depending on how much credit was given to participation in class discussion." The author continued, "Shyness followed me far into my life. I didn't conquer it until I was well into adulthood, middle age, actually." Greenfield found solace in reading—she joined a book club at the Langston branch of the public library and later noted in *SAAS* that her reading "took me to faraway places, some of them magical, and to earlier times"—and in music. She learned to play the piano, sang in the glee club and in a harmony group, and went to concerts and shows. Writing in *Childtimes,* Greenfield commented that music is "so much a part of me that if you could somehow subtract it from who I am, I would be a stranger to myself."

When she was nine, Greenfield and her family moved to Langston Terrace, a housing project in northeast Washington that was one of the first such developments in the nation. For her and her siblings, Langston Terrace was, the author recalled in *Childtimes,* "a good growing-up place. Neighbors who cared, family and friends, and a lot of fun. Life was good. Not perfect, but good. We knew about problems, heard about them, saw them, lived through some hard times ourselves, but our community wrapped itself around us, put itself between us and the hard knocks, to cushion the blows." Among the major difficulties faced by the residents of Langston Terrace was racism. For example, most of the pools in the city were only for white children; instead of waiting in long lines at one of the city's few pools for blacks, some children were forced to swim in the city's Kingman Lake. "Almost every summer," Greenfield wrote in *SAAS,* "the police would drag nearby Kingman Lake—

From Daydreamers, *written by Greenfield and illustrated by Tom Feelings.*

we called it a river—and bring up the body of a boy who had drowned. He would be a black boy, most likely from some part of northeast Washington. He would be a boy for whom fireplug showers were not enough. And because he wanted to swim, he would have died in the filthy water of Kingman Lake." Washington, the author noted, "was a city for white people. But inside that city, there was another city. It didn't have a name and it wasn't all in one area, but it was where black people lived. As with all places, there were both good and bad things about our city within a city. We had all the problems that the other Washington had, plus the problems caused by racism." However, Greenfield concluded, there "was always, in my Washington, a sense of people trying to make things better."

After graduating from high school, Greenfield attended Miner Teacher's College (now part of the University of the District of Columbia) with plans to become an elementary school teacher. "I had always enjoyed explaining things to little children," she wrote in *SAAS.* "I would be happy as a teacher. I didn't know about the spotlight that came with that." After two years of battling her shyness in class, Greenfield decided to leave college. In 1949, she became a clerk-typist at the U.S. Patent Office, where she was later promoted to supervisory patent assistant. She married Robert Greenfield, a young man she had known from Langston Terrace, in 1950; the couple, now separated, have two children, Steven and Monica. Greenfield began writing rhymes in her spare time and then moved on to songs, some of which she submitted to television programs such as

Songs for Sale, The Perry Como Show, and *The Fred Waring Show.* Although none of them were accepted, Greenfield looks upon her songs as important in her development as a writer. She stated in *SAAS,* "In fact, they were awful. But I'm glad I wrote them. They ... helped to put me on the right track." Greenfield once told *Something about the Author (SATA),* "Writing was the farthest thing from my mind when I was growing up. I loved words, but I loved to read them, not write them. I loved their sounds and rhythms, and even some of their aberrations, such as homonyms and silent letters.... I wish I could remember just what it was that made me sit down one day and write my very first rhyme. But I can't. I remember only that I was a young wife and mother working full-time as a clerk-typist, and that for some reason I began to write."

After experimenting with songs, Greenfield began writing short stories. "I wrote three," she told *SATA,* "and they were promptly rejected. It was obvious that I had no talent, so I gave up writing forever. Forever lasted five or six years, during which time I learned what writing was—that it was not the result of talent alone, but of talent combined with skills that had to be developed. So I set about practicing them." She brought home two or three books a week on the craft of writing and, she noted in *SAAS,* "studied and wrote, and studied and wrote, and submitted my work to publishers." In 1960, Greenfield retired from the Patent Office. In 1962, she published her first poem, "To a Violin," in Connecticut's *Hartford Times.* The author wrote, "That was the beginning.

Greenfield's series of poems explore life in an urban African-American neighborhood. (From Night on Neighborhood Street, *illustrated by Jan Spivey Gilchrist.)*

Throughout the sixties, I had one or two pieces published a year." Greenfield joined the D.C. Black Writers' Workshop in 1971, later becoming director of its children's literature division and co-director of its adult fiction division. She became friends with Sharon Bell Mathis, a highly respected writer for young people who was then head of the Workshop's children's literature division; Greenfield told Rosalie Black Kiah of *Language Arts* that Mathis "talked so passionately about the need for good black books that it was contagious. Once I realized the full extent of the problems, it became urgent for me to try, along with others, to build a large collection of books for children. It has been inspiring for me to be a part of this struggle."

Greenfield published her first book for children, *Bubbles* (later reprinted as *Good News*), in 1972. A picture book about a small boy who can't find anyone to share his joy in learning to read until his baby sister laughs with him, *Bubbles* was rejected by ten publishers before being accepted by Drum and Spear Press in Washington, D.C. A reviewer in *Interracial Books for Children Bulletin* noted that *Bubbles* "can help children deal with the times when adults are unable to give them the attention they want. It can also help youngsters understand that families adopt different lifestyles for survival." When Sharon Bell Mathis suggested to Greenfield that she write a biography in picture book form, the author recreated the life of Rosa Parks for young children as her second contribution to juvenile literature. Greenfield depicts Parks's childhood, her refusal to give up her bus seat in Montgomery, Alabama, and the resulting Supreme Court decision to end Jim Crow rule in transportation; in addition, she outlines the social situation that contributed to Parks's action. *Rosa Parks* was generally praised by critics: Judy Richardson of the *Journal for Negro Education* commented that the biography "beautifully captures the sense of urgency [that] prevailed at the time and gives young readers a good feeling for the early movement days of the Montgomery bus boycott," while Betty Lanier Jenkins of *School Library Journal* called it "a valuable addition for elementary school and public libraries needing supplementary material on the Civil Rights Movement."

After the success of *Rosa Parks,* which received the first Carter G. Woodson Award in 1974, Greenfield was faced with a dilemma. She wrote in *SAAS,* "Could I hold to my plan to be a reclusive writer while other people were speaking out about racism, and some were putting their lives on the line? The answer was 'No.' Not if I wanted to face myself in the mirror and respect the person I saw there." Greenfield began making public appearances, including television interviews; by telling herself to concentrate on the things that needed to be said and by acting as if she was a person who was not shy, she was able to conquer her fear of public speaking. Following *Rosa Parks,* the author wrote biographies about other notable contemporary African Americans— Paul Robeson and Mary McCloud Bethune—with the goal, she told Kiah of *Language Arts,* of making "children aware of the people who have contributed to the struggle for black liberation." Written in simple but expressive language and noted for their objectivity, Greenfield's biographies were acknowledged as important contributions to black literature for children. Writing in *Twentieth-Century Children's Writers,* Denise Murcko Wilms commented that the biographies "were, in a sense, groundbreaking books, for they presented strong black men and women little written about in a format easily accessible to younger readers. They were a significant contribution toward easing the dearth of black history material available for young readers."

While writing her biographies, Greenfield continued to publish well-received picture books. Her second contribution to the genre, *She Come Bringing Me That Little Baby Girl,* describes how little Kevin, disappointed because his new sibling is a sister instead of a brother, changes his attitude when his mother tells him that she needs his help in caring for the new arrival and that her own older brother protected her when she was a baby. Writing in *Bulletin of the Center for Children's Books,* Zena Sutherland noted, "There have been many books like this ... but there's always room for another when it's well done, and this is: the story catches the wistful pathos of the child who is feeling displaced." *Africa Dream,* a book published in 1977, is a prose poem that depicts a child's dream of going back to long-ago Africa and being welcomed by relatives and friends. Writing in the *Negro History Bulletin,* Thelma D. Perry called *Africa Dream* "a fantastic book" and noted that it "is a pure delight to recommend this lovely book of poignant text."

In *Talk about a Family,* a picture book published the next year, Greenfield describes an African American family facing the pain of divorce. With the help of her relatives and neighbors, small Genny realizes that families come in all shapes and that the concept of family is always changing. A critic in *Kirkus Reviews* noted that Genny's feelings, the interactions of her relatives, and her conversations with an old neighbor are "sensitive enough to make this one of the more honest and effective entries in its limited, problem/consolation genre," while Christine McDonnell of *School Library Journal* commented that the book's characters "are remarkably well developed, especially considering the confines of 64 pages." In her review of the revised edition of *Talk about a Family,* Beryle Banfield of *Interracial Books for Children Bulletin* commented, "You have to care about the people Eloise Greenfield writes about. You have to feel about them...."

Greenfield published her first collection of poetry, *Honey, I Love and Other Love Poems,* in 1978. In sixteen poems written in rhyme and blank verse, the author explores the warm and loving relationships that a young African American girl shares with her family, friends, and schoolmates; the title poem was reissued as a picture book with illustrations by Jan Spivey Gilchrist in 1995. Noting that the child in the poems loves both others and herself and is confident in the expression of her love, Banfield of *Interracial Books for Children Bulletin* commented that Greenfield's manner "gives a definite Afro-American emphasis on universal experi-

ence" and called the book "a must for classroom and school libraries." Greenfield has continued to write books of verse for children. Among her most popular titles is *Nathaniel Talking,* a volume that delineates the philosophy, observations, and opinions of nine-year-old Nathaniel B. Free, a boy whose mother has just died but who presents a thoughtful, positive world view. Nathaniel characterizes each member of his extended family with a poetic tribute written in the musical style of a form associated with their generation: for instance, his father is depicted in a twelve-bar blues, while his grandmother is sketched in a form that imitates the sound of bones, a folk instrument with African origins. Nathaniel himself is characterized by a poem in the rap idiom, and Greenfield is often credited for being the first writer for children to publish a poem written in this form. In her review in *School Library Journal,* Kathleen T. Horning called *Nathaniel Talking* "a stellar collection." Writing in the *Horn Book,* Mary M. Burns commented, "It is not often that a book of poetry can successfully contain a variety of verse forms while simultaneously maintaining the sense of a single voice. Eloise Greenfield meets the challenge brilliantly...." Gale W. Sherman of *Bookbird* noted of Greenfield, "With the importance music has played in her life since childhood, it was natural for her to pioneer the use of the rap rhyme scheme and verse form in children's literature." Evaluating Greenfield's verse for children, *Children's Books and Their Creators* contributor Sheila McMorrow Geraty claimed that Greenfield's poetry "remains her strongest contribution to children's literature.... When read aloud, her lyrical words almost dance, each stanza expressing a powerful sense of setting and character. Through her poignant images of family, friends, and neighborhood, Greenfield reveals a child's emotional reality without sentiment or nostalgia."

Perhaps Greenfield's most highly regarded book is *Childtimes,* the memoir that she wrote with her mother, Lessie Jones Little. An autobiography written with contributions by both authors and dictations from Greenfield's grandmother Patricia Ridley Jones, the book links three individual childhoods to represent the challenges facing African Americans and to demonstrate how they can be transcended by love, loyalty, and family support. In her essay in *Twentieth-Century Children's Writers,* Denise Murcko Wilms called *Childtimes* "Greenfield's most ambitious and mature work," adding that its "intimacy, pride, and reverence are compelling. It's a moving story that embodies all of its author's aims in a manner that qualifies as both art and living history." Quoting Greenfield's words, Mary M. Burns of *Horn Book* commented, "'There's a lot of crying in this book, and there's dying, too, but there's also new life and laughter. It's all part of living.' Few books have conveyed that message more memorably or more artistically." Geraldine L. Wilson of *Interracial Books for Children Bulletin* concluded, "Parents, teachers, family members, get this book into classrooms, homes, churches. Read it yourselves, read it to young children; older children will read it by themselves. Then bow down, low! And to the writers, continue to 'Speak the

For the love of the game

of my life

I live.

Greenfield uses the story of two impressionable eleven-year-olds along with images of basketball great Michael Jordan to encourage children to follow their dreams. (From For the Love of the Game: Michael Jordan and Me, *illustrated by Jan Spivey Gilchrist.)*

Truth to the people,' about the importance of child-times."

In addition to her contributions to other genres, Greenfield has written stories for primary and middle graders and young adults, easy readers, and a series of board books, concept books, and works that feature African American children involved in familiar activities. These titles, which include a volume about the arrival of a new sibling, alphabet and counting books, and stories with rhyming text about a lively little girl, Kia Tanisha, are credited with filling a need for simple but effective works about and for black preschoolers. *For the Love of the Game: Michael Jordan and Me,* a picture book published in 1997, is considered somewhat of a departure for Greenfield: the poetic text and illustrations by Jan Spivey Gilchrist—an artist whose pictures have graced several of the author's works—use images of the basketball great to encourage children to follow their dreams. Writing in *Booklist,* Susan Dove Lempke noted that Greenfield and Gilchrist "work together here like a winning ball team. The exultant text is a teacher's dream.... This book will set children soaring." Calling *For the Love of the Game* "a book that celebrates the human spirit," *School Library Journal* contributor Connie C. Rockman concluded that its overall effect is "a powerful blending of words and pictures that delivers a message that needs to be heard by children growing up in a hostile world." Greenfield has worked with a number of distinguished artists; in addition to Gilchrist, her collaborators include John Steptoe, Moneta Barnett, Tom Feelings, Leo and Diane Dillon, Carole Byard, Jerry Pinkney, Pat Cummings, and Floyd Cooper.

In an essay for *Horn Book* written near the beginning of her career, Greenfield stated, "Writing is my work. It is work that is in harmony with me; it sustains me. I want, through my work, to help sustain children." The author concluded, "I want to be one of those who can choose and order words that children will want to celebrate. I want to make them shout and laugh and blink back tears and care about themselves. They are our future. They are for loving." In her essay in *SAAS,* a piece written in the early 1990s, Greenfield commented, "From where I stand, at this point in my life, I can look back and see growth. And I have a clear view now of the winding path that brought me here. There might have been a shorter path, but I enjoyed all the steps, the process of learning to write. And even now, it is writing, not being a writer, that brings me the deepest satisfaction." She concluded, "I'm glad I chose this work. I would still like to produce children's plays someday—write, direct, and produce them, sometimes interweaving music to carry out the themes. I hope I get to do that. But there are only so many hours in one lifetime, and if I never get to do those things, I will still be happy that I was able to spend so much of my life in a love affair with words."

Works Cited

Banfield, Beryle, review of *Honey, I Love and Other Love Poems, Interracial Books for Children Bulletin,* Volume 9, number 2, 1978, p. 19.

Banfield, Beryle, review of *Grandmama's Joy* and *Talk about a Family, Interracial Books for Children Bulletin,* Volume 11, number 8, 1980, pp. 16-17.

Review of *Bubbles, Interracial Books for Children Bulletin,* Volume 6, numbers 5 and 6, 1975, p. 9.

Burns, Mary M., review of *Childtimes, Horn Book,* December, 1979, p. 676.

Burns, Mary M., review of *Nathaniel Talking, Horn Book,* September-October, 1990, p. 613.

Geraty, Sheila McMorrow, essay on Greenfield in *Children's Books and Their Creators,* edited by Anita Silvey, Houghton Mifflin, 1995, p. 285.

Greenfield, Eloise, "Something to Shout About," *Horn Book,* December, 1975, pp. 624-26.

Greenfield, Eloise, comments in *Something about the Author,* Volume 61, Gale, 1990.

Greenfield, Eloise, essay in *Something about the Author Autobiography Series,* Volume 16, Gale, 1993, pp. 173-85.

Greenfield, Eloise, and Lessie Jones Little, *Childtimes: A Three-Generation Memoir,* Harper, 1979.

Horning, Kathleen T., review of *Nathaniel Talking, School Library Journal,* August, 1989, p. 146.

Jenkins, Betty Lanier, review of *Rosa Parks, School Library Journal,* April, 1974, p. 50.

Kiah, Rosalie Black, "Profile: Eloise Greenfield," *Language Arts,* September, 1980, pp. 653-59.

Langton, Jane, "Five Lives," *New York Times Book Review,* May 5, 1974, p. 16.

Lempke, Susan Dove, review of *For the Love of the Game, Booklist,* February 15, 1997, p. 1024.

McDonnell, Christine, review of *Talk about a Family, School Library Journal,* May, 1978, pp. 67-68.

Perry, Thelma D., review of *Africa Dream, Negro History Bulletin,* January-February, 1978, p. 801.

Richardson, Judy, "Black Children's Books: An Overview," *Journal of Negro Education,* summer, 1974, pp. 380-400.

Rockman, Connie C., review of *For the Love of the Game, School Library Journal,* March, 1997, pp. 174-75.

Sherman, Gale W., "Hip-Hop Culture Raps into Children's Books," *Bookbird,* spring, 1995, pp. 21-25.

Sutherland, Zena, review of *She Come Bringing Me That Little Baby Girl, Bulletin of the Center for Children's Books,* March, 1975, p. 113.

Review of *Talk about a Family, Kirkus Reviews,* April 15, 1978, p. 436.

Wilson, Geraldine L., review of *Childtimes: A Three Generation Memoir, Interracial Books for Children Bulletin,* Volume 11, number 5, 1980, pp. 14-15.

Wilms, Denise Murcko, essay on Greenfield in *Twentieth-Century Children's Writers,* edited by Laura Standley Berger, 4th edition, St. James Press, 1995, pp. 410-11.

For More Information See

BOOKS

Children's Literature Review, Gale, Volume 4, 1982, pp. 95-103, Volume 38, 1996, pp. 76-96.

Fifth Book of Junior Authors and Illustrators, edited by Sally Holmes Holtze, Wilson, 1983.

PERIODICALS

Booklist, April, 1998, p. 1320.
Bulletin of the Center for Children's Books, March, 1997, p. 248.
Horn Book, March-April, 1997, p. 209; September-October, 1998, pp. 607-08.
Publishers Weekly, April 6, 1998, p. 77.
School Library Journal, August, 1998, p. 139; January, 1999, p. 140.

—Sketch by Gerard J. Senick

*   *   *

GRIFFIN, Adele 1970-

Personal

Born July 29, 1970, in Philadelphia, PA; daughter of John Joel Berg (a business manager) and Priscilla Sands Watson (a school principal); married Erich Paul Mauff (an investment banker). *Education:* University of Pennsylvania, B.A. (English), 1993. *Politics:* Democrat. *Hobbies and other interests:* "I am currently enrolled in an introduction to physics/astronomy course at 'The New School,' which has been keeping me quite fascinated, as well as sharpening my (little-used) math skills."

Addresses

Home—154 West 18th St., #7D, New York, NY 10011. *Electronic mail*—erichmauff@aol.com *Office*—215 Park Ave. So., New York, NY 10003. *Agent*—Charlotte Sheedy, c/o Sterling Lord Literistic, 65 Bleecker St., New York, NY 10012.

Career

Children's author. Clarion Books, New York, NY, assistant editor, 1996-98, freelance manuscript reader, 1996—. *Member:* Society of Children's Book Writers and Illustrators, "Young Penn Alum," Friends of the New York Public Library, 92nd Street Young Men's Christian Association (YMCA) of New York.

Awards, Honors

National Book Award nomination, National Book Foundation, 1997, and Notable Book citation, American Library Association (ALA), 1997, both for *Sons of Liberty;* Books for the Teen Age, New York Public Library, 1997, and *Parenting Magazine* Award, 1997, both for *Split Just Right;* Blue Ribbon designation, *Bulletin of the Center for Children's Books,* Best Books, *Publishers Weekly* and *School Library Journal,* Notable Book, ALA, Best Books for Young Adults, ALA, and 100 Titles for Reading and Sharing, New York Public Library, all 1998, all for *The Other Shepards.*

Writings

Rainy Season, Houghton Mifflin, 1996.
Split Just Right, Hyperion, 1997.
Sons of Liberty, Hyperion, 1997.
The Other Shepards, Hyperion, 1998.

Work in Progress

Dive, a middle-grade novel to be published in the fall of 1999.

Sidelights

Adele Griffin told *SATA:* "One of my most treasured childhood memories is the excitement I felt going book shopping before summer vacation. I looked forward to our family's annual visit to New York City and trip to Brentano's, where I was allowed to purchase as many books as I wanted, a joyful extravagance. I knew what I liked: stories about princesses, tough heroines who, defying all odds, would rise from a garret or cottage adjacent to the requisite bog to become a mogul—usually of a department store. I did *not* like science fiction, fantasy, or books about boys.

"While my books are not science fiction or fantasy, I do like to write about both girls *and* boys. (Perhaps age and marriage have helped with that particular aversion.) The voices in my writing are those of the children I have listened to hear and have strained to remember, voices that speak from the secret world we too soon leave. My goal, as I continue my career, is to write books for all young people, even boys, who look forward to a trip to the library or bookstore with great joy, and who are companioned by the friendship of a favorite book."

Griffin's well-received debut novel, *Rainy Season,* was lauded in a *Publishers Weekly* review as "ambitiously conceived and sharply observed." The story follows Lane Beck, a fearful twelve-year-old girl, and her

Adele Griffin

belligerently bold younger brother Charlie through a single transformative day. The Beck family is living on an army base in the Panama Canal Zone in 1977, when resentment of American imperialism is at its peak. The story's setting is key mainly for its contribution of danger and suspense, but the history and politics relevant to the Canal Zone are also discussed in an author's note. *Horn Book* reviewer Nancy Vasilakis wrote that the Panama setting "adds a faint aura of decadence to the narrative." Janice M. Del Negro of the *Bulletin of the Center for Children's Books* maintained that the story's atmosphere is "strongly evoked but never intrusive," adding that "the politics are present but always in the background" of Griffin's work. In anticipation of a battle with the children on the opposite side of the Zone, the Beck children and their friends begin building a fort. Tensions escalating outside the family are paralleled by the strains existing within the family. Lane is prone to panic attacks, Charlie to bully-like behavior, and both children's problems are being deliberately ignored by their parents. Lane's concern for her brother forces her to break the family's pathological silence about the grief they feel over older sister Emily's death in a car accident. *School Library Journal* contributor Lucinda Lockwood commented favorably on Griffin's "evocative" writing and the author's ability to "capture the setting and the nuances of adolescent relationships." A *Publishers Weekly* critic commended the way "Griffin unfolds the events of the day and lets the reader make sense of them," revealing the nature of the tragedy "deep into her story without resorting to melodrama or otherwise manipulating the characterizations." Del Negro concluded that "[T]he image of Lane opening a box of photographs and reclaiming the older sister she loves is one that will remain with readers long after the book is closed."

In an interview with Elizabeth Devereaux for *Publishers Weekly,* Griffin explained that *Rainy Season* was not an autobiographical novel. Griffin did, however, make frequent summer visits to Panama as a child, after her parents divorced and her father moved to Central America. She tackled the subjects of divorce and a girl's experience of life without her father in her next book, *Split Just Right. Horn Book* reviewer Nancy Vasilakis noted that the "sunny" tone of this novel "differ[s] markedly from the somber, interior voice that characterized Griffin's first novel, *Rainy Season.*" *Bulletin of the Center for Children's Books* reviewer Janice M. Del Negro also commented on the "more relaxed, humorous tone" of *Split Just Right,* commending the "natural easy flow" with which Griffin portrays central protagonist Danny's interpersonal relationships. A well-grounded fourteen-year-old who enjoys writing, Danny (otherwise known as Dandelion Finzimer) lives with her flamboyant, single, part-time waitress/actress/drama-teacher mother. With no memory of her father, Danny is unsure whether she should trust her mother's view of him and longs to learn about—or perhaps even meet—him. By way of a mix-up, Danny does get to meet her father, and in the process discovers much about her parents, her work as a burgeoning writer, and the line between fact and fiction. *School Library Journal* contributor Carol A.

Edwards asserted that in this work, Griffin "takes one of the most tired plots in current fiction and gives it fresh zip." *Booklist's* Ilene Cooper praised the book for successfully "tack[ling] a number of interesting issues, including class distinction and family relationships."

Griffin's next book, *Sons of Liberty,* again adopts the more serious tone of her first novel. Through seventh-grader Rock Kindle, Griffin seriously examines the complicated issues faced by members of a dysfunctional family. Rock has always looked up to his father, and in imitation of his father's behavior, has become a bully. Rock's older brother, Cliff, has lost patience with their father's clearly warped sense of militancy, which prescribes regular doses of humiliation and such bizarre punishments as waking the boys up in the middle of the night to do chores and calisthenics. When the family shatters, no longer able to stand the strain, Rock is forced to choose between loyalty to his father and loyalty to his newly discovered sense of self. In a starred review, a *Publishers Weekly* critic praised Griffin's use of "pointedly jarring dialogue" and her "keen ear for adolescent jargon." *Horn Book* reviewer Kitty Flynn credited the development of Rock's character with providing "the tension in what could have been a superficial treatment of the issues."

With *The Other Shepards,* Griffin created a supernatural teen romance about a girl named Holland and her obsessive-compulsive sister Geneva. The two are passing their adolescent years in a world that is haunted by the memory of three older siblings who died before the two sisters were even born. In the guise of Annie, a mural painter, the spirit of the older sister breathes color into the moribund Shepard family. A *Publishers Weekly* critic wrote that Griffin "spins a taut story of two girls . . . who must confront the unknown in order to liberate themselves. . . . Griffin's story offers a resounding affirmation that fears are to be faced, not denied, and life is to be lived, not mourned." In a *Booklist* review, Ilene Cooper lauded the way Griffin "paints Annie so carefully she seems as real as a kiss from a first boyfriend, and what can be more real than that?" Cooper concluded her positive assessment of *The Other Shepards* by asserting: "[C]arefully crafted both in plot and language, this book shows the heights that popular literature can scale."

In her 1996 *Publishers Weekly* interview, Griffin admitted, "I have no life . . . I leave work, go to the gym, come home and have dinner, and I write, every night. I talk to my mother, and then I go to bed . . . . I don't even have a plant." Offering an outlook on her writing future, Griffin said, "I don't think I want to do this my whole life, but right now, while I still feel so passionate about putting all my spare time into writing, I'll do it."

Works Cited

Cooper, Ilene, review of *The Other Shepards, Booklist,* August, 1998, p. 1999.

Cooper, Ilene, review of *Split Just Right, Booklist,* June 1 and 15, 1997, pp. 1702-03.

Del Negro, Janice M., review of *Rainy Season, Bulletin of the Center for Children's Books,* February, 1997, p. 207.

Del Negro, Janice M., review of *Split Just Right, Bulletin of the Center for Children's Books,* September, 1997, p. 11.

Devereaux, Elizabeth, interview with Griffin in "Flying Starts: Six First-Time Children's Book Authors Talk about Their Fall '96 Debuts," *Publishers Weekly,* December 16, 1996, p. 32.

Edwards, Carol A., review of *Split Just Right, School Library Journal,* June, 1997, p. 117.

Flynn, Kitty, review of *Sons of Liberty, Horn Book,* January-February, 1998, p. 72.

Lockwood, Lucinda, review of *Rainy Season, School Library Journal,* November, 1996, pp. 104-05.

Review of *The Other Shepards, Publishers Weekly,* September 21, 1998, p. 86.

Phelan, Carolyn, review of *Sons of Liberty, Booklist,* September 15, 1997, p. 235.

Review of *Rainy Season, Publishers Weekly,* October 14, 1996, p. 84.

Review of *Sons of Liberty, Publishers Weekly,* September 8, 1997, p. 77.

Vasilakis, Nancy, review of *Rainy Season, Horn Book,* March-April, 1997, p. 198.

Vasilakis, Nancy, review of *Split just Right, Horn Book,* July-August, 1997, p. 455.

For More Information See

PERIODICALS

Kirkus Reviews, April 1, 1997, p. 555; August 15, 1997, p. 1305.

New York Times Book Review, March 14, 1999, p. 31.

Publishers Weekly, April 7, 1997, p. 93.

*   *   *

GUTHRIE, Donna W. 1946-

Personal

Born May 15, 1946, in Washington, PA; daughter of Wallace Lyde (a lumberman) and Opal (a homemaker; maiden name, Daque) Winnett; married Michael Beck Guthrie (a physician) June 8, 1973; children: Carly Elizabeth, Colin Wallace. *Education:* Rider College, B.A., 1968; Ravenhill Academy, AMI Montessori degree, 1971. *Politics:* Independent. *Religion:* Methodist.

Addresses

Home and office—7622 Eads Ave., La Jolla, CA 92037.

Career

Teacher in Paulsboro, NJ, Colorado Springs, CO, and Philadelphia, 1968-75; Colorado Springs Montessori School, Colorado Springs, vice president of education, 1976-77; scriptwriter of pilot video series about hospitalization, 1979; Kids Corner Ltd. (audio visual company),

Colorado Springs, founder and president, 1980-1990. President, board of trustees, Pikes Peak Library District, Colorado Springs; lay member, El Paso County Bar Association fee dispute committee. Writer, 1980—. *Member:* Society of Children's Book Writers and Illustrators, The Author's Guild.

Awards, Honors

Best Parenting Video, 1982, and Best Video, 1982, 1983, National Council of Family Relations, all for *I'm a Little Jealous of That Baby; The Witch Who Lives Down the Hall* was selected one of *School Library Journal's* Twenty Best Children's Books, 1985; Arts Business Education Award of Colorado Springs, 1985, for "A Visit from History." Recognized as one of eight families of merit in a feature story highlighting volunteer work both locally and nationally, *USA Weekend Magazine,* 1991. Chosen by the Points of Light Foundation as one of three families to participate in the White House Conference on Volunteers in America, 1992. Best Books for Children, *Ideals,* 1992; *Parents Page* Magazine Award, 1993; Parents Press Best Books for Children, 1994, all for *Nobiah's Well.*

Writings

PICTURE BOOKS

The Witch Who Lives Down the Hall, illustrated by Amy Schwartz, Harcourt, 1985.

Grandpa Doesn't Know It's Me, illustrated by Katy Keck Arnsteen, Human Sciences Press, 1986.

Donna W. Guthrie

This Little Pig Stayed Home, illustrated by Arnsteen, Price Stern, 1987.

While I'm Waiting, illustrated by Marsha Howe, Current Press, 1988.

A Rose for Abby, illustrated by Dennis Hockerman, Abingdon (Nashville, TN), 1988.

Mrs. Gigglebelly Is Coming for Tea, illustrated by Arnsteen, Simon & Schuster, 1989.

The Witch Has an Itch, illustrated by Arnsteen, Simon & Schuster, 1990.

Not for Babies, illustrated by Arnsteen, Simon & Schuster, 1993.

Nobiah's Well: A Modern African Folk Tale, illustrated by Rob Roth, Ideals (Nashville, TN), 1993.

One Hundred and Two Steps, illustrated by Meg Kelleher Aubrey, Cool Kids Press (Boca Raton, FL), 1995.

The Secret Admirer, illustrated by Tony Sansevero, Ideals, 1996.

OTHER

(With Arnsteen) *I Can't Believe It's History! Fun Facts from around the World,* Price Stern, 1993.

Frankie Murphy's Kiss List (chapter book), Simon & Schuster, 1993.

(With Nancy Bentley) *The Young Author's Do-It-Yourself Book: How to Write, Illustrate, and Produce Your Own Book,* illustrated by Arnsteen, Millbrook Press, 1994.

The Better Letter Book, Learning Works (Goleta, CA), 1994.

(With Bentley) *The Young Producer's Video Book: How to Write, Direct, and Shoot Your Own Video,* Millbrook Press, 1995.

Donna Guthrie: An Author's Story, Chip Taylor Communications (Derry, NH), 1995.

(With Joy N. Hulme) *How to Write, Recite, and Delight in All Kinds of Poetry,* Millbrook Press, 1996.

(With Bentley) *Putting on a Play: The Young Playwright's Guide to Scripting, Directing, and Performing,* illustrated by Arnsteen, Millbrook Press, 1996.

(With Jan Stiles) *Real World Math: Money and Other Numbers in Your Life,* illustrated by Robyn Kline, Millbrook Press, 1998.

(With Bentley) *The Young Journalist's Book: How to Write and Produce Your Own Newspaper,* illustrated by Arnsteen, Millbrook Press, 1998.

Mysteries, Mats, and Monsters: A Kid's Guide to Writing Mysteries, Travel, Fantasy and Much, Much More, Millbrook Press, 1999.

Supermarket Math, Millbrook Press, 1999.

Contributor of stories and articles to periodicals including *Turtle, Mature Living, American Library Journal, Parent's Plus, L.A. Parent, Hopscotch Magazine for Girls,* and *San Diego Parent.* Author of radio program "Mr. Vanatoli and the Magic Pumpkin Seeds," *Children Unlimited,* 1983; author of videos *Jasper Enters the Hospital, The Day of Jasper's Operation, Wellness: It's Not Magic!, I'm a Little Jealous of That Baby, My Brother Is Sick,* and *Thea's Story: A Young Woman's Life with Lupus;* creator of classroom presentations "Make Mine a Mystery!," "Nine Nice Newberys and a Couple of Caldecotts," "A Visit from History," and "A Time to Live and a Time to Die," and a series of public service announcements and health spots for the National Poison Control Center.

Sidelights

A former schoolteacher, Donna W. Guthrie is the author of several imaginative picture books as well as books for older readers. *The Witch Who Lives Down the Hall,* with striking Halloween-toned illustrations by Amy Schwartz, will capture the interest of preschoolers as they are carried along with the overactive imaginings of the bright young narrator as he discovers witch-like attributes in an eccentric neighbor. For older readers, the foibles of a sixth grader trying to look cool in *Frankie Murphy's Kiss List* make the book "a guaranteed hit," according to *School Library Journal* contributor Connie Pierce. In addition to fiction, Guthrie has also co-authored several do-it-yourself books designed to help budding novelists, poets, playwrights, videographers, and nonfiction writers alike perform everything from writing and illustrating to editing and presenting their work.

"'Bookworm' is the word my family used to describe me as a child," Guthrie once revealed to *SATA.* Born in Washington, Pennsylvania, in 1946, Guthrie was, by her family's standards, "a hopeless 'dingbat.' I always had my nose in a book. Every time they turned around, I was off in some corner reading." Guthrie's parents were conservative farmers. "I was the fifth of six children (three girls and three boys)," the author recalled, "and according to my family, I lived with my head in the clouds. They had difficulty understanding my vivid imagination and love of reading. They saw it as a waste of time when there was so much work to do."

While she enjoyed story writing as an outlet for her imagination during elementary school, in high school Guthrie started to take the craft of writing more seriously. The encouragement of a supportive English teacher caused Guthrie to begin thinking about writing as a possible career. In college, she majored in journalism, despite the objection of her parents, who believed that teaching or nursing was a far more practical career for a young woman. Ultimately, her parents won out, and Guthrie turned to the study of education.

After earning her bachelor's degree and beginning work on her certification to teach Montessori school, Guthrie taught school in New Jersey. Married in 1973, she and her husband moved to Colorado, then to Philadelphia, where she continued teaching and eventually worked in an administrative position for a Montessori school. However, the love of writing was still with her, and by 1980, Guthrie had decided to begin a freelance writing career. She also started a company that produced videos for children.

As she juggled the roles of wife, mother, friend, community volunteer, businesswoman, and writer, Guthrie noted that "writer" was always last. "I used to tell myself that when everything else was accomplished, then and only then, could I turn on my electric typewriter and write," she remembered of those years. While her early writing met with little success, Guthrie refused to give up on her dream. She joined the Society of Children's Book Writers, and attended a writers conference in the summer of 1983. "I left my young family with a freezer full of casseroles and headed [to California] with my latest manuscript. I'd made a firm decision that unless I received a 'sign' of some sort at that conference, I would unplug my electric typewriter and go back to being a full-time wife, mother, friend, and volunteer." Fortunately, a book editor from Harcourt Brace Jovanovich read her manuscript and took a liking to it; *The Witch Who Lives Down the Hall* was soon published, with more books to follow.

The Witch Who Lives Down the Hall concerns the wariness of a small boy who lives down the hall from Ms. McWee, whose odd habits, "magic potions," and cranky black cat, lead the boy to the conclusion that his neighbor is a witch. His mom tries to dispel his suspicions, until Halloween night when they are confirmed, "to the delight of readers who will count on his adventure adding to the thrills of spook evening for

Young aspiring authors are given in-depth direction on writing, editing, illustrating, and the assembly, binding, and promotion of books in Guthrie's nonfiction work. (Cover illustration by Katy Keck Arnsteen.)

years to come," affirmed a *Publishers Weekly* reviewer. Anne E. Mulherkar, writing in *School Library Journal,* applauded the charming characters and said, "The illogical logic and underlying humor of this picture story make it a compelling tale to read, and one which is sure to please young listeners."

In the picture book *Grandpa Doesn't Know It's Me,* Guthrie focuses on a more realistic, albeit difficult, situation as a young girl attempts to understand the changes occurring in her grandfather as he moves into the later stages of Alzheimer's disease. Targeting primary graders, Guthrie uses a straightforward writing style to instruct young readers about the disease without frightening them. A contributor to the *Bulletin of the Center for Children's Books* maintained that *Grandpa Doesn't Know It's Me* "does a good job of explaining Alzheimer's disease and of explaining the disorientation it causes so that children realize that there is no rejection of them." *Booklist* critic Ilene Cooper called the book a "satisfying introduction" to understanding the disease, and one that reflects the conflicting emotions involved while stressing to young children the important message that "love can make a difference."

Other picture books by Guthrie include *Nobiah's Well: A Modern African Folktale,* about a young boy whose generosity in giving the last of his water to thirsty animals is repaid when those animals help him dig a well and find enough water for his whole drought-

A sophisticated sixth-grade newcomer is forced to make good on his bluff that he is an expert at kissing girls, with humorous results. (Cover illustration by Christian Potter Drury.)

stricken village. And *One Hundred and Two Steps* finds a curious young girl lost in an unfamiliar town after she wanders away from the house of a family relative with whom she is spending the summer.

Guthrie's first chapter book, *Frankie Murphy's Kiss List,* finds a sophisticated sixth-grade newcomer forced to make good on his bluff that he is an expert on kissing girls, with humorous results. When another boy in the small-town school calls former city resident Frankie's bluff, Frankie is forced to bet he can kiss all the girls in the sixth grade by the end of the school year. "Believable, endearing characters, snappy dialogue, and a good story" render *Frankie Murphy's Kiss List* "an authentic, funny slice of pre-junior high life," according to a contributor to *Kirkus Reviews,* while a *Publishers Weekly* reviewer stated, "Guthrie's prose and dialogue are entertaining and credible." Connie Pierce, writing in *School Library Journal,* asserted that "Guthrie gives readers characters with whom they can identify, and a valuable lesson in friendship and loyalty."

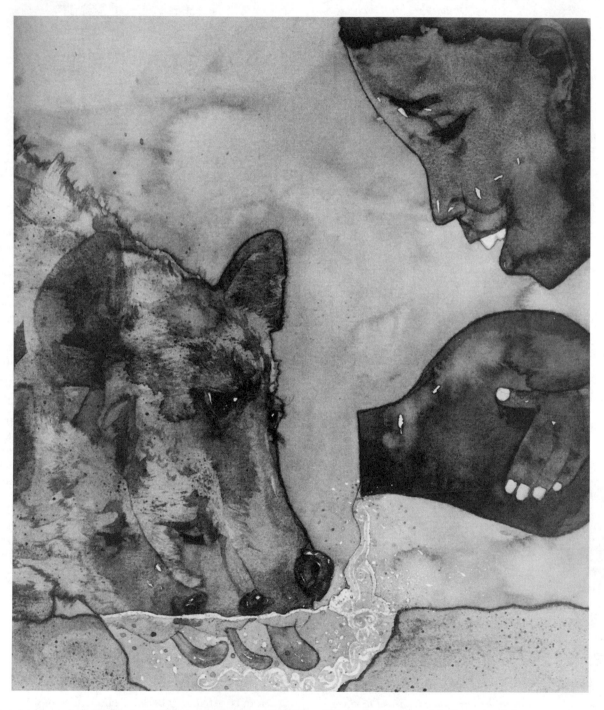

Guthrie's proceeds from this book about a caring boy who shares his precious water with the animals have been donated to Lifewater International, a group that builds wells in arid areas. (From Nobiah's Well: A Modern African Folktale, *illustrated by Rob Roth.)*

Guthrie has also penned several books, alone and with collaborators, that teach young people all the details of how to execute such "hands-on" projects as writing and producing plays, putting together and publishing a newspaper, and even practical applications for the math they are learning in school. One title, *The Young Author's Do-It-Yourself Book* gives elementary-school-age aspiring authors in-depth direction on how to write fiction and nonfiction, plus editing, illustration, assembly, binding, and promotion. Pamela K. Bombay stated in *School Library Journal* that "would-be writers couldn't be anything but successful if they use this concise manual."

Guthrie once cited three things that continue to be of prime importance in her life: "my family, my work, and my friends, but not always in that order. In the future, I hope to grow and mature as a writer. And I'm more than willing to risk and change, to read and study, to write and rewrite so that growth can occur in my life. My wish is to touch the minds and hearts of today's children through my writing, and with a little luck, perhaps leave something for tomorrow's 'bookworms.'"

Works Cited

Bombay, Pamela, review of *The Young Author's Do-It-Yourself Book: How to Write, Illustrate and Produce Your Own Book, School Library Journal,* April, 1994, p. 138.

Cooper, Ilene, review of *Grandpa Doesn't Know It's Me, Booklist,* August, 1986, p. 1687.

Review of *Frankie Murphy's Kiss List, Kirkus Reviews,* October 15, 1993, p. 1330.

Review of *Frankie Murphy's Kiss List, Publishers Weekly,* September 27, 1993, p. 64.

Review of *Grandpa Doesn't Know It's Me, Bulletin of the Center for Children's Books,* July-August, 1986, p. 208.

Mulherkar, Anne E., review of *The Witch Who Lives Down the Hall, School Library Journal,* October, 1995, p. 154.

Pierce, Connie, review of *Frankie Murphy's Kiss List,* September, 1993, p. 232.

Review of *The Witch Who Lives Down the Hall, Publishers Weekly,* August 9, 1985, p. 74.

For More Information See

PERIODICALS

Booklist, April 15, 1994, p. 1530.

Bulletin of the Center for Children's Books, January, 1986, p. 86; February, 1994, p. 188.

Kirkus Reviews, June 15, 1986, p. 937.

Publishers Weekly, August 9, 1993, p. 477.

School Library Journal, January, 1994, p. 90; March, 1996, p. 174.

Voice of Youth Advocates, February, 1994, p. 367.

H–I

HAAS, Dan 1957-

Personal

Born March 19, 1957, in New York, NY; son of Frank (a government official) and Mary (a librarian) Haas; married Vanessa Park (an English teacher), August, 1986; children: Win, Maggie. *Education:* Bard College, B.A., 1980; received master's degree in special education from State University of New York-New Paltz, 1986. *Politics:* Democrat. *Religion:* Unitarian Universalist. *Hobbies and other interests:* Hiking, playing guitar, sports.

Addresses

Home—Box 600, Copake, NY 12516. *Office*—Box AA, Millbrook, NY 12545. *Agent*—Liza Voges, Kirchoff-Wohlberg, 866 United Nations Plaza, New York, NY 10017. *Electronic mail*—parkhaas@taconic.net

Career

Writer and teacher. Millbrook Central Schools, Millbrook, NY, special education teacher, 1987—. Vice-chair, Harlem Valley Rail Trail Association. *Member:* Society of Children's Book Writers and Illustrators.

Awards, Honors

Hoyns Writing Fellowship, University of Virginia, 1984.

Writings

You Can Call Me Worm, Houghton Mifflin (Boston), 1997.

Work in Progress

The Opposite of Anchovies, a novel for middle-grade readers about a 15-year-old basketball athlete; researching an adult novel about a rock musician.

Dan Haas

Sidelights

Dan Haas told *SATA:* "In 1978 I hiked the Appalachian Trail end to end, 2,000 miles through mountains. In *You Can Call Me Worm,* the main character, Worm, hikes about 15 miles along a creek that winds through subdivisions. But the Appalachian Trail hike was an inspiration for the fictional hike." Haas, a special-education teacher in New York State, sends his title character, an eleven-year-old with a troubled family life, on a journey of self-discovery in his well-received debut novel. Worm and his thirteen-year-old brother Todd live with their mother in suburban Washington, D.C. Their parents are separated, and an eighth-grader whose cousin lives near Worm's father relates the news that their father has been sitting on the roof of his house for the past two days. Worm, adventurous and somewhat of a nonconformist, tags along when Todd decides to make the trek to their father's home via a creek that winds through the suburbs. During their journey, the two negotiate a variety of adventures and perils, including an encounter with a group of teens who steal their camping gear and food rations. Worm deals ably with these situations, and thinks about the odd world of adults and families during quieter moments in wry interior monologues. But the two brothers also argue about their father and what course of action they should take when they reach his house. Todd eventually injures his hand and returns home, while Worm forges ahead, witnessing quite a spectacle on his arrival. "It is not until then that [Worm] accepts the fact that his father has a mental illness," wrote Marlyn Roberts in *Voice of Youth Advocates.* Roberts called Haas "a marvelous writer," adding: "He is profound and very funny." A *Kirkus Reviews* commentator praised Haas's characterization of Worm, describing him as "an interesting creation: a self-aware, clumsy daydreamer who spouts bad poetry, worse jokes, and riddles." "[It's] Worm who readers will take to their hearts and remember," remarked Janice M. Del Negro in a *Bulletin of the Center for Children's Books* review.

Haas told *SATA:* "I love that sense of going places, something unclear and half-imaginary ahead, and it doesn't really matter what your destination is. Worm's walk was just as long a journey as mine was, but it was as much an interior trek as a physical one. I think all traveling is like that. The journey to getting a book published was a long one for me, almost twenty years and six unpublished novels along the way, but you learn more from an uphill climb."

Works Cited

Del Negro, Janice M., review of *You Can Call Me Worm,* *Bulletin of the Center for Children's Books,* January, 1998, p. 161.

Roberts, Marlyn, review of *You Can Call Me Worm,* *Voice of Youth Advocates,* February, 1998, p. 386.

Review of *You Can Call Me Worm,* *Kirkus Reviews,* October 15, 1997, p. 1582.

For More Information See

PERIODICALS

Booklist, October 15, 1997, p. 397.
School Library Journal, November, 1997, p. 118.

HARPER, Piers 1966-

Personal

Born July 8, 1966, in Romford, Essex, England; son of Ronald Harper (an overseas telegrapher) and Bel Harper-Gillard (a teacher; maiden name, Stephens). *Education:* Sheffield University, B.A. (dual honours), 1988. *Politics:* Labour. *Religion:* Church of England. *Hobbies and other interests:* "Ancient and classical history, listening to music, mountain climbing, eating vast amounts of chocolate."

Addresses

Home—40 Marne Ave., Ravenstown, Flookburgh, Grange-Over-Sands, Cumbria LA11 7LH, United Kingdom.

Career

Author and illustrator of children's books, 1991—. Editor and advisor, Walker Books Ltd.

Writings

ILLUSTRATOR

Patricia Borlenghi, *From Albatross to Zoo: An Alphabet Book in Five Languages,* ABC (London), 1992, Scholastic (New York), 1992.
Tim Chadwick, *Cabbage Moon,* ABC (London), 1993, Orchard (New York), 1994.
Nigel Nelson, *Looking into Space,* J. Morris (Westport, CT), 1998.
Wendy Body, *Anna's Amazing Multi-Colored Glasses,* Longman (Harlow), 1998.

Piers Harper

AUTHOR AND ILLUSTRATOR

(Reteller) *How the World Was Saved,* ABC, 1994.

Turtle Quest, Walker Books (London), 1997, Candlewick Press (Cambridge, MA), 1997.

Snakes and Ladders (And Hundreds of Mice): A Weird and Wonderful Tower Maze, Walker Books, 1997, Candlewick Press, 1997.

If You Love a Bear, Walker Books, 1998, Candlewick Press, 1998.

Checkmate at Chess City, Walker Books, in press, Candlewick Press, in press.

Cabbage Moon is published in Germany as *Der Kohlkopfmond; Turtle Quest,* also published in Germany, is *Das Ratsel der Maya; Snakes and Ladders* is published in Denmark as *Stiger Og Slanger.*

Work in Progress

A series of comparative history books for children ages seven to eleven, a puzzle book based on perspective and/or Sinbad.

Sidelights

Piers Harper told *SATA:* "Although I had always loved children's books (I love to see words and pictures on the same page), it never occurred to me to try and illustrate them. After leaving university, I had no idea what to do for a job until someone asked me what my ideal job would be. I answered—a children's book illustrator. I started from there."

Harper won praise for his creative collaboration with writer Patricia Borlenghi in his debut title, *From Albatross to Zoo: An Alphabet Book in Five Languages.* The 1992 work features an animal per page along the "E

Then they jump out of bed
and run to the kitchen to make breakfast.

Through a little boy's friendship with a bear, Harper shows very young readers that our friends and family have likes and dislikes different from our own. (From If You Love a Bear, *written and illustrated by Harper.)*

is for Elephant" formula, but stands out for featuring twenty-five terms whose words begin with the same letter in an astounding five different languages—English, German, French, Italian, and Spanish. The multilingual aspect was deemed an excellent learning tool for children who were already studying a second language, and Harper won especial praise for his illustrations, which possess a "frantic charm," noted Ann Welton in *School Library Journal*. Harper and Borlenghi also managed to insert into *From Albatross to Zoo* a simple narrative about a bird who is attempting to fly from one end of the book to the other. A *Publishers Weekly* reviewer appreciated the book's attractive design, noting that it "skillfully blends illustrations and type to create many gamesome touches, such as a dolphin diving through the letter *D* and the letter *R* getting stuck in a reindeer's antlers."

Harper noted that: "One of my biggest influences is Maurice Sendak. I love his way of making things eerie and charming at the same time and making improbable things seem right." Some of Sendak's influence may be seen in Harper's illustrations for Tim Chadwick's 1994 tale *Cabbage Moon*, which won glowing, near-unanimous praise. Aimed at the three-to-six-year-old reader, the book features Albert, a curious bunny with numerous questions about the world around him and outside his window. He also despises that staple of the rabbit diet, cabbage. One night, he looks up at the moon and wonders how it can shift shape from week to week so dramatically if, as his parents have informed him, it is made up of rocks and sand? Suddenly a beam transports him there, where he meets an army of bunnies busily chomping away, as they do nightly, on the moon itself—which is actually a giant cabbage. Here Albert learns to love his roughage, knowing now that his enjoyment will help make the magic of the moon visible to earth-dwellers. Reviewers praised the bunny world that Albert returns to, where everything from slippers to buildings are made from carrots, and even Albert's cozy quilt is decorated with the vegetable. "Harper's art features endearing, yet not overly cute, bunnies, and many winsome details," wrote *School Library Journal* reviewer Lisa S. Murphy, and *Booklist's* Deborah Abbott noted that the details "enhance the humor of the lighthearted story."

Harper suffered some tough reviews, however, for his 1994 book *How the World Was Saved: And Other Native American Tales*, for which he served as both illustrator and reteller. The work presents eight creation myths from a plethora of Native American cultures, from Kwakiutl to Algonquin to Navajo. One critic, Judy Constantinides, opined in *School Library Journal* that she found the illustrations "somewhat garish," and ventured that the text would have been more instructive if more interpretive details had been included. A *Publishers Weekly* reviewer echoed those sentiments, but commented that the "tales themselves are cleanly told."

In 1997, Harper wrote the text and drew the clever illustrations for two puzzle books: *Turtle Quest* and *Snakes and Ladders (And Hundreds of Mice): A Weird and Wonderful Tower Maze*. Both received excellent reviews for the intricacy of the challenges presented. "Apart from my first book the books I have worked on have been triggered by something I am interested in. *Turtle Quest* was written because I had fallen in love with the Maya of Central America. *Snakes and Ladders* came about after a conversation with my editor. I said that all puzzle books were basically like mazes where the reader is led along a set path. As an example I used the game Snakes and Ladders and my editor said, 'Good idea! Do a book based on it.'"

His book *If You Love a Bear* was also singled out for especial praise for the manner in which it presents a little boy and his friendship with a bear, showing very young readers that our friends and family can have different likes and dislikes from ourselves. "If you love a bear, you will know that bears like to be woken up gently," Harper begins. The text and drawings present "the spectrum of toddler emotions," noted Tana Elias in *School Library Journal*, and overall invites readers into "an intimate atmosphere." A *Publishers Weekly* reviewer praised Harper for a work that "manages to both flatter a child's sense of competence and teach the rewards of thinking about others."

Harper, who earned a dual honors degree in ancient history and classical civilization from Sheffield University, is working on a series of comparative history books for young readers, among other projects. He discussed his daily routine with *SATA*: "I work at my desk and rarely elsewhere. It's next to a window so I can use natural light as much as possible—I can also see mountains at the same time, which is bliss. I tend to swing from one extreme to another—either working too much or not at all. Someday I hope to strike a happy medium."

Works Cited

Abbott, Deborah, review of *Cabbage Moon, Booklist,* June 1 & 15, 1994, pp. 1835-36.

Constantinides, Judy, review of *How the World Was Saved: And Other Native American Tales, School Library Journal,* June 1995, p. 102.

Elias, Tana, review of *If You Love a Bear, School Library Journal,* September 1998, p. 173.

Review of *From Albatross to Zoo, Publishers Weekly,* September 28, 1992.

Review of *How the World Was Saved: And Other Native American Tales, Publishers Weekly,* May 8, 1995, p. 276.

Review of *If You Love a Bear, Publishers Weekly,* June 15, 1998, p. 58.

Murphy, Lisa S., review of *Cabbage Moon, School Library Journal,* April, 1994, p. 101.

Welton, Ann, review of *From Albatross to Zoo, School Library Journal,* September, 1992, pp. 214-15.

For More Information See

PERIODICALS

Booklist, October 1, 1992, p. 334.
Kirkus Reviews, November 15, 1997, p. 1707.
Northern Echo, June 7, 1997.
Publishers Weekly, December 6, 1993, p. 72.

*   *   *

HARRIS, Christine 1955-

Personal

Born August 5, 1955, in South Australia; daughter of Glenn (a carpenter) and Martha (a homemaker; maiden name, Gallacher) Brown; married David William Harris (a writer) July 6, 1989; children: Samuel Reynolds, Jennifer Reynolds. *Education:* Graduated from Dover Gardens Girls' Technical High School; College of Technical and Further Education, certificate (creative writing). *Hobbies and other interests:* Cottage gardening, swimming, bush-walking, shi ba shi.

Addresses

Office—P.O. Box 478, Mt. Barker, South Australia 5251. *Agent*—Lyn Tranter, Australian Literary Management, 2-A Booth Street, New South Wales 2041, Balmain, Australia. *Electronic mail*—harris @ books.mtx.net.

Career

Myer Bookstore, Adelaide, South Australia, sales assistant, 1990-94; writer, 1995—. Also works occasionally as a photographer, with work published in newspapers including *Australian, Herald Sun,* and *Australian Airways Magazine. Member:* Australian Society of Authors, South Australian Writers' Centre, Ekidnas (children's book writers' group), Royal Geographical Society.

Awards, Honors

Golden Gateway Literary Award; Australia Council Literature Board grant, 1991, for *Trees in My Ears;* Department for Arts and Cultural Development grants, 1993, for *Strike!,* 1995, for *Baptism of Fire;* Children Rate Outstanding Writers (CROW) Awards, shortlist, 1993, for *Outer Face,* and 1994, for *Buried Secrets;* Notable Book designation, Children's Book Council, for *Outer Face, Strike!, Party Animals, Baptism of Fire,* and *Sleeping In;* KROC Award runner-up, 1996; Western Australian Young Readers Book Award shortlist, 1997, for *Party Animals;* ArtSA grant, 1997, for *Foreign Devil;* Christian Schools Award nomination, 1998, for *Baptism of Fire.*

Writings

SHORT STORY COLLECTIONS

Outer Face, Random House, 1992.
Buried Secrets, Random House, 1993.

Christine Harris

Widdershins, Random House, 1995, published as *Party Animals,* 1997.
(With Clare Carmichael and Margaret Clark) *Deadly Friends,* Random House, 1997.
Fortune Cookies, Random House, 1998.

NOVELS; FOR YOUNG ADULTS

Strike!, Random House, 1994.
Baptism of Fire, Random House, 1996.
Pitt Man, Random House, 1996.
Torture Chamber, Random House, 1997.
Slime Time, Hodder, 1997.
Foreign Devil, Random House, 1999.

"VIBES" SERIES; SCIENCE-FICTION NOVELS

Suspicion, Hodder Headline, 1998.
Masks, Hodder Headline, 1998.
Jigsaw, Hodder Headline, 1998.
Shadows, Hodder Headline, 1998.

EDITOR; NON-FICTION

No Bed of Roses, Wakefield Press, 1993.
Old Yanconian School Daze, Wakefield Press, 1995.
What a Line! (History of Hills Hoists), Hills Industries, 1995.
In Looking-Glass Land, Seaview Press, 1996.

OTHER

Trees in My Ears: Children from around the World Talk to Christine Harris, Wakefield Press, 1992.
Countdown (novel), Omnibus, 1995.
A Real Corpse, HarperCollins, 1997.

Sleeping In (picture book), illustrated by Craig Smith, Random House, 1997.

Odd Balls: Jokes and Funny Stories, illustrated by David Mackintosh, Random House, 1998.

I Don't Want to Go to School (picture book), illustrated by Craig Smith, Random House, 1999.

The Little Book of Elephants (humor and nonfiction), Hodder Headline, 1999.

Adaptations

Several of Harris's short stories were adapted as the dance performance, "Second Hand," produced by Outlet Dance, for performance at the space theatre and in South Australian schools, 1995.

Sidelights

Australian author Christine Harris has drawn upon her highly developed imagination, as well as her skills as a writer and her sense of fun, to create a body of short stories and novels that have gained a large following in her native country. Reviewing Harris's collection *Outer Face* in *Magpies,* Kevin Steinberger maintained: "While acknowledging the established appeal of bizarre humour and ironic twists, [Harris] is also analytical, descriptive, and reflective. There is something for everyone in her ... stories." In addition to writing fiction, Harris has also edited several volumes of short fiction, and has served as the compiler of *Trees in My Ears,* a collection of narrations by children living in a variety of countries. The subjects covered in the book range from family life, friendship, school, and pets to heroes and aging. *Trees in My Ears* "provides a quite remarkable insight into how young minds and hearts interpret and respond to life as it unfolds around them," stated *Magpies* contributor Cathryn Crowe.

Born in South Australia in 1955, Harris grew up with a love of books. "As a child I escaped into other worlds via the written page and pretended I was a character in the story," she told *SATA.* "I still do this, but now I write down my own versions of what that character does. For many years, it seemed to some of my relatives that I had a book welded to my hands, whatever I was doing: cooking, ironing (yes, I actually used to iron once), in the bath, and even when walking (but keeping half an eye open for potholes and vehicles)."

After graduating from an all-girls technical high school near her home, Harris knew she wanted to advance her writing skills, but living in the country limited her options. So she enrolled in a home-study course with South Australia's College of Technical and Further Education, eventually earning a certificate in their creative writing program. She worked for several years in a bookstore in Adelaide, South Australia, before the success of such short story collections as *Outer Face* and the young adult novel *Strike!* gave her the confidence to devote full-time attention to writing.

Outer Face served as a book-buyer's introduction to Harris's work. A collection of fourteen short stories,

Outer Face features such selections as "Knocked Out," about a young man who finds his newly acquired ability to read minds is a mixed blessing; "Mirror Door," in which a young woman enters a ghostly dimension through a portal that opens only on Halloween; and "A Bad Year," which showcases a farming family forced to lose its stock of sheep because of a severe drought. *Outer Face* "announces a new talent that will find a comfortable place" in the children's short story genre, noted *Magpies* reviewer Steinberger.

The short stories in the collection *Buried Secrets* help to establish a Harris trademark: each features a likeable teen protagonist, a slightly off-beat problem, and a dash of bizarre humor. Here the author introduces a wide variety of new characters, including a boy who sees through people's clothes, a woman who takes on the personality of the ruthless Black Widow spider, and even a young man who suspects his date of being a horrible monster. Praising the volume as being suitable for even reluctant teen readers, *Magpies* contributor Alf Mappin called *Buried Secrets* entertaining and asserted that "Harris's style, with its lightness and, one suspects,

Harris's story collection focuses on the differences between Australians of European descent and Asian immigrants as these two cultures attempt to coexist. (Cover photo by Reece Scannell.)

tongue-in-cheek attitude to what is being related, works well."

While Harris does write for her young readers with an eye toward entertainment, she occasionally uses her writing to make a point. "Sometimes I feel strongly about something and want to highlight a message through the medium of a story," Harris explained to *SATA.* "Among the themes I have chosen are freedom of thought (*Baptism of Fire*), loyalty (*Strike!*), communication and understanding of other cultures (*Fortune Cookies*)." Reviewing *Fortune Cookies* in *METaphor* magazine, Bill Simon called Harris's ten-story collection "extremely moving" in its focus on the differences between Australians of European descent and that continent's growing number of Asian immigrants and the attempts of these two cultures to coexist.

When she is writing, Harris becomes completely absorbed in her fictional world, to the point that she even *dreams* about her characters. "For example, when I was halfway through writing *Baptism of Fire,* I was about to write a scene involving a fire when I dreamt the fire. I heard the crackle of flames on the thatched Fijian roofs, felt the heat and smelt the smoke. When I woke, I was sure that I could still smell smoke. I went straight to the computer and wrote that scene in one passionate sitting."

Harris frequently suffers from insomnia, so a great deal of her writing is accomplished during sleepless nights, particularly in the quiet hours between midnight and 3 a.m. "But on days when I write in daylight hours, I clean up, get dressed, and switch on the computer by 9 a.m., just as if I was going out to an office to work," Harris explained.

Having become familiar with many of the books available to young readers through her work in a local bookstore, Harris maintains that a great deal of quality writing exists for young readers. "And that's good," she told *SATA,* "because we compete with television, the internet, computer games, sport and all the other activities that fill and enrich children's lives. But [writers] have to be good, entertaining, and thought-provoking if we are to keep a place for books."

What is Harris's advice to young students thinking about becoming writers someday? "I would say read, read, and then read some more. Don't give up. It is not always the best writers who are published. Sometimes, it is the most determined. Train yourself to be observant, keep instincts. Keep your eye on market trends and listen to readers when they speak about the kinds of stories they like to read. Make time. Follow your heart. And be prepared to rewrite, take advice and keep polishing until the story is the best it can be. And hope for a bit of luck."

Works Cited

Crowe, Cathryn, review of *Trees in My Ears, Magpies,* September, 1993, p. 4.

Mappin, Alf, review of *Buried Secrets, Magpies,* July, 1993, p. 4.

Simon, Bill, review of *Fortune Cookies, METaphor.*

Steinberger, Kevin, review of *Outer Face, Magpies,* July, 1992, p. 4.

For More Information See

PERIODICALS

Lollipops, July-August, 1998, p. 15.
Magpies, March, 1997, p. 33.

*   *   *

HASELEY, Dennis 1950-

Personal

Surname rhymes with "paisley"; born June 28, 1950, in Cleveland, OH; son of Robert Carl (a sales executive) and Margaret (an account supervisor; maiden name, Boigner) Haseley; married Claudia Eleanore Lament (a child psychoanalyst), October 12, 1986; children: Connor McMurray. *Education:* Oberlin College, A.B., 1972; New York University, M.S.W., 1982; attended the New York University Psychoanalytic Institute. *Hobbies and other interests:* Tennis, skiing, running.

Dennis Haseley

Addresses

Home—Brooklyn, NY.

Career

Teacher and author. Worked variously as a professional fund raiser and a community organizer. Jewish Board of Family and Children's Services, New York City, therapist, 1982-86; author of books for children, 1982—; private practice in psychotherapy, 1984—. *Member:* Society of Children's Book Writers and Illustrators, Authors Guild.

Awards, Honors

The Old Banjo was named among New York Public Library's Children's Books, Child Study Association of America's Children's Books of the Year, and as a Pick of the Lists by American Booksellers, all 1983; Parents' Choice Remarkable Book for Literature, Parents' Choice Foundation, 1983, for *The Scared One; The Kite Flier* was chosen a Notable Book in the Field of Social Studies, National Council for Social Studies, and as a Pick of the Lists, American Booksellers, both 1986, and named among Child Study Association of America's Children's Books of the Year, 1987; *Shadows* was chosen as a Pick of the Lists by American Booksellers, and named one of the books of the year by the Library of Congress, both 1991; fiction grant, New York Foundation for the Arts, 1994.

Writings

FOR CHILDREN

The Scared One, illustrated by Deborah Howland, Warne, 1983.
The Old Banjo, illustrated by Stephen Gammell, Macmillan, 1983.
The Pirate Who Tried to Capture the Moon, illustrated by Sue Truesdell, Harper, 1983.
The Soap Bandit, illustrated by Jane Chambless-Rigie, Warne, 1984.
The Kite Flier, illustrated by David Wiesner, Aladdin Books, 1986.
The Cave of Snores, illustrated by Eric Beddows, Harper, 1987.
My Father Doesn't Know about the Woods and Me, illustrated by Michael Hays, Atheneum, 1988.
Ghost Catcher, illustrated by Lloyd Bloom, Harper, 1989.
The Thieves' Market, illustrated by Lisa Desimini, Harper-Collins, 1991.
Horses with Wings, illustrated by Lynn Curlee, HarperCollins, 1993.
Crosby, illustrated by Jonathan Green, Harcourt Brace, 1996.
Bear, illustrated by Jim LaMarche, Harcourt Brace, in press.

The Scared One and *The Old Banjo* have been translated into French and Spanish, and *The Pirate Who Tried to Capture the Moon* has been translated into French.

YOUNG ADULT NOVELS

The Counterfeiter, Macmillan, 1987.
Shadows, illustrated by Leslie Bowman, Farrar, Straus, 1991.
Dr. Gravity, Farrar, Straus, 1992.
Getting Him, Farrar, Straus, 1994.

Dr. Gravity has been translated into Chinese.

Adaptations

The Old Banjo was adapted as a filmstrip with cassette, Random House, 1986; *The Cave of Snores* was included in the video recording *Return to the Magic Library. Norbert, Snorebert,* TVOntario (Chapel Hill, NC).

Sidelights

Psychotherapist Dennis Haseley has written extensively for children; his works include picture books, middle-grade, and young adult novels. Known for their unusual and imaginative subject matter, symbolism, and lyrical prose, Haseley's books have long captured the attention of reviewers. Among the most critically acclaimed are *The Old Banjo, Ghost Catcher,* and *Shadows.*

Haseley grew up in Brecksville, Ohio, where at the age of seven he wrote his first poem. While a student in high school and at Oberlin College, he renewed and developed his talent for writing, working with novelist and screenwriter William Goldman during a semester in New York City. After graduation, Haseley published verse in literary magazines and came to the realization that children's books offered an opportunity for him to showcase his talent. His first book for children, 1983's *The Scared One,* is a prose poem picture book about the rites of passage of a timid young Native American boy who has been nicknamed the Scared One by his playmates. "It is gravely told, and touching" wrote a reviewer in the *Bulletin of the Center for Children's Books,* while a *Publishers Weekly* critic remarked that the story "resonates with the cadences of heroic legends."

Many of Haseley's subsequent picture books caught the attention of reviewers. In *The Old Banjo,* which a *Publishers Weekly* critic termed a "sensitive ballad" and a "memorable story" and a *Booklist* reviewer called "a mystical, magical fantasy," a boy discovers on a Depression-era farm some forgotten musical instruments that magically come alive. Describing the book written by Haseley and illustrated by Stephen Gammell, George A. Woods concluded in the *New York Times Book Review* that "the combo of Mr. Haseley on words and Mr. Gammell on pencil have produced a modest piece that will strike a responsive chord in most readers." Likewise, *School Library Journal* contributor Ellen D. Warwick declared that "this beautiful book has something important to say about the nature of hope and the persistence of dreams."

In 1983's *The Pirate Who Tried to Capture the Moon,* a lonely, island-bound pirate captures all the ships that

Jamie encounters his aunt's disapproval when he tries to build a relationship with his grandfather, who wants to acquaint Jamie with the memory of his deceased father. (Cover illustration by Leslie Bowman.)

pass until he is himself captivated by the moon, an ending that a *Kirkus Reviews* contributor deemed "a satisfactory surprise." David Gale, writing in *School Library Journal,* noted that the text is "lyrical at times." Published the following year, Haseley's *The Soap Bandit* is, in the words of a *Publishers Weekly* critic, a "gentle allegory." Karla Kuskin in the *New York Times Book Review* commented on the "imaginative and humorous touches" in the book. *The Soap Bandit* revolves around a mysterious stranger who steals all the soap from a quaint seaside town, changing the character of the inhabitants.

Many of Haseley's picture books deal with unusual subjects or are allegories. For example, *The Kite Flier* tells the tale of a man who is a stonemason by day and a kite maker by night. When his wife dies after their son is born, the man stops making kites until his son shows an interest in them. As the child grows, the father makes kites that symbolize his son's development. Years later, when his son is a young man ready to be launched into the world, he and his son make a special kite together and release it. While noting that the book's symbolism

would be lost on a young readership, "the book may have special appeal to an older audience," judged Maria B. Salvadore in *School Library Journal.* Similarly, a *Booklist* critic predicted, "This quiet story is for the special reader; older children especially will respond to its formal language."

Another book by Haseley that commentators thought more appropriate for an older audience is *The Cave of Snores,* which concerns a shepherd's son who wishes that his father would not snore so loudly. Several critics praised Haseley's prose in this book. Karen K. Radtke, writing in *School Library Journal,* noted that the book's language "properly captures the tall-tale boastfulness of Arabian folklore." Tim Wynne-Jones of the Toronto *Globe and Mail* described *The Cave of Snores* as a "cleverly contrived coming-of-age allegory," and called Haseley's language "lyrical and bursting with life."

My Father Doesn't Know about the Woods and Me relates how a boy, walking in the woods with his father, feels like he is transformed into the animals he sees. This "possibility weaves a magic spell over readers and listeners," wrote David Gale in *School Library Journal.*

Donald befriends Harold and takes advantage of his trust in Haseley's mysterious coming-of-age novel. (Cover illustration by Mark Elliott.)

A lonely, fatherless boy finds solace, friendship, and freedom when he repairs and flies a broken kite. (*From* Crosby, *written by Haseley and illustrated by Jonathan Green.*)

Describing *My Father Doesn't Know* as a "magical story," a *Booklist* critic likewise remarked that the book "offers possibilities to tweak children's imaginations." Another fantasy, *The Thieves' Market,* revolves around a group of thieves who open up a market outside a town where children come at night to choose their dreams. *Booklist* contributor Leone McDermott highly praised the metaphor of the market and the "eerie beauty" of the text, describing the work as "unusual and affecting" and "filled with insight and respect for children's inner lives." This is a story that "may intrigue the curious, the lovers of mystery and magic" remarked Shirley Wilton in *School Library Journal.*

Rona Berg, writing in the *New York Times Book Review,* called Haseley's 1989 storybook *Ghost Catcher* the author's "most ambitious and original work," a parable about "the pull of community and the power of love." The story tells of a solitary man called Ghost Catcher who has no shadow and so avoids forming relationships with the people of his Hispanic village. Because he has no shadow, he can bring people back from the brink of death. When Ghost Catcher is tempted by curiosity to visit the land of shadows, he is trapped and must be rescued by the villagers who, through their compassion

and efforts, show what it is to depend upon one another. "American children, used to a heavier does of realism or a lighter flight of fantasy, may find this story confusing," maintained Berg. However, Berg concluded that *Ghost Catcher* can be read and enjoyed on several levels. A *Publishers Weekly* reviewer voiced similar comments, noting that while *Ghost Catcher* may be too difficult for some children, it is still "an intriguing, thoughtful collaboration" and a "highly atmospheric parable."

If *Ghost Catcher* is steeped in fantasy, 1993's *Horses with Wings* is more down-to-earth. The book is based on a historical event: Leon Gambetta's balloon escape from besieged Paris during the Franco-Prussian War. Stephen Fraser of *Five Owls* praised *Horses with Wings* highly, declaring Haseley's work to be "nonfiction the way it should be: accessible, engaging, and alive." *Booklist* contributor Kay Weisman suggested that while "young children may miss the understated messages about war and peace" in the work, middle-school students could use the book as a discussion starter. A critic for *Kirkus Reviews* called *Horses with Wings* "an interesting vignette, though the lack of a historical note is curious."

Haseley's most recent picture book is *Crosby*. With *Crosby*, Haseley returned to the subject of kites. This time, a lonely fatherless boy finds solace and freedom when he repairs and flies a broken kite. "It's a thoughtful, unusual picture book, more complex than most, and deserving of a close look," wrote a *Publishers Weekly* reviewer. A critic for *Kirkus Reviews,* remarked that *Crosby* "is a strange story" for such young readers, and also admitted that the book offers "an emotionally satisfying ending." Writing in *School Library Journal,* Judith Constantinides praised *Crosby* as "a feast for both the eye and the ear."

Although Haseley once admitted to *SATA* that, after concentrating on picture books, "it was rather frightening to take on a novel," he has written several longer works for young adult readers. *The Counterfeiter* and *Dr. Gravity* are humorous treatments, while *Shadows* and *Getting Him* strike a more serious, responsive note. *The Counterfeiter* describes how would-be artist James falls in love with Heather, a cheerleader, and makes counterfeit currency in order to afford to take her on a date. James is a protagonist who "convincingly embodies the peculiar blend of frustration, cynicism and giddy optimism" characteristic of teens, according to a critic for *Publishers Weekly.* Reviewing *The Counterfeiter* in *School Library Journal,* Robert E. Unsworth noted that the book contains "lots of laughs and insight into the perplexities of adolescence."

With its focus on a man who releases townspeople from the force of gravity and faces weighty consequences, *Dr. Gravity* is a "rambling, old-fashioned novel" and "a graceful, carefully developed fantasy," according to a *Horn Book* contributor. Comparing the work to that of noted children's author Roald Dahl, Catherine M. Dwyer of *Voice of Youth Advocates* proclaimed that "Haseley has written a wonderful fantasy. *Dr. Gravity* is full of gentle humor and peopled with well-drawn characters." The *Horn Book* critic also maintained that "there is much humor in the story," adding that "Haseley's skilled use of description creates a convincing setting for fantastic events." As Dwyer concluded, young readers "will love this tale."

Shadows, a short novel written for middle-grade readers, deals with subtle ideas. Young protagonist Jamie wonders about his absent father and learns about him through stories his grandfather tells by casting shadows on a wall. *Shadows* elicited high praise from Liz Rosenberg, who reviewed the book in the *New York Times Book Review.* Haseley, Rosenberg contended, "possesses an acute sense of childhood's pathos," putting his talent to good effect in this "beautifully written novel." Rosenberg added that *Shadows* "combines realism and fantasy," and "is strong and powerfully appealing," a story "perfect for reluctant readers, as well as all those who love good books."

Set in a small Ohio town in the late 1950s, *Getting Him* is a story of revenge against an eccentric sixth grader named Harold who has accidentally injured the dog of another boy named Donald. Because precocious Harold, who is only eight years old, believes in the existence of extraterrestrials, Donald and several of his friends perpetrate an elaborate hoax involving "aliens." Citing the work as a combination science-fiction novel, fantasy, morality tale, and coming-of-age story, a *Publishers Weekly* commentator wrote, "Haseley creates a mysterious stark world of preadolescent confusion." In a *School Library Journal* review of *Getting Him,* Tim Rausch noted that while "readers may enjoy the details of the boys' prank and the mysterious elements of the plot," the book's characters, except for Harold, "are flat, stereotypical, and basically unlikable." A *Horn Book* contributor, on the other hand, described *Getting Him* as "a thoughtful, complex story with an intriguing plot and rich, believable characters."

Haseley once commented: "I often start a story—whether for a picture book or a novel—with an image or metaphor that captures me. For instance, for *Dr. Gravity,* it was the idea of a town that could float. *Shadows* began when I came upon a reprinted nineteenth-century book instructing the reader how to make various hand shadows. *Crosby* grew from the images of a kite's tail made of old socks and scuffed shoes that looked like turtles. Starting with a key, evocative image, I try to reach in some way into my own experiences and emotions and build a story that becomes for the reader—and for me—something that's new."

Works Cited

Berg, Rona, review of *Ghost Catcher, New York Times Book Review,* April 26, 1992, p. 25.

Constantinides, Judith, review of *Crosby, School Library Journal,* September, 1996, p. 180.

Review of *The Counterfeiter, Publishers Weekly,* November 27, 1987, p. 86.

Review of *Crosby, Kirkus Reviews,* August 1, 1996, p. 1153.

Review of *Crosby, Publishers Weekly,* September 2, 1996, p. 131.

Review of *Dr. Gravity, Horn Book,* March-April, 1993, pp. 211-12.

Dwyer, Catherine M., review of *Dr. Gravity, Voice of Youth Advocates,* December, 1992, p. 292.

Fraser, Stephen, review of *Horses with Wings, Five Owls,* September-October, 1993, pp. 10-11.

Gale, David, review of *My Father Doesn't Know about the Woods and Me, School Library Journal,* October, 1988, p. 121.

Gale, David, review of *The Pirate Who Tried to Capture the Moon, School Library Journal,* August, 1983, p. 51.

Review of *Getting Him, Horn Book,* January-February, 1995, pp. 59-60.

Review of *Getting Him, Publishers Weekly,* November 7, 1994, pp. 79-80.

Review of *Ghost Catcher, Publishers Weekly,* July 25, 1991, p. 54.

Review of *Horses with Wings, Kirkus Reviews,* September 1, 1993, p. 1145.

Review of *The Kite Flier, Booklist,* October 1, 1986, p. 272.

Kuskin, Karla, review of *The Soap Bandit, New York Time Book Review,* September 9, 1984, p. 43.

McDermott, Leone, review of *The Thieves Market, Booklist,* March 15, 1991, p. 1505.

Review of *My Father Doesn't Know about the Woods and Me, Booklist,* January 1, 1989, p. 788.

Review of *The Old Banjo, Booklist,* October 1, 1983, p. 294.

Review of *The Old Banjo, Publishers Weekly,* October 14, 1983, p. 54.

Review of *The Pirate Who Tried to Capture the Moon, Kirkus Reviews,* February 1, 1983, p. 117.

Radtke, Karen K., review of *The Cave of Snores, School Library Journal,* April, 1987, pp. 82-83.

Rausch, Tim, review of *Getting Him, School Library Journal,* November, 1994, pp. 102-103.

Rosenberg, Liz, review of *Shadows, New York Times Book Review,* October 20, 1991, p. 53.

Salvadore, Maria B., review of *The Kite Flier, School Library Journal,* November, 1986, p. 78.

Review of *The Scared One, Bulletin of the Center for Children's Books,* January, 1984, p. 88.

Review of *The Scared One, Publishers Weekly,* September 16, 1983, p. 125.

Review of *The Soap Bandit, Publishers Weekly,* June 22, 1984, p. 99.

Unsworth, Robert E., review of *The Counterfeiter, School Library Journal,* October, 1987, pp. 138-39.

Warwick, Ellen D., review of *The Old Banjo, School Library Journal,* November, 1983, p. 64.

Weisman, Kay, review of *Horses with Wings, Booklist,* November 15, 1993, pp. 630-31.

Wilton, Shirley, review of *The Thieves Market,* May, 1991, p. 78.

Woods, George A., review of *The Old Banjo, New York Times Book Review,* September 18, 1983, p. 39.

Wynne-Jones, Tim, review of *The Cave of Snores,* Toronto *Globe and Mail,* May 30, 1987.

For More Information See

PERIODICALS

Booklist, December 15, 1994, p. 747; November 15, 1995, p. 546.

Bulletin of the Center for Children's Books, December, 1994, p. 129.

Canadian Materials, September, 1988, p. 182.

Horn Book, July-August, 1991, p. 456.

Interracial Books for Children Bulletin, January, 1984, p. 36.

Kirkus Reviews, February 15, 1987, p. 301; October, 15, 1987, p. 1515; September 1, 1991, p. 1160; November 15, 1994, p. 1530.

New York Times Book Review, March 29, 1987, p. 26.

Publishers Weekly, January 19, 1983, p. 112; April 10, 1987, p. 95; September 13, 1993, pp. 132-33.

School Library Journal, January, 1984, p. 77; April, 1984, p. 102; June, 1991, p. 106; November, 1991, p. 117; December, 1992, p. 133; December, 1993, pp. 88-89.

Voice of Youth Advocates, October, 1987, p. 201; December, 1994, p. 274.

HASKINS, James S. 1941-
(Jim Haskins)

Personal

Born September 19, 1941, in Demopolis, AL; son of Henry and Julia (Brown) Haskins. *Education:* Georgetown University, B.A., 1960; Alabama State University, B.S., 1962; University of New Mexico, M.A., 1963; graduate study at New School for Social Research, New York, 1965-67, and Queens College of the City University of New York, 1967-68.

Addresses

Home—325 West End Ave., Apt. 7D, New York, NY 10023. *Office*—Department of English, University of Florida, Gainesville, FL 32611.

Career

Smith Barney & Co., New York City, stock trader, 1963-65; New York City Board of Education, teacher, 1966-68; New School for Social Research, New York City, visiting lecturer, 1970-72; Staten Island Community College of the City University of New York, associate professor, 1970-77; University of Florida, Gainesville, professor of English, 1977—. New York *Daily News,* reporter, 1963-64. Elisabeth Irwin High School, visiting

James S. Haskins

lecturer, 1971-73; Indiana University/Purdue University-Indianapolis, visiting professor, 1973-76; College of New Rochelle, visiting professor, 1977. Union Mutual Life, Health and Accident Insurance, director, 1970-73. Member of board of advisors, Psi Systems, 1971-72; member of board of directors, Speedwell Services for Children, 1974-76. Member of Manhattan Community Board No. 9, 1972-73, academic council for the State University of New York, 1972-74, New York Urban League Manhattan Advisory Board, 1973-75, and National Education Advisory Committee and vice-director of Southeast Region of Statue of Liberty-Ellis Island Foundation, 1986. Consultant, Education Development Center, 1975—, Department of Health, Education and Welfare, 1977-79, National Research Council, 1979-80, and Grolier, Inc., 1979-82. Member of National Education Advisory Committee, Commission on the Bicentennial of the Constitution. *Member:* National Book Critics Circle, Authors League of America, Authors Guild, 100 Black Men, Phi Beta Kappa, Kappa Alpha Psi.

Awards, Honors

Notable Children's Book in the Field of Social Studies citations from *Social Education,* 1971, for *Revolutionaries: Agents of Change,* from *Social Studies,* 1972, for *Resistance: Profiles in Nonviolence* and *Profiles in Black Power,* and 1973, for *A Piece of the Power: Four Black Mayors,* from National Council for the Social Studies-Children's Book Council, 1975, for *Fighting Shirley Chisholm,* and 1976, for *The Creoles of Color of New Orleans* and *The Picture Life of Malcolm X,* and from Children's Book Council, 1978, for *The Life and Death of Martin Luther King, Jr.;* World Book Year Book literature for children citation, 1973, for *From Lew Alcindor to Kareem Abdul-Jabbar;* Books of the Year citations, Child Study Association of America, 1974, for *Adam Clayton Powell: Portrait of a Marching Black* and *Street Gangs: Yesterday and Today;* Books for Brotherhood bibliography citation, National Council of Christians and Jews book review committee, 1975, for *Adam Clayton Powell: Portrait of a Marching Black;* Spur Award finalist, Western Writers of America, 1975, for *The Creoles of Color of New Orleans;* Coretta Scott King Award and Books Chosen by Children citation, Children's Book Council, both 1977, both for *The Story of Stevie Wonder;* Woodson Outstanding Merit Award, National Council for the Social Studies, 1980, for *James Van DerZee: The Picture-Takin' Man;* American Society of Composers, Authors and Publishers-Deems Taylor Award, 1980, for *Scott Joplin;* Ambassador of Honor book, English-Speaking Union Books-Across-the-Sea, 1983, for *Bricktop;* Coretta Scott King Honorable Mention, 1984, for *Lena Horne;* American Library Association (ALA) Best Books for Young Adults citation, 1987, for *Black Music in America: A History through Its People;* Alabama Library Association best juvenile work citation, 1987, for "Count Your Way" series; "Bicentennial Reading, Viewing, Listening for Young Americans" citations, ALA and National Endowment for the Humanities, for *Street Gangs: Yesterday and Today, Ralph Bunche: A Most Reluctant Hero,* and *A Piece of the Power: Four Black Mayors;* certificates of appreciation, Joseph P. Kennedy Foundation, for work with the Special Olympics program; Coretta Scott King honor book for text, 1991, for *Black Dance in America: A History through Its People;* Parents Choice picture book award, 1992, and Hungry Mind YA nonfiction award, 1993, for *Rosa Parks: My Story;* Carter G. Woodson Award, 1994, for *The March on Washington,* and 1997, for *The Harlem Renaissance; Washington Post*/Children's Book Guild Nonfiction Award, 1994; Coretta Scott King honor book for text, 1997, for *The Harlem Renaissance* and 1998, for *Bayard Rustin: Behind the Scenes of the Civil Rights Movement;* Carter G. Woodson merit books, 1998, for *I Am Rosa Parks* and *Bayard Rustin: Behind the Scenes of the Civil Rights Movement.*

Writings

FOR YOUNG PEOPLE

Resistance: Profiles in Nonviolence, Doubleday, 1970.
Revolutionaries: Agents of Change, Lippincott, 1971.
The War and the Protest: Viet Nam, Doubleday, 1971.
Religions, Lippincott, 1973.
Witchcraft, Mysticism, and Magic in the Black World, Doubleday, 1974.
Street Gangs: Yesterday and Today, Hastings House, 1974.
Jobs in Business and Office, Lothrop, 1974.
The Creoles of Color of New Orleans, illustrated by Don Miller, Crowell, 1975.
The Consumer Movement, F. Watts, 1975.
Who Are the Handicapped?, Doubleday, 1978.
(With J. M. Stifle) *The Quiet Revolution: The Struggle for the Rights of Disabled Americans,* Crowell, 1979.
The New Americans: Vietnamese Boat People, Enslow, 1980.
Black Theater in America, Crowell, 1982.
The New Americans: Cuban Boat People, Enslow, 1982.
The Guardian Angels, Enslow, 1983.
(With David A. Walker) *Double Dutch,* Enslow, 1986.
Black Music in America: A History through Its People, Crowell, 1987.
(With Kathleen Benson) *The 60s Reader,* Viking, 1988.
(Editor) *Religions of the World,* Hippocrene Books, 1991.
The March on Washington, introduction by James Farmer, HarperCollins, 1993.
(Reteller) *The Headless Haunt and Other African-American Ghost Stories,* illustrated by Ben Otero, HarperCollins, 1994.
The Scottsboro Boys, Holt, 1994.
The Freedom Rides: Journey for Justice, Hyperion, 1995.
(With Kathleen Benson) *African Beginnings,* illustrated by Floyd Cooper, Lothrop, 1998.
Distinguished African American Political and Governmental Leaders, Oryx Press, 1999.
(With Kathleen Benson) *Bound for America: The Forced Migration of Africans to the New World,* illustrated by Floyd Cooper, Lothrop, 1999.
History of Rap, Hyperion, in press.
History of Reggae, Hyperion, in press.

BIOGRAPHIES; FOR YOUNG PEOPLE

A Piece of the Power: Four Black Mayors, Dial, 1972.
Profiles in Black Power, Doubleday, 1972.

Deep Like the Rivers: A Biography of Langston Hughes, 1902-1967, Holt, 1973.

Adam Clayton Powell: Portrait of a Marching Black, Dial, 1974.

Babe Ruth and Hank Aaron: The Home Run Kings, Lothrop, 1974.

Fighting Shirley Chisholm, Dial, 1975.

The Picture Life of Malcolm X, F. Watts, 1975.

Dr. J: A Biography of Julius Erving, Doubleday, 1975.

Pele: A Biography, Doubleday, 1976.

The Story of Stevie Wonder, Lothrop, 1976.

Always Movin' On: The Life of Langston Hughes, F. Watts, 1976.

Barbara Jordan, Dial, 1977.

The Life and Death of Martin Luther King, Jr., Lothrop, 1977.

From Lew Alcindor to Kareem Abdul-Jabbar, Lothrop, 1978.

George McGinnis: Basketball Superstar, Hastings, 1978.

Bob McAdoo: Superstar, Lothrop, 1978.

Andrew Young: Man with a Mission, Lothrop, 1979.

I'm Gonna Make You Love Me: The Story of Diana Ross, Dial, 1980.

"Magic": A Biography of Earvin Johnson, Enslow, 1982.

Sugar Ray Leonard, Lothrop, 1982.

Katherine Dunham, Coward-McCann, 1982.

About Michael Jackson, Enslow, 1985.

Diana Ross: Star Supreme, Viking, 1985.

Leaders of the Middle East, Enslow, 1985.

Corazon Aquino: Leader of the Philippines, Enslow, 1988.

The Magic Johnson Story, Enslow, 1988.

Shirley Temple Black: Actress to Ambassador, illustrated by Donna Ruff, Viking, 1988.

Sports Great Magic Johnson, Enslow, 1989.

I Am Somebody!: A Biography of Jesse Jackson, Enslow, 1992.

Thurgood Marshall: A Life for Justice, Holt, 1992.

The First Black Governor: Pinckney Benton Stewart Pinchback, Africa World Press, 1996.

Bayard Rustin: Behind the Scenes of the Civil Rights Movement, Hyperion, 1997.

FOR YOUNG PEOPLE; AS JIM HASKINS

Jokes from Black Folks, Doubleday, 1973.

Ralph Bunche: A Most Reluctant Hero, Hawthorn, 1974.

Your Rights, Past and Present: A Guide for Young People, Hawthorn, 1975.

Teen-Age Alcoholism, Hawthorn, 1976.

The Long Struggle: The Story of American Labor, Westminster, 1976.

Real Estate Careers, photographs by Chuck Freedman, F. Watts, 1978.

Gambling—Who Really Wins?, F. Watts, 1979.

James Van DerZee: The Picture-Takin' Man, illustrations by James Van DerZee, Dodd, Mead, 1979.

(With Pat Connolly) *The Child Abuse Help Book,* Addison-Wesley, 1981.

Werewolves, F. Watts, 1981.

(Editor) *The Filipino Nation,* three volumes, Grolier International, 1982.

(With J. M. Stifle) *Donna Summer: An Unauthorized Biography,* Little, Brown, 1983.

(With Kathleen Benson) *Space Challenger: The Story of Guion Bluford: An Authorized Biography,* Carolrhoda Books, 1984.

Break Dancing, Lerner, 1985.

The Statue of Liberty: America's Proud Lady, Lerner, 1986.

Bill Cosby: America's Most Famous Father, Walker, 1988.

(With Helen Crothers) *Scatman: An Authorized Biography of Scatman Crothers,* Morrow, 1991.

Outward Dreams: Black Inventors and Their Inventions, Walker, 1991.

Christopher Columbus: Admiral of the Ocean Sea, illustrated by Joe Lasker, Scholastic, 1991.

(With Rosa Parks) *Rosa Parks: My Story,* Dial, 1992.

Colin Powell: A Biography, Scholastic, 1992.

One More River to Cross: The Story of Twelve Black Americans, Scholastic, 1992.

I Have a Dream: The Life and Words of Martin Luther King, Jr., Millbrook Press, 1992.

The Day Martin Luther King, Jr. Was Shot: A Photo History of the Civil Rights Movement, Scholastic, 1992.

Amazing Grace: The Story Behind the Song, Millbrook Press, 1992.

Against All Opposition: Black Explorers in America, Walker, 1992.

Get on Board: The Story of the Underground Railroad, Scholastic, 1993.

(With Joann Biondi) *From Afar to Zulu: A Dictionary of African Cultures,* Walker, 1995.

The Day Fort Sumter Was Fired On: A Photo History of the Civil War, Scholastic, 1995.

Black Eagles: African Americans in Aviation, Scholastic, 1995.

(With Kathleen Benson) *Mario Lemieux: Beating the Odds,* Lerner, 1996.

Louis Farrakhan and the Nation of Islam, Walker, 1996.

The Harlem Renaissance, Millbrook Press, 1996.

Separate, but Not Equal: The Dream and the Struggle, Scholastic, 1997.

Power to the People: The Rise and Fall of the Black Panther Party, Simon and Schuster, 1997.

Spike Lee: By Any Means Necessary, Walker, 1997.

(With Rosa Parks) *I Am Rosa Parks,* illustrated by Wil Clay, Dial, 1997.

(Reteller) *Moaning Bones: African-American Ghost Stories,* illustrated by Felicia Marshall, Lothrop, 1998.

Black, Blue, & Grey: African Americans in the Civil War, Simon and Schuster, 1998.

(Editor) Otha Richard Sullivan, *African American Inventors,* Wiley, 1998.

African American Military Heroes, Wiley, 1998.

African American Entrepreneurs, Wiley, 1998.

The Exodusters, Millbrook Press, 1999.

(Editor) Brenda Wilkinson, *African American Women Writers,* Wiley, 1999.

The Geography of Hope: Black Exodus from the South after Reconstruction, Millbrook Press, 1999.

FOR CHILDREN; AS JIM HASKINS; "COUNT YOUR WAY" SERIES

Count Your Way through China, illustrated by Dennis Hackerman, Carolrhoda Books, 1987.

... *through Japan,* illustrated by Martin Skoro, Carolrhoda Books, 1987.

... *through Russia,* illustrated by Vera Mednikov, Carolrhoda Books, 1987.

... *through the Arab World,* illustrated by Dana Gustafson, Carolrhoda Books, 1987.

... *through Mexico,* illustrated by Helen Byers, Carolrhoda Books, 1989.

... *through Canada,* illustrated by Steve Michaels, Carolrhoda Books, 1989.

... *through Africa,* illustrated by Barbara Knutson, Carolrhoda Books, 1989.

... *through Korea,* illustrated by Dennis Hockerman, Carolrhoda Books, 1989.

... *through Israel,* illustrated by Rick Hanson, Carolrhoda Books, 1990.

... *through India,* illustrated by Liz Brenner Dodson, Carolrhoda Books, 1990.

... *through Italy,* illustrated by Beth Wright, Carolrhoda Books, 1990.

... *through Germany,* illustrated by Helen Byers, Carolrhoda Books, 1990.

(With Kathleen Benson) ... *through Ireland,* illustrated by Beth Wright, Carolrhoda Books, 1996.

(With Kathleen Benson) ... *through Greece,* illustrated by Janice Lee Porter, Carolrhoda Books, 1996.

(With Kathleen Benson) ... *through France,* illustrated by Andrea Shine, Carolrhoda Books, 1996.

(With Kathleen Benson) ... *through Brazil,* illustrations by Liz Brenner Dodson, Carolrhoda Books, 1996.

OTHER NONFICTION; AS JIM HASKINS

Diary of a Harlem Schoolteacher, Grove, 1969, 2nd edition, Stein & Day, 1979.

(Editor) *Black Manifesto for Education,* introduction by Mario Fantini, Morrow, 1973.

(With Hugh F. Butts) *The Psychology of Black Language,* Barnes & Noble, 1973.

Snow Sculpture and Ice Carving, Macmillan, 1974.

The Cotton Club, Random House, 1977, 2nd edition, New American Library, 1984.

(With Kathleen Benson and Ellen Inkelis) *The Great American Crazies,* Condor, 1977.

Voodoo & Hoodoo: Their Tradition and Craft as Revealed by Actual Practitioners, Stein & Day, 1978.

(With Kathleen Benson) *The Stevie Wonder Scrapbook,* Grosset & Dunlap, 1978.

Richard Pryor, a Man and His Madness: A Biography, Beaufort Books, 1984.

Queen of the Blues: A Biography of Dinah Washington, Morrow, 1987.

OTHER

Pinckney Benton Stewart Pinchback, Macmillan, 1973.

A New Kind of Joy: The Story of the Special Olympics, Doubleday, 1976.

(Contributor) Emily Mumford, *Understanding Human Behavior in Health and Illness,* Williams & Wilkins, 1977.

(With Kathleen Benson) *Scott Joplin,* Doubleday, 1978.

(Contributor) *New York Kid's Catalog,* Doubleday, 1979.

(Contributor) *Notable American Women Supplement,* Radcliffe College, 1979.

(With Bricktop) *Bricktop,* Atheneum, 1983.

Lena Horne, Coward-McCann, 1983.

(With Kathleen Benson) *Lena: A Personal and Professional Biography of Lena Horne,* Stein & Day, 1984.

(With Kathleen Benson) *Nat King Cole,* Stein & Day, 1984.

(Contributor) Jerry Brown, *Clearings in the Thicket: An Alabama Humanities Reader,* Mercer University Press, 1985.

(With Kathleen Benson) *Aretha: A Personal and Professional Biography of Aretha Franklin,* Stein & Day, 1986.

Mabel Mercer: A Life, Atheneum, 1987.

Winnie Mandela: Life of Struggle, Putnam, 1988.

(With N. R. Mitgang) *Mr. Bojangles: The Biography of Bill Robinson,* Morrow, 1988.

(With Lionel Hampton) *Hamp: An Autobiography,* Warner, 1989, reissued with discography by Vincent H. Pelote, Pengin, 1993.

India Under Indira and Rajiv Gandhi, Enslow, 1989.

Black Dance in America: A History through Its People, Crowell, 1990.

The Methodists, Hippocrene, 1992.

(With Joann Biondi) *Hippocrene U.S.A. Guide to Historic Black South: Historic Sights, Cultural Centers, and Musical Happenings of the African-American South,* Hippocrene, 1993.

(With Joann Biondi) *Hippocrene U.S.A. Guide to Black New York,* Hippocrene, 1994.

Also contributor to *Author in the Kitchen* and to *Children and Books,* 4th edition, 1976. Contributor of articles and reviews to periodicals, including *American Visions, Now, Arizona English Bulletin, Rolling Stone, Children's Book Review Service, Western Journal of Black Studies, Elementary English, Amsterdam News, New York Times Book Review, Afro-Hawaii News,* and *Gainesville Sun.*

Adaptations

Diary of a Harlem Schoolteacher has been recorded by Recordings for the Blind; *The Cotton Club* inspired the 1984 film of the same name.

Work in Progress

Blacks in Colonial America, for Lothrop.

Sidelights

James S. Haskins is the award-winning author of scores of nonfiction titles for young readers. His topics have ranged from current affairs to biography, his subjects from the Civil Rights movement to Stevie Wonder. "Most of my books and articles are about black subjects—black history, black people," Haskins wrote in an entry for *Something about the Author Autobiography Series (SAAS).* "Partly that's because I remember being a child and not having many books about black people to read. I want children today, black and white, to be able to find books about black people and black history in case they want to read them." In the same *SAAS* entry,

Haskins noted his preference for "fact" books over fiction: "I have always liked true stories better than made up ones," Haskins wrote. "Every single one of my books is nonfiction and I have no desire whatever to write fiction, although I admire the people who write fiction well."

Haskins's preference for black subjects, as well as his penchant for the facts, are direct results of his upbringing in the segregated South in the 1940s and 1950s. With no black hospitals available to his family, Haskins was born at home in Demopolis, Alabama, in 1941. No record was kept of his birth and he had no birth certificate until later in life, when he needed such an affidavit for practical matters such as a Social Security card or a passport. But white society was not merely indifferent to blacks. "I was born into a society in which blacks were in deep trouble if they forgot about the real world," Haskins noted in *SAAS*. "For if they daydreamed and were caught off-guard, they could pay dearly." As a child, Haskins had to be ever vigilant not to wander into white neighborhoods and not to enter white diners or drink from whites-only water fountains. Haskins's youth

SCHOLASTIC BIOGRAPHY

COLIN POWELL

A BIOGRAPHY

JIM HASKINS

SCHOLASTIC

Award-winning biographer Haskins penned the story of the much-admired contemporary African-American military leader. (Cover photo by Cindy Karp.)

was indeed overshadowed by the cold, hard facts of racial discrimination.

Education was segregated as well, and not only in the schools. Denied access to the public library, Haskins found reading material in the volumes of an encyclopedia his mother slowly acquired at the local supermarket as a reward for buying a certain amount of groceries. More books came his way from a white woman for whom Haskins's mother worked, but from early on his interest was primarily in matters of fact and nonfiction. His formal education emphasized blacks' contributions to the world, for in the absence of adequate books, his teachers used contemporary materials—magazine and newspaper articles—to teach their pupils about the world. During Haskins's youth, teaching was the highest profession to which most blacks could aspire, and he looked up to those who taught him, unconsciously viewing them as role models.

When he was in high school, Haskins and his mother moved to Boston, where he attended the prestigious Boston Latin School; but upon graduation he decided to return to the South, to the all-black Alabama State University in Montgomery. Here he first became politically and personally involved in the Civil Rights movement, taking part in the Montgomery Bus Boycott when Rosa Parks refused to give up her bus seat to a white man and was arrested. He came into contact with a young Baptist minister, Martin Luther King, Jr., who led the boycott and later was a dominant force in the Civil Rights movement. Arrested for marching in protest in downtown Montgomery after the incarceration of several civil rights activists, Haskins was expelled from Alabama State and subsequently enrolled in Georgetown University in Washington, DC, where he earned his undergraduate degree. Unfinished business drew him back to Alabama State where he earned a second degree, in history. After graduate studies in New Mexico, Haskins settled in New York where he worked as a journalist and stock broker. Soon, however, he realized that what he really wanted to do was teach.

It was his teaching career that initially led Haskins to writing. Working in special education at a Harlem school, he became aware of the shortage of information for young readers about current events. He was also intensely concerned about youth welfare, so much so that, at the instigation of a social worker, he began recording his impressions of teaching disadvantaged children in Harlem. The subsequent account was published as an adult book, *Diary of a Harlem Schoolteacher,* in 1969, and won praise from many critics, including Ronald Gross who remarked in the *New York Times Book Review* that while the book was "plain, concrete, unemotional, and unliterary," it commanded concern by its "truthfulness alone." Gross concluded that Haskins's diary "is like a weapon—cold, blunt, painful."

Publication of this first book opened other literary doors for Haskins when publishers approached him to see if he would be interested in writing books for children. Haskins knew immediately the sort of books he would write: "books about current events and books about important black people, so that students could understand the larger world around them through books written at a level they could understand," as he explained in *SAAS*. Early books dealt with subjects such as nonviolent protest; with profiles of black political leaders; with studies of social phenomena such as gangs, gambling, the disabled, and child abuse; and with all aspects of contemporary African-American history.

Haskins's first work for younger readers was *Resistance: Profiles in Nonviolence,* an attempt to place the nonviolent tactics of Martin Luther King, Jr. into historical perspective. This was followed by *A Piece of the Power: Four Black Mayors* and a historical work, *The Creoles of Color of New Orleans.* Such books set the tone for Haskins's subsequent work—well-crafted and informative examinations of the black experience in America. Though Haskins's works reflect the entire racial spectrum, it is this exploration and illumination of African Americans that continues to be his hallmark. His 1974 adult title, *The Cotton Club,* looked at the famous Harlem nightclub of the same name and was later adapted for a film of the same title. Meanwhile, Haskins moved from teaching in public high schools to college-level instruction in nonfiction writing and juvenile literature, eventually taking a professorship in English at the University of Florida at Gainesville.

Biography soon became a major focus of Haskins's works, and his subjects have included not only political figures but also sports heroes and entertainers. He has written books on Rosa Parks, Martin Luther King, Jr., Malcolm X, Adam Clayton Powell, Ralph Bunche, Shirley Chisholm, and Barbara Jordan among others, initially avoiding the common sports biography. "But when Hank Aaron's home-run total started creeping up on Babe Ruth's record, and so many people seemed to be taking sides as to who was the better hitter, and the better man, I could not resist doing *Babe Ruth and Hank Aaron: The Home Run Kings,*" Haskins explained in his *SAAS* entry. "I got more 'fan mail' from children who had read that book than I had gotten for all the other books put together," Haskins commented in *SAAS*. "That saddened me a bit, but eventually I realized that it doesn't matter so much *what* kids read as it does *that* they read."

Some of Haskins's most popular biographies are focused primarily on black sports figures and entertainers. His biography of the rock singer Diana Ross, *I'm Gonna Make You Love Me,* brings the reader not only into the singer's professional life, but also into the era that shaped her. "Haskins creates a vivid picture of Detroit," noted Diane Haas in *School Library Journal,* "of the South and the conditions which forced blacks to migrate northward." Likewise lauded was Haskins's biography of Lena Horne which *Voice of Youth Advocates* dubbed a "moving story of a beautiful and sensitive dancer, singer, and actress," and his *Bill Cosby: America's Most Famous Father,* which *Kirkus Reviews* called an "unconventional biography of a multi-faceted performer." For his *The Story of Stevie Wonder,* Haskins spent

Haskins compiled accounts of more than thirty African Americans from the eighteenth century to the present who have fought bigotry and adversity to become successful entrepreneurs.

several days with the blind musician, amazed by Wonder's continual emphasis on rhythm, even in the smallest aspects of his life. Haskins recalled in *SAAS* that Wonder was fond of "beating on the table with a fork or making rhythms with his feet on the steps."

Haskins's sports biographies have included a look at basketball players, such as in *"Magic": A Biography of Earvin Johnson.* Linda W. Callaghan commented in a *Booklist* review that "Coaches, teammates, Johnson, and his family are portrayed with warmth and depth, becoming real people, not just personalities." Other sports figures Haskins has profiled include the boxer Sugar Ray Leonard, and baseball great Bob McAdoo, while other popular subjects that have found illumination at Haskins's hands deal with black culture. His *Black Theater in America* was later joined by the award-winning *Black Music in America,* which traced musical roots from slave times through spirituals, ragtime, blues, jazz, gospel and soul. Jeffrey Cooper, writing in *Kliatt,* announced that "It's difficult to imagine the library that could not find a place in its shelves for this clear and concise history of African-American music." The story of African-American contributions to the world of dance was also documented in *Black Dance in America.* Other books dealing with music include biographies of Mr. Bojangles and Scott Joplin, along with studies of reggae and rap. Haskins investigated the origins of a popular hymn in his 1992 *Amazing Grace: The Story Behind the Song,* a book which *Booklist*'s Ilene Cooper called "unique and uplifting." In his *Spike Lee: By Any Means Necessary,* Haskins put together a profile of the well-known filmmaker.

Yet Haskins also continues to give expression to the full gamut of black achievement, both in the U.S. and around the world. The story of an apartheid activist was chronicled in *Winnie Mandela: Life of Struggle,* a book, *Kirkus Reviews* concluded, that "readers won't forget." Important figures in the Civil Rights movement such as Rosa Parks and Martin Luther King, Jr., have been profiled more than once by Haskins. His *The Day Martin Luther King, Jr. Was Shot* uses that attention-grabbing title to present "a photo history of the African American struggle from the time of slavery through today," according to Hazel Rochman in *Booklist.* The life of the first African American Supreme Court Justice was presented in *Thurgood Marshall: A Life for Justice.* Marshall, who fought segregation and racism through the courts, was involved in such landmark cases as

Brown v. The Board of Education, which dealt with school desegregation. *Publishers Weekly* commented that this "energetic portrait of the venerable jurist is also an overview of civil rights advances since 1908," while *Booklist*'s Karen Hutt concluded that the "historical, social, and political perspective Haskins incorporates makes the work an illuminating, in-depth portrait of a courageous leader as well as an excellent resource for study of the civil rights movement." In *I Am Somebody!,* the contemporary political leader, Jesse Jackson, is profiled in an "incisive biography that relates its subject's strengths and flaws in a balanced manner," according to Jeanette Lambert in *School Library Journal.*

Haskins has also written a score of books centered on pivotal historical times and issues. *The March on Washington* recounts that momentous occasion in 1963 when a quarter million people marched from the Washington Monument to the Lincoln Memorial in

Haskins and coauthor Benson employ the Portuguese words for the numerals from one to ten to teach young readers about the country of Brazil. (Cover illustration by Liz Brenner Dodson.)

support of racial equality, and according to *Horn Book*'s Ellen Fader, "Haskins provides a lucid, in-depth, and moving study" of the march and the work that led up to it. Cultural history was at the heart of *The Harlem Renaissance*, Haskins's recreation of the flowering of black music, dance, theater, and literature that took place between 1916 and 1940. Kathleen Murphy Campbell, writing in *Voice of Youth Advocates*, commented that this book is "well-written and informative" and "will capture the interest of anyone who enjoys art or history." In *Power to the People*, Haskins turned to the rise and fall of the Black Panther Party, the radical 1960s political organization, in a book that is a "unique source of information on an important period of our history," according to *School Library Journal* reviewer Jonathan Betz-Zall. Haskins has also focussed on the hidden history of African Americans and their contributions to society. In *Black, Blue, & Grey,* he examined the participation of African American soldiers in the American Civil War, a book marked by "diligent research and intelligent writing," according to *Kirkus Reviews*. In the *African American Entrepreneurs* and *African American Military Heroes*, Haskins carried his black-history lesson even further.

Whatever his subject, Haskins sticks to the facts. As the saying goes, "the truth will set you free," and James Haskins has spent a career setting the historical record straight about the achievements of African Americans. In doing so, he has also attempted to give a balanced and fair picture of lives and times. "Whoever I write about," Haskins explained in *SAAS*, "I try very hard to make that person seem like a real person, with troubles as well as triumphs, and it pleases me that, more often than not, when a young person writes to me about a book, he or she mentions the grit along with the glitter. They are inspired as much by hardships overcome as by victories won. To inspire young people to overcome the obstacles that confront them is, next to simply inspiring them to read, my purpose in writing these books."

Works Cited

Betz-Zall, Jonathan, review of *Power to the People: The Rise and Fall of the Black Panther Party, School Library Journal,* March, 1997, p. 201.

Review of *Bill Cosby: American's Most Favorite Father, Kirkus Reviews,* June 1, 1988, pp. 827-28.

Review of *Black, Blue, & Grey: African Americans in the Civil War, Kirkus Reviews,* December 1, 1997, pp. 1775-76.

Callaghan, Linda W., review of *"Magic": A Biography of Earvin Johnson, Booklist,* February 1, 1982, pp. 709-10.

Campbell, Kathleen Murphy, review of *The Harlem Renaissance, Voice of Youth Advocates,* December, 1996, p. 288.

Cooper, Ilene, review of *Amazing Grace: The Story Behind the Song, Booklist,* January 15, 1992, p. 115.

Cooper, Jeffrey, review of *Black Music in America: A History through Its People, Kliatt,* May, 1993, p. 36.

Fader, Ellen, review of *The March on Washington, Horn Book,* July-August, 1993, pp. 477-78.

Gross, Ronald, review of *Diary of a Harlem Schoolteacher, New York Times Book Review,* December 6, 1970.

Haas, Diane, review of *I'm Gonna Make You Love Me: The Story of Diana Ross, School Library Journal,* November, 1980, p. 86.

Haskins, Jim, essay in *Something about the Author Autobiography Series,* Volume 4, Gale, 1987, pp. 197-209.

Hutt, Karen, review of *Thurgood Marshall: A Life for Justice, Booklist,* July, 1992, p. 1939.

Lambert, Jeanette, review of *I Am Somebody!: The Biography of Jesse Jackson, School Library Journal,* August, 1992, pp. 181-82.

Review of *Lena Horne, Voice of Youth Advocates,* April, 1984, pp. 46-47.

Rochman, Hazel, review of *The Day Martin Luther King, Jr. Was Shot: A Photo History of the Civil Rights Movement, Booklist,* February, 1992, p. 1024.

Review of *Thurgood Marshall: A Life for Justice, Publishers Weekly,* July 20, 1992, p. 252.

Review of *Winnie Mandela: Life of Struggle, Kirkus Reviews,* April 15, 1988, p. 618.

For More Information See

BOOKS

Black Authors and Illustrators of Children's Books, Garland, 1992.

Brown, Jerry, *Clearings in the Thicket: An Alabama Humanities Reader,* Mercer University Press, 1985.

Children's Literature Review, Volume 39, Gale, 1996, pp. 29-73.

Sixth Book of Junior Authors and Illustrators, edited by Sally Holmes Holtze, Wilson, 1989, pp. 115-17.

PERIODICALS

Booklist, September 1, 1996, p. 116; February 15, 1997, p. 1020; March 15, 1997, p. 1233; May 1, 1997, p. 1488; February 15, 1998, p. 995.

Bulletin of the Center for Children's Books, July, 1996, p. 375; May, 1997, p. 323; April, 1998, p. 281.

Kirkus Reviews, January 15, 1998, pp. 111, 112; December 1, 1998, p. 1733.

New York Times Book Review, February 16, 1997, p. 25.

Publishers Weekly, December 8, 1997, p. 74; February 2, 1998, p. 92.

School Library Journal, January, 1999, p. 142.

Voice of Youth Advocates, October, 1994, p. 230; February, 1995, p. 358; June, 1995, p. 132; August, 1995, p. 182; August, 1996, p. 150; August, 1997, p. 202; October, 1997, p. 264; February, 1998, p. 402.

—*Sketch by J. Sydney Jones*

*   *   *

HASKINS, Jim
See HASKINS, James S.

HIGGINS, Simon (Richard) 1958-

Personal

Born November 21, 1958, in Aldershot, England; son of Aubrey Charles Roff (a military officer) and Marjorie Helen (a stenographer; maiden name, Stevens) Higgins; married Anne Catherine Ennis (a visual artist), October 27, 1979; children: Bronwyn, James. *Hobbies and other interests:* History, archaeology, Oriental and Native American culture, experimental technology, martial arts, science fiction, Shakespearean tragedy, computer game design, rain forest restoration and terra-forming.

Addresses

Home—P.O. Box 140, Murwillumbah, New South Wales 2484, Australia. *Agent*—Jenny Darling and Associates, P.O. Box 235, Richmond, Victoria 3121, Australia.

Career

Police officer working as patrol officer, breath analyst, and prosecutor, Adelaide, Australia, 1986-94, leaving service as senior constable; private investigator, Adelaide, 1994-96; novelist, 1996—. *Member:* Queensland Writers' Centre, Gold Coast Writers, Inc., Northern Rivers Writers' Centre.

Writings

Doctor Id (young adult mystery novel), Random House (Milsons Point, Australia), 1998.

Contributor to magazines, including *Police Journal* and *South Australian Manager,* and *Viewpoint.*

Work in Progress

Cybercage, a technological crime thriller and sequel to *Doctor Id; Thunderfish,* a young adult sea adventure; *Beyond the Shaking Time,* a young adult adventure fantasy.

Sidelights

Simon Higgins told *SATA:* "Writing became an obsession for me at an early age, I think because my mother read to me—a rich literary diet of Greek and Celtic hero myths and classic adventure stories. My mother was a gifted storyteller herself, and I grew up hearing fascinat-

Simon Higgins

ing tales of my parents' lives in India, Africa, Cyprus, and other exotic locations. Both the cooking and conversation at our house were multicultural and, like our decor and ornaments, they were incidental facts of life, neither a fad nor an issue. My parents would sometimes banter in Hindi, yet they were also very British in both speech and personal culture. It was a great atmosphere for an embryonic writer, and I remain grateful to them for it to this day.

"I was first published at the age of ten in a national poetry contest, but then, like many teenagers lurching uneasily into adulthood, I proceeded to lose track of my inner self, somehow bumbling, after a decade of drifting, into the unlikely world of law enforcement. A respected police partner once summed up my time in that scene most deftly, with a quote from Dickens: 'It was the best of times, it was the worst of times.'

"Fortunately, I garnered some useful life skills from that decade before relocating the real me and reinventing myself as a writer. Because of this long journey back to identity, I often sign books for young adults with my maxim, 'Chase that dream!' I have no regrets, however, as those 'bests' and 'worsts' of that season in my life have made me who I am, and memory-driven inspirations are now allies, not personal demons, though the transformation took time and the love and support of my family to achieve.

"While writing as an adult began for me as self-prescribed therapy for stress, it is now a joyful, consuming passion. My abiding interest is the impact of technology and societal change on the human condition, particularly our ancient drives which pull us—at times—in opposite directions. In moments they make us the hero or civilized, conscience-bound peacemaker of our own unique story, at other times the villain or guest barbarian. I am fascinated by the timely dynamics thrown into that timeless mix: is our destiny marriage to the machine, or is the next step in human evolution a more spiritual and enlightened one, perhaps in direct reaction to the silicon invasion we all face?

"As a writer I strive to examine these and related issues, and to use them as a context for creating intelligent entertainment—and hopefully in some small fragments, even art. I try to look at our current turning point in history with insight, compassion, and optimism. I also take perverse pride in relentlessly doing something periodically unfashionable or politically incorrect: unashamedly highlighting—through fictional characters—the defiant, wonderful *positives* about human nature and the hope they offer for the future. I think writers like myself, so eminently qualified by their backgrounds to be *pessimists,* are the logical people to underscore these truths.

"My work has one predominant message. There will be battles, some of them terrible and costly, but in the end our species will grow up, to a future worth fighting for. It will be a future richly deserved by our children, and by the brave, hopeful child within us all."

HILTON, Margaret Lynette 1946- (Nette Hilton, Virginia Baxter, Anne Hilton-Bruce)

Personal

Born September 9, 1946, in Traralgon, Victoria, Australia; daughter of Stanley James (a carpenter and builder) and Margaret Irene (a bookkeeper and artist) Davidson; first marriage dissolved; second marriage to Ronald James Hilton (a teacher); children: (first marriage) Lachlan Barney, Emily Kathleen; (second marriage) Nicolette Anne, Melissa June (stepdaughter). *Education:* Alexander Mackie Teachers' College, Wollongong, Australia, teaching certificate, 1969. *Religion:* Christian. *Hobbies and other interests:* Music, playing the guitar.

Addresses

Home and office—Lot 3, Broken Head Rd., Broken Head, New South Wales, Australia 2481. *Electronic mail*—nette@om.com.au.

Career

Author and educator. New South Wales Department of Education, primary school teacher, 1967-91. Full-time writer, 1995—. Worked variously as a governess, a receptionist for an Italian company, a clerk for a taxation department, and a receptionist/telephonist for a chain store. Has also held school workshops and seminars on writing. *Member:* Author's Guild, Children's Book Council of Australia, Fellowship of Australian Writers, Australian Society of Authors.

Awards, Honors

Honor Book, Children's Book Council of Australia, 1988, for *The Long Red Scarf,* and 1993, for *The Web;* Shortlist, Australian Picture Book of the Year, 1990, for *A Proper Little Lady.* Hilton has also been awarded a literary fellowship from the Australian Arts Council, 1990, and a New Zealand Family Workers prize.

Writings

PICTURE BOOKS; AS NETTE HILTON

The Long Red Scarf, illustrated by Margaret Power, Omnibus (Adelaide), 1987, Orchard (New York City), 1988.

Dirty Dave the Bushranger, Five Mile Press (Knoxfield, Australia), 1987, Orchard, 1988.

Toys, illustrated by Craig Smith, Macmillan (Melbourne), 1988, Nelson, 1991.

Prince Lachlan, illustrated by Ann James, Omnibus, 1989, Orchard, 1990.

A Proper Little Lady, illustrated by Cathy Wilcox, HarperCollins, 1989, Orchard, 1990.

A Monstrous Story, illustrated by Donni Carter, Five Mile Press, 1989.

Good Morning, Isobel, illustrated by Robert Roennfeldt, Rigby (Australia), 1989.

The Ombly-Gum Chasing Game, illustrated by Lucinda Hunnam, Mimosa (Australia), 1990.

Alison Wendlebury, illustrated by Virginia Barrett, Mimosa, 1990.

Would You?, illustrated by David Legge, Hodder & Stoughton (Australia), 1991.

The Gift, illustrated by Craig Smith, Mimosa, 1991.

Andrew Jessup, illustrated by Cathy Wilcox, Walter McVitty, 1991, Ticknor & Fields (New York City), 1993.

FICTION FOR CHILDREN; AS NETTE HILTON

The Friday Card, Angus & Robertson, 1988, HarperCollins, 1988.

Everybody Dances, Victorian Department of Education (Australia), 1990.

First Impressions, Victorian Department of Education, 1990.

Carnations, Curriculum Development (Australia), 1990.

Boomers, Curriculum Development, 1990.

Competitions, Victorian Department of Education, 1990.

Square Pegs (young adult fiction), Angus & Robertson, 1991, HarperCollins, 1991.

The Web, illustrated by Kerry Millard, Angus & Robertson, 1991, HarperCollins, 1991.

My Great Grandma, Hodder & Stoughton, 1992.

The New Kid, Angus & Robertson, 1991, HarperCollins, 1991.

The Belonging of Emmaline Harris, Penguin (London), 1994.

A Frilling Time, Angus & Robertson, 1994, HarperCollins, 1994.

Hiccups, Angus & Robertson, 1994, HarperCollins, 1994.

The Foundling, illustrated by Gwen Harrison, Angus & Robertson, 1995, HarperCollins, 1995.

Four Eyes, Angus & Robertson, 1995, HarperCollins, 1995.

Seeing Things, Angus & Robertson, 1995, HarperCollins, 1995.

FICTION FOR YOUNG ADULTS; AS VIRGINIA BAXTER

Abigail, Angus & Robertson (Sydney, Australia), 1995, HarperCollins, 1995.

Desley, Angus & Robertson, 1995, HarperCollins, 1995.

Fran, Angus & Robertson, 1995, HarperCollins, 1995.

Lainie, Angus & Robertson, 1995, HarperCollins, 1995.

Sandy, Angus & Robertson, 1995, HarperCollins, 1995.

Molly, Angus & Robertson, 1995, HarperCollins, 1995.

FICTION FOR ADULTS; AS ANNE HILTON-BRUCE

Someone Came Knocking, Macmillan, 1995.

Somebody's Watching, Macmillan, 1996.

Whisper Who Dares, Macmillan, 1997.

OTHER

Jonathan's Story, Omnibus, 1989.

What a Ball, Omnibus, 1990.

Wrinkles, Omnibus, 1990.

Wake Up, Isobel!, Macmillan, 1996.

Tough Lester, Omnibus, 1997.

Hothouse Flowers, HarperCollins, 1997.

Strays, Koala Press, 1997.

Margaret Lynette Hilton

Clouded Edges: Five Teenagers, Five Stories, Five Lives Take Shape, HarperCollins, 1997.

A Stuffy Old Bear, Koala Press, 1998.

A Ghost of a Chance, Penguin, 1998.

Watch Out, William, Omnibus, 1998.

Contributor of short stories to anthologies, including *Bittersweet,* Penguin, 1992; *Bizarre,* Omnibus, 1992; *The Blue Dress,* Octopus, 1992; *State of the Heart,* Penguin, 1992; *Weird,* Omnibus, 1992; *Clever Company and Other Stories,* Curriculum Development, 1992; *Bedtime Stories,* Hodder & Stoughton, 1997. Author of *Napoleon,* a picture book commissioned by Film Australia to accompany the release of a film by the same name. *The Web* was translated into German by Cecilie Dressler Veelag (Hamburg), 1995, and into Spanish by Cecilia Olivares Mansuy, Fondo de Cultura Economica (Mexico), 1997.

Adaptations

Square Pegs was serialized on ABC Radio, Western Australia, 1992, and *The Web* was released on audio cassette in 1994. *The Belonging of Emmaline Harris* was adapted for the stage.

Work in Progress

The Collecting of Timothy Taylor, a picture book, for HarperCollins; *Urban Fever* (working title), a picture book; *The Appleyard Animals,* juvenile fiction; *Dear Dead Brother,* for HarperCollins, and *Fee Donnelly* (working title), both adult novels; *The Hicksville Horror,* for Lothian; a young adult novel featuring aboriginal history; a book on teenage runaways; a study of aboriginal life in contemporary Australia.

Sidelights

An Australian author of picture books and fiction who creates books for preschoolers, primary graders, and adolescents as well as adults, Nette Hilton is praised as a writer of range and variety whose works celebrate equality and individuality in a sympathetic, stylish manner. Although only a handful of her titles—mainly picture books—have been published in the United States, the prolific author, who is considered a major writer in Australia, has achieved popularity in this country and in the United Kingdom as well as in her native land. Hilton is often acknowledged for creating witty tales, both realistic and fantastic, that feature child and adult protagonists who perform capably while remaining true to themselves. In addition, the author, who is often praised for her observant and perceptive qualities, writes sensitive stories dealing with relationships among young people as well as young people and adults. Hilton's books, according to Liza Bliss in *School Library Journal,* go "beyond limitations traditionally accorded to gender and age." The author, whose signature themes center on self-reliance and nonstereo-

Hilton challenges traditional gender roles in her story about Grandpa, who decides to knit a scarf for himself when no one else will do it. (From The Long Red Scarf, *illustrated by Margaret Power.)*

typical behavior, often features boys and girls who possess self-confidence and ingenuity and adults who challenge traditional sexual roles. For example, Hilton's first work, *The Long Red Scarf,* is a picture book that describes how Grandpa learns to knit. Her next book, *Dirty Dave the Bushranger,* also features a man with a nontraditional talent: sewing. In *A Proper Little Lady,* tomboy Annabelle, who attempts to become refined by dressing in formal attire, learns that she can still be "a proper little lady" in jeans and sneakers.

Often noted for her inventive use of language, Hilton favors spare texts that incorporate onomatopoeia, sound effects, rhythm, and repetition, elements noted for making her books enjoyable both for individual reading and reading aloud; she has also written short stories as well as tales in rhyme. As Millicent Jones noted in *Reading Time,* "Nette Hilton has a flair for writing so that stories and reading are fun." Hilton's books are often graced with pictures by some of Australia's most prominent illustrators, such as Margaret Power, Roland Harvey, and Cathy Wilcox. Acknowledged for her humor, which ranges from restrained to rollicking, Hilton is also credited for the panache and poignancy of several of her works. Hilton is generally considered an author of charming, captivating books that acknowledge the feelings of children and young people while introducing them to the possibilities beyond traditional roles.

In her essay in *Something about the Author Autobiography Series (SAAS),* Hilton wrote, "I think it took a long time for me to find my place in space, to find the little hole in the world that has all the right bends and bumps to fit me, Nette Hilton. Even now I sometimes find a rough corner or edge that seems to be nudging too hard at me, and I have to rethink who I am and what I am in order that I might be comfortable again. When I was young, a child, this was something I hadn't discovered— I think I must have always been trying to fit into someone else's space and so, when I look back, it seems as though I never really fitted anywhere at all. I was not unhappy. It's just that when I think back over my childhood this is the way that I see myself."

Born in the small town of Traralgon in Victoria, Australia, Hilton was the daughter of a builder, Stanley Davidson, which meant, as the author wrote in her essay, "that we moved around when I was young." Until she was eleven, Hilton lived in Bairnsdale, Victoria, and she later wrote that "my years there in school were possibly the happiest that I can remember." One of her teachers, Miss Martin, read the class *Snugglepot and Cuddlepie,* a story by May Gibbs about bush fairies that is considered a classic of Australian children's literature. Hilton noted, "So well did May Gibbs illustrate her books, making use of her own new landscape, this strange foreign country that she took to be her own, that they have always stayed with me, and even now I take care walking through the bush for fear that the bad Banksia men may get me." When she became a teacher, Hilton read *Snugglepot and Cuddlepie* to her own first graders. When she was in sixth grade, Hilton wrote plays and original stories under the guidance of her teacher Mr. Macklehenny, who, the

The protagonist of Hilton's picture book is downcast when her best friend moves away, until the possibility for a new friendship arises. (From Andrew Jessup, *written by Hilton and illustrated by Cathy Wilcox.)*

author wrote in *SAAS,* "gave us the opportunity to read our own stories (we called them compositions) aloud to the class, and our efforts were always applauded. We really were just a bunch of country kids and he did very well to have us all so involved with art and literature." In addition to her literary pursuits, Hilton spent a lot of time in imaginative play, pretending with her friends that she was one of the "Famous Five," the child detectives from the Enid Blyton mysteries; putting on concerts for the neighborhood preschoolers; and having adventures in corrals and on the local race course.

Hilton wrote in her autobiographical essay, "We [Hilton, her sister Anne, and her brother Jim] certainly had great support from my parents." Her mother, Margaret David-son, was a talented artist who, the author mused, "must have been forever making dress-up clothes for us," while her father Stanley Davidson took great joy in introduc-ing his children to the flora and fauna of the Australian bush, much of which he would bring home. Hilton

wrote, "I have inherited my father's love of the environment. It wasn't called environment back then. It was simply nature study, but we always seemed to be involved in some way with animals or plants and it was always with pleasure." Developing a passion for reading, Hilton spent many hours in the town library. Whenever she would get a book, the author noted in *SAAS,* "I simply zoned out and would live, along with the characters, whatever adventure they were involved in at the time." When Hilton was about ten, she became ill and had to recuperate for a long time in the hospital and at home. "I believe," she wrote in *SAAS,* "all that time in bed certainly improved my imagination. So many hours I could fill making up stories in my head with me as the hero." She added, "I don't think I ever really fitted the role of the princess in distress—there wasn't a whole lot to do while you were waiting to be rescued. Much better fun to be the rescuer."

At eleven, Hilton moved to Sydney, New South Wales, where it was hoped that the warmer climate would improve her health. "In many ways," she wrote in her autobiographical essay, "leaving Bairnsdale was leaving behind my childhood. All those easy days of friends and knowing everyone and flip-flopping along and not being afraid of high school vanished when I became the newcomer in the city." Hilton found adjustment to city life difficult and new friendships hard to make. It took her almost a full year to make friends who were more than acquaintances, but when she met Beth and Sue, two girls who shared the carriage with Hilton on her way to high school, they became lifelong friends. The girls experimented with makeup and shared books like *Gone with the Wind* with one another. "In retrospect," the author wrote, "Sue and Beth and I were probably all misfits and I marvel that we found each other." When Hilton finished high school in 1963, she was the youngest person in her class. "I guess," she noted in *SAAS*, "this explains to me now why I seemed to be so out of step with everyone else."

While in high school, Hilton had written a comic play that was received poorly by her teacher, an experience that made her put aside creative writing for a while. However, in her senior year, a different instructor gave her an "A" on her term paper in English and the same final grade in the course; she later described this in *SAA* as "the first inkling that perhaps my talents lay in writing." After graduation, Hilton went to work in various businesses, including a taxation office, before traveling to the outback of New South Wales to become the governess for a five-year-old boy. Although she was homesick, Hilton threw herself into her job; finished with lessons by lunchtime, she became a catcher for lamb markings, a tractor driver, a cook, and a first-aid officer, all without any training. Anxious to hear news from home and to share what she called in *SAAS* "the experiences that were so foreign to all that we knew" with her family, Hilton began corresponding with her grandmother Rene, who, Hilton noted, "had a style that brought home right to me, almost as if she were beside me speaking, and I tried hard to bring to her the same feeling in my own letters. I think this was the first time that I remember the joy of writing."

Returning home to Sydney, Hilton was offered a scholarship to Wollongong Teachers' College; this was, she wrote in *SAAS,* "the beginning of a very long and happy relationship with teaching and learning." She added, "In teaching children to know about themselves I was also learning about myself; and the more I learnt the more, it seemed, I needed to know." During her first years as a teacher, Hilton was married to her first husband and had two children, Lachlan and Emily. Her life, Hilton noted in *SAAS,* "became a whirlwind of schoolwork, parenting, work, and housework . . . ." After divorcing, Hilton rediscovered her love of letter writing. "I could," she recalled, "write things that somehow made me feel better and happier. I was too unhappy for awhile to be able to read very much, but I wrote . . . . And so I survived." She added, "I think, at the end of the

Jenny's loving respect for her unconventional great-grandmother inspires her to protest against removing the old woman from her beloved home. (From The Web, *written by Hilton and illustrated by Kerry Millard.)*

bad time, my place in space started to feel a little more comfortable."

When her children were eleven and seven, Nette married her second husband, teacher Ron Hilton. One of their first homes, a ramshackle country house by the sea that was supposed to be haunted, later provided her with material for her books: "Often now," she wrote in *SAAS,* "when I need to think of something mysterious to work into my books, I go back to that house, in my mind, and work from there." After moving to another home, one which was filled with dogs and cats and frequented by both domestic and wild animals, Hilton became interested in the way children learn language. "I have always felt," she claimed in *SAAS,* "that anything is possible if the words necessary are able to be found. I had, for a long time, tried to work this into my teaching and spent a long time working up little stories to tell with number problems, or whatever it was that needed to be explained." When her daughter Emily suddenly began to hate school, Hilton searched in vain for a book about a child with similar feelings. This prompted her to write her first story, *I Don't Want to Go,* for her daughter. "I believed then, as I believe now," Hilton wrote in *SAAS,* "that books validate our feelings—they make true the problems we have that are causing us such pain, and sometimes they even give us a way to find an answer. I felt sure that if Em could read a story about a child who didn't want to go to school, she would begin to understand her own feelings about it." Emily was delighted with the story and settled down to her school life. Although *I Don't Want to Go* is unpublished, an editor at Omnibus Books in Australia who saw the work invited Hilton to send her another manuscript; this became *The Long Red Scarf,* her first published book.

The Long Red Scarf was inspired by a boy that Hilton had taught in the small community of Dungay. A talented knitter, Flawn was ridiculed when he moved to a city school, which eventually caused him to stop knitting. Hilton wrote in *SAAS,* "It seemed to me a shame that [the children in Flawn's new school] didn't understand that anyone can do anything if they really want to. It shouldn't matter if you are a boy or a girl." *The Long Red Scarf* features Grandpa, a fisherman who learns to knit in order to provide himself with a warm scarf for his fishing trips; not only does Grandpa create a long red scarf for himself, he also makes one for newborn Baby Susan. Writing in *Reading Time,* Judith Hall commented, "This beautifully written, very non-sexist book is full of warmth and colour.... Every home and library should have a long red scarf for family reading time and fishing excursions!" Noting the book's themes of "old age, loneliness, and self-sufficiency," Janeen Webb of *Magpies* claimed that there is "a great deal of warmth and sympathy in this family story," while Liza Bliss, writing in *School Library Journal,* called *The Long Red Scarf* a "fresh story that vibrates with positive energy." Bliss added that Hilton's "refusal to acknowledge stereotypes accounts for some of the book's vivacity." One of Hilton's most popular works, *The Long Red Scarf* was named an honor book by the Children's Book Council of Australia in 1988.

Hilton's second picture book, *Dirty Dave the Bushranger,* is also one of her most well-received creations. The title character, one of Australia's toughest stagecoach robbers, comes from a family equal to or even tougher than he is. However, Dave's dad, Dan, stays at home designing clothes while the rest of the family is out shooting it up. After the passengers of a plundered stagecoach are impressed by the clothing worn by the bandits, Dan is launched into a profitable business while Dirty Dave and the rest of his family find new careers as models for Dan's designs. Writing in *School Library Journal,* Marcia Hupp commented that Hilton's "rollicking tale is thoroughly entertaining, with a clear message to 'follow your bliss.'" *School Librarian* contributor Anne Everall noted, "The book's tongue-in-cheek use of role reversal and its challenge to traditional stereotypes regarding male/female jobs and behaviour will make it useful in helping to counterbalance books which offer more traditional images."

Hilton's picture book *A Proper Little Lady* features Annabella Jones, a red-haired, freckle-faced girl who decides to become a sophisticate. Leaving her house in a dress with a bow, a frilly petticoat, shiny black shoes, and a long gold chain, Annabella rescues a cat in a tree, teaches two children to race a go-cart, and joins her friends in a game of football. Arriving home in a disheveled state, Annabella is gently told by her mother that she might enjoy being a proper lady in her more familiar casual clothes, advice that she quickly accepts. Called a "wry look at ladylike deportment" by Dorothy Houlihan in *School Library Journal, A Proper Little Lady* was named "a useful addition to any picture storybook collection" by Cynthia Anthony of *Magpies.* The book, which was shortlisted for the Australian Picture Book of the Year Award in 1990, was inspired by Hilton's daughter Nicolette, who once put on her best dress to go out and ride the family horse. Writing in *SAAS,* Hilton recalled, "[I]t made me smile and I remembered other times in my life when my own mother had dressed us up ready to go out on an outing. I guess I was probably better at staying put in my good clothes but my sister always seemed to get out and climb fences or play tag with the dog. I think there's probably a lot of my sister, Anne, in *Proper Little Lady* and a lot of Nicolette, my own little girl...."

One of Hilton's most well-received picture books is *Andrew Jessup,* a story that demonstrates the importance of friendship to small children. The unnamed protagonist—a bespectacled little girl—is sad when her best friend Andrew Jessup moves away; she is unsure about

Fatherless Cecilia deliberates over the rightful recipient of her homemade Father's Day card. (From The Friday Card, *written by Hilton and illustrated by George Aldridge.)*

who will take his place until a new girl, Madeleine, moves into Andrew's old house. When a new friendship evolves, Andrew becomes the narrator's best "faraway" friend. Noting Hilton's "usual perception and humour" and "clear expressive text," Cathryn Crowe of *Magpies* concluded that *Andrew Jessup* is a "sensitive and amusing story." Karen James of *School Library Journal* said that the "accessible and appealing" story "offers hope that new friends can be made, and that a special feeling can be retained for old ones," while Denia Hester of *Booklist* commented, "This is a sensitively written account of a situation many children face sooner or later. The author and illustrator [Cathy Wilcox] keep a sense of humour about the proceedings.... At the same time, this on-target story shows exactly how important best friends are to boys and girls."

Andrew Jessup and *Square Pegs,* Hilton's first novel for young adults, were published the same year. In *Square Pegs,* the friendship that teenager Denny shares with Stephen, a flamboyant, charming schoolmate, causes him to doubt his sexuality. Ostracized by his basketball friends, who tease him about being gay, Denny is also pressured by his father, who tries to break up his relationship with Stephen. Writing in *Magpies,* Kevin Steinberger commented that Hilton "is well in command of her subject. She demonstrates a fine understanding of the dynamics of adolescent society, the aspirations of youth, and the pressures against which teenagers must struggle to develop and maintain their individuality." The critic concluded that among recent novels exploring teenage sexuality, *Square Pegs* is "a rewarding read." In addition to the books written under her own name, Hilton is the creator of a series of young adult novels written as Virginia Baxter. She once told *Something about the Author (SATA)*, "I adore teenagers—they are such a wonderful, seething mass of vitality, urges, and emotion. It is such a difficult time. In my work, I try to provide an outlet for some of the concerns teenagers have which are often not easily spoken about."

The Web, a story for primary graders published in 1993, is considered one of the author's best works of fiction. Called by *Magpies* contributor Jane Connolly a "charming and poignant story of a young girl's unconditional love, acceptance, and understanding of her elderly great-grandmother," *The Web* features a young girl, Jenny, and her great-grandmother, Violet Anne, who are joined to each other by mutual love and respect. Hilton, who weaves her story around the last weeks of Violet Anne's life, describes the special relationship shared by the two women as well as Jenny's attempt to save her great-grandmother from being ejected from her beloved home. The title of the book refers to the web spun by a spider who lives in Violet Anne's house as well as the plan by Jenny's mother to place Violet Anne, whom she feels is losing her faculties, into a nursing home. Connolly concluded her review by praising *The Web* as "a work of quality for young readers."

Hilton once told *SATA,* "I have always believed that many of our dilemmas, problems, and concerns can be given added dimension and perspective by relating them to a character in a book." She added, "I also adore the ridiculousness of life, its silly rules and social customs. I love dragons and monsters (harmless ones) and suffer (oh! I suffer) for the poor, brave individuals that are pitted against them. I try, always, to see the humor in situations." In conclusion, Hilton claimed, "I hope to continue writing. I hope I can produce something of real merit, something that people will smile about and cherish, much as I cherish my favorite books." Writing in *SAAS,* she said, "A great deal of my inspiration (or ideas, or research) comes from my own experiences growing up. When I look around now and listen to kids talking, very often their problems are the ones that I remember so well. I talk about my understanding of this with my husband, who works with teenagers, to make sure that I am hearing it right, and before long I feel as though I can work this into a book." She continued, "Between my first book and the ones that I am working on now has been a lot of learning, and most of it I've had to teach myself." Hilton concluded, "I will go on writing. I don't believe I will ever stop.... You see, it did take me a long time to learn about my place in space and I know, oh I know, how very lucky I was to have the opportunity to find it.... It feels very comfortable and cozy indeed."

Works Cited

Anthony, Cynthia, review of *A Proper Little Lady, Magpies,* July, 1990, pp. 25-26.

Bliss, Liza, review of *The Long Red Scarf, School Library Journal,* March, 1991, p. 173.

Connolly, Jane, review of *The Web, Magpies,* March, 1993, p. 29.

Crowe, Cathryn, review of *Andrew Jessup, Magpies,* May, 1993, p. 26.

Everall, Anne, review of *Dirty Dave the Bushranger, School Librarian,* November, 1989, p. 145.

Hall, Judith, review of *The Long Red Scarf, Reading Time,* Volume 31, number 4, 1987, p. 36.

Hester, Denia, review of *Andrew Jessup, Booklist,* December 13, 1993, p. 764.

Hilton, Nette, *Something about the Author Autobiography Series,* Volume 21, Gale, 1996, pp. 205-23.

Houlihan, Dorothy, review of *A Proper Little Lady, School Library Journal,* May, 1990, p. 86.

Hupp, Marcia, review of *Dirty Dave the Bushranger, School Library Journal,* April, 1990, p. 91.

James, Karen, review of *Andrew Jessup, School Library Journal,* October, 1993, p. 101.

Jones, Millicent, review of *Prince Lachlan, Reading Time,* Volume 28, number 4, 1989, pp. 14-15.

Steinberger, Kevin, review of *Square Pegs, Magpies,* March, 1993, p. 32.

Webb, Janeen, review of *The Long Red Scarf, Magpies,* May, 1988, p. 27.

For More Information See

BOOKS

Children's Literature Review, Volume 25, Gale, 1991, pp. 59-61.

PERIODICALS

Australian Book Review, February, 1993, p. 56; February, 1994, p. 56.
Magpies, March, 1993, p. 29; May, 1994, p. 30; July, 1997, p. 37.
Publishers Weekly, February 9, 1990, p. 58.
School Librarian, August, 1990, p. 101.

—*Sketch by Gerard J. Senick*

* * *

HILTON, Nette
See HILTON, Margaret Lynette

* * *

HILTON-BRUCE, Anne
See HILTON, Margaret Lynette

HOGG, Gary 1957-

Personal

Born March 5, 1957, in Burley, ID; son of Paul and LuAnn Hogg; children: Jackson, Jonah, Annie, Boone. *Education:* Brigham Young University, B.A.

Addresses

Home—1015 North 7300 E., Huntsville, UT 84317.

Career

Writer. Creator and presenter of the program *Writing Is Exciting!*

Writings

"HAPPY HAWK GOLDEN THOUGHT" SERIES

I Heard of a Nerd Bird, illustrated by Gary R. Anderson, Little Buckaroo Books, 1992.
Sir William the Worm, illustrated by Anderson, Little Buckaroo Books, 1992.
The Half-hearted Hare, illustrated by Anderson, Little Buckaroo Books, 1992.
The Lion Who Couldn't Roar, illustrated by Anderson, Little Buckaroo Books, 1992.
Lizzie Learns about Lying, illustrated by Anderson, Little Buckaroo Books, 1992.

Gary Hogg

Friendship in the Forest, illustrated by Anderson, Little Buckaroo Books, 1992.

"SPENCER'S ADVENTURES" SERIES

Garbage Snooper Surprise, illustrated by Dale Kilbourn, Scholastic, 1996.
Hair in the Air, illustrated by Kilbourn, Scholastic, 1997.
Stop That Eyeball!, illustrated by Kilbourn, Scholastic, 1997.
The Great Toilet Paper Caper, Scholastic, 1997.
Don't Bake That Snake!, Scholastic, 1997.
Let Go of That Toe!, Scholastic, 1998.
Scrambled Eggs and Spider Legs, Scholastic, 1998.

OTHER

Beautiful Buhla's Day at the Zoo, illustrated by Anderson, Little Buckaroo Books, 1993.

Work in Progress

Bears, Scares, and Underwear; The Nincompoop Troop and the Great School Gross Out.

Sidelights

Gary Hogg told *SATA:* "As a nineteen-year-old, I was writing one night and composed the picture book, *I Heard of a Nerd Bird.* After writing that story, I decided that a career of creating books for children would be a dream come true. Since then, I have dedicated myself to creating funny, insightful books for young people. It took years to be able to support my family from my writing, but I never lost sight of my goal. Even when I was working at other jobs to pay the bills, I would always list my occupation as 'children's book author.'

"One of my favorite activities as an author is speaking to thousands of children each year. Over the past ten years, I have visited an average of 150 elementary schools per year. In that time I have entertained more than a million boys and girls. I feel a responsibility to help young people see that writing can be an exciting part of their lives. My school presentations focus on the creative abilities that we all possess.

"My four children are my best friends and the greatest assets to my writing. They inspire me and help me get my stories just right. For the past several years, I have been concentrating on writing 'chapter books.' I love this category of fiction and have plans for many new and funny stories for the second-, third-, and fourth-grade audience."

*   *   *

HOOK, Brendan 1963-

Personal

Born September 20, 1963, in Tasmania, Australia; son of Geoffrey Raynor (a cartoonist/illustrator) and Pauline Beryl (a teacher; maiden name, Lowe) Hook; married Molly Brumm (an actress); children: Maeve Maire, Beatrice Therese. *Education:* Melbourne University, B.A.

Addresses

Home—5 McLean Ave, Bentleigh 3204.

Career

Moonee Valley Instrumental Music Program, primary and junior high music teacher, 1991—. Saxophonist.

Writings

Harry the Honkerzoid, illustrated by Jeff Hook, Penguin, 1997.
Planet of the Honkerzoids, illustrated by Jeff Hook, Penguin, 1998.

Work in Progress

A third addition to the Honkerzoid series.

Sidelights

Brendan Hook told *SATA:* "I grew up watching my father work as a well-known cartoonist and picture book illustrator. He opened my eyes to the possibilities in children's literature.

"I became a musician and then went into music teaching. My experiences over a seven-year-period working with primary age students prompted me to begin writing for

Brendan Hook

them. My stories feature music and are for children with an interest in or love of music. Coupled with this was the fact that I knew I could ask a great illustrator to help me realize the story. So far my father and I have worked on two stories—with more to follow."

For More Information See

PERIODICALS

Magpies, July, 1997, p. 31.

*   *   *

ISLE, Sue 1963-

Personal

Born September 17, 1963, in Fremantle, Western Australia. *Education:* Western Australian Institute of Technology (now Curtin University), B.A.

Addresses

Home—Perth, Western Australia. *Electronic mail*—rat-fan@newton.dialix.com.au. *Agent*—Angela Graham, Literature Connection.

Career

Court reporter, 1992—. *Member:* Australian Society of Authors, Horror Writers Association.

Writings

Scale of Dragon, Tooth of Wolf, Hodder Headline (Rydal-mcre, Australia), 1996.
Wolf Children, the Real Feral Kids: An Extraordinary Story, Omnibus Books (Norwood, Australia), 1998.

Work in Progress

Dragons Fly South, a sequel to *Scale of Dragon, Tooth of Wolf.*

Sidelights

Sue Isle told *SATA:* "I have been reading science fiction and fantasy since the age of about eleven, starting with books like *The Hobbit* and Robert A. Heinlein's *Citizen of the Galaxy.* It's my favorite area of writing as well as reading. Other interests include cycling, conservation, and the Internet, and I generally have at least two pet rats around, plotting to take over the world.

"People often speculate about things, but most don't have the urge to write stories about them. They can wonder what it would be like to have a baby aboard the Space Shuttle without trying to create a world where this happens. Or, they can fly a glider without translating the experience into what it might feel like to ride a dragon. I cannot, and maybe that's what makes me a writer.

Sue Isle with her pet rat, "Ari."

"*Scale of Dragon, Tooth of Wolf* is set in an imaginary Elizabethan-type land where a young girl named Amber is recruited by an order of witches. Amber is mc, with a double dose of attitude, but then she has to survive in a rougher environment that I ever had to do. My local police force is nothing to the Inquisition!

"In *Wolf Children,* the children, who are adopted by wolves, are another kind of alien. They have no human language and copy the wolves in all things. When they are brought back from the forest or the jungle, the children are strangers and remain alien, never recovering language or understanding.

"To write about the future, I have to understand the present and the past as well as I can. Maybe I don't write about the people in my neighborhood in their everyday lives, but I must understand them or my projection—my story of the future or the sideways past—isn't going to make any sense. Amber's story is that of a girl who must train her magic in a society hostile to witches, but she's also a teenager alienated from her family, a teenager looking for the place where she belongs. Fantasy and science fiction must be a blend of the mundane and the strange, the real and the might-be dreams.

"I think writing is a vocation like that of the religious orders. You do it because you can't bear not to, because the voices won't let you alone. If you wanted a lot of money, there are much better and surer ways to make it."

K

KING, Jeanette (Margaret) 1959-

Personal

Born May 14, 1959, in Hokitika, New Zealand; daughter of Ross (a printer) and Thora (a midwife; maiden name, McDougall) King; children: two. *Education:* University of Canterbury, B.A., 1983, B.A. (with honors), 1993.

Jeanette King

Addresses

Office—Maori Department, University of Canterbury, Private Bag 4800, Christchurch, New Zealand. *Electronic mail*—j:king@maori.canterbury.ac.nz.

Career

Teacher at a girls' high school in Christchurch, New Zealand, 1982-87; University of Canterbury, Christchurch, tutor, 1988-92, lecturer in Maori department, 1993—. St. Albans Primary School, chairperson of management committee for bilingual unit. University of Canterbury, Harassment Prevention Committee, convener. *Member:* Te Kohanga Reo o Rehua Whanau.

Writings

E Pirangi Ana Koe?, Learning Media (Wellington, New Zealand), 1994.
E Haere Mai Ana Nga Manuhiri, Learning Media, 1994.
One Sleepy Day, Learning Media, 1998.
Te Pu Harakeke, Learning Media, 1998.

Author of the poetry collection *Maramara,* 1999. Short stories written in Maori are represented in school anthologies. Contributor to periodicals.

Work in Progress

Research on Maori language revitalization among adults.

Sidelights

Jeanette M. King told *SATA:* "I have been learning *te reo Maori,* an indigenous language of New Zealand, for more than twenty years. I am committed to its revitalization, particularly since my involvement with the Maori language preschool movement (*Te Kohanga Reo*) from 1989, when my children began attending school. Most of my writing for children has been in Maori."

KLEIN, Rachel S. 1953-

Personal

Born December 23, 1953, in Ann Arbor, MI; daughter of Lawrence R. (an economist) and Sonia (an economist; maiden name, Adelson) Klein; married Lyle C. Rexer, May 11, 1979; children: Raisa, Norah, Jonah. *Education:* University of Michigan, B.A., 1974, M.A., 1976. *Religion:* Jewish. *Hobbies and other interests:* "The natural world."

Addresses

Home—112 Park Pl., Brooklyn, NY 11217.

Career

Writer.

Awards, Honors

Hopwood Awards, University of Michigan, 1972, 1977.

Writings

FOR CHILDREN

Moonlight and Music (juvenile art book), illustrated by Gayleen Aiken, Abrams, 1997.

OTHER

(With Lyle Rexer) *One-Hundred-Twenty-Five Years of Expedition and Discovery: The American Museum of Natural History,* Abrams (New York City), 1995.

Contributor of fiction to *Chicago Review.*

Work in Progress

The Princess of the Sands, for children, with illustrations by Gracia Alzamora; *Legends of Good Women,* short stories; *Ernessa,* a novel; a musical play for children, with music by Nancy Harrow.

Sidelights

Rachel S. Klein comments: "My work is not limited to a category. Fiction, nonfiction, children's literature, dramatic writing are all forms in which I have found meaningful stories. In my writing for children, both stage plays and fiction, my mission is to provide an inner challenge. There is a battle going on for children's imaginations—a battle between marketers and therapists. I want to offer alternatives to the mass-produced packaging that both sides offer.

"Collaboration with other artists is essential. *Moonlight and Music* was a joint effort, with the self-taught artist Gayleen Aiken, to present to children and adults a visual and written record of [Aiken's] unique life and creative power. I am now working with the jazz composer Nancy Harrow on a musical for children, for which I adapted Waldemar Bonsels's classic novel *The Adventures of Maya the Bee.* This collaboration has also involved jazz musicians and puppet makers from the Theatre Bayh in Warsaw, Poland. In another ongoing project, the Peruvian artist Gracia Alzamora is illustrating *The Princess of the Sands,* a novel that I wrote for children. These projects have an appeal beyond children to adults who have not lost touch with their own childhood mythologies.

"In my adult fiction, my mission has been similar. I have tried, in a simple style, to rediscover depths of thought and feelings that others ignore. In this endeavor, I have been influenced by the great writers of this century: Marcel Proust, Franz Kafka, Hermann Broch, Maxim Gorky, Thomas Bernhardt, S. Y. Agnon, and Shusaku Endo, among others. They have all served as models of uncompromised prose writers and thinkers."

* * *

KOPPER, Lisa (Esther) 1950-

Personal

Born April 8, 1950, in Chicago, IL; moved to England, 1970.

Addresses

Home—1 Peary Place, London, England.

Career

Illustrator and author.

Awards, Honors

Wilfred Radio Memorial Award, 1970, for best studio work; Premio per la Poesia, 1980; Best of British Illustrations Award, 1982; Short listed for the Annecy Awards, 1990, for the "Barney" television series; Parent's Choice Award, 1990, for *Jafta: The Wedding;* French Libraries Award, 1991, for *Jafta: My Mother* and *Jafta: My Father.* Victoria and Albert Museum Art Illustration Award short list, 1995, for *I'm a Baby, You're a Baby.* Kate Greenaway Medal long short list, 1994, and *She* magazine Brilliant Book of the Year, 1996, for *Daisy Is a Mummy;* also selected as a Capitol Choice, 1998, as *Daisy Is a Mommy.*

Writings

SELF-ILLUSTRATED

Daisy Thinks She Is a Baby, Hamish Hamilton (London), 1993, Knopf, 1994.
I'm a Baby, You're a Baby, Hamish Hamilton, 1994, Viking, 1995.
My Pony Ride, Hamish Hamilton, 1995.
Daisy Is a Mummy, Hamish Hamilton, 1996, published as *Daisy Is a Mommy,* Dutton, 1997.
Daisy Knows Best, Hamish Hamilton, 1998, Dutton, 1999.

ILLUSTRATOR

Ted Harriott, *Black Bear, White Bear,* Evans Bros. (London), 1979.

Leonard Clark, compiler, *The Way the Wind Blows: A Book of Poetry,* Evans Bros., 1979.

Hugh Lewin, *Jafta,* Evans Bros., 1981, Carolrhoda, 1983.

Hugh Lewin, *Jafta: My Father,* Evans Bros., 1981, Carolrhoda, 1983.

Hugh Lewin, *Jafta: My Mother,* Evans Bros., 1981, Carolrhoda, 1983.

Hugh Lewin, *Jafta: The Wedding,* Evans Bros., 1981, Carolrhoda, 1983.

Victoria Whitehead, *Katie Moves House,* Dinosaur (Cambridge, England), 1982.

Ruth Silcock, *Posy and Sam,* Dinosaur, 1982.

Sylvia Barrett and Sheena Hodge, selectors, *Tinder-box: Sixty-six Songs for Children,* A. & C. Black (London), 1982.

Leonard Clark, *The Corn Growing: Poems and Verses for Children,* Hodder & Stoughton, 1982.

Hugh Lewin, *Jafta: The Town,* Evans Bros., 1983, Carolrhoda, 1984.

Hugh Lewin, *Jafta: The Journey,* Evans Bros., 1983, Carolrhoda, 1984.

Christine Parker, *Rebekah and the Slide,* Dinosaur, 1983.

Jules Older, *Hank Prank and Hot Henrietta: Stories for Younger Children,* Heinemann, 1984.

Mollie Clarke, reteller, *The Chief's Son: A Story from South Africa,* Collins Educational (London), 1984.

Mollie Clarke, reteller, *The Wonderful Wigwam: A Story from North America,* Collins Educational, 1984.

Sheila Lavelle, *The Big Stink,* Heinemann, 1984.

Peter Bonnici, *Festival,* Mantra (London), 1984, published as *The Festival,* Carolrhoda, 1985.

Peter Bonnici, *First Rains,* Mantra, 1984, published as *The First Rains,* Carolrhoda, 1985.

Hugh Lewin, *An Elephant Came to Swim,* Hamish Hamilton, 1985.

Sheila Lavelle, *The Disappearing Granny,* Heinemann, 1985, Barron's, 1989.

Peter Bonnici, *Amber's Other Grandparents,* Bodley Head, 1985.

Jules Older, *Hank Prank in Love,* Heinemann, 1985.

Ted Harriott, *Coming Home: A Dog's True Story,* Gollancz (London), 1985.

Olly N. Stanford and Esmee E. Mejias, *The New Ibis Readers,* Collins Caribbean, 1985.

Kate Petty, *What's That [Color?] [Feel?] [Noise?] [Number?] [Shape?] [Size?] [Smell?] [Taste?],* F. Watts, 1986.

Ruth Silcock, *Posy and Sam Go on a Picnic,* Dinosaur, 1986.

Leila Berg, *Having Friends,* Methuen, 1987.

Leila Berg, *Loving Jonathan Jones,* Methuen, 1987.

Leila Berg, *Call That a Hat!,* Methuen, 1987.

Leila Berg, *Rosie and Mister Brown,* Methuen, 1987.

Kate Petty, *Going to the Doctor,* F. Watts, 1987.

Kate Petty, *Moving House,* F. Watts, 1987.

Kate Petty, *The New Baby,* F. Watts, 1987.

Kate Petty, *Starting School,* F. Watts, 1987.

Althea, *When Uncle Bob Died,* Dinosaur, 1988.

Kate Petty, *Splitting Up,* F. Watts, 1988.

Lisa Kopper

Kate Petty, *Staying Overnight,* Gloucester Press, 1988.

Kate Petty, *Taking Care with Strangers,* F. Watts, 1988, published as *Being Careful with Strangers,* Gloucester Press, 1988.

Peter Bonnici, *Barney's TV Act,* Methuen, 1988.

Peter Bonnici, *The Present,* Hodder & Stoughton, 1988.

Peter Bonnici, *The Village Show,* Hodder & Stoughton, 1988.

Peter Bonnici, *The Special Event,* Hodder & Stoughton, 1988.

Peter Bonnici, *Lost in Town,* Hodder & Stoughton, 1988.

Peter Bonnici, *Barney's Christmas Surprise,* Magnet (London), 1988.

Peter Bonnici, *Barney's Hungry Day,* Methuen, 1988.

Peter Bonnici, *Barney's Treasure Hunt,* Magnet, 1988.

Kate Petty, *Going to the Dentist,* Gloucester Press, 1988.

Peter Bonnici, *Barney's Balloon Ride,* Little Mammoth, 1989.

Peter Bonnici, *Barney's Day at the Seaside,* Little Mammoth, 1989.

Peter Bonnici, *Barney's Forgotten Birthday,* Magnet, 1989.

Peter Bonnici, *Barney's Big Book of Stories,* Methuen, 1989.

Peter Bonnici, *Barney's Big Spring Clean,* Magnet, 1989.

Jules Older and Effin Older, *Hot Henrietta and Nailbiters United,* Puffin, 1989.

Hugh Lewin, *A Bamboo in the Wind,* Hamish Hamilton, 1989.

Hugh Lewin, *A Flower in the Forest,* Hamish Hamilton, 1989.

Hugh Lewin, *A Shell on the Beach,* Hamish Hamilton, 1989.

Hugh Lewin, *A Well in the Desert,* Hamish Hamilton, 1989.

Sheila Lavelle, *Chaill Sinn Granaigh,* (Stornoway, Scotland) Acair, 1989.

Ten Little Babies, Dutton, 1990.

Jules Older and Effin Older, *Hank and Henrietta Take Off!*, Heinemann, 1991.

Sheila Fraser, *I Can Play Football*, F. Watts, 1991, published as *I Can Play Soccer*, Barron's, 1991.

Sheila Fraser, *I Can Ride a Bike*, Barron's, 1991.

Sheila Fraser, *I Can Roller Skate*, Barron's, 1991.

Sheila Fraser, *I Can Swim*, Barron's, 1991.

Debbie MacKinnon, *Babies' Favourites*, F. Lincoln, 1992.

Hugh Lewin, *Jafta's Mother*, Hamish Hamilton, 1992.

Charles Causley, *Bring in the Holly*, F. Lincoln, 1992.

Hugh Lewin, *Jafta: The Homecoming*, Hamish Hamilton, 1992, Knopf, 1994.

Hush-a-Bye Baby: Bedtime Poems and Lullabies, Grosset & Dunlap, 1992.

Happy Birthday!, Grosset & Dunlap, 1992.

Peek-a-Boo Kitty, Grosset & Dunlap, 1993.

Peek-a-Boo Teddy, Grosset & Dunlap, 1993.

Peek-a-Boo Baby, Grosset & Dunlap, 1993.

Margaret Greaves, *Stories from the Ballet*, F. Lincoln, 1993.

Grace Hallworth, *Sleep Tight*, Cambridge University Press, 1996.

Jules Older, *Anita! The Woman Behind the Body Shop*, Charlesbridge (Watertown, MA), 1998.

Richard Brown and Kate Ruttle, selectors, *Out and About*, illustrated with Amanda Harvey, Cambridge University Press, 1998.

"BABY SHAPE" BOARD BOOKS; WITH TONY BRADMAN

The Baby's Bumper Book, Methuen, 1987.

Bedtime, Methuen 1987.

The Cuddle, Methuen, 1987.

Our Cat, Methuen, 1987.

Baby's Best Book, Harper & Row, 1987.

"SMALL WORLD" SERIES; BY LEILA BERG

Worms, Methuen, 1983.

Bees, Methuen, 1983.

Blood and Plasters, Methuen, 1983.

Dogs, Methuen, 1983.

Cars, Methuen, 1985.

Ducks, Methuen, 1985.

Rainbows, Methuen, 1985.

Vacuum Cleaners, Methuen, 1985.

OTHER

For television, Kopper illustrated the stories for "What's Inside," a British Broadcasting Corporation (BBC) series for young children. She has created characters for the award-winning animated "Barney" series. She has also produced work for the BBC "Watch" and "Storytime" series. Also contributor to *Books for Keeps* and *Women and Creativity,* published by Women's Press.

Sidelights

Lisa Kopper is a prolific illustrator of children's picture books who has also begun a career as a children's author. Working hard to break down cultural stereotypes, Kopper portrays people of color as unique individuals. She has illustrated numerous books that feature children of a variety of ethnic backgrounds. Among her most celebrated illustration projects in a career spanning more than two decades is the "Jafta" series that describes the South African childhood of the author, Hugh Lewin. For these books, Kopper was praised for "conveying the emotions and spirit of these South African people," by *School Library Journal* contributor Barbara Williams. In addition to illustrating the works of other authors, Kopper has illustrated several of her own stories, including a series of picture books starring Daisy, an endearingly drawn bull terrier who is treated like one of the human members of her family.

Born in Chicago, Illinois, Kopper's childhood was deeply influenced by the philosophy and social activism of the civil rights movement. Due to her parents' involvement in the move towards political and social equality between the races that characterized that era, Kopper was made aware of social issues, poverty, and discrimination from an early age. In 1970, a few years after completing her high school degree, she decided to relocate from the United States to England, where she began her career as an illustrator. Eight years later, Kopper's first published illustrations appeared in "Children of Soweto," a pamphlet condemning apartheid, the racist policies that separate blacks and whites in South Africa.

Continuing to focus on apartheid, Kopper collaborated with author Hugh Lewin on the highly praised "Jafta" series. One of the volumes, *Jafta: The Homecoming*, relates the story of a family torn apart by apartheid. Jafta's father has been working in the mines, far away from the village. Political changes in South Africa will allow him to return to his family. Jafta is joyous at his return and reflects on all that his father has missed. A *Publishers Weekly* reviewer stated that "Kopper rises to the demands of the text," and *Booklist* critic Hazel Rochman said the "realistic sepia-toned illustrations evoke energy and longing in the rural community."

Among Kopper's numerous other illustration projects are Leila Berg's "Small World" series, which includes the volumes *Bees, Dogs,* and *Worms;* Mollie Clarke's retelling of a Native American legend in *The Wonderful Wigwam;* and Tony Bradman's "Baby Shape Board Books" series.

Kopper also writes and illustrates her own works. Of her illustrations for the counting book *Ten Little Babies*, a *Publishers Weekly* reviewer noted that "Kopper's pastel drawings give these multicultural moppets distinct characterizations, and her choices of wardrobe and props are nearly as amusing as the babies themselves." "It is a book to read, share, chant, play with, laugh over and enjoy and will appeal to a wide age range," enthused Sue Smedley in *School Librarian.*

Critics have called Kopper's pastel-toned *I'm a Baby, You're a Baby,* which she wrote and illustrated, a sweet book. On the left-hand pages, multiethnic toddlers and baby farm animals engage in playtime activities. The names of the baby animals, from ducklings, to piglets, to foals, appear on the right-hand pages with groupings of

So does Daisy.

Kopper's popular canine protagonist takes on the responsibilities of motherhood in **Daisy Is a Mommy,** *illustrated by the author.*

the animals and their siblings. *Booklist* contributor Stephanie Zvirin commented that *I'm a Baby, You're a Baby* "is the kind of book toddlers will want to 'read'" repeatedly. "This attractively designed title should ... be a popular choice," commented Linda Wicher, writing in *School Library Journal.*

In *My Pony Ride,* author/illustrator Kopper follows a young girl and her father as they encounter various natural obstacles—including ditches, streams, and fields—during their horseback ride through the countryside. Calling *My Pony Ride* "an attractive and appropriate book to read at bedtime," *School Librarian* contribu-

tor Margaret Mallett added that the spare, descriptive text in Kopper's book will encourage discussion of contrasts such as large and small, soft and hard, and bumpy and smooth, between young listeners and their storytellers. Deeming the book "delightful," Liz Waterford in *Books for Keeps* stated that, "The pictures are clear and uncluttered in soft colours which let the reader concentrate on the people and animals and their environment."

Young readers first meet the lovable canine character of Daisy in *Daisy Thinks She Is a Baby.* In Kopper's humorous book, a toddler is forced to compete for space

I'm a baby.   You're a baby.

Human and animal babies play together in Kopper's self-illustrated picture book **I'm a Baby, You're a Baby.**

on Mom's lap, in the stroller, and even in the high chair with a dog who is convinced that she is really one of the family. Finally, Daisy is put in her place when it is discovered that she is going to have a litter of puppies; Daisy isn't a baby any more! *School Library Journal* contributor Caroline Parr described *Daisy Thinks She Is a Baby* as "an inviting story that will be fun to read aloud," and praised Kopper's cheerful colored-pencil drawings. Kopper's sequels, *Daisy Is a Mommy* and *Daisy Knows Best,* both received similar praise. In *Daisy Is a Mommy,* Daisy the four-legged mommy is now as busy tending to puppies Little Daisy, Morris, and Delores as the human mommy who bustles about caring for her human baby, in a book that *Booklist* reviewer Zvirin characterized as "loaded with charm." "An easy and enjoyable tale for preschool story hours as well as for beginning readers," noted *School Library Journal* contributor Christy Norris, who also called attention to Kopper's "irresistible illustrations."

Winner of the Wilfred Radio Memorial Award in 1970 for best studio work, Kopper has also received the Premio per la Poesia in 1980 and the Best of British Illustrations in 1982. In addition to her work as a children's picture book writer and illustrator, Kopper has also contributed to the anthology *Women and Creativity,* published by Women's Press.

Works Cited

Review of *Jafta: The Homecoming, Publishers Weekly,* November 29, 1993, p. 64.

Mallett, Margaret, review of *My Pony Ride, School Librarian,* February, 1996, p. 40.

Norris, Christy, review of *Daisy Is a Mommy, School Library Journal,* February, 1997, p. 82.

Parr, Caroline, review of *Daisy Thinks She Is a Baby, School Library Journal,* August, 1994, pp. 138-39.

Rochman, Hazel, review of *Jafta: The Homecoming, Booklist,* December 1, 1993, p. 700.

Smedley, Sue, review of *Ten Little Babies, School Librarian,* November, 1990, p. 143.

Review of *Ten Little Babies, Publishers Weekly,* October 26, 1990, p. 66.

Waterford, Liz, review of *My Pony Ride, Books for Keeps,* September, 1997, pp. 20-21.

Wicher, Linda, review of *I'm a Baby, You're a Baby, School Library Journal,* April, 1995, pp. 103-04.

Williams, Barbara, review of *Jafta: The Homecoming, School Library Journal,* March, 1994, pp. 203-04.

Zvirin, Stephanie, review of *I'm a Baby, You're a Baby, Booklist,* January 1, 1995, p. 824.

Zvirin, Stephanie, review of *Daisy Is a Mommy, Booklist,* December 1, 1996, p. 668.

For More Information See

PERIODICALS

Kirkus Reviews, May 15, 1994, p. 701.
Magpies, March, 1997, p. 26.
School Library Journal, February, 1991, p. 72.

L

LaFAYE, A(lexandria R. T.) 1970-

Personal

Born March 9, 1970, in Hudson, WI; daughter of Patrick (an airline mechanic) and Rita (an insurance staff agent) LaFaye. *Education:* University of Minnesota-Twin Cities, B.A. (summa cum laude); Mankato State University, M.A. (creative writing and multicultural literature); University of Memphis, M.F.A.; Hollins College, M.A.

A. LaFaye

(children's literature). *Politics:* "Democratic Socialist." *Religion:* "Non-denominational Christian." *Hobbies and other interests:* Movies, storytelling, fine arts.

Addresses

Home—Upstate New York. *Electronic mail*—alafaye @netscape.net. *Agent*—Marcia Wernick, Sheldon Fogelman Agency, 10 East 40th Street, New York, NY 10016.

Career

Writer, educator. Roanoke College, Salem, VA, instructor in English, 1997-98; visiting professor, Plattsburgh State University, NY, 1998—. *Member:* Society of Children's Book Writers and Illustrators.

Awards, Honors

Books in the Middle: Outstanding Titles of 1998, *Voice of Youth Advocates,* 1999, for *The Year of the Sawdust Man.*

Writings

The Year of the Sawdust Man, Simon & Schuster, 1998.
Edith Shay, Viking Penguin, 1998.
Strawberry Hill, Simon & Schuster, 1999.
Nissa's Place, Simon & Schuster, 1999.

Work in Progress

Farlington, an adult novel; a fantasy novel for young people.

Sidelights

A. LaFaye told *SATA:* "I am a prose writer who is inspired by an intense interest in knowing more. I was obsessed with learning from a young age, often hunting down odd little historical facts, like what exactly is a 'coffin corner'? My thirst for knowledge is funneled into my writing as I explore subjects that exist outside my own experience. My first novel, *The Year of the Sawdust*

Man, is set in rural Louisiana in the Depression Era—a far cry from the rural Wisconsin community where I grew up. I treat writing as a form of literary acting, stepping into the roles of my characters to explore the possibilities of their fictional lives.

"Forever inventing stories in my head, I was inspired to begin writing by a sixth-grade teacher who said I had the talent to become a writer. Writing throughout middle school and high school, I launched into my college career in history because I thought it would be 'practical,' but my love for writing won out before I graduated from the University of Minnesota.

"In my graduate work, I devoted myself to the study of literature from a writer's perspective. An avid fan of writers like Gabriel Garcia Marquez, Toni Morrison, Robert Cormier, and Patricia MacLachlan, I aspired to create realistic stories about everyday life in the past.

"Frustrated by pejorative attitudes toward the literary quality of books for child readers, I strive to create tales with literary and psychological depth. *The Year of the Sawdust Man* deals with parental abandonment, while *Edith Shay* chronicles a young woman's struggle for identity and independence following the Civil War. I have also explored the lighter side of fiction with a humorous fantasy novel that tells the story of a young boy whose father goes into a coma only to return to the house as a ghost."

LaFaye's well-received debut novel, *The Year of the Sawdust Man,* was inspired by a television documentary the author viewed about the Great Depression. "I wondered what would happen if a parent told a child that they had to leave home and could only take one suitcase," LaFaye told Cindi Di Marzo in a *Publishers Weekly* interview. "And then I wondered how a child might feel if her mother left home with one suitcase." Set in Louisiana during the 1930s, LaFaye's story explores the plight of young Nissa Bergen, who comes home from school one afternoon to find that her free-spirited mother has departed, leaving the distraught eleven-year-old narrator in the care of her father. "The author creates a believable set of characters and a realistic environment, and sustains them well with a lyrical and leisurely use of language," maintained *School Library Journal* contributor Darcy Schild. Calling *The Year of the Sawdust Man* a "searching, character-driven debut," a *Kirkus Reviews* critic asserted: "LaFaye depicts complex, profoundly disturbed characters with a sure hand, and this turbulent story joins Ruth White's *Belle Prater's Boy* as a cut above the rest." A *Publishers Weekly* commentator noted that LaFaye's novel "is filled with poignant insights into a hurt child's fragile psyche and resilient spirit." The same critic commended the author for "lighten[ing] the story with Nissa's memories of her mother's refreshingly candid and whimsical nature," and concluded: "This bittersweet, moving debut reveals a writer capable of plumbing the depths of a painful situation to surface triumphantly with compassion and humor."

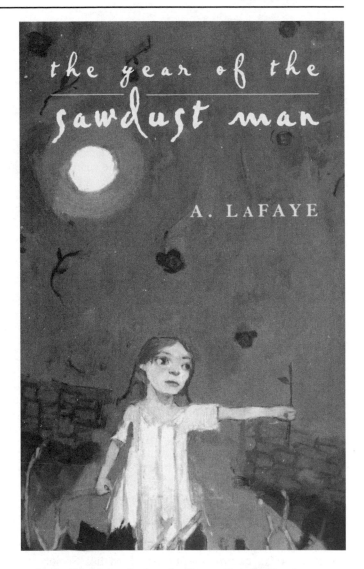

Set in Louisiana during the Depression, LaFaye's story explores the plight of young Nissa Bergen, who comes home from school one afternoon to find that her free-spirited mother has departed, leaving the distraught eleven-year-old narrator in the care of her father. (Cover illustration by Natalie Ascensios.)

LaFaye's second novel, *Edith Shay,* is a character study set in post-Civil War America that blends travel and adventure with the coming-of-age of young Katherine Lunden. Assuming the name she has found on an abandoned suitcase, sixteen-year-old Katherine leaves her home in a small Wisconsin town and travels by train to Chicago, where she takes a job as a seamstress. Katherine later determines to find the real Edith Shay and return her suitcase, a mission that takes her to Richmond, Virginia, by way of Philadelphia and Washington, DC. "While Katherine does travel far and has many adventures, there is more introspection than action," maintained *School Library Journal* contributor Bruce Anne Shook, who added: "The book's main appeal will be to readers who can identify with her independent spirit." A *Publishers Weekly* critic asserted that in *Edith Shay* "LaFaye offers a multi-dimensional portrait of a young woman in transition, one capable of seeing her flaws and rising above them, revealed in poetic and poignant language."

Strawberry Hill focusses on Raleia Pendle, who is spending the summer in Tidal, Maine—the ideal anti-dote to the turbulent, free-spirited 1970s in which she lives. Tidal looks almost exactly as it did in 1911, when a tidal wave crushed the town and killed more than one hundred people. It is the ideal place for Raleia to live out her daydreams about life at the turn of the century and to avoid her cranky pregnant mother and her self-absorbed father. In Tidal, Raleia believes she has found her living link to the past in Ian Rutherford, the reclusive old man on the hill who has hardly left home since the tidal wave hit. As their friendship grows, Raleia discovers that the past was not the golden time she imagined. Of the book, LaFaye said that she was inspired by the age-old question, "What if?" During the Vietnam War, her father served in the navy as a mechanic on an aircraft carrier, and her mother worked as a clerk in a county auditor's office. As a child, LaFaye wondered what it would be like to be raised by "hippies," and *Strawberry Hill* is one possible answer to that question.

LaFaye's next project was a sequel to *The Year of the Sawdust Man*. After finishing *Sawdust*, LaFaye wanted to give Nissa the same self-awareness and independence that Heirah Rae acquired in the first book. Nissa needed to learn to live for herself and not her mother. In *Nissa's Place*, she does just that. After a revelation in a Chicago library while visiting Heirah Rae, Nissa discovers a way to stake her independence back home in Harper, Louisiana.

A self-described "method writer," LaFaye reflects on her work habits in comments published on her Society of Children's Book Writers and Illustrators (SCBWI) webpage. "I go on writing binges," she relates. "Sitting down in front of the computer in the late afternoon, I immerse myself into the world I create in words and write until dawn. I often write so fast that I go back and reread my work with a sense of wonder, saying, 'Did I really write that?'"

Works Cited

Di Marzo, Cindi, interview with LaFaye, "Flying Starts: Seven Children's Authors Talk about Their Spring Debuts," *Publishers Weekly*, June 29, 1998, p. 26.

Review of *Edith Shay, Publishers Weekly*, October 12, 1998, p. 78.

LaFaye, A., comments published on website, http:// bergen stein.com/SCBWI/lafaye/lafaye.htm.

Schild, Darcy, review of *The Year of the Sawdust Man, School Library Journal*, July, 1998, p. 97.

Shook, Bruce Anne, review of *Edith Shay, School Library Journal*, October, 1998, p. 138.

Review of *The Year of the Sawdust Man, Kirkus Reviews*, May 15, 1998, p. 740.

Review of *The Year of the Sawdust Man, Publishers Weekly*, June 1, 1998, p. 63.

For More Information See

PERIODICALS

Bulletin of the Center for Children's Books, December, 1998, p. 137.

Kirkus Reviews, October 1, 1998, pp. 1460-61.

* * *

LANE, Dakota 1959-

Personal

Born September 23, 1959, in Brooklyn, NY; children: Alex Kamin, Hailey Pearson. *Education:* Attended San Francisco State University.

Addresses

Home—P.O. Box 591, Woodstock, NY 12498.

Career

Freelance writer, c. 1996—; creative writing instructor, 1996—.

Writings

Johnny Voodoo, Delacorte, 1996.

Johnny Voodoo was also recorded on audio cassette by Recorded Books, 1997.

Contributor to periodicals, including the *Village Voice, Entertainment Weekly, Interview,* and the *Woodstock Times.*

Dakota Lane

When Deirdre moves to the Louisiana bayou soon after her mother dies, her fascination with mysterious Johnny Vouchamps causes tension between her and her father. (Cover photos by James Joern and Michel Legrou.)

Sidelights

Brooklyn native Dakota Lane's first novel, *Johnny Voodoo,* was published in 1996. The book's protagonist is Deirdre, a sixteen-year-old young woman who has just suffered the loss of her mother. As the story opens, she is uprooted by her artist father from her familiar home in New York City and taken to live with him in a rural community in Louisiana. Deirdre finds it hard to adjust to her new home and school and begins to rebel against her father. However, she soon meets the boy described by Lane's title, whose real name is Johnny Vouchamps. Johnny has a mysterious, exotic quality that attracts Deirdre, and he is rumored by the other students to be homeless. Deirdre's father tries to discourage the rela-

tionship, causing more tension between parent and child. As Johnny's behavior becomes increasingly strange, however, Deirdre begins to take her father's advice more seriously. The story concludes with Deirdre becoming closer to her family and classmates. Deirdre decides that "the love she had for her mother and for Johnny will live forever in her heart," wrote *Voice of Youth Advocates* contributor Mary Hedge.

Critics responded favorably to *Johnny Voodoo.* Margaret Cole, writing in *School Library Journal,* hailed the novel as "a well-paced story filled with symbolism, emotion, and intriguing characters," while a *Publishers Weekly* commentator observed that the book's "mood is perfect." Deborah Stevenson, writing in the *Bulletin of the Center for Children's Books,* commended Lane's "incisive accuracy about various cliques and patterns in the high-school social world."

Comments about Lane's keen insight into the world of her young characters are not surprising, since the author drew details directly from her own experiences. In a *Publishers Weekly* interview, Lane explained that as a child she attended some twenty-five schools. At one school, according to interviewer Cindi DiMarzo, Lane "was the only white girl ... [and] she experienced firsthand the intense bathroom scenes described in *Johnny Voodoo,* in which the popular girls try to intimidate anyone who dares to be different." Lane also incorporated other experiences from her childhood in the novel, including "stories about the bayou that were told to her by a babysitter," explained DiMarzo.

Despite the success of her debut novel, Lane, a single mother of two, still participates in a variety of writing projects, including writing adult fiction and teaching creative writing.

Works Cited

Cole, Margaret, review of *Johnny Voodoo, School Library Journal,* November, 1996, p. 123.

DiMarzo, Cindi, "Flying Starts: Six First-Time Children's Book Authors Talk about Their Fall '96 Debuts," *Publishers Weekly,* December 16, 1996, p. 32.

Hedge, Mary, review of *Johnny Voodoo, Voice of Youth Advocates,* October, 1996, p. 210.

Review of *Johnny Voodoo, Publishers Weekly,* November 18, 1996, pp. 76-77.

Stevenson, Deborah, review of *Johnny Voodoo, Bulletin of the Center for Children's Books,* January, 1997, p. 178.

For More Information See

PERIODICALS

Booklist, September 15, 1996, p. 232.

Teaching and Learning Literature, September-October, 1997, pp. 95-96.

M

MAZER, Anne 1953-

Personal

Born April 2, 1953, in Schenectady, NY; daughter of Harry (a writer) and Norma (a writer; maiden name, Fox) Mazer; children: Max and Mollie Futterman. *Education:* Attended State University of New York at Binghamton, Syracuse University, and the Sorbonne.

Addresses

Agent—Elaine Markson, Elaine Markson Literary Agency, 44 Greenwich Ave., New York, NY 10011.

Career

Freelance writer, 1982—. *Member:* Authors Guild, Authors League of America.

Awards, Honors

Keystone to Reading Book Award for books for younger children, 1992, ABC Children's Choice Award, Reading Rainbow Feature Selection, and Pick of the Lists, American Booksellers Association, all for *The Salamander Room;* Editor's Choice Award, *Booklist,* 1992, for *Moose Street;* Notable Book, American Library Association (ALA), 1993, and notable children's trade book in the field of social studies citation, both for *The Oxboy;* finalist, Hungry Mind Best Young Adult Book, 1993, and Best Book for Teens, New York Public Library, both for *America Street: A Multicultural Anthology of Stories;* Best Book for Teens citation from ALA and from New York Public Library, both for *Working Days: Stories about Teenagers and Work.*

Writings

Watch Me, illustrated by Stacey Schuett, Knopf, 1990.
The Yellow Button, illustrated by Judy Pedersen, Knopf, 1990.

Anne Mazer

The Salamander Room, illustrated by Steve Johnson, Knopf, 1991.
Moose Street, Knopf, 1992.
The Oxboy, Knopf, 1993.
(Editor) *America Street: A Multicultural Anthology of Stories,* Persea, 1993.
The Accidental Witch, Hyperion, 1995.
(Editor) *Going Where I'm Coming From: Memoirs of American Youth,* Persea, 1995.

Goldfish Charlie and the Case of the Missing Planet,
    illustrated by Jerry Harston, Troll Communications,
    1996.
A Sliver of Glass and Other Uncommon Tales, Hyperion,
    1996.
(Editor) *Working Days: Stories about Teenagers and Work,*
    Persea, 1997.
(Editor) *A Walk in My World: International Short Stories
    about Youth,* Persea, 1998.
The Fixits, illustrated by Paul Meisel, Hyperion, 1999.

Work in Progress

The No-Nothings and Their Baby, picture book, for
Scholastic.

Sidelights

Raised in a family of children's book authors, Anne
Mazer has made her own mark on the field of children's
literature, writing several highly praised picture books
and young adult novels. "Mazer writes with such clarity
and perception, it can sometimes take your breath away,
the same way an unexpected punch does," noted
Booklist contributor Ilene Cooper of Mazer's young
adult novel, *Moose Street.* Other titles to Mazer's credit
include the picture books *The Salamander Room* and
Watch Me and the novel *The Oxboy.* She has also
compiled several anthologies of short fiction for teens
that showcase diversity of both socio-economic culture
and ethnic heritage.

Mazer has loved books ever since she can remember. As
she once told *SATA:* "From the earliest age, I would
devour anything that could be read—from comic books
to cereal boxes to encyclopedias. I loved boys' books,
girls' books, mysteries, adventures, humor, and historical fiction. As a young girl, I stood in front of the
shelves of books that lined our walls, and hungrily
pulled out volumes. The same scene was repeated
countless times in libraries, where I would wander
among the stacks almost intoxicated by so many books.
When I got older, I crept into my closet late at night,
where I stuffed towels under the door and read until well
past midnight."

As a teen, Mazer's love of books far surpassed her love
of school. She admitted to leaving school after attendance was taken in homeroom and walking the four
miles to her town library to spend the day reading. Even
though her parents were both published writers by this
time, Mazer never considered making the transition from
avid reader to writer. "My love of books was private,"
she recalled.

Following her graduation from high school, Mazer spent
several years in Paris where she studied French language
and literature and began to write. Her first book, a novel
for young adults set in Paris, was never published. After
her son was born, she began to write for younger
children, and by 1987 had completed three picture
books. Her first book, *Watch Me,* was released in 1990.

From **Goldfish Charlie and the Case of the Missing
Planet,** *written by Mazer and illustrated by Jerry
Harston.*

Watch Me was Mazer's reaction to watching her then-
two-year-old son playing on her bed. "'Look at me,
Mom! Look at me!,'" Mazer recalled him saying. "I
wrote the words on my blank piece of paper. In a few
minutes 'look at me' had changed to 'watch me,' and I
was off." Despite its simple text, Mazer reworked each
verse of *Watch Me* numerous times before she felt she
had gotten it right. "Some of the verses came out
smoothly and easily, but most were the result of hours of
trial and error," she recalled. "The phrase 'watch me'
seemed such a universal theme for small children that I
couldn't believe half a dozen people hadn't thought of it
already."

Unlike *Watch Me, The Yellow Button* grew easily out of
the author's childhood memories. "When I was a small
child, I often tried to encompass infinity within my own
mind," Mazer explained. "I would dazzle myself with
visions of unlimited space, and then return to my room,
my self, my own small, but somehow newly expanded
and enlivened reality. This mental game—a kind of
contemplation really—used to give me great pleasure.
One night I was sitting at the typewriter, when a picture
popped into my mind of a button sitting in a pocket. As I
wrote down the words, describing the picture I clearly
saw, one image seemed to flow from another. In a very

short time, the book was written—and I made few changes in it.

"My third book *The Salamander Room,* was triggered by a remark a little boy made while we were on a nature hike," explained Mazer. "I no longer remember the original conversation, but the boy wanted to bring a salamander home." From the boy's comment, Mazer developed the story of a boy named Brian who is determined to bring home a new pet salamander. Despite his mother's practical questions, like "Where will the salamander sleep?" "Brian's cozy bedroom is gradually transformed into a dark green forest that overflows the pages" as he imagines his pet's ideal home, according to *School Library Journal* contributor Louise L. Sherman. Praising both the story and its illustrations, a *Publishers Weekly* reviewer commented that "Mazer's text offers fitting tribute to a child's perseverance and imagination."

In addition to picture books, Mazer has written several novels for older readers. In *Moose Street,* eleven-year-old Lena Rosen feels like a loner in her neighborhood because she is the only Jewish child on the block. Her isolation provides her with a different perspective on the people around her, and she shares her heightened sensitivity to people's secret side through a series of interrelated vignettes. Cooper commended Mazer for portraying the "exquisite torture Lena feels when she's made to suffer for a religion she barely believes in, or when she's asked to participate in the torture adolescents excel at, picking on the most vulnerable child around." In another novel, *The Accidental Witch,* Mazer assembles "an imaginative, action-packed plot and a fine cast of characters" in a "light, fun-filled fantasy," according to *Booklist* contributor Lauren Peterson. Fifth-grader Phoebe discovers that she has gained the witch-like powers she always wanted but can't quite figure out how to focus them, in a novel that Anne Connor described in *School Library Journal* as "a lively fantasy [that] creates a world very much like our own," where Phoebe "fulfills her dream through persistence and good will."

In *The Oxboy,* Mazer weaves together fantasy and social commentary to create a world in which animals and humans can marry. The "mixed-bloods" of these unions—which are outlawed by the intolerant humans—must attempt to pass as wholly human because the offspring of such unions, if discovered, are executed. Within this world, a boy whose disguised father is actually a noble ox refuses to oppress other, more obvious mixed-bloods, even though his actions will result in his imprisonment. Mazer's "allegorical world is compelling," noted a *Kirkus Reviews* critic, who found *The Oxboy* to be a "provocative, unusually imaginative tale." According to *Booklist* contributor Hazel Rochman, "Mazer writes with poetic restraint about the glory of pushing boundaries to understand 'the language of stones and stars and moss and roses.'"

Although Mazer has expanded her works beyond picture books in recent years—in addition to her writing she has acted on her desire to promote tolerance of cultural differences among young people by editing such anthologies as *Going Where I'm Coming From: Memoirs of American Youth*—she still respects picture books as a medium far more complicated than it might seem to the casual reader. "Though the text has to be done with the utmost simplicity, I find that I can express many complex and profound emotions such as joy, love and contentment. I also love the spareness of the picture book. There is no waste in a good picture book. Each word counts and each word must be placed exactly right."

Works Cited

Connor, Anne, review of *The Accidental Witch, School Library Journal,* January, 1996, p. 110.

Cooper, Ilene, review of *Moose Street, Booklist,* November 1, 1992, p. 510.

Review of *The Oxboy, Kirkus Reviews,* December 1, 1993, p. 1526.

Peterson, Lauren, review of *The Accidental Witch, Booklist,* November 1, 1995, p. 473.

Rochman, Hazel, review of *The Oxboy, Booklist,* November 1, 1993, p. 523.

Review of *The Salamander Room, Publishers Weekly,* January 11, 1991, p. 101.

Sherman, Louise L., review of *The Salamander Room, School Library Journal,* April, 1991, p. 100.

For More Information See

PERIODICALS

Booklist, September 1, 1993, p. 50; January 15, 1995, p. 910; September 15, 1996, p. 242.

Bulletin of the Center for Children's Books, November, 1993, p. 90; November, 1996, p. 107.

Horn Book, December, 1997, p. 682.

Publishers Weekly, December 5, 1994, p. 78; May 26, 1997, p. 86; March 8, 1999, p. 67.

School Library Journal, October, 1990, p. 143; November, 1992, p. 96; November, 1993, p. 110; February, 1997, p. 104; September, 1997, p. 220.

Voice of Youth Advocates, December, 1993, p. 317; December, 1997, p. 318.

*   *   *

MAZER, Harry 1925-

Personal

Born May 31, 1925, in New York, NY; son of Sam (a dressmaker) and Rose (a dressmaker; maiden name, Lazevnick) Mazer; married Norma Fox (a novelist), February 12, 1950; children: Anne, Joseph, Susan, Gina. *Education:* Union College, B.A., 1948; Syracuse University, M.A., 1960.

Addresses

Agent—Marilyn Marlow, Curtis Brown Ltd., 10 Astor Pl., New York, NY 10003.

Career

New York Central Railroad, brake man and switchtender, 1950-55; New York Construction, Syracuse, sheet metal worker, 1957-59; Central Square School, Central Square, NY, English teacher, 1959-60; Aerofin Corp., Syracuse, welder, 1960-63; full-time writer, 1963—. *Military service:* U.S. Army Air Force, 1943-45; became sergeant; received Purple Heart and Air Medal with four bronze oak leaf clusters. *Member:* Authors Guild, Authors League of America, Society of Children's Book Writers and Illustrators, American Civil Liberties Union.

Awards, Honors

Best of the Best Books list, American Library Association (ALA), 1970-73, for *Snow Bound; Kirkus* Choice list, 1974, for *The Dollar Man;* Best Books for Young Adults, ALA, 1977, and Children's Choice, International Reading Association-Children's Book Council, 1978, both for *The Solid Gold Kid;* Best Books for Young Adults, ALA, and Dorothy Canfield Fisher Children's Book Award nomination, Vermont Congress of Parents and Teachers-Vermont Department of Libraries, both 1979, both for *The War on Villa Street;* Best Books, *New York Times,* 1979, Books for the Teen Age, New York Public Library, 1980, Best Books for Young Adults, ALA, 1981, and Best of the Best Books list, ALA, 1970-83, all for *The Last Mission; Booklist* Contemporary Classics list, 1984, and "Preis der Lesseratten" (West Germany), both for *Snow Bound;* Arizona Young Readers Award nomination, Arizona State Library Association, 1985, for *The Island Keeper: A Tale of Courage and Survival;* Best Books for Young Adults, ALA, 1986, for *I Love You, Stupid!;* Books for the Teen Age, New York Public Library, 1986, and International Reading Association-Children's Book Council Young Adult Choice list, 1987, both for *Hey, Kid! Does She Love Me?;* Best Books for Young Adults, ALA, 1987, Iowa Teen Award Master list, Iowa Educational Media Association, 1988, and West Australian Young Reader's Book Award, Australian Library and Information Association, 1989, all for *When the Phone Rang;* Best Books for Young Adults, ALA, Books for Reluctant Young Adult Readers, ALA, 1988, and Books for the Teen Age, New York Public Library, 1988, all for *The Girl of His Dreams;* Books for the Teen Age, New York Public Library, 1989, for *Heartbeat;* Books for Reluctant Young Adult Readers, ALA, 1989, for *City Light;* Quick Picks for Reluctant Young Adult Readers, ALA, 1998, for *Twelve Shots: Outstanding Stories about Guns;* Best Books, *School Library Journal,* 1998, and Fanfare list, *Horn Book,* 1999, both for *The Wild Kid.*

Writings

NOVELS; FOR YOUNG ADULTS

Guy Lenny, Delacorte, 1971.
Snow Bound, Delacorte, 1973.
The Dollar Man, Delacorte, 1974.
The War on Villa Street, Delacorte, 1978.
The Last Mission, Delacorte, 1979.

Harry Mazer

The Island Keeper: A Tale of Courage and Survival, Delacorte, 1981.
I Love You, Stupid!, Crowell, 1981.
Hey, Kid! Does She Love Me?, Crowell, 1984.
When the Phone Rang, Scholastic, 1985.
Cave under the City, Crowell, 1986.
The Girl of His Dreams, Crowell, 1987.
City Light, Scholastic, 1988.
Someone's Mother Is Missing, Delacorte, 1990.
Who Is Eddie Leonard?, Delacorte, 1993.
(Editor) *Twelve Shots: Outstanding Short Stories about Guns,* Delacorte, 1997.
The Dog in the Freezer: Three Novellas, Simon & Schuster, 1997.
The Wild Kid, Simon & Schuster, 1998.

WITH NORMA FOX MAZER

The Solid Gold Kid, Delacorte, 1977.
Heartbeat, Bantam, 1989.
Bright Days, Stupid Nights, Bantam, 1992.

Adaptations

Snow Bound was produced as a National Broadcasting Company (NBC) "After School Special" in 1978. *Snow Bound* and *The Last Mission* were recorded on audio cassette by Listening Library, 1985.

Sidelights

In addition to being part of a writing family that includes wife Norma Fox Mazer and daughter Anne Mazer, novelist Harry Mazer has received critical acclaim for his many young adult novels—including *The Island Keeper, Cave under the City,* and *Who Is Eddie Leonard?*—which illustrate the values of perseverance, self-esteem, and inner fortitude. Noting that, "despite their predicaments, Mazer's protagonists usually emerge morally victorious," *Twentieth-Century Young Adult Writers* contributor Mary Lystad cited as Mazer's strength his depiction of the "emotional turmoil, the humor and pain" of adolescence. "His characters are resilient and strong," Lystad continued. "His endings emphasize compassion, understanding, resourcefulness, and honesty."

"A dream is made by real effort," Mazer once explained in an essay in *Something about the Author Autobiography Series* (*SAAS*). Mazer was in his mid-thirties when he and his wife began to write every day; they wrote for the "women's true confessions" market, using the money to support the family. "My writing dismayed me," the author revealed; "I had dark moments when I wondered why I was going on with this . . . . I wrote a lot about my feelings, interpreting my dreams, trying to keep myself together." In 1971 Mazer's "real effort" resulted in *Guy Lenny,* his first novel, and since then, many of his novels have been translated into German, French, Finnish, and Danish. Kenneth L. Donelson asserted in *Voice of Youth Advocates* that "Mazer writes about young people caught in the midst of moral crises, often of their own making. Searching for a way out, they discover themselves, or rather they learn that the first step in extricating themselves from their physical and moral dilemmas is self-discovery. Intensely moral as Mazer's books are," continued Donelson, "they present young people thinking and talking and acting believably," a characteristic that accounts for Mazer's continued popularity among readers and critics alike.

The son of hard-working Polish-Jewish immigrants, Mazer grew up in an apartment building in the Bronx, New York. The building was part of a two-block complex called the Coops, and Mazer recalled in *SAAS* that "you could feel the optimistic spirit that built these houses—in the central courtyards with their gardens and fountains, in the library, the gymnasium, and the kindergarten. The Coops were special, an island, a community, a village in a great city built on a shared dream of cooperation and social justice." Mazer shared the bedroom of the two-room apartment with his brother, while his parents slept in the living room, which also served as a dining room and kitchen. The halls and the stairs were Mazer's playground, and he grew up between two worlds—the park and the street—both of which he would later use in his novels. "The park was mine, so big it was limitless," recalled Mazer. The many games that the street offered, such as marbles and chalk-drawing, also appealed to Mazer, as did the huge fires built in empty lots after dark.

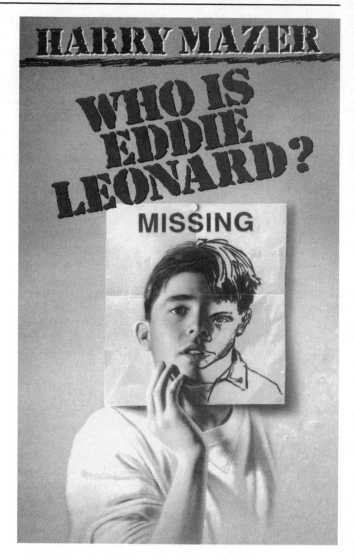

Fifteen-year-old Eddie seeks to find the truth about his birth and reunite with his parents in Mazer's moving story.

Lack of money was always a problem for Mazer during these years. While he did not retain many memories of his school days, he remembered reading *The Gingerbread Man* and *Little Black Sambo,* for reading was among his favorite pastimes. "I read and ate," he noted, recalling memories of lying on the couch with his nose in a book and "a pile of apple cores on the floor." Mazer read everything from series books and adventure stories to the collected works of Charles Dickens. "Two of my all-time favorite books were *Robinson Crusoe,* the story of a man alone on a desert island, and *Tarzan of the Apes,*" stated Mazer in *SAAS.*

Changes loomed large in Mazer's life when he entered his high-school years. Questions about his future occupied his mind; jobs were scarce at the time, and many employers wouldn't hire Jews. If he had been a dutiful son, Mazer later reflected, he would have become a teacher; "but I was in rebellion. I was impatient. I wanted to be great, famous . . . . My secret desire was to be a writer, but I knew nothing about how to make it happen. I had the idea that if I could only write it down, if I could only put all my feelings into words, I would finally figure everything out (whatever everything was)." Mazer took the competitive exam for the Bronx High School of Science and got in, but the courses that most interested him were English and history, and the questions concerning his future still lingered.

World War II was on Mazer's mind also. At age seventeen he qualified to join the U.S. Army Air Force Cadets, but had to wait until he was eighteen to serve. "I prayed that the war didn't end before I got in," Mazer remembered in his *SAAS* essay. While he waited, he started attending college classes, only to quit after less than a week. The army finally called him, and Mazer served for two and a half years. Starting out as an airplane mechanic, he volunteered for aerial gunnery school, training as a ball-turret and waist gunner. After training, Mazer was assigned to a crew on a B-17 bomber. In December of 1944 the young crew headed for Europe and flew their first mission two months later. Their last mission was flown in April when the plane was shot down over Czechoslovakia; only Mazer and one other crew member survived. "I remember thinking afterward that there had to be a reason why I had survived," recalled Mazer. "I didn't think it was God. It was chance. Luck. But why me? Chance can't be denied as a factor in life, but I clung to the thought that there was a reason for my survival."

Mazer was discharged from the army in October of 1945, and days later began attending classes at a liberal arts college. He began writing, but his work "was too serious and self-conscious. I turned each word over in my head before I allowed it out into the open.... I wrote, but I was full of doubt, my standards were miles higher than my abilities. I suffered over what I wrote and didn't write any more than I had to." Graduating with a liberal arts degree, Mazer took a blue-collar job while struggling to define himself as a writer. A three-month course in welding resulted in a job in an auto-body shop. "I was dramatizing myself," Mazer later admitted, "imagining myself a leader of the downtrodden, pointing the way to the future.... I was idealistic. I was unrealistic. Most of all I was avoiding the real issues of my life. I didn't have the belief or the nerve to say I was a writer, to begin writing and let everything else take care of itself."

Politics also interested Mazer during this period; it was while working on a campaign that he met Norma Fox for the second time. He had met her two years earlier when she was fifteen and he was twenty-one, but it was the second meeting that started their on-again, off-again romance. A year later Norma began college, but Mazer pressed her to get married. "Norma said yes, we'd get married, then she said no," Mazer remembered. "When she was with me it was yes, but when she went back to school it was no again." The couple finally married and settled in a tiny apartment in New York City, but soon moved back upstate to Schenectady, and then to Utica, finally settling in Syracuse. Mazer worked at various jobs, doing welding, sheet metal work, and track work for the railroad. "I was moody and didn't talk and I wasn't nice to be around," he recalled of these years. "I didn't know what was bothering me. I only knew I had to get out, move, walk off the mood. I'd walk along the railroad tracks and pick wild asparagus or I'd go to Three Rivers, where I'd sit under a tree and watch birds. I thought if I could only write down what I was feeling—if only I could put thought to paper—I'd know what I ought to do. But I didn't know how to start."

After ten years of factory work, Mazer became a teacher. It was at this point that he and Norma talked, discovered that they both longed to be writers, and began writing every day. Mazer lost his teaching job and returned to factory work, taking paperbacks with him, trying to understand how a story worked. The insurance money from an accident finally enabled him to quit his job and begin writing full-time; the couple were soon writing two confession stories a week. "These stories demanded that I develop a character, a plot, action that rose to a climax, and a satisfying ending. And I had to do it every week, week after week. It was a demanding school. I was being forced to write to stay out of the factory," Mazer wrote in *SAAS*. He also tried other forms of writing, including television scripts and pieces for literary magazines. The Mazers' agent finally suggested they try the children's field.

A piece in a "Dear Abby" column gave Mazer the idea for his first children's book. The column was about a boy who was concerned about an older girl he liked. She was going with someone else who was no good for her, and the boy wanted to know how he could break them up. "It was the germ that started my first book, *Guy Lenny*," Mazer revealed in his essay. *Guy Lenny* is the story of a boy whose parents are divorced, a subject that children's books of the time did not deal with. His mother has left him, and he is living with his father when she returns to claim him. "It's a children's story because it's about a boy and is told from his point of view," explains Mazer in *SAAS*; "it's also an adult story because it's about growing up and having to live with some of the hard, intractable things of life. And that's what made it a young-adult book, a new category of fiction that was still to be named." Norma's novel *I, Trissy* had just been accepted for publication; Mazer sent his book off reluctantly, expecting the worst. "There is no moment to equal the moment when your first book is taken," Mazer claimed, recalling the call from his agent saying that his book had found a publisher.

Many of Mazer's novels use characters from earlier books, and father-and-son relationships appear again and again. "I've gone about the work of writing like a bird building a nest each year with the bits of thread and paper I snatch up in the street, but also from the scraps of memory I weave together in book after book," the novelist noted in *SAAS*. "I didn't have a plan, there was no agenda, no burning purpose, no passion about injustice," he continues. "There was passion, but it was a passion for the characters, for the world they lived in."

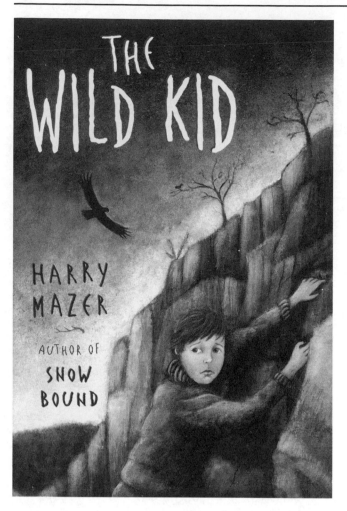

Rebellious Kevin and twelve-year-old Sammy, who has Down's Syndrome, begin to trust and assist one another in Mazer's story of their move toward a reluctant friendship. (Cover illustration by Deborah Lanino.)

A *Publishers Weekly* contributor maintained that Mazer "creates credible characters ... and incorporates splashes of humor while maintaining the established mood and tone." In the novel *The Girl of His Dreams,* for example, Mazer relates the romance of Willis and Sophie, two ordinary young adults, with "a credibility apart from [the book's] fairy-tale ending," in the opinion of Marianne Gingher in the *Los Angeles Times.* Willis is a factory worker and dedicated runner who has a clear vision of exactly what the girl of his dreams should be like. Sophie does not fit this image, and their relationship develops slowly and awkwardly. "No run-of-the-mill, boy meets girl story here," stated Libby K. White in *School Library Journal,* adding that the novel "is romantic without being either mushy or explicitly sexual. Willis and Sophie are attractive characters who will interest and involve readers."

Snow Bound is another tale of two mismatched teens who are caught unprepared for a New York blizzard and must cooperate to survive. Tony is a spoiled rich kid who sets out to get revenge on his parents for not letting him keep a stray dog. He steals his mother's car and

takes off in the middle of a snowstorm, picking up hitchhiker Cindy along the way. Besides getting lost, Tony wrecks the car in a desolate area, and he and Cindy must save themselves from the cold and a pack of wild dogs. "The relationship that develops between the two of them is sensitively handled, never foolishly romanticized, and will probably be an easy thing for young readers to identify with," maintains Tom Heffernan in *Children's Literature. New York Times Book Review* contributor Cathleen Burns Elmer concluded that "the final measure of the book's capacity to enthrall lies in the *mature* reader's willingness to suspend disbelief. 'Snow Bound' is a crackling tale; Mazer tells it with vigor and authority."

Highly praised by critics, *The Last Mission,* based in part on Mazer's own experiences in World War II, "represents an amazing leap in writing, far surpassing anything [the author] had written before," according to Donelson. Jewish fifteen-year-old Jack Raab is so desperate to fight against Hitler that he borrows his older brother's identification to enlist in the U.S. Army Air Forces. Jack is trained as a gunner, and he and his fellow crew members fly more than twenty missions out of England before being hit by enemy fire. Jack bails out and is the only one to survive—but ends up a German prisoner of war. While war stories are common, Donelson maintained that *The Last Mission* "conveys better than any other young adult novel, and better than most adult novels, the feeling of war and the desolation it leaves behind.... This book is a remarkable achievement, both for its theme and its portrait of a young man who searches and acts and finds the search futile and the actions incoherent." Paxton Davis asserted in the *New York Times Book Review:* "Mazer is a prize-winning writer for young people."

The main character in *I Love You, Stupid!* is faced with more typical adolescent problems. A senior in high school, Marcus wants to be a writer and is obsessed with sex. *School Library Journal* contributor Kay Webb O'Connell pointed out that Marcus's erotic dreams include almost every young female he meets—everyone but Wendy, a girl he knew in grade school. Marcus even goes so far as to babysit for a young divorced woman, hoping she'll become his lover. Wendy and Marcus finally make love, but Marcus, looking for a reason to do it every day, drives Wendy away. By the end of the book, they are back together, and Marcus realizes the importance of friendship and love. "It takes most of the book to get them together, but it's better that way; Marcus and Wendy are friends who become lovers," observed O'Connell, concluding that "they're honest and humorous; their conversations and adventures are fresh and funny."

Who Is Eddie Leonard? introduces readers to the fifteen-year-old title character, who lives with an eccentric elderly woman he calls "Grandmother." When she dies, he is left alone, feeling that he must belong somewhere. A poster of a missing child named Jason Diaz changes everything for Eddie. Seeing the resemblance between himself and the missing boy, and calculating that Jason would now also be fifteen years old, Eddie hunts down the boy's family and introduces himself as their missing son. Now divorced and having given up their son as lost forever, Jason's parents are skeptical, and the missing boy's sister, Miller, is happy as an only child. Eddie becomes involved in this new family, and when the truth about his birth is finally discovered, he must suffer further loss. "Mazer has written a book teens will respond to," maintained *Voice of Youth Advocates* contributor Ruth E. Dishnow, "a story about the often painful search for self-identity." While *School Library Journal* reviewer Lucinda Snyder Whitehurst felt that Mazer's terse, detached style makes *Who Is Eddie Leonard?* more a "series of strong character studies" than a cohesive story, Chris Sherman had praise for the novel, writing in *Booklist* that Mazer's is "an emotionally charged story that readers will not be able to put down."

The Wild Kid finds twelve-year-old Sammy, who has Down's Syndrome, building a reputation as a no-good kid. Leaving the house without permission, Sammy gets his bike stolen and becomes lost in the woods outside of town while following the thief. In the forest he meets Kevin, a teen on the run. First Kevin's prisoner, Sammy gradually becomes the wild teen's friend, and Kevin ultimately helps the younger boy find his way home. Mazer's story was praised by several reviewers for its positive portrayal of a child with Down's Syndrome. *School Library Journal* contributor Carol A. Edwards asserted: "Vividly and with a fast pace, Mazer describes Sammy's world, his awful predicament, his magnificent spirit, and his incredible determination." Edwards concluded that *The Wild Kid* is "for anyone looking for an adventure, a survival story on many levels, or a compelling read."

Other novels by Mazer include *The War on Villa Street,* about a boy's attempts to find stability in a family where his father's alcoholism and his mother's passivity mean constant upheaval and relocation. Ultimately his own passivity and sense of shame at his father's abuse cause the boy to fight back, building his own self-confidence in the process. *The War on Villa Street* was called "a moving, fast-paced story that once more proves Mazer's understanding of adolescence" by *School Library Journal* contributor Robert Unsworth. Also set in an urban area, *Cave under the City* takes place during the Great Depression, as two brothers find themselves parentless after their father's departure in search of work and their mother's subsequent collapse and hospitalization. When social workers attempt to separate the boys, they flee and live among New York City's homeless population until their father returns. *School Library Journal* contributor Christine Behrmann noted that *Cave under the City* contains "resonances of the plight of today's homeless." In addition to novel-length books and a few collaborative efforts with his wife, Mazer has also written *The Dog in the Freezer,* a collection of three novellas. Focusing on dogs, the boys who own them, and the fathers who rule the family home, each of the stories has a slightly quirky perspective. In "My Life as a Boy," the family dog trades places with his human master for a

day, while "Puppy Love" weaves a teen boy's summer crush on a pretty dog trainer with his growing affection for the puppy he adopted as a way of gaining the young woman's attention. "The Dog in the Freezer" finds a boy struggling to figure out how to bury a neighbor's dead dog rather than leave it lying on the street. While of the opinion that Mazer is more adept at longer fiction, a *Kirkus Reviews* contributor praised *The Dog in the Freezer* as "an interesting departure."

Drawing on his personal concerns about modern society, Mazer served as editor of *Twelve Shots: Outstanding Short Stories about Guns,* which was released in 1997. Inviting a dozen authors to write stories concerning "not the politics of the gun, not the heated arguments or the polemics, but the way guns are present in people's lives," Mazer assembles works by such well-known children's authors as Walter Dean Myers, Chris Lynch, Frederick Busch, and Rita Williams-Garcia, as well as contributing his own short story, based on his novel *The Last Mission.* While the stories included range from serious commentary on the devastation wrought by gun-related violence in modern society to humorous folk-like tales, Mazer's own anti-gun slant is made clear. "De-

From a slightly quirky perspective, each of Mazer's three novellas focuses on dogs and the boys who own them. (Cover illustration by Christopher Buzelli.)

struction clearly outweighs redemption in the bulk of these stories," Elizabeth Bush commented in the *Bulletin of the Center for Children's Books,* "with manipulative power, paranoia, or profound despair generally behind the trigger." Including statistics about guns and other helpful information, *Twelve Shots* is "timely and thought provoking" as well as "an excellent springboard for discussion," according to *Booklist* contributor Helen Rosenberg.

From his novels to his shorter works of fiction, Mazer's writing has been characterized by reviewers as containing a belief in the essential goodness of people, particularly young people. As *Horn Book* reviewer Margaret A. Bush observed, Mazer's "characters are down to earth, very ordinary people who are flawed, inept, good. Their eccentricities, loneliness, and dreams are lightly touched with humor." In his *SAAS* essay, Mazer concluded: "I think underlying all my writing has always been the belief that beneath the surface of our differences there is a current, a dark stream that connects all of us, readers and writers, parents and children, the young and the old. Despite the erosion of time the child in us never dies. The search for love never ends, the need for connection, the desire to know who we are, and the need to find someone of our own to love. How else do I keep writing for young readers?"

Works Cited

Behrmann, Christine, review of *Cave under the City,* School Library Journal, December, 1986, pp. 105-06.

Bush, Elizabeth, review of *Twelve Shots: Outstanding Short Stories about Guns,* Bulletin of the Center for Children's Books, October, 1997, p. 61.

Bush, Margaret A., review of *The Girl of His Dreams,* Horn Book, March-April, 1988, pp. 209-10.

Davis, Paxton, review of *The Last Mission,* New York Times Book Review, December 2, 1979, p. 41.

Dishnow, Ruth E., review of *Who Is Eddie Leonard?,* Voice of Youth Advocates, April, 1994, p. 29.

Review of *The Dog in the Freezer: Three Novellas,* Kirkus Reviews, March 15, 1997, p. 466.

Review of *The Dog in the Freezer: Three Novellas,* Publishers Weekly, February 10, 1997, p. 84.

Donelson, Kenneth L., "Searchers and Doers: Heroes in Five Harry Mazer Novels," *Voice of Youth Advocates,* February, 1983, pp. 19-21.

Edwards, Carol A., review of *The Wild Kid,* School Library Journal, October, 1998, p. 140.

Elmer, Cathleen Burns, review of *Snow Bound,* New York Times Book Review, August 12, 1973, p. 8.

Gingher, Marianne, "A Boy Who Runs Meets a Girl Anxious to Catch Up," *Los Angeles Times,* March 12, 1988.

Heffernan, Tom, review of *Snow Bound,* Children's Literature, edited by Francelia Butler, Volume 4, Temple University Press, 1975, p. 206.

Lystad, Mary, *Twentieth-Century Young Adult Writers,* St. James Press, 1994, pp. 429-31.

Mazer, Harry, essay in *Something about the Author Autobiography Series,* Volume 11, Gale, 1991, pp. 223-40.

O'Connell, Kay Webb, review of *I Love You, Stupid!,* School Library Journal, October, 1981, p. 152.

Rosenberg, Helen, review of *Twelve Shots: Outstanding Short Stories about Guns,* Booklist, August, 1997, p. 1899.

Sherman, Chris, review of *Who Is Eddie Leonard?,* Booklist, November 15, 1993, p 615.

Unsworth, Robert, review of *The War on Villa Street,* School Library Journal, December, 1978, p. 62.

White, Libby K., review of *The Girl of His Dreams,* School Library Journal, January, 1988, pp. 86-87.

Whitehurst, Lucinda Snyder, review of *Who Is Eddie Leonard?,* School Library Journal, November, 1993, p. 125.

For More Information See

BOOKS

Children's Literature Review, Volume 16, Gale, 1989, pp. 125-33.

Nilsen, Alleen Pace, and Kenneth L. Donelson, *Literature for Today's Young Adults,* Scott, Foresman, 1985.

Reed, Arthea J. S., *Presenting Harry Mazer,* Twayne, 1996.

PERIODICALS

Booklist, March 15, 1997, p. 1236.

Bulletin of the Center for Children's Books, November, 1997, p. 109.

Kirkus Reviews, July 1, 1997, p. 1033.

Publishers Weekly, August 10, 1990, p. 446.

Voice of Youth Advocates, August, 1997, p. 190.

*   *   *

MAZER, Norma Fox 1931-

Personal

Born May 15, 1931, in New York, NY; daughter of Michael and Jean (Garlen) Fox; married Harry Mazer (a novelist), February 12, 1950; children: Anne, Joseph, Susan, Gina. *Education:* Attended Antioch College, 1949-50, and Syracuse University, 1957-59. *Politics:* "I believe in people—despise institutions while accepting their necessity." *Religion:* "Jewish by birth, pantheistic by nature." *Hobbies and other interests:* Reading, racquetball, gardening.

Addresses

Agent—Elaine Markson, 44 Greenwich Avenue, New York, NY 10012; Abner Stein, 10 Roland Gardens, London SW7 3PH, England.

Career

Writer, 1964—. Has worked as a secretary at a radio station, punch press operator, waitress, and cashier.

Awards, Honors

National Book Award nomination, 1973, for *A Figure of Speech;* Lewis Carroll Shelf Award, University of Wisconsin, 1975, for *Saturday, the Twelfth of October;* Christopher Award, *New York Times* Outstanding Books of the Year, Best Books, *School Library Journal,* Best Books for Young Adults, American Library Association (ALA), Notable Book, ALA, and Lewis Carroll Shelf Award, all 1976, all for *Dear Bill, Remember Me? and Other Stories;* Best Books for Young Adults, ALA, 1977, Children's Choice, Children's Book Council-International Reading Association, 1978, and 100 Best of the Best Books, ALA, 1993, all for *The Solid Gold Kid;* Best Books for Young Adults, ALA, 1979, Best Books, *School Library Journal,* 1979, and Best of the Best Books list, ALA, 1970-83, all for *Up in Seth's Room;* Austrian Children's Books list of honor and German Children's Literature prize, both 1982, both for *Mrs. Fish, Ape, and Me, the Dump Queen;* Edgar Award, Mystery Writers of America, 1982, and California Young Readers Medal, California Reading Association, 1985, both for *Taking Terri Mueller;* Best Books for Young Adults, ALA, 1983, for *Someone to Love;* Best Books for Young Adults, ALA, *New York Times* Outstanding Books of the Year list, and Books for the Teen Age, New York Public Library, all 1984, all for *Downtown;* Iowa Teen Award, Iowa Educational Media Association, 1985-86, for *When We First Met;* Children's Choice, Children's Book Council-International Reading Association, 1986, for *A, My Name Is Ami;* Newbery Honor Book, Best Books, *School Library Journal,* Notable Book, ALA, Best Books for Young Adults, ALA, Children's Choice, Canadian Children's Books Council, *Horn Book* Fanfare selection, and Association of Booksellers for Children Choice, all 1988, all for *After the Rain;* Best Books for Young Adults, ALA, 1989, Iowa Teen Award, 1991, and One Hundred Best of the Best Books, 1968-93, ALA, all for *Silver;* Children's Choice, Children's Book Council-International Reading Association, German Literature Prize, and Books for the Teen Age, New York Public Library, all 1989, all for *Heartbeat;* Books for the Teen Age, New York Public Library, 1989, for *Silver* and *Heartbeat* and 1990, for *Waltzing on Water: Poetry by Women* and *Babyface;* Pick of the Lists, American Booksellers Association, 1990, for *Babyface, Bright Days, Stupid Nights, Out of Control,* and *Missing Pieces;* Best Books for Young Adults, ALA, 1994, for *Out of Control;* Best Books, *School Library Journal,* Editor's Choice, *Booklist,* both 1997, Best Books for Young Adults, ALA, 1998, all for *When She Was Good.*

Writings

NOVELS; FOR YOUNG ADULTS

I, Trissy, Delacorte, 1971.
A Figure of Speech (also see below), Delacorte, 1973.
Saturday, the Twelfth of October, Delacorte, 1975.
Dear Bill, Remember Me? and Other Stories, Delacorte, 1976.
Up in Seth's Room, Delacorte, 1979.
Mrs. Fish, Ape, and Me, the Dump Queen, Dutton, 1980, reissued as *Crazy Fish,* Morrow, 1998.
Taking Terri Mueller, Avon, 1981.
When We First Met (sequel to *A Figure of Speech;* also see below) Four Winds, 1982.
Summer Girls, Love Boys, and Other Short Stories, Delacorte, 1982.
Someone to Love, Delacorte, 1983.
(With Axel Daimler) *When We First Met* (screenplay based on novel of same title), Learning Corporation of America, 1984.
Downtown, Morrow, 1984.
Supergirl (novelization), Warner, 1984.
A, My Name Is Ami, Scholastic, 1986.
Three Sisters, Scholastic, 1986.
B, My Name Is Bunny, Scholastic, 1987.
After the Rain, Morrow, 1987.
Silver, Morrow, 1988.
C, My Name Is Cal, Scholastic, 1990.
Babyface, Morrow, 1990.
D, My Name Is Danita, Scholastic, 1991.
E, My Name Is Emily, Scholastic, 1991.
Out of Control, Morrow, 1993.
Missing Pieces, Morrow, 1995.
When She Was Good, Arthur A. Levine, 1997.
Good Night, Maman, Harcourt, 1999.

WITH HARRY MAZER

The Solid Gold Kid, Delacorte, 1977.
Heartbeat, Bantam, 1989.
Bright Days, Stupid Nights, Bantam, 1992.

Norma Fox Mazer

OTHER

(Editor with Margery Lewis) *Waltzing on Water: Poetry by Women,* Dell, 1989.

(Editor with Jacqueline Woodson) *Just a Writer's Thing: A Collection of Prose and Poetry from the National Book Foundation's 1995 Summer Writing Camp,* National Book Foundation, 1996.

Contributor to anthologies, including *Sixteen: Short Stories by Outstanding Writers for Young Adults,* edited by Donald R. Gallo, Delacorte, 1984; *Short Takes: A Short Story Collection for Young Readers,* edited by Elizabeth Segal, Lothrop, 1986; *Visions: Nineteen Short Stories by Outstanding Writers for Young Adults,* edited by Donald R. Gallo, Delacorte, 1987; *Hot Flashes: Women Writers on the Change of Life,* edited by Lynne Taetzsch, Faber and Faber, 1995; *Night Terrors: Stories of Shadow and Substance,* edited by Lois Duncan, Simon & Schuster, 1996; *When I Was Your Age: Original Stories about Growing Up,* edited by Amy Ehrlich, Candlewick, 1996; *Stay True: Short Stories for Strong Girls,* edited by Marilyn Singer, Scholastic, 1998; *Places I Never Meant to Be: Original Stories By Censored Writers,* edited by Judy Blume, Simon & Schuster, 1999. Also contributor of stories and articles to magazines, including *Jack and Jill, Ingenue, Calling All Girls, Child Life, Boys and Girls, Redbook, English Journal, Voice of Youth Advocates, Signal, Top of the News,* and *ALAN Review.*

Adaptations

When We First Met was made into a movie for HBO in 1984. Mazer's novels recorded on audio cassette and released by Listening Library include *Taking Terri Mueller,* 1986, *Dear Bill, Remember Me? and Other Stories,* 1987, and *After the Rain,* 1988.

Sidelights

Norma Fox Mazer has garnered numerous awards, as well as high praise from critics, for novels like *Silver, After the Rain,* and *Saturday, the Twelfth of October* that depict teenagers in everyday situations, experiencing common problems. "At her best," observed Suzanne Freeman in the *Washington Post Book World,* "Mazer can cut right to the bone of teenage troubles and then show us how the wounds will heal. She can set down the everyday scenes of her characters' lives in images that are scalpel sharp.... What's apparent throughout all of this is that Mazer has taken great care to get to know the world she writes about. She delves into the very heart of it with a sure and practiced hand." It took many years of discipline for Mazer to become such a writer, and even longer for her to consider herself one; it wasn't until she was writing her 1976 novel *Dear Bill, Remember Me? and Other Stories* that Mazer actually believed she was a real author. In an essay in *Something about the Author Autobiography Series (SAAS),* she recalled that "during the months I spent working on [*Dear Bill*], I somehow lost time, I began to believe fearlessly in the endless vitality of that mysterious source from which my imagination is constantly replenished."

Mazer grew up in Glens Falls, New York, the middle daughter in a family of three girls. Her father was a route driver, delivering such things as milk and bread, and the family lived in a succession of various apartments and houses. "The year we lived on Ridge Street, when I was eight," stated Mazer in her autobiographical essay, "I learned to ride a two-wheeler, changed my name (briefly, because I kept forgetting I'd changed it) to the more glamorous Diane, made up triplet brothers in the Navy to impress my new girlfriend, and was caught stealing." School, reading, and boys were her childhood loves, and it was in a new apartment on First Street that she may have realized the possibilities of her imagination: "A girlfriend and I are playing near ... wooden steps. I have forgotten the game, although I made it up, but not her words. 'Norma Fox! What an imagination!' And perhaps it was precisely then that I realized that my imagination had some other function than to torment me with witches in doorknobs and lurking figures in the shadows of the stairs."

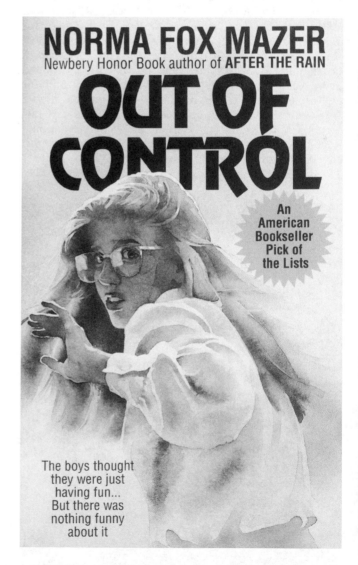

High school student Rollo Wingate must face the humiliation and trauma he caused when he participated in the sexual harassment of a classmate in Mazer's insightful novel.

During Mazer's teen years, her family started calling her the "Cold One," as she began to live more and more in her own world. Feeling like an outsider, Mazer admitted in *SAAS* that "were I to be asked to use one word to describe myself then and for years afterward, it would be—eyes. There's a picture of me around thirteen, sitting in a high-backed leather chair, looking out of the corner of my eyes, looking around, watching, a little frightened smile on my face. Along about then, it struck me, a bone-aching truth, that grown-ups—adults, these powerful mysterious people—were all play-acting; they weren't, in fact, any older, any more grown-up than I was."

A job with the school newspaper gave Mazer her first opportunity to write for publication, and writing soon became the focus of her existence at school. "But I wanted to write more than newspaper articles. There was a longing in me, vague, . . . but real, almost an ache," the novelist recalled. When she was fifteen, Mazer met her future husband, Harry Mazer, for the first time. He was a friend of her older sister, and at the age of twenty-one, he seemed ancient to Mazer. Two years later, they met again, and a much more confident Mazer was determined that Harry should fall in love with her. Harry thought that Mazer was too young, though, and she had to work at making him notice her—the couple fell in and out of love and quarreled many times before finally getting married.

During the early part of their marriage, the Mazers worked at "boring" jobs and tried to learn how to cook. Three children soon became part of the family, and Mazer took on the role of Mommy. "I had almost forgotten Norma," she remembered. "One day, looking around at the houseful of kids and listening to the never ending cries of Mommy! Mom! Mama!, it occurred to me that the day I'd been both putting off and waiting for—the day when I was all grown up—had arrived without my noticing. Indeed, it must have been here for quite a while. And that famous question 'What are you going to do when you grow up?' had not gone away." A serious talk with her husband followed, and both Mazers revealed a desire to be a writer. They decided that if they were really serious about writing, they had to do at least a little every day. So, for three years, the Mazers spent an hour at the end of each day writing. Money from an insurance settlement finally enabled them to write full-time. "It was mildly terrifying," revealed Mazer in her autobiographical essay. "I had some days when I sat in front of the typewriter and shook because I couldn't think of what to write next."

To support the family, the Mazers wrote for the "women's true confessions" market. These stories were presented as first-person confessions of women who had made serious mistakes in their lives, but were actually the work of professional writers. During the following years, the Mazers each wrote one of these 5,000-8,000 word stories every week, leaving little time to devote to the writing of novels. In 1970 Mazer managed to find the time to write the novel *I, Trissy,* and it was published the following year. *A Figure of Speech* came two years

later and received a National Book Award nomination. "I remember meeting a member of the National Book Award committee some time after *A Figure of Speech* had received a . . . nomination and hearing him say to me, '. . . and you just came out of nowhere.' I laughed. My 'nowhere' had been the ten years I'd spent writing full time and learning the craft."

Mazer has been particularly noted for her young adult novels, some of which she has written with her husband. *Taking Terri Mueller,* for example, earned her an Edgar Award from the Mystery Writers of America, although she had not intended it as a mystery. The book follows Terri Mueller and her father as they wander from town to town, never staying in one place for more than a year. Although Terri is happy with her father, she is old enough to wonder why he will never talk about her mother, who supposedly died ten years before; an overheard discussion leads Terri to discover that she had been kidnapped by her father after a bitter custody battle. "Skillfully handling the deeply emotional situation, the author portrays Terri's conflicting feelings as well as the feelings of both her parents," remarked a *Horn Book* reviewer, who added: "The unfolding and the solution of the mystery are effectively worked; filled with tension and with strong characterization . . . we believe in just about everything Terri does, because Mazer's writing makes us willing to believe. She wins us completely with this finely wrought and moving book."

In the novel *Babyface,* Mazer handles another parent/daughter relationship that is threatened by secrets. Toni Chessmore believes she has perfect parents and an ideal best friend. During the summer of Toni's fourteenth year, though, her opinions begin to change when her father has a heart attack and she goes to stay with her sister in New York. Toni learns shocking secrets about her parents' past, and has a hard time dealing with them when she returns home. A *Publishers Weekly* contributor felt that "Toni's inner growth and increasing awareness . . . are realistically portrayed," and that "Mazer offers a thorough, sensitive exploration of parent/teen relationships."

In both *A Figure of Speech* and *After the Rain,* Mazer deals with the relationship between a young girl and her grandfather. Jenny, the granddaughter in *A Figure of Speech,* feels like an outsider in her own family. The only one she relates to is her grandpa, who lives in an apartment in the basement, neglected by the rest of the family. When Jenny's older brother returns home with a young wife and wants to move into Grandpa's apartment, the family decides to put Grandpa in a nursing home. Grandpa runs away, and Jenny goes with him, sharing the last days of his life. "The fine definition of all characters, the plausibility of the situations and the variety of insights into motivation make [the novel] almost too good to be true," Tom Heffernan asserted in *Children's Literature. A Figure of Speech* was followed by the sequel *When We First Met* in 1982.

Family relationships are also the focus of Mazer's *Missing Pieces*. Raised by her mother with help from her elderly aunt Zis after her father abandoned the family over a decade before, fourteen-year-old Jessie Wells wishes she had a "normal" family, and this wish has become almost an obsession. During the process of trying to get her mom to talk about the reasons for her dad's disappearance and then attempting to relocate him, Jessie gains a new understanding of family structure, using this new knowledge to help balance relationships among her friends. "Between snappy dialogue and tangy insights, Mazer thoughtfully explores issues of loyalty, compassion and forgiveness," noted a *Publishers Weekly* contributor.

In *After the Rain* Rachel's grandfather, Izzy, has cancer, so Rachel begins to go with him on his long afternoon walks. Izzy's crusty exterior has often prevented his family from getting close to him. Rachel is the youngest member of her family, half the age of her older brother, and her parents embarrass her and seem incredibly old. During the walks with her grandfather, Rachel comes to know and love him before he dies. When he is gone, she

Em Thurkill, rendered emotionally fragile by the abusive treatment of her dysfunctional family, struggles forward with courage and determination. (Cover illustration by S. Saelig Gallagher.)

is able to deal with the death and loss, and even teach her parents a few things. A *Kirkus Reviews* contributor asserted that *After the Rain* is "beautifully and sensitively written, sounding the basic chords of the pleasures and pains of family relationships."

Growing up in a single-parent family is given an unpleasant twist in *When She Was Good,* which was published in 1997. Em Thurkill's mother died years ago, and her stepmother doesn't want to deal with her husband's children by his first marriage. When older sister Pamela moves out on her own, Em follows her, and becomes captive to Pamela's controlling personality, drastic mood swings, and daily outbursts of violent temper. After four years, Pamela's unexpected death leaves seventeen-year-old Em on her own, with no one to tell her what to do. Beginning her story after Pamela's death, as a newly liberated Em looks back at the unfortunate circumstances that brought her to this point and her sometimes self-destructive attempts to deal with the emotional void in her life, Mazer "conveys both the emotional poverty such daily abuse incurs and the victim's need for some sort of interior solution or healing in addition to the cessation of abuse," according to Deborah Stevenson of the *Bulletin of the Center for Children's Books.* "Using language at once fierce and unpretentious, Mazer captures ... not only Em's vulnerability and inner struggle but also Pam's quirky madness," added Stephanie Zvirin in *Booklist,* concluding that *When She Was Good* is a "believably rendered testament to the resiliency of the human spirit."

Published in 1993, Mazer's *Out of Control* features a male protagonist named Rollo Wingate, whose friendship with the wrong crowd brings him into a situation bordering on the tragic. Rollo becomes a tagalong member of a group of three high-school juniors who dub themselves the Lethal Threesome. The trio corner fellow student Valerie Michon in a deserted part of the school and grope her. Eventually discovered and reprimanded, Rollo is uncertain why his actions so disgust his father and upset the school administration, and can't fathom why his attempt at an apology is rejected by a traumatized Valerie. In the opinion of *Voice of Youth Advocates* reviewer Kevin Kenny, *Out of Control* "is an exemplary exploration of an essentially random act of violence which by today's jaded standards might be written off by too many.... This is a work of real strength, a book in which every character, every facet of plot, suggests credibility and provokes introspection." Echoing Kenny's praise in *Booklist,* Janice Del Negro praised the novel as "deal[ing] directly and realistically with the complexities of sexual harassment."

Less intense in plot than most of her YA novels are the books in the growing series that includes *A, My Name Is Ami* and *B, My Name Is Bunny.* Written for a slightly younger, less emotionally sophisticated audience, the books touch upon the everyday problems and situations encountered by average American teens. In *D, My Name Is Danita,* for example, Mazer's thirteen-year-old protagonist finds her image of the perfect family destroyed when she runs into a previously unknown half-brother at the mall. Other problems also enter the mix, including boy trouble, ups and downs with her best friend Laredo, and the antics of a younger sibling. In *E, My Name Is Emily,* the boy trouble cheerfully encouraged by the title character is offset by Emily's mother's interest in a man Emily can't stand, in a novel that *School Library Journal* contributor Susan Oliver called "an entertaining step up from those ever-present series books."

Along with her novels, Mazer has also written several short-story collections. The eight short stories in *Dear Bill, Remember Me? and Other Stories* deal with young girls going through a period of crisis. In "Up on Fong Mountain," Jessie strives to be accepted as something other than an extension of her boyfriend. Eighteen-year-old Louise in "Guess Whose Friendly Hands" knows she's dying of cancer, and merely wishes that her mother and sister would accept it as she has. The stories in this collection "are clearly broadcast on a young teenager's wavelength, with the signal unobtrusively amplified as in good YA novels," contended a *Kirkus Reviews* contributor. The stories in Mazer's second collection, *Summer Girls, Love Boys, and Other Short Stories,* are connected by the setting of Greene Street. In "Do You Really Think It's Fair?," Sarah tells about the death of her younger sister and questions the existence of justice. Another story, "Amelia Earhart, Where Are You When I Need You?," relates the short vacation a young girl spends with her eccentric Aunt Clare. "Each story has a strength and a sharpness of vision that delights and surprises in its maturity," commented Ruth I. Gordon in the *New York Times Book Review.* Gordon added that "Mazer has the skill to reveal the human qualities in both ordinary and extraordinary situations as young people mature."

By the time *Dear Bill, Remember Me? and Other Stories* was published, Mazer had enough successes under her belt, including thirteen years as a freelancer and two published books, to finally consider herself a "real writer." With their children grown, she and her husband purchased an old farmhouse for use as a weekend getaway. "No windows, no plumbing, no heating, no electricity. Even the outhouse had fallen in on itself and was useless. We loved it. It took every cent we had to buy it, but we wanted it too much to care," Mazer recalled in *SAAS.* The farmhouse was eventually fixed up, just in time for the Mazers to discover Canada. They sold the house and bought seventeen acres of woods and scrub on a cliff one hundred feet above a small lake in Canada. Many of Mazer's books involve memories of those summers spent camping. "Each one, in its own way, took me over," she reflected. "I lived in the world I was creating; it became real to me. Sometimes I'm asked about 'writer's block.' I don't have it and I don't fear it. Those years of writing pulp fiction taught me that there are always more words. And writing my own novels taught me that there are things inside me waiting to come out that I hardly know are there."

Mazer pointed out in her autobiographical essay that there is "a kind of mystery" in all of her books: "I write and my readers read to find out the answers to questions,

Previously published as **Mrs. Fish, Ape, and Me, the Dump Queen,** *Mazer's story centers on young Joyce, whose unconventional lifestyle brings ridicule from her schoolmates, but love and support from her makeshift family. (Cover illustration by Elizabeth Sayles.)*

secrets, problems, to be drawn into the deepest mystery of all—someone else's life." Freeman asserted that "in its sharpest moments, Mazer's writing can etch a place in our hearts," and in her *Top of the News* essay, Mazer declared: "I love stories. I'm convinced that everyone does, and whether we recognize it or not, each of us tells stories. A day doesn't pass when we don't put our lives into story. Most often these stories are ... of the moment. They are the recognition, the highlighting of ... our daily lives.... In my own life, it seems that events are never finished until I've either told them or written them."

Works Cited

Review of *After the Rain, Kirkus Reviews,* May 1, 1987, p. 723.

Review of *Babyface, Publishers Weekly,* July 27, 1990, p. 235.

Review of *Dear Bill, Remember Me?, Kirkus Reviews,* October 1, 1976, pp. 1101-02.

Del Negro, Janice, review of *Out of Control, Booklist,* June 1-15, 1993, p. 1804.

Freeman, Suzanne, "The Truth about the Teens," *Washington Post Book World,* April 10, 1983, p. 10.

Gordon, Ruth I., review of *Summer Girls, Love Boys, and Other Short Stories, New York Times Book Review,* March 13, 1983, p. 29.

Heffernan, Tom, review of *A Figure of Speech, Children's Literature,* No. 4, edited by Francelia Butler, Temple University Press, 1975, pp. 206-207.

Kenny, Kevin, review of *Out of Control, Voice of Youth Advocates,* August, 1993, p. 154.

Mazer, Norma Fox, "Growing up with Stories," *Top of the News,* winter, 1985, pp. 157-167.

Mazer, Norma Fox, essay in *Something about the Author Autobiography Series,* Volume 1, Gale, 1986, pp. 185-202.

Review of *Missing Pieces, Publishers Weekly,* June 12, 1995, p. 62.

Oliver, Susan, review of *E, My Name Is Emily, School Library Journal,* November, 1991, p. 120.

Stevenson, Deborah, review of *When She Was Good, Bulletin of the Center for Children's Books,* October, 1997, p. 61.

Review of *Taking Terri Mueller, Horn Book,* April, 1983, pp. 172-73.

Zvirin, Stephanie, review of *When She Was Good, Booklist,* September 1, 1997, p. 118.

For More Information See

BOOKS

Children's Literature Review, Volume 23, Gale, 1991, pp. 214-34.

Holtze, Sally Holmes, *Presenting Norma Fox Mazer,* Twayne, 1987.

Holtze, Sally Homes, editor, *Fifth Book of Junior Authors and Illustrators,* H. W. Wilson, 1983, pp. 204-06.

PERIODICALS

Booklist, September 15, 1990, p. 157; October 15, 1990, p. 437.

Bulletin of the Center for Children's Books, May, 1991, p. 223; May, 1992, p. 232; April, 1993, p. 259.

Kirkus Reviews, April 1, 1995, p. 472.

Publishers Weekly, September 16, 1996, p. 85; July 21, 1997, p. 202.

School Library Journal, March, 1991, p. 193; July, 1992, p. 90.

Voice of Youth Advocates, June, 1987, p. 80; August, 1992, p. 168.

*　　　*　　　*

McLAREN, Clemence 1938-

Personal

Born November 3, 1938, in New Jersey; daughter of Edward (a packaging engineer) and Grayce (Berg) Dobson; married Robert Alfred McLaren (a lawyer and teacher), June, 1960; children: Kevin, Heather. *Education:* Received B.A. from Douglass College/Rutgers University (magna cum laude); received Ed.D. from University of Hawaii. *Religion:* "Quaker attender."

Addresses

Home—2009 McKinley St., Honolulu, HI 96822. *Office*—Kamehameha Schools, Honolulu, HI. *Agent*—Linda Allen, Green St. #5, San Francisco, CA.

Career

Pan American Airlines, flight attendant, 1960-61; teacher in Dover, NJ, Guam, Saudi Arabia, and Maui, Hawaii, 1962-84; affiliated with Johns Hopkins University as a summer program dean, 1987—; occasional stints as a professor and researcher with the University of Hawaii, 1987-95; teacher of senior English, Kamehameha Secondary Schools, Honolulu, HI, 1993—. *Member:* Phi Beta Kappa.

Awards, Honors

Books for the Teen Age, New York Public Library, 1997, and Best Books for Young Adults, American Library Association, 1997, both for *Inside the Walls of Troy.*

Writings

Inside the Walls of Troy: A Novel of the Women Who Lived the Trojan War, Atheneum, 1996.
Dance for the Land, Atheneum, 1999.
Waiting for Odysseus, Atheneum, in press.

Contributor to popular magazines and professional journals. Contributor to *Cat Heaven,* Island Heritage Press, 1998.

Work in Progress

The Pygmalion Premise (play).

Sidelights

Clemence McLaren told *SATA:* "As a child hooked on the myths, I always wondered what the mythological characters were feeling about what was happening to them. That dimension was missing from so many of the written sources. When I became a teacher, I used to tell these stories to my students, always embroidering on the characters' personalities. (I still tell stories to my students.) My students actually encouraged me to start writing them down."

McLaren is referring to the myths of classical Europe and the body of literature that grew out of them. *The Iliad* is considered the first epic poem in Western civilization, ascribed to the Greek writer Homer, and tells the story of an actual historical event that occurred during the Trojan War. For many years, McLaren and her husband worked as teachers in exotic locales across the globe. Their experiences living in rural Greece, near the island where the warrior of *The Iliad,* Achilles, was born, gave her the inspiration for her first book, *Inside the Walls of Troy: A Novel of the Women Who Lived the Trojan War.* Here McLaren puts herself inside the great fortress at the ancient city of Troy and tells a story through the eyes of two young women: Helen, a famed beauty who enters into an arranged marriage to Menelaus, and then elopes with the Trojan prince Paris; and Cassandra, who holds the gift of prophecy and the curse of never being believed.

This romantic conflict allegedly brought about the Trojan War, and events prior to it are recounted by Helen in the first-person, and then by Cassandra in the book's latter half. Cassandra is able to predict the future, but is unable to help Helen with her romantic dilemma. Writing in *School Library Journal,* Patricia Lothrop Green noted that McLaren's descriptions of the palace intrigue, despite an outcome already known through *The Iliad,* "still manage to be suspenseful, and the ending is particularly deft." Susan Dove Lempke, reviewing the work for *Booklist,* praised McLaren as a "promising first-time author" with a talent for making these ancient tales "as fresh and vivid as any modern tale."

McLaren told *SATA* that *Inside the Walls of Troy* took her more than ten years to write, but she has learned how to focus better on her subject matter over time. Her next work, *Dance for the Land,* is set in the author's adopted home, the islands of Hawaii. The plot centers around Kate, a California girl with a father of Hawaiian heritage. Kate's life enters a new and difficult phase when her father decides to return with the family to his homeland. Kate must give up her dog, her school, and her friends in California, and deal with new troubles in a school where Hawaiian children tease her because of her mixed heritage. McLaren explained that her own personal experience served as inspiration for *Dance for the Land.* "In 1970, my family and I went to live on a small island in the Western Pacific," McLaren told *SATA.* "A grand adventure, but I was unprepared for the culture shock. This was my first experience of being a minority." Of the book, Janice M. DelNegro, writing in *Bulletin of the Center for Children's Books,* stated: "Politics is secondary to relationships here: characterization is sharp, with the emotional core of each scene played out honestly and sincerely."

"It turns out that Hawaii is unique in that every ethnic group (including native Hawaiians) is a minority. On the surface, we manage to live together harmoniously, but I gradually learned, as does Kate, the main character in this book, that some local people see *haoles* (Caucasians) as representatives of a ruling class that discriminated against and excluded all others. These layers of resentment are complex. My white skin reminds some Hawaiians of the 'superior' race that imposed on them a religion, a culture, and a language—people who, in the end, stole their land and their nation. The current Hawaiian sovereignty movement, which takes many forms, is about regaining that land and that almost-extinguished cultural pride—a lot of baggage for island children to inherit.

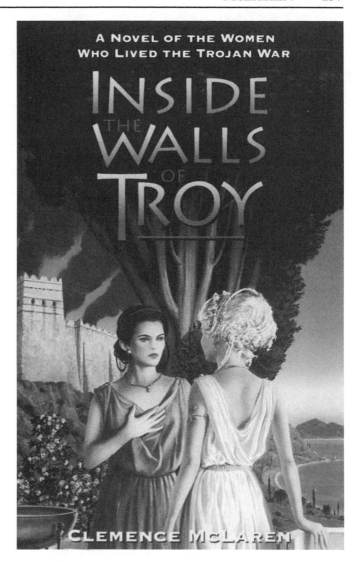

Clemence McLaren puts herself inside the great fortress at the ancient city of Troy to tell the story of Helen and Cassandra. (Cover illustration by Mark Harrison.)

"Now, twenty-nine years later, Hawaii is home. I've had the privilege of studying with a kumu hula who taught us, through her life and work, the healing power of aloha. I understand Pidgin English (although it's presumptuous for a haole to speak it). I'm studying the Hawaiian language, and hope one day to be able to navigate its subtle metaphors. I teach in a school for Hawaiian children, who are constructing their own versions of sovereignty. Most are *hapa* (mixed race), like Kate in my book. Almost all come with baggage.

"Books and films about Hawaii paint a picture of mixed-race people with flowers in their hair, laughing and dancing hula together. And this picture is often true, but there's much more underneath the surface. Living in a multicultural paradise—with all its ethnic baggage—is sometimes a messy business [but] also more interesting and more significant. I hope my book will address this messiness. Here as elsewhere, ethnic prejudice gets passed down through the generations. This book is about moving beyond the fears and stereotypes and learning to live together in aloha, a lesson I believe Hawaii can teach the world."

McLaren has also lived and taught in Saudi Arabia, but her third book will revisit another Homeric epic, *The Odyssey,* the tale of a warrior's long journey home. Though Homer also wrote of the wife and son who await the hero Odysseus's return, McLaren's *Waiting for Odysseus* will explore the family's story more fully. The author, who continues to live in Hawaii, told *SATA:* "Students who really want to be writers will, quite simply, put in the hours and hours obsessing, revising, dreaming, and living in their stories. They won't be able to help it. Writing is an addiction, that's why people do it. Very few writers make a lot of money or become famous, and writing is a tremendous amount of work. Still, for most of us it's a healthy addiction. The main advice I have for students is to prepare for a job that will support and even nourish this addiction. Don't expect it to pay the bills."

Works Cited

Del Negro, Janice M., review of *Dance for the Land, Bulletin of the Center for Children's Books,* March, 1999, p. 247.
Green, Patricia Lothrop, review of *Inside the Walls of Troy, School Library Journal,* October, 1996, p. 148.
Lempke, Susan Dove, review of *Inside the Walls of Troy, Booklist,* October 15, 1996, p. 414.

For More Information See

PERIODICALS

Booklist, October 15, 1996, p. 414.
School Library Journal, October 1996, p. 148.
Voice of Youth Advocates, February, 1997, p. 338.

N–O

NOLEN, Jerdine 1953-

Personal

Born April 6, 1953, in Crystal Springs, MS; daughter of Eugene (Sr.) and Eula (Lee) Nolen; married Anthony L. Harold (an administrator and educator), May 27, 1988; children: Matthew, Jessica. *Education:* Northeastern Illinois University, B.A. (special education), 1975; Loyola University, M. Ed., 1981.

Jerdine Nolen

Addresses

Electronic mail—jnolen@bcpl.net.

Career

Educator; writer. Special education teacher at James Weldon Johnson Elementary School, New Orleans, LA, 1974-75, Chicago Public Schools, 1975-76; elementary education teacher at Martin Luther King Experimental Laboratory School, Evanston, IL, 1976-85; Chicago Public Schools, learning disabilities resource teacher, 1986-87; Baltimore County Public schools, Maryland, special education teacher, 1987-94, English/language arts specialist, 1994-96, Title I and family involvement Specialist, 1996—. Also worked as a buyer and window designer for Arabesque Ladies' Clothing Boutique, Evanston, IL, 1980-87, and taught at several Maryland middle schools, 1987-94. *Member:* National Council of Teachers of English, Society of Children's Book Writers and Illustrators, Delta Kappa Gamma International Society of Teachers (Xi Chapter), Black Literary Umbrella (co-founder), Authors Guild, Maryland State Teachers Association, Chicago Reading Round Table, Baltimore Writers Alliance.

Awards, Honors

Northwood Institute Alden B. Dow Creativity Center Fellowship Award, 1981; Artist-in-Residence, Chicago Office of Fine Arts, 1985-86; Chicago Office of Fine Arts Block Grant Award, 1986, for "Writing Folktales"; Chicago Foundation for Education Grant Award, 1987, for "Black History: A Talking Book"; National Endowment for the Humanities Fellowship for Classroom Teachers, 1988, 1990, 1992; Council for Basic Education Fellowship, 1993; American Library Association (ALA) Notable Book, IRA/CBC Children's Choice Award, both 1995, Storytime "Storypick," Delaware Blue Hen Picture Book Award, Maryland Black Eyed Susan Picture Book Award, Kentucky Blue Grass Award, all 1996, Indiana Hoosiers Picture Book Award, Washington State Children's Choice Picture Book Award, 1997, and Arizona Young Readers' Award,

1998, all for *Harvey Potter's Balloon Farm;* Smithsonian Notable Book, Christopher Award, Oppenheim Platinum Award, and Best Book, *Newsweek,* all 1998, all for *Raising Dragons.*

Writings

Harvey Potter's Balloon Farm, illustrated by Mark Buehner, Lothrop, Lee & Shepard, 1994.
Raising Dragons, illustrated by Elise Primavera, Harcourt Brace/Silver Whistle, 1998.
In My Momma's Kitchen, illustrated by Colin Bootman, Lothrop, Lee & Shepard, 1999.

Nolen's story "The Story of the Skunk and Why He Has Such a Bad Smell" appeared in the anthology *Talk That Talk,* Simon and Schuster, 1989; "Jeremy's Dollar" appeared in the social studies text *People We Know* (Harcourt Brace), 1991, and "What Can You Do With a Statue?" was published in *Places We Know,* Harcourt Brace, 1991. Also contributor of stories to *Ebony, Jr!,* the poem "Branches" to *American Poetry Review,* and readings to *ENGLISH In Charge,* Scott Foresman. Nolen was the featured author in the May, 1998 issue of *Instructor Magazine.*

Adaptations

Disney adapted *Harvey Potter's Balloon Farm* for film as a "Wonderful World of Disney" made-for-television movie, entitled *Balloon Farm.*

Work in Progress

Picture books, including: *Big Jabe* and *Pitching In for Eubie* for Lothrop, Lee & Shepard; and *Hewitt Anderson's Big Life, The Quilt of Love, Max and Jax in Second Grade* (books I and II), *Lauren McGill's Pickle Museum,* and *Irene's Wish,* for Harcourt Brace/Silver Whistle.

Sidelights

Jerdine Nolen is an educator as well as the author of the popular picture books *Harvey Potter's Balloon Farm* and *Raising Dragons,* both of which chronicle marvelous and exuberant goings-on down on the farm. The two tales are told from the point of view of an African-American girl, and the language of the texts blends southern patois, rural colloquialisms, and big-hearted humor. *Harvey Potter's Balloon Farm* was the recipient of a number of awards and made first-time author Nolen something of an immediate success, her book being featured on the Columbia Broadcasting System (CBS) "Morning News" and in elementary classrooms around the country. Though Nolen's first book was an overnight success once published, the making of it was a slow and arduous process.

About her beginnings, Nolen told *SATA:* "While my mother was pregnant with me, she went South to care for her own mother, who was ill. That is how I came to be born in Crystal Springs, Mississippi. Sadly, my grand-

A young girl unlocks the secret of a balloon farmer's magical crop and grows up to carry on his legacy in Nolen's award-winning picture book. (From Harvey Potter's Balloon Farm, *illustrated by Mark Buehner.)*

mother died four months after I emerged into the world." After the death of her grandmother, Nolen's family returned to the North, where young Nolen was raised in Chicago with her five sisters and two brothers. A 1994 *Publishers Weekly* interview reported that Nolen credits her frequently praised "sharp ear for dialogue to her family's colorful expressions, which mingled with the new vernacular she learned in the North." Her family, with its confluence of Northern and Southern dialect, influenced not only her ear for speech patterns, but her sense of humor as well. "Growing up in such a large family, I had to have a good sense of humor—to make up for a lack of space," Nolen once commented. "My sisters and brothers were pretty funny, too—but my father said *I* was 'right witty.'"

Nolen remarked in her *Publishers Weekly* interview that she felt in some ways "like an immigrant" raised in the North, but she would later blend the life of the rural South into her works. Growing up, she was influenced by the work of such disparate writers, poets, and musicians as Paul Laurence Dunbar, Zora Neale Hurston, Dr. Seuss, Kenneth Patchen, Paul Simon, and Nina Simone. All these influences would merge into Nolen's own unique form of musical language. Her childhood also fostered her fertile imagination. "If we told our parents we were bored, they were sure to find some work for us to do," Nolen once said. "So we made sure to keep busy. We told stories; played 'rock teacher,' baseball, dodgeball, and Red Rover; had tea parties and puppet shows; and—my favorite—we dressed up in costumes and put on plays and musicals."

Imaginative child that she was, Nolen developed an early love of words. "I can't remember a time I wasn't writing and collecting words. *Cucumber* was a favorite word once, then *chutney*." Nolen would chant the word over and over until it lost all meaning and became pure sound. An inveterate writer from elementary school on, she published her first poem—a Thanksgiving verse—in her school paper as a second grader. "It was printed on pink paper," Nolen reminisced, "and I still remember the joy I felt to see my name in print."

Nolen's love of words took her to Northeastern Illinois University, where she majored in special education, and then, after teaching several years, to Loyola University, where she earned a masters degree in education in 1981. Nolen worked as an elementary and special education teacher in New Orleans, Louisiana and Chicago, Illinois before taking up duties at the Baltimore County Public Schools, where she has become an English and language arts specialist and a Title I specialist. (Title I is a federally sponsored entitlement program for schools with student body poverty rates of fifty percent or higher.) All the while, she has been writing—for her students, for textbooks, and for her own personal enjoyment.

Nolen's first book, *Harvey Potter's Balloon Farm,* grew out of a 1984 classroom assignment. Teaching a first and second grade combination class as part of a six-member team, Nolen conducted a unit on money. Elaborating for *SATA,* Nolen commented: "We taught the students what money was, what it looked like, and we explored what it was for. For a culminating activity, each of the six classrooms were turned into stores within a single community. There was a bakery, a movie theater, a popcorn store, a book store, a food store, and a balloon farm. Some products were: ballons, wind socks (made from paper), small kites, and antique balloons made from paper mache. That summer, as I was scrubbing the tiles in my shower, I got the first line of what later developed into *Harvey Potter's Balloon Farm:* 'Harvey Potter was a very strange fellow indeed.' At the time I was writing that line, I had no idea that Harvey Potter was strange because he grew balloons. That was a delightful surprise. I guess there really is no wasted motion in the universe."

A classroom hit, the story of Harvey Potter appeared in a reading anthology text in 1986, though Nolen retained the rights to further publication. In 1990, working with the publishers Lothrop, Lee & Shepard, Nolen began

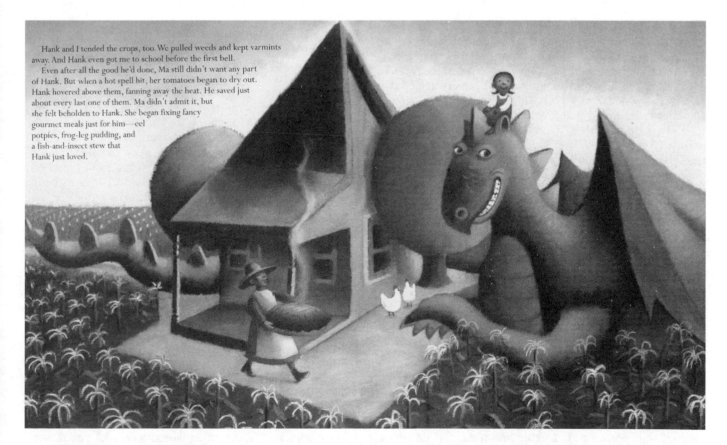

Hank and I tended the crops, too. We pulled weeds and kept varmints away. And Hank even got me to school before the first bell.

Even after all the good he'd done, Ma still didn't want any part of Hank. But when a hot spell hit, her tomatoes began to dry out. Hank hovered above them, fanning away the heat. He saved just about every last one of them. Ma didn't admit it, but she felt beholden to Hank. She began fixing fancy gourmet meals just for him—eel potpies, frog-leg pudding, and a fish-and-insect stew that Hank just loved.

After discovering a dragon egg, a young girl cares for the newly emerging creature, and her parents cease to object when the dragon becomes a helper on the family farm. (From Raising Dragons, *written by Nolen and illustrated by Elise Primavera.)*

preparing, for book format, another early story of hers, "Grandpa's Secret," which had appeared in the magazine *Ebony, Jr!* A new editor took over at the publishing company and decided that the story of the balloon farm was a better bet for a picture book. By this time, Nolen had tried over a dozen publishers with her story of the balloon farmer, with no luck. Finally, she had an editor who shared her vision of the story. The editor brought on illustrator Mark Buehner to create visuals for Nolen's tale. "I was really amazed Mark saw [the story] the way I saw it," Nolen noted in *Publishers Weekly*. "Mark lives in Salt Lake City and we have very different lives, but what I saw in the book was what I wanted." This serendipity of text and illustrations did not go unnoticed by reviewers.

Nolen's title character, Harvey Potter, is a farmer, but his crop is not something mundane like cucumbers or apples. Harvey grows multi-colored balloons atop long sturdy stalks lined up in resemblance to a corn field. Harvey's balloons are grown to order, shaped like clowns, monsters, and animals. A young African-American girl is determined to figure out how Harvey creates his balloon magic. She secretly watches Harvey dance at night in his field with his magic stick. Denounced by a jealous farmer and threatened by government inspectors, Harvey's future looks grim, but all turns out fine in the end; he retains his ranking as a government-certified balloon farmer. The little girl grows up to become a balloon farmer, as well, but in her case the balloons are a root crop.

Horn Book's Ann A. Flowers called this first book "an excellent story" with the added attraction of "vivid, air-brushed illustrations of balloons with expressive faces in every size, color, and shape...." Flowers concluded that the book was "lively and unusual." A *Kirkus Reviews* critic noted that "Nolen's writing has an oral lilt to it" in a book with a "wonderfully appealing premise, skillfully developed." *Booklist*'s Mary Harris Veeder thought that "Nolen's 'true truth' style contrast[ed] delightfully with the pictures of Harvey's crop," and that if the "dry narrative humor" did not reach all children, "the illustrations [would]n't be forgotten." Writing in *School Library Journal*, Kathleen Whalin commented that *Harvey Potter's Balloon Farm* is "the best sort of fantasy—imaginative, inventive, and believable." Whalin concluded her review by declaring that "this title should sail into every library shelf. May Nolen grow a bumper crop of books." An ALA Notable Book, *Harvey Potter's Balloon Farm* did indeed sow the seeds for Nolen's writing career.

Balancing the roles of wife, mother of two young children, educator, and writer, Nolen published her second picture book, *Raising Dragons*, in 1998. Again Nolen placed her story in a rural setting and featured a young African-American girl. Instead of balloons, there is an egg found near the young girl's farm. When it hatches, out pops a tiny dragon whom the girl proceeds, quite nonchalantly, to name Hank. "As I touched skin to scale, I knew I was his girl and he was my dragon," the girl comments. Her parents are more conservative about such matters and at first don't much care for Hank, not being particularly open-minded as far as dragons go. Their opinions change, however, when Hank starts helping out—sowing Pa's seeds and saving Ma's dying crop of tomato plants. Hank ultimately grows to the size of a barn, and is a genuine flying, fire-breathing dragon who can pop a whole field of corn with a single fiery breath. Soon forced by public opinion to flee to the volcanic island where other such creatures live, Hank leaves behind a special present for his human buddy—a wheelbarrow full of dragon eggs ready for the hatching.

A *Kirkus Reviews* critic commented, tongue-in-cheek, "Nolen unearths some unique livestock in this tale of a farmer's daughter who braves her parents' skepticism to hatch and raise a flying, fire-breathing dragon." Summarizing, the reviewer praised *Raising Dragons* as a "fresh and cheery tall tale, told in an appropriately matter-of-fact tone." Susan P. Bloom, building on the favorable mix of text and artwork, remarked in *Horn Book* that "Nolen's chimerical text meets its match in Primavera's imaginative and bold acrylic and pastel illustrations." Bloom went on to point out that "author and artist both reach their peak when Hank's enthusiastically planted corn crop overflows," inspiring "the first dragon-popped popcorn anybody ever saw or tasted." A reviewer for *Family Fun* noted that "The whole fantastical tale is told with an engaging mix of matter-of-factness and awe," while *Working Mother* commented: "Seldom is a story so fanciful told in a voice so plain and true." The critic for *Working Mother* went on to call Nolen's second publication "a lovely book about nurturing, accepting differences, and embracing magic." *Raising Dragons* earned a starred review in *Publishers Weekly*, whose critic called it an "enchanting blend of the real and unreal," appreciating that "Nolen adopts a comfortable pace and down-on-the-farm vernacular to tell this fantastic tale." The author's very understated tone, in the opinion of a *Publishers Weekly* critic, "adds a layer of humor" when contrasted to the very unusual circumstances happening in the book. This same reviewer concluded that "[y]oungsters will hanker to go on this journey; it will set their imagination soaring."

Soaring imaginations are Nolen's stock and trade. More humorous and homely tales, such as *In My Momma's Kitchen*—amalgams of her own childhood and an imagination honed on the precept of never saying you're bored—are rolling out of her mouth and pen. *In My Momma's Kitchen* is a celebration of African-American families and mothers and fathers, a story of a family's year as witnessed by events in the heart of the home—the kitchen. Despite her whimsical tall tales, Nolen told *Publishers Weekly*, "I'm really a very down-to-earth person." Stories are within each of us, Nolen contends, just waiting to get out. It is a matter of perseverance and hanging on to one's dreams that brings the stories out. "When I get in a writing jam, I ask myself, 'So, then what happens?' Your imagination won't let you down." Sage advice from a writer who typically autographs her books with the words, "Hold fast to your dreams as you would your balloons."

Works Cited

Bloom, Susan P., review of *Raising Dragons, Horn Book,* March-April, 1998, p. 217.

Flowers, Ann A., review of *Harvey Potter's Balloon Farm, Horn Book,* July-August, 1994, p. 442.

Frederick, Heather Vogel, Lynda Brill, Shannon Maughan, Sally Lodge, and Amy Umland Love, "Flying Starts: Seven Talents New to the Children's Book Scene Talk about Their Debuts," *Publishers Weekly,* July 4, 1994, pp. 36-41.

Review of *Harvey Potter's Balloon Farm, Kirkus Reviews,* March 15, 1994, p. 401.

Nolen, Jerdine, comments in a promotional release for Lothrop, Lee & Shepard.

Nolen, Jerdine, *Raising Dragons,* Harcourt Brace/Silver Whistle, 1998.

Review of *Raising Dragons, Kirkus Reviews,* March 1, 1998, p. 343.

Review of *Raising Dragons, Family Fun,* May, 1998, p. 116.

Review of *Raising Dragons, Publishers Weekly,* March 9, 1998, pp. 67-68.

Review of *Raising Dragons, Working Mother,* June 19, 1998, p. 62.

Veeder, Mary Harris, review of *Harvey Potter's Balloon Farm, Booklist,* April 15, 1994, p. 1541.

Whalin, Kathleen, review of *Harvey Potter's Balloon Farm, School Library Journal,* May, 1994, p. 102.

For More Information See

PERIODICALS

Entertainment Weekly, April 8, 1994, p. 69.
New York Times Book Review, September 11, 1994, p. 32.
Publishers Weekly, April 11, 1994, p. 65.
School Library Journal, April, 1998, p. 106.
Smithsonian, November, 1998, p. 26.

—Sketch by J. Sydney Jones

*   *   *

O'HARE, Jeff(rey A.) 1958-

Personal

Born February 4, 1958, in Brookhaven, NY; son of Edward J. and Eleanor O'Hare; married, wife's name Amy; children: Sarah, Edward, Morgan. *Education:* Suffolk County Community College, A.A.S.; New York University, B.S.; University of Southern California, M.P.W.

Addresses

Home—R.D. 3, Box 490, Honesdale, PA 18341. *Office*—Highlights for Children, 803 Church St., Honesdale, PA 18431. *Electronic Mail*—jeffhfc@aol.com.

Career

Writer and editor. *Suffolk County News,* Selden, NY, worked as sports reporter. Designer, producer, and director of CD-ROM and online computer games, including *Jonny Quest—New Adventures, Puzzlemania,* and *Highlights on CD.* Collaborator on the development of more than twenty games for manufacturers such as Parker Brothers, including "Balderdash," "Trivial Pursuit, Junior Edition," "Clue Home Party Game," "Rumble Dome," "Claim to Fame," and "Romantic Antics."

Awards, Honors

Parents' Choice Award for the CD-ROM game *Puzzlemania;* two Edpress Distinguished Achievement Awards, including one for *Cat and Dog Mysteries;* awards from Printing Industry Association for Excellence, for editing the magazine *The Fun Zone* and for writing *The World's Best Board Games.*

Writings

(With Ruth S. Pitt and Peter C. Fenlon, Jr.) *Creatures of Middle Earth,* illustrated by Jim Holloway and Angus McBride, Iron Crown Enterprises, 1988.

Knee Slappers, Side Splitters, and Tummy Ticklers: A Book of Riddles and Jokes, Boyds Mills Press (Honesdale, PA), 1992.

Searchin' Safari: Nature's Hidden Wonders, illustrated by Marc Nadel, Boyds Mills Press, 1992, published as *Searchin' Safari: Looking for Camouflaged Creatures,* Bell Books, 1992.

What Might I Be?, Bell Books, 1992.

Cat and Dog Mysteries: Fourteen Exciting Mini-Mysteries with Hidden Pictures, illustrated by R. Michael Palan, Boyds Mills Press, 1993.

Globe Probe: Exciting Geographical Adventures All around the World, illustrated by Carlos Carzon, Boyds Mills Press, 1993.

Hanukkah, Happy Hanukkah: Crafts, Recipes, Games, Puzzles, Songs, and More for the Joyous Celebration of the Festival of Lights, illustrated by Arthur Friedman, Boyds Mills Press, 1994.

Secret Codes and Hidden Messages, Boyds Mills Press, 1997.

Giant Book of Mazes, Boyds Mills Press, 1997.

Other books include *Puzzlemania Super Challenge, Mathmania, The World's Best Board Games,* and the sixty-volume series "Puzzlemania," all published by *Highlights for Children* (Honesdale, PA); author of *Doonesbury Trivia,* Warner Books (New York City). Stage plays include *Terminal,* produced in New York City, at New York University; and *Upstairs at the Unicorn,* produced in Selden, NY, at Suffolk County Community College. Author of the screenplays *Karen's Story,* released by Fries Entertainment, and *Miss Lonelyheart,* for American Film Institute. Writer for television programs, including *The Caption Center, The New Gidget, Dennis the Menace, He-Man and Masters of the Universe, Scooby-Doo,* and *Smurfs.* Author of scripts and songs for audio cassettes, *Highlights for Children.*

Columnist for the magazines *Comic Times, Media Showcase,* and *Wargaming;* feature columnist for the newspaper *Compass.* Contributor of articles and reviews to magazines and newspapers, including *Exceptional Parent, Games, Comics Arena,* and *Adam Film World.*

Writer for comic books, including *Marvel Adventure Coloring Books, R.I.P., Batman: Bonus Book,* and *L.I.F.E. Brigade.* Executive editor, *Fun Zone;* editor, *Hidden Pictures;* puzzle and games editor, *Highlights for Children;* contributing editor, *Wine Investor.*

P

PERERA, Hilda 1926-

Personal

Full name Hilda Perera Diaz; born September 11, 1926, in Havana, Cuba; emigrated to the United States, 1964; daughter of Jose Francisco Trujillo (a Supreme Court judge) and Hilda Soto (Barroso) Perera; married Saul Diaz, 1948 (died, 1984); married Juan Aguirre, 1987; children: Hilda Gonzalez, Saul Diaz. *Education:* Western College for Women (now part of Miami University, Oxford, Ohio), B.A., 1948; University of Havana, Ph.D., 1951; University of Miami, M.A., 1970.

Addresses

Home—8371 South West 5th St., Miami, FL 33144.

Career

Ruston Academy, Havana, Cuba, head of high school Spanish department, 1948-60; National Library of Havana, Cuba, course planning counselor, 1960-62; author of adult fiction and children's books, 1972—. Counselor of education, Cuban National Commission of UNESCO, 1960-62; consultant for Spanish Curricula Development Center, Miami, FL, 1972. Associate editor, *Buen Hogar* (Spanish language version of *Good Housekeeping*), 1965-66; editor, *Romances,* 1966-67. *Member:* Instituto Literario y Cultural Hispanico (honorary member), Coalition of Hispanic American Women, Phi Sigma Iota Honorary Society for Spanish, Cuban Roots Institute (honorary member), Cuban American Cultural Society of Maryland (honorary member), Cuban Women's Club.

Awards, Honors

First prize, Instituto Cultural Cubano Americano, 1948, for *Biografia de Lincoln;* first prize, Professional Women's Club of Cuba, 1948, for short story "Tixé"; first prize, National Children's Book Contest, Consejo Nacional de Cultura, 1960, for *Cuentos de Adli y Luas;* Lazarillo Award for Children's Literature, National

Hilda Perera

Institute of the Spanish Book and Ministry of Education, 1975, for *Cuentos para chicos y grandes,* and 1978, for *Podría ser que una vez;* "Dynamic Woman of the Year" citation, American Cancer Society, 1989; honor book citation, Spanish Catholic Commission for Children's Literature, 1992, for *Mumú;* special prize from Instituto de Cultural del Sur de la Florida, for literary achievements, 1992; certificate of recognition from city of Miami, Florida, and proclamation of Hilda Perera Day, state of Florida, in recognition of literary achievements, July, 1992; Nobel Prize for Literature nomination, 1993; Hispanic Heritage Award in Literature, 1994.

Writings

Biografia de Lincoln, Instituto Cultural Cubano-Norteamericano (Havana), 1947.
Cuentos de Apolo, Editorial Lex (Havana), 1947, 2nd edition, Imprenta L zaro y Hno. (Havana), 1960, 3rd edition, Franhil Enterprises, Inc. (Miami, FL), 1975, 4th edition, Editorial Everest (León, Spain), 1983.
Aspectos de "La Voragine" (criticism), Editorial Manigua (Santiago de Cuba), 1956.
La carta comercial, Imprenta L zaro y Hno., 1956, 2nd edition, Editorial Lex, 1958.
Ortografía, Imprenta L zaro y Hno., 1956, 5th edition, Minerva Books (New York), 1966, 12th edition, Minerva Books, 1977.
Cuentos de Adli y Luas, Editorial Lex, 1960.
Mañana es 26, Imprenta L zaro y Hno., 1960.
(Abridger) *Una niña bajo tres banderas,* Editora Nacional de Cuba (Havana), 1960.
Cómo escribir para adultos recién alfabetizados, Comisión Nacional Cubana de la UNESCO (Havana), 1961.
La lectura (Colección manuales técnicos), Biblioteca Nacional "José Martí" (Havana), 1961.
Ortografía b sica, Comisión Nacional Cubana de la UNESCO, 1961.
Acentuación y puntuación (first three editions originally published in Havana, Cuba), 4th edition, Minerva Books (New York), 1966.
Idapo: El sincretismo en los cuentos negros de Lydia Cabrera, Ediciones Universal (Miami, FL), 1971.
El sitio de nadie (novel), Editorial Planeta (Barcelona, Spain), 1972.
Cuentos para chicos y grandes, Editorial Miñón (Valladolid, Spain), 1976.
Felices Pascuas (novel), Editorial Planeta, 1977.
Podría ser que una vez, Editorial Everest, 1981.
(With Dr. Mana Fraga) *La pata Pita* (pre-primer; includes teacher's manual and workbook), Minerva Books (New York), 1981, revised edition, 1995.
Plantado (novel), Editorial Planeta, 1981, 2nd edition, Plaza y Janés (Barcelona, Spain), 1985.
Pericopín, Editorial Everest, 1981, new edition, 1997.
Rana Ranita, Editorial Everest, 1981, English translation published as *Froggie Frogette,* Lectorum Publications (New York), 1997.
Pepín y el abuelo, Editorial Everest, 1982, new edition, 1997.
Mai, Editorial Santa Maria (Madrid), 1983.
(With Dr. Fraga) *La pata Pita vuelve* (reading book; includes teacher's manual and workbook), Minerva Books (New York), 1984, revised edition, 1998.
Kike, Editorial Santa Maria, 1984, English translation by the author's daughter, Hilda Gonzales S., and Warren Hampton published as *Kiki: A Cuban Boy's Adventures in America,* Pickering Press (Coconut Grove, FL), 1992.
La fuga de los juguetes, Editorial Everest, 1986.

Los Robledal (novel), Editorial Diana (Mexico), 1987.
Mumú, Editorial Bruño (Madrid), 1990.
La jaula del unicornio, Editorial Noguer (Barcelona, Spain), 1991.
Javi, Editorial Everest, 1991.
El burrito que quería ser azul, Editorial Everest, 1992.
Tomasin y el cerdito, Editorial Everest, 1992.
La noche de Ina, Ediciones Libertarias (Madrid), 1993.
Perdido, Fondo de Cultural Económica (Mexico), 1994.
El automóvil del abuelo, Editorial Everest, 1995.
El duende y el mar, Centro de Información y Desarrollo de la Comunicación y la Literatura Infantiles (Mexico), 1995.
La media roja (published as part of *Un barco cargado de ... cuentos*), Ediciones S-M (Madrid), 1996.
Volver a empezar, Rigby (Crystal Lake, IL), 1997, English translation published as *To Begin Again,* Rigby, 1997.
De encuentros y despedidas, Ediciones Cocodrilo Verde (New York), 1997.

Several of Perera's works have been translated into other languages. *Cuentos de Apolo* was translated into Azerbayanian, Russian, Georgian, Moldavian, Estonian, and Ukranian. *Mumú* was translated into Galician, Euskeran, Catalonian, and German. *Rana ranita* was translated into Italian and Turkish. *Kike* and *Cuentos para chicos y grandes* were translated into French. *El burrito que quería ser azul* and *El automóvil del abuelo* were translated into Turkish. *La jaula del unicornio* was translated into German, and *Javi* was translated into Catalonian.

Work in Progress

Sergín; revised editions of *Cuentos de Apolo* and *Podría ser que una vez; Yo soy asi.*

Sidelights

Hilda Perera is perhaps the most prestigious Spanish-language writer for children. She has twice received Spain's illustrious Premio Lazarillo—"the most important prize in Spanish given to a Spanish author," she explained in an interview for *SATA*—once in 1975, for her story collection *Cuentos para chicos y grandes,* and again in 1978, for *Podría ser que una vez.* She left her native Cuba following the Castro revolution in 1959, and she has lived in Miami, Florida, since 1964. She was honored by the city of Miami for her contributions to literature in 1992, and in July of that same year the governor of Florida proclaimed a Hilda Perera Day in recognition of her literary achievements. In 1993 she was nominated for the Nobel Prize in literature, and in 1994 she received the celebrated Hispanic Heritage Award in Literature.

Perera was born in Havana, Cuba, one of two daughters of a Supreme Court judge and his wife. "Mine was an upper-middle class family," she told *SATA.* "My father was a Supreme Court judge in Cuba and my mother was 'just' a mother, which was plenty. I went to an Episcopalian school called Cathedral School because my mother was very keen on our studying English when we were young. I didn't seem to show any particular talents for writing until I was about twelve. Then I wrote something and it caught the attention of the teacher, and from then on they started asking me to write.

"We lived in a very beautiful house when I was very young, and we lived there for many years. We got the Depression around 1932, and we just didn't have enough money to keep the big house. I remember when we had to move to a small apartment, and I wrote a poem about that. It was like a palace for me, because I had my animals—my cats, my rabbits and my hens. And of course in an apartment I couldn't keep them.

"It was at that time that my father was elected to become a Supreme Court judge. But his salary was only 490 dollars a month. It was at the time when things were very, very bad economically, and we had to make sacrifices. Later things improved in Cuba in general, and consequently the family situation improved. My father's salary had been cut almost to half of what he should have gotten, but it was restored. World War II did not affect us as much, except for not having certain things: shortages were encountered. I wrote about the war in a story, and it hurt me to see the magazine pictures of the people dying, but the war did not affect me personally."

During the early 1940s, Perera entered high school in Havana. In Cuba, she recalled in her *SATA* interview, "you have to pass a test to get into high school, but not into college. The Cathedral school prepared us very well; it was very tough. But I was really very well prepared, and besides that I studied like a fiend. I enjoyed studying tremendously. My favorite subjects were literature (of course), and chemistry (which doesn't seem to go very well with me), and algebra." "I had a knack for writing; it was easy for me," she told *SATA*. "My family was completely devoted to us—my sister and I—and they were very understanding about any vocation we might have. So I really didn't have to struggle at all with my writing. My sister did not go into writing; she went into ballet. I tried to share her dancing, but the professor told me I wasn't fit for it, and I was asked to leave the class."

"I was *very* social in high school. There were always dances going on," the author remembered, "and picnics and all kinds of social activities. But they weren't organized by the school, they were organized by the students. There was some interest in sports, but not as much as here [in the United States]. Most of my friends from those days have come to live in the United States after the Revolution in Cuba. I married one of my close friends (he took French so that he could be in class with me). The rest of us also stayed very close."

It was around this time that Perera began emerging as a professional writer. "I won a very important prize when I was seventeen in an international contest with a story called 'Apolo.' After that, I started writing again on the same subject and finally the stories came out as a book when I was twenty-one years old." That book, published in 1947 as *Cuentos de Apolo,* she said in her *SATA*

From Javi, *written by Perera and illustrated by Ana G. Lartitegui.*

interview, "was the first fiction that I wrote for children." She published one more book of stories for children, *Cuentos de Adli y Luas,* which "won the first prize in a contest by the Ministry of Education in Havana," before she left Cuba for the United States in 1964.

After high school, Perera moved on to study at the University of Havana. "I specialized in literature," she told *SATA*. "I couldn't maintain my interest in algebra or chemistry because there were no classes in my major I could take that would go with my specialty." After three years, she won a scholarship sponsored by the Cuban American Institute in Havana to attend Western College for Women, a small private school in southwestern Ohio. "There was a contest to write about Abraham Lincoln, and I won, and the prize was a scholarship to go to Western College. I was very fortunate—they said they would pay for everything and they did," she said. Her prize-winning entry was published in 1947 under the title *Biografia de Lincoln.*

"I was very fond of Western [College]. It was a wonderful experience, and I loved having contact with so many people from different countries. I stayed at one of the dorms and I had a roommate, Ann Waterfield. We became quite close; I visited her family and stayed with them for a few days, so I got to know them well. I majored in English because the school gave me credit for the subjects I had studied in Havana. My scholarship was for one year, so I had to make up all the English requirements in that time. That was quite tough, because I hadn't had English since the fifth grade, but the instructors were very good and very helpful, and I was practicing my English all day. There was no one to speak Spanish to! I was grateful for the opportunity to make up for all those years that I had not had English. I completed the degree in one year, but it was a great effort. Then I went back to Havana to get married."

"As soon as I graduated from both Western College and the University of Havana, I went to look for a job," Perera told *SATA*. "The first day I got one at Ruston Academy, teaching Spanish to English speakers. The English I had learned came in very handy. Later I became head of the Spanish department. Ruston Academy gave me liberty to continue to study—the headmaster was very understanding—and I got that privilege."

Perera also got the opportunity to begin writing for children again, starting with her own son and daughter. "My two children started asking for stories, and I started creating the stories for them," she explained to *SATA*. "That was the beginning. They loved stories about animals, so I started with that. Practically all of the animals I had as a child have become part of these stories at one time or another. Then I went on to write about children. Many of those stories were fictional, but I kept them and eventually the books I made out of them won the Premio Lazarillo. They awarded me that prize twice: once for *Cuentos para chicos y grandes,* and the second time for a book called *Podría ser que una vez.*"

"After Ruston Academy closed in 1959, I went on to the Library of Havana and gave some courses there as an educational consultant with the Cuban National Commission of UNESCO. This person who was very well placed in the communist party happened to be a friend of mine. He offered me the secretariat of UNESCO, but I told him, 'Look, if I accept a post from you, I'll have to cater to your taste and to your opinions, and I don't want that,' and he said, 'So why don't you take a post as consultant, and you will be totally free,' and I accepted that. I wrote a book on alphabetization for UNESCO called *Cómo escribir para adultos recién alfabetizados.*"

Despite the opportunities that were emerging for writers after Fidel Castro's Communist revolution, Perera found herself becoming disillusioned with the new regime. "I was all for the revolution in the beginning, 1960, 1961 ... but then I started seeing things I didn't like, and that's when I decided to withdraw. It was very painful. I was very much against Batista too, but I never thought the revolution would turn out the way it did. Castro ruined so many lives. He is an extremely bright individual, and he has many ways of influencing propaganda. Generally in Cuba public services like health care had been very good even before Castro, so he has been able to develop good clinics, especially for foreigners. These are not open to the Cubans."

Finally in 1962, Perera explained to *SATA*, "I decided the revolution wasn't for me, because of the many cases I had seen of lack of *habeas corpus,* the many friends I had that were in prison, and because the whole setup of the revolution didn't agree with me. Also, I had written a novel about the revolution called *Tomorrow is 26* (*Mañana es 26*), and after I had written it, they came to my house and confiscated it. Apparently they wanted *Tomorrow is Communism,* not *Tomorrow is 26.*"

Perera ran into many difficulties trying to leave Cuba and emigrate to the United States. "Being a writer, I had been assigned to certain positions I had to resign from, and I had a great deal of trouble getting out. My mother was still living at that time; my father had died. Curiously enough, she was the one that took the lead in leaving the country, because she said that it was not Cuba any more," she told *SATA*. "Also, I was a writer, and the United States is very careful about which writers it admits. We went to Mexico for a few months and got our papers ready to enter the United States. At the time we left—in 1964—it was easier to get papers of residence in Mexico than in the United States. They went through the whole of my work, and the consulate in Mexico revised practically everything I had written to be sure that there wasn't any communism involved. But it wasn't too much trouble getting into the United States. It was worse getting out of Cuba."

Perera found a niche for her skills as a Spanish-language writer in the United States. She served as an associate editor for *Buen Hogar* (a Spanish-language edition of *Good Housekeeping*) and then as an editor for *Romances,* a women's magazine. She also began working on her masters degree at the University of Miami. Her thesis, she told *SATA*, "was about Lydia Cabrera, a very well-noted ethnologist and writer" who specialized in African cultures. Perera's masters work, published as *Idapo,* helped her become friends with the ethnologist. "Cabrera was a very charming person," Perera said to *SATA*. "She was very funny, and I enjoyed talking to her."

It was after 1970 that Perera's career as a writer for children and young adults really took off. "I continued writing stories by myself after my own children grew up," Perera explained to *SATA*. "Then I realized the amount of Spanish-speaking children who need books in Spanish in the United States." The result has been a number of highly regarded books for children, including fantasies (such as *Rana Ranita* and *El duende y el mar*), realistic stories, young adult novels (such as *Mai* and *Perdido*), and Spanish language textbooks (including *La pata Pita* and *La pata Pita vuelve*). The Spanish Catholic Commission for Children's Literature cited her 1992 children's book *Mumú* for special recognition as an honor book. "*Mai* has been a best-seller in Spain; it sold more than 180,000 copies, which is a lot for Spain," the author stated. "It has been translated into English, and I've sent it recently to see if I can get it published in English. I'm also working on a book about the people who come from Cuba in makeshift boats. They say that only about one of every two people who come that way make it to the United States."

One of the most popular of Perera's books available in English translation is the story called *Kike* in its Spanish version and *Kiki: A Cuban Boy's Adventures in America* in English translation. *Kike* tells the story of seven young boys who escape from Cuba without their parents, who are refused permission to leave the country. "It's about what [Kike] has to confront being a non-English speaker, the changes in family he has to undergo, and his adaptation to the United States," Perera explained to *SATA*. "Kike has a slip of paper with the address of his grandfather, who lives in Miami," declared on-line magazine *Booktalk* contributor Mark Hall. "When they arrive in the United States, they move in with their grandfather, but the reunion with their parents gets delayed. The parents still can't leave Cuba, and they weren't counting with the fact that grandfather was very poor and incapable of taking care of so many kids alone."

The boys respond to the combined abuse and neglect by essentially declaring war on Kike's grandfather. The old man responds in turn by locking himself in his room and leaving the boys to fend for themselves. "They have no money, and only enough food for a few days; they don't speak English, and they don't know anyone," Hall concluded. *Kike* "was based on the experiences of many of the boys I knew who had come by themselves in what they called the 'Peter Pan Project,'" Perera explained. "It was quite a tragic experience."

The English-language version of the story differs from the Spanish version in substance as well as in title. "I wrote it originally as *Kike*," Perera explained in her *SATA* interview. "I have a Jewish friend and he called me and asked why I had named my book 'Kike,' which is a quite derogatory term for Jewish people. I told him that it didn't occur to me, but I changed the English title to *Kiki*."

There were also changes that had to be made because of cultural differences between Spanish- and English-language readers. "My editor pointed out that I should change some things," the author told *SATA*. "For instance, there was a scene in the original book where the American girl tries to teach the little boy to kiss. My editor thought that it would be a mistake to say that he kissed her on the mouth. I debated whether I should or not, and then I thought it was okay to say that he kissed her on the brow."

Perera has also written highly regarded Spanish-language fiction for adults. *El sitio de nadie*, which was originally published in Spain and was a best-seller there for two years, "deals with disenchantment with the Cuban revolution," she told *SATA*. It was a runner-up in the Planeta International Novel contest, as was a later book, *Felices Pascuas*. In 1993, she told *SATA*, she was significantly honored for her contributions to literature. "Ten professors nominated me for a Nobel Prize for my body of work. I didn't really expect anything of it, but I

was very honored that they thought of me. It was very exciting."

Works Cited

Hall, Mark, review of *Kiki: A Cuban Boy's Adventures in America, Booktalk,* http://www.booktalk.com.

Perera, Hilda, telephone interview with Kenneth R. Shepherd for *Something about the Author,* April 6, 1998.

For More Information See

BOOKS

Contemporary Spanish-Speaking Writers and Illustrators for Children and Young Adults: A Biographical Dictionary, edited by Isabel Schon, Greenwood Press (Westport, CT), 1994.

Who's Who among Hispanic Americans, 3rd edition, Gale, 1994.

PERIODICALS

Booklist, December 15, 1992, pp. 738-39.
Publishers Weekly, May 26, 1997, pp. 85-86.
School Library Journal, February, 1993, p. 94.

* * *

PERRY, Ritchie (John Allen) 1942- (John Allen)

Personal

Born January 7, 1942, in King's Lynn, Norfolk, England; son of Hubert John (a teacher) and Ella (Allen) Perry; married Lynn Mary Charlotte Barton, November 23, 1976; children: Tina Elizabeth, Sara Charlotte. *Education:* St. John's College, Oxford, B.A. (honors), 1964.

Addresses

Agent—Peters, Fraser & Dunlop, 5th Floor, The Chambers, Chelsea Harbour, Lots Rd., London SW10 0XF, England.

Career

Bank of London & South America Ltd., Brazil, managerial trainee, 1964-66; assistant teacher in Norfolk, England, 1966-74, and in Luton, England, 1975—.

Writings

FOR YOUNG PEOPLE

Brazil: The Land and Its People (nonfiction), Macdonald Educational (London), 1977, Silver Burdett (Morristown, NJ), 1978.
George H. Ghastly, illustrated by Priscilla Lamont, Hutchinson (London), 1981.
George H. Ghastly to the Rescue, illustrated by Chris Winn, Hutchinson, 1983.
George H. Ghastly and the Little Horror, Hutchinson, 1985.

Fenella Fang, illustrated by Jean Baylis, Hutchinson, 1986.
Fenella Fang and the Great Escape, illustrated by Jean Baylis, Hutchinson, 1987.
Fenella Fang and the Wicked Witch, illustrated by Jean Baylis, Hutchinson, 1989.
The Creepy Tale, Hutchinson, 1989.
Fenella Fang and the Time Machine, Hutchinson, 1991.
The Runton Werewolf, illustrated by Doffy Weir, Hutchinson, 1994, Chivers North America, 1997.
Haunted House, Ginn (Aylesbury), 1995.
The Runton Werewolf and the Big Match, Hutchinson, 1996.
The Shadow (children's play), illustrated by Stephen Player, Ginn, 1997.

FOR ADULTS; MYSTERY NOVELS

The Fall Guy, Houghton (Boston), 1972.
A Hard Man to Kill, Houghton, 1973, published in England as *Nowhere Man,* Collins (London), 1973.
Ticket to Ride, Collins, 1973, Houghton, 1974.
Holiday with a Vengeance, Collins, 1974, Houghton, 1975.
Your Money and Your Wife, Collins, 1975, Houghton, 1976.
One Good Death Deserves Another, Collins, 1976, Houghton, 1977.
Dead End, Collins, 1977.
Dutch Courage, Collins, 1978, Ballentine, 1982.
Bishop's Pawn, Pantheon, 1979.
Grand Slam, Pantheon, 1980.
Fool's Mate, Pantheon, 1981.
Foul Up, Doubleday, 1982.
MacAllister, Doubleday, 1984.
Kolwezi, Doubleday, 1985.
Presumed Dead, Doubleday, 1987.
Comeback, Doubleday, 1991.

UNDER PSEUDONYM JOHN ALLEN

Copacabana Stud, R. Hale (London), 1978.
Up Tight, R. Hale, 1979.

Sidelights

Older readers of mystery novels may associate British author Ritchie Perry's name with his numerous "Philis" novels. A series of crime/mystery works originating in 1972 with *The Fall Guy,* the novels center on tough protagonist Philis—a once small-time smuggler in Brazil turned secret agent. Younger readers, however, may recognize Perry's name from his collections of spooky yet humorous tales featuring friendly ghosts, vampires, and werewolves.

George H. Ghastly (the "H" is for Horrible) is the first book in a trilogy of the same name and Perry's first work for middle-school readers. It stars George as a recent ghost academy graduate who can't seem to scare anyone. In fact, he makes people laugh, particularly the family he is sent to frighten. When Wizard Yuck gives George a fearsome scream to improve his scaring skills, George winds up scaring himself as well. Eventually, "George is relieved to settle down with Mr. Merryfellow, a lonely man whose attitude to George's technique is kindly, if a little derisive," maintained Margery Fisher

of *Growing Point.* A *Junior Bookshelf* critic appreciated Perry's "agreeably light touch," and the way the author "uses language precisely and with wit."

For his next slapstick series, Perry employs an unusual family of vampires, including Beatrice Bite, Uncle Samuel Suck, and young Fenella Fang, to keep readers in stitches. In *Fenella Fang,* Fenella becomes acquainted with a human girl (newly nicknamed Heinz Beans) who has snuck into Fenella's crypt. Since Fenella prefers HBS (Human Blood Substitute) to warm-blooded humans, the two are able to become friends. Coming to Heinz's aid, Fenella helps the girl find her lost dog and teaches Heinz's mean cousin a valuable lesson. "It is all off-beat fun, with plenty of gruesome detail," wrote a *Junior Bookshelf* reviewer, who added that the "excessive fantasy ensures smiles instead of cold shivers, giggles instead of nightmares." In *Fenella Fang and the Great Escape* Fenella saves Uncle Sam from becoming a new attraction at nasty Spiro Pasto's zoo. "Not very demanding ... but it's fast, verbal slapstick and kids will love it!" exclaimed *British Book News* contributor Bill Boyle.

And then there are the Cunninghams of Perry's "Runton Werewolf" stories. In *The Runton Werewolf,* twelve-year-old Alan Cunningham is disappointed to learn that he and his family are not humans but werewolves from another planet. However, he eventually grows accustomed to the idea, especially when he masters his newly found powers to squelch a bully at school and to help his school's football team in the sequel *The Runton Werewolf and the Big Match.* "Creepy yet comfortingly absurd," deemed a reviewer in *Junior Bookshelf* of the first novel, which Mary Crawford, writing in *School Librarian,* called "an entertaining read." Another *Junior Bookshelf* reviewer called the sequel "realistic" and its characters "contemporary in their attitudes, actions, interests and responses," adding that *The Runton Werewolf and the Big Bookshelf* is "a book well in touch with today's youngsters."

Perry once explained to *SATA* how he began his writing career. "It was ingrained laziness which helped to start me writing—while I was sitting at a typewriter, nobody asked me to help with the household chores. Eventually the cynics around me (i.e., those doing all the chores) demanded some proof of my writing abilities, and pride forced me to deliver. Hence my first book, back in 1972. However, the dilettante in me remains and I seldom work at my writing for more than ten hours a week. Indeed, I find it very difficult to take my books seriously as I have never, ever considered myself a creative person. A lot of my readers would probably agree with me."

Works Cited

Boyle, Bill, review of *Fenella Fang and the Great Escape, British Book News Children's Books,* September, 1987, p. 31.
Crawford, Mary, review of *The Runton Werewolf, School Librarian,* February, 1995, p. 23.

Review of *Fenella Fang, Junior Bookshelf,* December, 1986, p. 227.

Fisher, Margery, review of *George H. Ghastly, Growing Point,* May, 1981, p. 3877.

Review of *George H. Ghastly, Junior Bookshelf,* August, 1981, p. 151.

Review of *The Runton Werewolf and the Big Match, Junior Bookshelf,* October, 1996, p. 205.

Review of *The Runton Werewolf, Junior Bookshelf,* December, 1994, p. 230.

For More Information See

BOOKS

St. James Guide to Crime and Mystery Writers, fourth edition, St. James Press (Detroit), 1996.

PERIODICALS

Books for Keeps, June, 1987, p. 18; November, 1987, p. 21.

British Book News Children's Books, December, 1986, p. 27.

School Librarian, December, 1983, p. 360.*

R

REES, (George) Leslie (Clarence) 1905-

Personal

Born December 28, 1905, in Perth, Australia; married Coralie Clarke (a writer), 1931 (died, 1972); children: Megan, Dymphna. *Education:* University of Western Australia, Nedlands, B.A., 1929; graduate study at University College, University of London, 1930. *Hobbies and other interests:* Travel, nature.

Leslie Rees

Addresses

Home—4/5 The Esplanade, Balmoral Beach 2088, New South Wales, Australia.

Career

Writer, editor, and drama critic. *Era,* London, England, senior drama critic, 1931-35; Playwrights Advisory Board, Sydney, New South Wales, Australia, co-founder, 1937, honorary chairman, 1938-63; Australian Broadcasting Commission, Sydney, chief drama editor, 1937-57, assistant director of drama, 1957-66. Sydney Centre of International PEN, President, 1967-75; Mt. Lawley College of Advanced Education, Perth, Australia, writer-in-residence, 1975; Curtin University, Perth, writer-in-residence, 1988. *Member:* Sydney Centre of International PEN, honorary member.

Awards, Honors

Children's Book of the Year Award, Children's Book Council of Australia, 1946, for *The Story of Karrawingi the Emu;* Award from Townsville Literary Foundation, 1978, for *A History of Australian Drama;* named member of the Order of Australia, 1981.

Writings

FOR CHILDREN

Digit Dick on the Barrier Reef, illustrated by Walter Cunningham, Sands (Sydney, Australia), 1942, published as *Digit Dick on the Great Barrier Reef,* Hamlyn (Sydney, Australia), 1969.

Gecko: The Lizard Who Lost His Tail, illustrated by Cunningham, Sands, 1944.

The Story of Shy the Platypus, illustrated by Cunningham, Sands, 1944.

Digit Dick and the Tasmanian Devil, illustrated by Cunningham, Sands, 1946.

The Story of Karrawingi the Emu, illustrated by Cunningham, Sands, 1946.

The Story of Sarli, the Barrier Reef Turtle, illustrated by Cunningham, Sands, 1947.

Bluecap and Bimbi: The Blue Wrens, illustrated by Cunningham, Trinity House (Sydney, Australia), 1948.

Mates of the Kurlalong, illustrated by Alfred Wood, Sands, 1948.

The Story of Shadow, the Rock Wallaby, illustrated by Walter Cunningham, Sands, 1948.

The Story of Kurri Kurri the Kookaburra, illustrated by Margaret Senior, Sands, 1950.

Quokka Island, illustrated by Arthur Horowicz, Collins, 1951.

Digit Dick in Black Swan Land, illustrated by Walter Cunningham, Sands, 1952.

The Story of Aroora the Red Kangaroo, illustrated by John Singleton, Sands, 1952.

Two-Thumbs: The Story of a Koala, illustrated by Margaret Senior, Sands, 1953.

Danger Patrol: A Young Patrol Officer's Adventures in New Guinea, Collins, 1954.

Digit Dick and the Lost Opals, illustrated by Tony Hutchings, Sands, 1957.

The Story of Koonaworra the Black Swan, illustrated by Margaret Senior, Sands, 1957.

Australian Nature Tales: Shy the Platypus, Aroora the Red Kangaroo, Sarli the Turtle, Sands, 1958.

The Story of Wy-Lah the Cockatoo, illustrated by Walter Cunningham, Sands, 1959.

The Story of Russ, the Australian Tree Kangaroo, illustrated by Cunningham, Sands, 1964.

Boy Lost on a Tropic Coast: Adventure with Dexter Hardy, illustrated by Frank Beck, Ure Smith (Sydney, Australia), 1968.

The Big Book of Digit Dick, illustrated by Tony Hutchings, Hamlyn, 1973.

Mokee, the White Possum, illustrated by Tony Oliver, Hamlyn, 1973.

Panic in the Cattle Country, Rigby (Adelaide, Australia), 1974.

A Treasury of Australian Nature Stories, illustrated by Walter Cunningham, John Singleton, and Margaret Senior, Sands, 1974.

Bluecap and Bimbi; Gecko; and Mokee, illustrated by Tony Oliver, Hamlyn, 1975.

Digit Dick and the Magic Jabiru, illustrated by Sandra Laroche, Lansdowne (Sydney, Australia), 1981.

Digit Dick and the Zoo Plot, illustrated by Walter Cunningham, Angus & Robertson (Sydney, Australia), 1982.

Billa, the Wombat Who Had a Bad Dream, illustrated by Penny Walton, Child & Associates (Brookvale, New South Wales), 1988.

(With Margaret Wilson) *The Seagull Who Liked Cricket,* University of Western Australia Press (Nedlands, Western Australia), 1997.

The Story of Karrawingi the Emu has also been published in Armenian and Russian.

FOR ADULTS; NONFICTION

English Drama: Is It Dead or Dying?, Australian English Association (Sydney, Australia), 1936.

Drama in Our Lives, from "Discussion Pamphlet" series, Australian Army Education Service (Melbourne, Australia), 1944-46.

Towards an Australian Drama, Angus and Robertson, 1953; revised edition published as *The Making of Australian Drama from the 1830s to the Late 1960s,* 1973.

A History of Australian Drama (two volumes, containing revised versions of *The Making of Australian Drama* and *Australian Drama in the 1970s*), Angus and Robertson, 1973-1978.

Australian Drama in the 1970s: A Historical and Critical Survey, Angus and Robertson, 1978; revised edition published as *Australian Drama 1970-1985: A Historical and Critical Survey,* 1987.

PLAYS

(Contributor) *Six Australian One-Act Plays by Louis Esson ... [and others],* Mulga (Sydney, Australia), 1944.

(Editor) *Australian Radio Plays,* Angus and Robertson, 1946.

(Contributor) *Australian Youth Plays,* Angus and Robertson, 1948.

(Adapter) *The Man with the Money: A Comedy by Philip Abson,* adapted from radio play, "Leave it to George," by Philip Abson, Angus and Robertson, 1948.

(Editor) *Modern Short Plays,* Angus and Robertson, 1951.

(Editor) *Mask and Microphone: Plays Selected and Edited by Leslie Rees,* Angus and Robertson, 1963.

OTHER

(With Coralie Rees) *Spinifex Walkabout: Hitch-hiking in Remote North Australia,* Australasian (Sydney, Australia), 1953.

(With C. Rees) *Westward from Cocos: Indian Ocean Travels,* Harrap, 1956.

(With C. Rees) *Coasts of Cape York: Travels Around Australia's Pearl-tipped Peninsula,* Angus and Robertson, 1960.

(With C. Rees) *People of the Big Sky Country,* Ure Smith, 1970.

Here's to Shane (novel), Wentworth (Sydney, Australia), 1977.

Hold Fast to Dreams: Fifty Years in Theatre, Radio, Television, and Books (memoir), Alternative Publishing Cooperative (Sydney, Australia), 1982.

Sidelights

Leslie Rees once commented: "I think children like exploring, recognising, discovering; they like adventure, meeting strange and interesting people, animals, and birds; they like laughing, play-acting, and narrow escapes; but in the long run feeling secure with someone and something to put their faith in. I like these things too, because there's still a child and still a boy in me. I also like sharing with children the fun and excitement I've had while travelling and getting to know Australian creatures of the wild, and reaching unusual Australian places. And with this emphasis and this incentive I go to work finding a method and an idiom that will catch the interest of the young. I am gratified to find that some of my books have reached young audiences in most English-speaking countries, and in some non-English-speaking countries, with especially large audiences in Russia."

Common vehicles for Rees's communication with young readers include fantasy and adventure stories, often centering Australian wildlife. Rees's first book for children, *Digit Dick on the Barrier Reef*, embraces the universal appeal of diminutive creatures. In this story, Rees presents an Australian variation of Tom Thumb, whimsically recounting his adventures on the Great Barrier Reef and in other remote areas of the continent. Several of Rees's adventure stories are geared toward an audience of older boys. *Danger Patrol*, for example, is based on a young patrol officer's adventures in New Guinea. *Panic in the Cattle Country* explores the troubling mystery of who or what is slaughtering cattle and leaving their mutilated carcasses in the Outback. Evident in this book is Rees's fascination with the geology of an ancient continent, its aboriginal inhabitants, and the white men who live in its remote vastness. The story's rugged scenery and Australian flavour, according to H. M. Saxby, "belong firmly in the tradition of the robust boys' adventure story."

Perhaps best known for his enthusiasm for wildlife, Rees, who has enjoyed the process of discovery while writing travel books, has gone to great lengths to further the study of Australia's natural wonders. He has crafted his wealth of experiential learning into a series of nature tales for young people. Before writing *Shy the Platypus*, the first book in the series, Rees and illustrator Walter Cunningham visited the gullies, forests, and streams of the Blue Mountain region. Unobtrusive descriptions of observations made on this trip are featured in *Shy the Platypus*, the story of a platypus who must turn from her cherished pool to the dark entrance of her sub-terranean tunnel in order to fulfill her role as a mother. Remaining popular with children for decades, *Shy the Platypus* has been reprinted in various forms. Another book in Rees's nature series, *The Story of Karrawingi the Emu*, was the first to receive the Australian Children's Book of the Year Award. This book addresses birth and parenthood, telling of an emu who races through the bush at midnight, proclaiming his fatherhood—of eighteen oval eggs. More than half a century after writing *Karrawingi*, Rees published *The Seagull Who Liked Cricket*, a well-received book that was considered for another Book of the Year Award.

Mr. Rees offered *SATA* the following comments about his love for Australian life: "The full variety of indigenous creature-life of our continent, so different from that of all other lands, had hardly begun in the 1940s to be transmuted by writers and artists into agreeable forms for new generations who ought, so I believed, to have the chance of knowing and accepting all this Australian life as their essential heritage."

Works Cited

Rees, Leslie, comments in *Twentieth-Century Children's Writers*, Fourth Edition, St. James, 1995.

Saxby, H. M., essay on Rees in *Twentieth-Century Children's Writers*, Fourth Edition, St. James, 1995.

* * *

ROBINSON, Sue
See ROBINSON, Susan Maria

* * *

ROBINSON, Susan Maria 1955-
(Sue Robinson)

Personal

Born April 10, 1955, in Brisbane, Australia; married Eric Edward Robinson, 1977. *Education:* University of Sydney, B.Sc., 1975; Sydney Teachers College, Diploma in Education, 1976. *Hobbies and other interests:* Writing letters, history, gardening, travel, languages.

Addresses

Home—London, England and Monclergerie, France.

Susan Maria Robinson

Career

High school mathematics teacher in Australia, New Zealand, and England, 1977-90; teacher, writer and researcher, 1990—.

Writings

UNDER NAME SUE ROBINSON

The Lyrebird's Tail, Thomas C. Lothian (Port Melbourne, Australia), 1998.
The Cannibal Virus, illustrated by Peter Gouldthorpe, Thomas C. Lothian, 1998.
Edward's Magic Paintbox, illustrated by Gregory Rogers, Thomas C. Lothian, 1998.

Sidelights

Susan Maria Robinson told *SATA:* "I accompanied my husband to Moscow in 1990, then to Prague in 1992. I lived in Moscow during the dying years of the Soviet Union, the time of *glasnost, perestroika,* and empty shops. It was difficult to find birthday presents for my nephews, who lived in Australia, so I started writing stories to send as gifts. I became addicted to writing. Even now, years later, the stories I write are still communications with my family in Australia. They receive the first draft of any new work, complete with idiosyncrasies which we enjoy, and which I usually eliminate before sending the work to the publisher."

*   *   *

ROCHMAN, Hazel 1938-

Personal

Born April 13, 1938, in Johannesburg, South Africa; daughter of Maurice (a physician) and Ekkie (a bookkeeper; maiden name, Sloshberg) Fine; married Hymie Rochman (a professor), October 14, 1959; children: Danny, Simon. *Education:* University of the Witwatersrand, Johannesburg, South Africa, B.A.; University of Chicago, M.A.

Addresses

Home—5429 Eastview Park, Chicago, IL, 60615. *Office*—*Booklist*, American Library Association, 50 East Huron St., Chicago, IL, 60611.

Career

Journalist, South Africa; English teacher, England, 1963-72; school librarian, University of Chicago Laboratory Schools, Chicago; American Library Association, Chicago, assistant editor and book reviewer for *Booklist*, 1984—.

Awards, Honors

G. K. Hall Award for Library Literature, American Library Association (ALA), 1994, for *Against Borders:*

Hazel Rochman

Promoting Books for a Multicultural World; Best Books for Young Adults, ALA, for *Somehow Tenderness Survives: Stories of Southern Africa, Who Do You Think You Are?: Stories of Friends and Enemies, Bearing Witness: Stories of the Holocaust,* and *Leaving Home: Stories.* Rochman has been selected to deliver the May Hill Arbuthnot Lecture in the year 2000.

Writings

Tales of Love and Terror: Booktalking the Classics, Old and New, American Library Association, 1987.
(Editor) *Somehow Tenderness Survives: Stories of Southern Africa,* HarperCollins, 1988.
Against Borders: Promoting Books for a Multicultural World, American Library Association, 1993.

EDITOR; WITH DARLENE Z. MCCAMPBELL

Who Do You Think You Are?: Stories of Friends and Enemies, Little, Brown, 1993.
Bearing Witness: Stories of the Holocaust, Orchard, 1995.
Leaving Home: Stories, HarperCollins, 1997.

Also author of a monthly book review column for *Sesame Street Parents' Magazine.*

Sidelights

Born and raised in Johannesburg, South Africa, Hazel Rochman grew up under apartheid. She once commented in her *Against Borders: Promoting Books for a Multicultural World:* "Book and press censorship was fierce; radio was state controlled; there was no television at all. Multiculturalism was against the law." Rochman and her husband became involved in opposition to apartheid, a decision that eventually caused her to turn to literature as a source of stability in her life. "In 1963 we left South Africa on a one-way passport and were not allowed back until the 1990s," Rochman recalled. "We were stateless. Books—reading, talking, sharing, arguing, reviewing books—have helped me find a home. I believe that reading makes immigrants of us all."

Nowhere is Rochman's devotion to literature more evident than in *Tales of Love and Terror: Booktalking the Classics, Old and New.* In this work, Rochman describes many aspects of booktalking as a way of teaching young people about literature. Topics include the importance of talking about quality books, ways to integrate the classics with new books, a procedure for selecting titles, and how to prepare a booktalk session. *School Library Journal* reviewer Barbara A. Lynn noted, "it is hard to read *Tales of Love and Terror* and not be touched by Rochman's enthusiasm, commitment, and love of books." Writing in *Voice of Youth Advocates,* Dorothy M. Broderick declared that "there isn't any

15 distinguished authors explore personal journeys

Amy Tan
Sandra Cisneros
Tim O'Brien
Allan Sherman
Charles Mungoshi
Vickie Sears
Edward P. Jones
Annette Sanford
David St. John
Francisco Jiménez
Judith Ortiz Cofer
Norma Fox Mazer
Tim Wynne-Jones   Stories selected by
Gary Soto   Hazel Rochman
Toni Morrison   & Darlene Z. McCampbell

Rochman's selection of stories by prominent authors focuses on the experiences of young people when they first strike out on their own. (Cover photo by Donovan Reese.)

Rochman compiled this collection about friendship, bringing together the works of more than a dozen writers, including Maya Angelou, Ray Bradbury, and Richard Peck. (Cover photo by Christine Rodin.)

booktalker in the field, beginner or old-timer, who cannot benefit from Rochman's advice and example."

Rochman and colleague Darlene Z. McCampbell tackle an important historical topic with their compilation *Bearing Witness: Stories of the Holocaust,* a collection that contains "much of the most evocative writing about the Holocaust," according to a critic in *Kirkus Reviews.* Selections include passages from the works of noted Jewish writers such as Elie Wiesel, Art Spiegelman, and Primo Levi; but also pieces that speak directly to young readers, such as excerpts from Carl Friedman's *Nightfather.* The *Kirkus Reviews* commentator concluded that "these selections are hard—even elusive for young readers—but collected here have a power that may prove unforgettable." Elizabeth Bush, writing in the *Bulletin of the Center for Children's Books,* maintained: "The breadth of experiences and diversity of voices featured in this shrewdly compiled anthology virtually assure that no reader will escape untouched."

Rochman and McCampbell also teamed up for two other anthologies, *Who Do You Think You Are?: Stories of*

Friends and Enemies and *Leaving Home.* The former, a collection of tales by modern American authors with a theme that is of universal relevance to young people, includes selections from Ray Bradbury, Joyce Carol Oates, Maya Angelou, and Sandra Cisneros, among others. In a review for *Horn Book,* Ellen Fader called the book "an artfully arranged collection of exceptional depth," declaring that "Rochman and McCampbell have chosen an enticing array of stories." *Five Owls* contributor Cathryn M. Mercier praised the editors' awareness of their audience, stating, "Rochman and McCampbell trust young adult readers to listen at their own pace, to hear their own voice among the many, to mine their own questions, to discover their own resolutions." *Leaving Home* presents more than a dozen poems, essays and stories from prominent contemporary authors centering on the emotions occasioned by an extended or permanent departure from home. "Definitions of home and experiences of departure are as varied as the characters populating this expertly chosen multicultural anthology," asserted a *Publishers Weekly* commentator, who added: "While some voices here reverberate with eagerness to break new ground, others resonate with the regret of leaving loved ones behind." Elizabeth Bush of the *Bulletin of the Center for Children's Books* noted that the works featured in *Leaving Home,* "drawn together in one volume ... offer combined insight into the comforts and challenges of home and leavetaking."

Rochman received the G. K. Hall Award for Library Literature for her well-received solo anthology *Against Borders: Promoting Books for a Multicultural World.* Reviewing the compilation for the *Journal of Youth Services in Libraries,* contributor Sara Miller offered high praise, maintaining: "With enthusiasm, sensitivity, and clarity, [Rochman] promotes a wide spectrum of literature for young adults that introduces many cultures and points of view, plus provides us with an extraordinary introduction that fights against the narrowness of political correctness." A *Voice of Youth Advocates* contributor similarly declared that *Against Borders* "introduces both sensitivity and sanity into the entire multiculturalism discussion."

Works Cited

Review of *Against Borders, Voice of Youth Advocates,* October, 1997, p. 226.
Review of *Bearing Witness: Stories of the Holocaust, Kirkus Reviews,* October 15, 1995, p. 1500.
Broderick, Dorothy M., review of *Tales of Love and Terror: Booktalking the Classics, Old and New, Voice of Youth Advocates,* October, 1987, p. 192.
Bush, Elizabeth, review of *Bearing Witness: Stories of the Holocaust, Bulletin of the Center for Children's Books,* October, 1995, pp. 66-67.
Bush, Elizabeth, review of *Leaving Home, Bulletin of the Center for Children's Books,* March, 1997, pp. 256-57.
Fader, Ellen, review of *Who Do You Think You Are?: Stories of Friends and Enemies, Horn Book,* September-October, 1993, p. 605.
Review of *Leaving Home, Publishers Weekly,* January 13, 1997, p. 77.

Lynn, Barbara A., review of *Tales of Love and Terror: Booktalking the Classics, Old and New, School Library Journal,* September, 1987, p. 134.
Mercier, Cathryn M., review of *Who Do You Think You Are?: Stories of Friends and Enemies, The Five Owls,* September-October, 1993, pp. 15-16.
Miller, Sara, review of *Against Borders, Journal of Youth Services in Libraries,* spring, 1994, pp. 304-05.
Rochman, Hazel, *Against Borders: Promoting Books for a Multicultural World,* American Library Association, 1993.

For More Information See

PERIODICALS

Bulletin of the Center for Children's Books, June, 1993, pp. 327-28.
Horn Book, March-April, 1996, pp. 232-33; May-June, 1997, pp. 327-28.
Hungry Mind Review, spring, 1997, p. 36.
Kirkus Reviews, June 1, 1993, p. 727.
Publishers Weekly, November 13, 1995, pp. 62-63.
School Library Journal, May, 1993, p. 128; September, 1995, p. 228.

*   *   *

RUBINSTEIN, Gillian (Margaret) 1942-

Personal

Born August 29, 1942, in Potten End, Berkhamstead, Hertfordshire, England; daughter of Thomas Kenneth (a research chemist) and Margaret Jocelyn (Wigg) Hanson; married Ion Will (marriage ended); married Philip Eli Rubinstein (a health educator), 1973; children: Matthew, Tessa, Susannah. *Education:* Lady Margaret Hall, Oxford, B.A. (with honors), 1964; Stockwell College, London, post-graduate certificate of education, 1973.

Addresses

Home—29 Seaview Road, Lynton, SA 5062, Australia. *Agent*—Caroline Lurie, Australian Literary Management, 2-A Armstrong St., Middle Park, Victoria 3206, Australia.

Career

London School of Economics, London, England, research assistant, 1964-65; Greater London Council, London, administrative officer, 1965-66; Tom Stacey Ltd., London, editor, 1969-71; freelance journalist and film critic, 1971-74; freelance writer, 1986—. Writer-in-residence, Magpie Theatre, 1989. *Member:* Australian Society of Authors, National Book Council (Australia).

Awards, Honors

Honour Book, Children's Book Council of Australia (CBCA), 1987, Children's Literature Peace Prize, 1987,

Gillian Rubinstein

Adelaide Festival of Arts National Children's Book Award, 1988, and Young Australians Best Book Award, 1990, all for *Space Demons;* Australia Council Literature Board senior fellowship, 1988, 1989-92; New South Wales Premier's Award, 1988, and CBCA honour book, 1989, both for *Answers to Brut;* CBCA honour book, 1989, and Highly Recommended, New South Wales Family Therapy Association Family Award for Children's Books, 1989, both for *Melanie and the Night Animal;* CBCA Book of the Year for Older Readers, 1989, Adelaide Festival of Arts National Children's Book Award, 1990, and shortlist, Victorian Premier's Alan Marshall Prize, all for *Beyond the Labyrinth;* shortlist, CBCA Book of the Year, 1990, and CBCA notable book citation, both for *Skymaze;* CBCA notable book citation, for *Flashback, the Amazing Adventures of a Film Horse,* and 1992, for *Squawk and Screech;* CBCA notable book citation, 1992, shortlist, New South Wales State Literary Award, and Victorian Premier's Alan Marshall Prize, all for *At Ardilla;* shortlist, CBCA Book of the Year, 1992, and CBCA notable book citation, both for *Dog In, Cat Out;* CBCA honour book, 1993, Books for the Teen Age citation, New York Public Library, 1996, shortlist, Victorian Premier's Alan Marshall Prize, and Young Reader's Choice Award nominee, 1998, all for *Galax-Arena;* shortlist, CBCA Book of the Year, 1994, and CBCA notable book citation, 1994, both for *The Giant's Tooth;* CBCA Book of the Year, 1995, shortlist, New South Wales State Literary Awards, 1995, and shortlist, Victorian Premier's Alan Marshall Prize, all for *Foxspell;* CBCA notable book citation, 1996, for *Jake and Pete;* shortlist, CBCA Book of the Year Awards, 1997, for *Sharon, Keep Your Hair On!*

Writings

FOR YOUNG PEOPLE

Space Demons (novel), Omnibus/Penguin (Adelaide, Australia), 1986, Dial Books (New York), 1988.
Melanie and the Night Animal, Omnibus/Penguin, 1988.
Answers to Brut, Omnibus/Penguin, 1988.
Beyond the Labyrinth (novel), Hyland House (Melbourne), 1988, Orchard (New York), 1990.
Skymaze, Omnibus/Penguin, 1989, Orchard, 1991.
Flashback, the Amazing Adventures of a Film Horse, Penguin, 1990.
At Ardilla, Omnibus, 1991.
Keep Me Company, illustrated by Lorraine Hannay, Penguin, 1991.
Squawk and Screech (chapter book), illustrated by Craig Smith, Omnibus, 1991.
Dog In, Cat Out, illustrated by Ann James, Omnibus, 1991, Ticknor and Fields (New York), 1993.
Mr. Plunkett's Pool (picture book), illustrated by Terry Denton, Mark Macleod/Random House (Milson's Point, Australia), 1992.
Galax-Arena, Hyland House (Melbourne, Australia), 1992, Simon & Schuster, 1995.
The Giant's Tooth (chapter book), illustrated by Craig Smith, Viking, 1993.
Foxspell, Hyland House, 1995, Simon & Schuster, 1996.
Jake and Pete (chapter book), illustrated by Terry Denton, Random House, 1995.
Peanut the Pony Rat (chapter book), Heinemann (London), 1995.
Shinkei, Omnibus, 1995.
Sharon, Keep Your Hair On!, illustrated by David Mackintosh, Random House, 1996.
Witch Music (collected short stories), Hyland House, 1996.
Annie's Brother's Suit (collected short stories), Hyland House, 1996.
Jake and Pete and the Stray Dogs (chapter book), Random House, 1997.
Under the Cat's Eye: A Tale of Morph and Mystery (novel previously called *Nexhoath Nine*), illustrated by Victor Lee, Hodder Headline (Sydney, Australia), 1997, Simon & Schuster, 1998.
Pure Chance (junior novel), Walker Books (London), 1998.
Hurray for the Kafe Karaoke, illustrated by David Mackintosh, Random House, 1998.
The Fairy's Wings, illustrated by Craig Smith, Penguin, 1998.
The Pirate's Ship, illustrated by Craig Smith, Viking, forthcoming.

PLAYS

New Baby, for Magpie Theatre, 1989.
Alice in Wonderland (adaptation) for Magpie Theatre, 1989.
Melanie and the Night Animal (adaptation) for Patch Theatre, 1990.
Paula, for Patch Theatre, 1992.
Galax-Arena (adaptation) for Come Out 95, Patch Theatre, and Adelaide Festival Centre Trust (AFCT), 1995.

Wake Baby, for Out of the Box and Company Skylark, first presented at the Queensland Festival of Early Childhood, 1996.

Jake and Pete (adaptation) for Theatre of Image, first presented at the Sydney Theatre Company, 1997.

Each Beach (original play) for Patch Theatre, first presented at the Adelaide Festival Centre, 1997.

OTHER

(Compiler) *After Dark,* Omnibus/Penguin, 1988.
(Compiler) *Before Dawn,* Omnibus/Penguin, 1988.

Has also contributed numerous short stories to anthologies including *After Dark, State of the Heart, Dream Time, Bizarre, Landmarks, The Pattern Maker,* and *Celebrate,* and several articles for periodicals including *Magpies, Literacy for the New Millennium, Island Magazine,* and *Australian Magazine.*

Adaptations

Space Demons was adapted for the stage by Richard Tulloch and performed in Australia in 1989.

Work in Progress

Across the Nightingale Floor, a fantasy with a Japanese historical setting; *South Road,* a novel about families and horses in the southern part of Adelaide.

Sidelights

Australian author Gillian Rubinstein is best known for her science fiction and fantasy stories in which young people learn through fantastic, often otherworldly experiences the importance of community and shared responsibility. Her many works for children and young adults focus principally on family and peer relationships, reflecting the author's belief that "the most pain and the most pleasure and the most intense emotions" reside within the family. Rubinstein's protagonists learn to grapple with strong emotions—including fear, love, and hate—and feelings of insecurity in a manner that is considered forthright, positive, and constructive. "Many of my books have the underlying theme that 'we must love one another or die,'" Rubinstein once told *SATA.* "I don't think human beings have a very good track record in this area, and sometimes I despair of us ever getting it right, but I keep plugging away at the idea that if we love and respect the planet we live on, the other species we share it with, and each other, then our lives won't have been wasted." In books such as *Space Demons* and its sequel *Skymaze, Beyond the Labyrinth, Galax-Arena,* and *Foxspell,* Rubinstein investigates the boundaries between childhood and adulthood as well as between imagination and reality. "Her tightly plotted narratives move seamlessly from reality to fantasy," *Twentieth-Century Young Adult Writers* contributor Agnes Nieuwenhuizen stated, "and, while they incorporate tough issues, they do so in ways that seem to both entertain and empower readers."

Much of the material Rubinstein draws on comes from her own life. She was born in the village of Potten End, near Berkhamstead in Hertfordshire, England, during World War II. "My husband says that after I was born, things started looking up for the Allies," the author once wrote. "But it must have been an anxious time for my parents, starting a family. My father, as a research chemist, was considered to be on essential war work, so he stayed at home throughout the war. The only major excitement was when his laboratory was bombed by mistake by a German plane dropping its bombs too late and missing London." "As a child," she continued, "I was always in some dramatic state or other, either deliriously happy or desperately miserable. I cried easily and fell into terrible rages. My parents described me as exasperating, or more kindly, as highly strung."

Rubinstein describes her own family life as uneasy. Her parents were not well-matched, and they had many personality conflicts. Her father was a scholar who had entered Oxford University on scholarships and earned his Ph.D. there. He also, Rubinstein once revealed, had a serious drinking problem. Her mother, on the other hand,

Four young people are drawn into a computer game's alternate reality until timid Mario overcomes his fears in time to release himself and the other three. (Cover illustration by Jon Weiman.)

was a very social woman, partly handicapped by a childhood bout of osteomyelitis. "She had to undergo many painful operations and spend long periods in hospital, and had to wear a leg brace. She was left with a deep scar and ongoing arthritis," the author explained. "But her spirits were undamaged. She was a very attractive woman who loved company and parties. She was also strong-willed and sharp-tongued.... With only bridge and charity work for outlets, she had too much energy to be a comfortable person to live with. I spent a lot of time as a child studying her to find out what sort of mood she was in."

Gillian and her sister, Jocelyn, found additional support outside their immediate family. Lavendar Helen Hatt-Cook, her husband John, and her two children, Mark and Pippa, became close family friends. The two families originally met during World War II, and formed a close attachment. "When the war ended and we started going away on summer holidays," Rubinstein once explained, "we always went with the Hatt-Cooks, to Devon, Cornwall or Guernsey in the Channel Islands. Later, when my mother and my stepfather went to live in Nigeria, my sister and I made our home with the Hatt-Cooks, and they became like a foster family to us. I drew on this situation for some of the feelings Victoria has in *Beyond the Labyrinth*." The same summer holidays supplied memories later recalled by Rubinstein in her novel *At Ardilla*. Similar childhood recollections of English village life also inspired her picture book *Mr. Plunkett's Pool*.

The tension between Rubinstein's parents led to their divorce in the mid-1950s. "Their relationship had deteriorated beyond saving," the author recalled, "and the fights and arguments had escalated." After her father left, she remembers, the tension in the house lessened, but other pressures emerged. "Even though the atmosphere in the house was better and my mother did all she could to soften the shock, I was devastated," Rubinstein stated. "No one else in my school, no one else I knew, had divorced parents. My strongest feeling was one of terrible shame. I couldn't bear to tell anyone." The shock of the revelation—divorce was regarded as disgraceful in England in the 1950s—may have contributed to the strong stammer Rubinstein developed during that time. Both her parents later remarried. Her mother and stepfather accepted a position in Nigeria, and her father died in an automobile accident a few years after his remarriage. Rubinstein and her sister stayed at boarding school in England, dividing their holidays between visiting their mother in Africa and staying with the Hatt-Cooks. "My parents spent eight years in Nigeria and the pattern of my life," Rubinstein once said, "became one of spending the long summer holidays with them in Kano, and later Lagos, the school terms at Queen Anne's [boarding school], until I went to Oxford in 1961, and the holidays at Whiteparish with the Hatt-Cooks."

Rubinstein did very well in her final exams at school, and won a place at Lady Margaret Hall at Oxford University to study modern language. She decided to read Spanish and French, influenced by the large French-speaking population she had met in Africa and the great love she developed for Spanish language and culture. At Oxford she was introduced to drama and began to work with the Worcester College Players and the Oxford University Dramatic Society (OUDS) as a props person and stage manager. "I enjoyed stage management for its own sake," she recalled, "but I was also fired with ambition to write for the theatre, and did in fact write a one-act play for an OUDS competition." After graduation, she turned to a succession of jobs, finally "ending up as the arts and entertainment editor on *Chambers's Encyclopaedia Year Book*" in London. During the early 1970s, she returned to school to earn her teaching certificate and "worked as a part-time cook in a 'stately home,' Oxenhoath in Kent, in return for a flat in the old servants' quarters."

In 1973, Rubinstein married Philip Rubinstein and the couple relocated to Australia. They settled first in Sydney, then in Byron Bay, and finally in Adelaide. Their three children were born in Australia, and Rubinstein credits them for influencing her decision to become an author of children's and young adult fiction. "I didn't know anything about Australian adult culture," she once said, "but my children were growing up as young Australians and I knew their world. I wanted to write books that they would enjoy reading, that spoke to them about their concerns and their problems, that didn't shy away from describing the world they lived in with all its cruelties and dangers but that gave them hope and confidence in the abiding human virtues of courage, compassion, and unselfishness."

The Australian culture also contributed to Rubinstein's development as a writer. "When my son was eleven he gave up reading novels—all he did was play computer games and read computer magazines," she told *SATA*. "There were simply no books around that he thought looked interesting. I thought I could write something that would appeal to him and in 1985 I gave myself three months to see if I could write a novel. At the end of three months I had a manuscript of 42,000 words—the first version of *Space Demons*. The first publisher I sent it to rejected it, but the second, Omnibus Books, said they would be interested in it if I could rewrite it. I went through two more versions before it was accepted—and it taught me the important lesson that books aren't written, they are rewritten!"

Space Demons was Rubinstein's first successful novel. It attracted critical attention for its forthright exploration of hatred and fear, and for the way its four young characters—Andrew, Ben, Mario, and Elaine—react to and deal with those emotions. *Space Demons* opens with Andrew Hayford, the neglected son of well-to-do parents, receiving a new computer game. Although the game has no instruction manual, Andrew guesses that its object is to destroy the video demons with his laser gun. "What he discovers later," said Susan Rogers in *School Library Journal*, "is that the game feeds on the preexisting alienation and hostility of its players in order to pull them into the reality level." Gradually Andrew and his companions are sucked into the reality of the

"Space Demons" game, and it is only after they learn to overcome their hostility and work together that they manage to escape from the game's alternate reality. *Skymaze* is the sequel to *Space Demons,* and once again it takes the four young people into an alternate reality where they are forced to confront their weaknesses, prejudices, and fears. "Each book," wrote John Foster in *Children's Literature in Education,* "illustrates the power of a negative emotion, hate in the former and fear in the latter."

All of the protagonists in *Space Demons* and *Skymaze* come from unhappy or broken families, like Rubinstein herself. "Andrew's parents break up in *Space Demons,*" Foster explained, "and he lives uneasily with his mother, stepfather, and troublesome stepbrother in *Skymaze;* Ben's parents are teachers and seldom at home, while his older brother bullies him, especially in the second novel; Mario's parents wished he had been a girl and his older brother makes fun of him; and Elaine's father is a drifter while her mother has run away, so that she is insecure in *Space Demons* and left with a foster family in *Skymaze.*" Each of the characters carries their emotional baggage into the gaming arena, where such anxieties can become deadly. "The growing understanding in the children that they must co-operate to defeat the dangerous game," Foster concluded, "leads inevitably to the improvement in their relationships in *Space Demons.*" In *Skymaze,* timid Mario must overcome his fears in order to release himself and the other three from the game. "Rubinstein convincingly melds the two worlds of fantasy and reality, revealing how inner and outer selves connect," wrote Cathi Dunn MacRae in *Wilson Library Bulletin.* "Her characters' authentic conflicts seem intense enough to set the maze in motion. Games are explored on several levels, from power struggles ... to dance exercises probing inner fears."

Rubinstein uses another game motif to probe fears, racism, and sexism in *Beyond the Labyrinth.* Fourteen-year-old Brenton Trethewan and his younger friend Victoria are the protagonists of the story. Brenton "is sharply different from his brothers and sister," stated *Horn Book* reviewer Ann A. Flowers, "and has become the outsider, the scapegoat, in his heedless, noisy, materialistic family." Victoria is a visitor; she has been sent to board with the Trethewans while her parents work in Africa. Brenton expresses his alienation through devotion to a "Dungeons and Dragons"-like role-playing game called *Labyrinth of Dead Ends.* "He bases all his decisions on the fall of the dice that he always carries with him," Flowers explained, "and plays 'Choose Your Own Adventure' games constantly." Trouble arises when Vicky and Brenton discover Cal, an alien anthropologist, on a nearby beach. "What is interesting," declared Foster, "is that Cal is both female and black, factors that affect others' reactions to her. Through this ploy, Rubinstein demonstrates the racism and sexism which underlie much of Australian society." When Cal falls ill with a viral infection, Brenton and Vicky realize that they must return her to her home planet. In a finish reminiscent of the "Choose Your Own Adventure" books Brenton loves, Rubinstein confronts the reader

Three young siblings who are kidnapped and taken to the planet Vexa to perform dangerous gymnastic feats execute a plan for escape in Rubinstein's psychological thriller. (Cover illustration by Joanne Pendola.)

with alternative endings that describe different futures for Cal, Brenton, and Vicky.

Beyond the Labyrinth attracted critical attention for its use of language as well as for its theme. While *Space Demons* and *Skymaze* are written in a relatively conventional format, *Beyond the Labyrinth* jumps backward and forward in time, mixing flashbacks with sections set in the current time—all of them written in present tense. The book also employs controversial language. "After it won its award," Foster explained, "a reporter for a television current-affairs program read excerpts from the novel to startled (and often horrified) members of the public in the main shopping street of Rubinstein's hometown, Adelaide, and asked them whether they would allow *their* children to be submitted to such material." Many libraries refused to shelve the book, citing its language as a factor in their decision. Despite this critical uproar, all three of Rubinstein's early novels have been popular with young adult audiences. *Space*

Demons in particular proved very popular with readers; it was dramatized and performed onstage throughout Australia in 1989.

Gaming, in the form of sports, again becomes an issue in *Galax-Arena,* Rubinstein's 1992 psychological thriller. *Galax-Arena* is the story of three young siblings, Peter, Joella, and Liane, who are kidnapped and taken by spaceship to the planet Vexa. Hythe, their trainer, begins preparing them for a life in the arena, where they will perform dangerous gymnastics for the amusement of the native Vexans. "Peter soon shows unrivalled gymnastic skills," stated Flowers in her *Horn Book* review of the title, "and Liane somehow turns her toy puppet, Bro Rabbit, into a menacing prophet of things to come." Joella, however, proves incompetent at gymnastics and is placed in a tank, where she is destined to become a sort of pet for the Vexans. However, this "situation," argued Chris Sherman in *Booklist,* "... allows her to learn the truth about her captivity and acquire the courage and means to escape. Rubinstein's *Galax-Arena* is chillingly real—from the Peb pidgin language to the

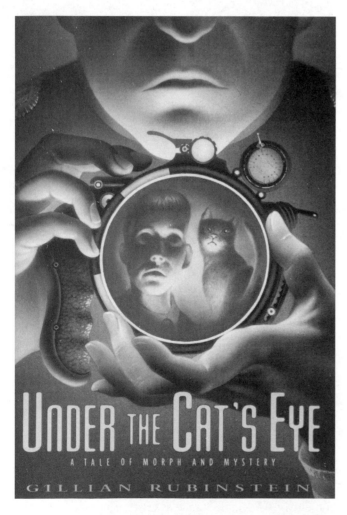

Mr. Drake, the headmaster of Jai's ominous new boarding school, turns out to be a demon who takes souls, and Jai finds himself pulled into the plot to stop Drake's spiritual vampirism. (Cover illustration by Victor Lee.)

children's gradual loss of innocence," the reviewer concluded. Flowers also praised the book, comparing it to William Golding's *Lord of the Flies.*

Alienation takes a fantastic twist in *Foxspell.* Twelve-year-old Tod is caught in a difficult family life. His father has deserted the family and his mother has been forced to move in with her mother to save money. Tod is facing extreme pressure to join a local teenage gang, and he finds escape in the wildlife of a local quarry. "Eventually," wrote Steven Engelfried in *School Library Journal,* "he meets a spirit fox that allows him to transform into an animal himself." Dan Russell, the fox spirit, "tempts Tod with an offer of peace and immortality if he will assume a fox shape forever," said *Booklist* reviewer Chris Sherman. Although Tod enjoys life as a fox, his human self is shaken by the animal violence that the shape unleashes in him. As a human, he enjoys the excitement and danger of gang life. "The harrowing climax takes place when one of his friends is accidentally killed during a gang escapade," declared Flowers in *Horn Book.* "The ending leaves the reader in doubt as to whether Tod can resolve the tension between a natural and a human life or escape permanently from his misery by becoming a fox." *Five Owls* contributor Christine Heppermann asserted: "Rubinstein does not depict one mode of existence as better than the other. Hers is more a plea for sympathy between species." Deborah A. Feulner, writing in *Voice of Youth Advocates,* maintained that Rubinstein "intertwines the two stories with skill, developing her characters fully."

For her novel *Under the Cat's Eye,* Rubinstein drew upon her memories of Oxenhouse—the stately manner in Kent where she once worked as a cook. The book "is based on this house," wrote the author in *Something about the Author Autobiography Series* (*SAAS*). "It was an extraordinary experience which I've always wanted to write about." In the novel, Jai Kala is sent to Nexhoath, a boarding school in Australia. It doesn't take him long to realize that something is not right at the institution—particularly with regard to the headmaster, Mr. Drake, Kitty, the housekeeper, and Roughly, the handyman. Jai's two new friends, Hugo and Seal, soon share with him their belief that Mr. Drake is some kind of spiritual vampire from another world. As it turns out, "Drake is using technology from ... [a] parallel world to suck the souls from individuals and extend his own life," explained Janice M. Del Negro in the *Bulletin of the Center for Children's Books.* Jai also discovers that Kitty and Roughly are shapechangers (a cat and a dog, respectively, who change into human form) from another parallel world. The two are looking for a lost child—their destined ruler—who they mistakenly believe is Jai. Eventually, Jai and Seal take on the difficult tasks of helping Kitty and Roughly find their real sovereign, rescuing Hugo who has become one of Drake's victims, and stopping Drake before everyone at Nexhoath is consumed by his evil power. "Rubinstein," asserted a *Publishers Weekly* reviewer, "employs the devices of classic fantasy with intelligence and authority." *Voice of Youth Advocates* contributor Susan Dunn enthused that with "mistaken identity, time travel, mystery, fantasy, and an animal story all rolled into one—this book has something for everyone."

Rubinstein continues to follow her stated goal of writing stories that draw and speak to alienated young readers. Yet the books she writes also serve as a connection with her own past. "Most of all," she concluded in *SAAS,* "when I write I want to spin the spell of words that enthralls the reader and takes them into the magic world of the imagination that inspired and consoled me when I was young. When I look back over my life, I can see that everything I've ever felt, whether it's been good or bad at the time, has all contributed to the emotion that goes into my writing."

Works Cited

Del Negro, Janice M., review of *Under the Cat's Eye: A Tale of Morph and Mystery, Bulletin of the Center for Children's Books,* November, 1998, p. 111.

Dunn, Susan, review of *Under the Cat's Eye: A Tale of Morph and Mystery, Voice of Youth Advocates,* October, 1998, p. 288.

Engelfried, Steven, review of *Foxspell, School Library Journal,* September, 1996, p. 206.

Feulner, Deborah A., review of *Foxspell, Voice of Youth Advocates,* December, 1995, p. 282.

Flowers, Ann A., review of *Beyond the Labyrinth, Horn Book,* January-February, 1991, pp. 75-76.

Flowers, Ann A., review of *Galax-Arena, Horn Book,* November-December, 1995, p. 206.

Flowers, Ann A., review of *Foxspell, Horn Book,* November-December, 1996, p. 747.

Foster, John, "'Your Part in This Adventure Is Over, You Have Lost': Gillian Rubinstein's Novels for Older Readers," *Children's Literature in Education,* June, 1991, pp. 121-27.

Heppermann, Christine, review of *Foxspell, Five Owls,* January-February, 1997, p. 62.

MacRae, Cathi Dunn, "The Young Adult Perplex: Reading Teenagers Enjoy," *Wilson Library Bulletin,* March, 1994, pp. 124-25.

Nieuwenhuizen, Agnes, "Gillian Rubinstein," *Twentieth-Century Young Adult Writers,* St. James Press, 1994, pp. 568-69.

Rogers, Susan, review of *Space Demons* and *Skymaze, School Library Journal,* March, 1992, p. 177.

Rubinstein, Gillian, essay in *Something about the Author Autobiography Series,* Volume 25, Gale, 1997.

Sherman, Chris, review of *Galax-Arena, Booklist,* October 15, 1995, p. 403.

Sherman, Chris, review of *Foxspell, Booklist,* October 15, 1996, pp. 414-15.

Review of *Under the Cat's Eye: A Tale of Morph and Mystery, Publishers Weekly,* September 21, 1998.

For More Information See

BOOKS

Children's Literature Review, Volume 35, Gale, 1995, pp. 207-13.

Twentieth-Century Children's Writers, fourth edition, St. James Press, 1995, pp. 844-45.

PERIODICALS

Bulletin of the Center for Children's Books, January, 1997, p. 184.

Horn Book, May-June, 1991, pp. 339-40; November-December, 1998, p. 741.

Kirkus Reviews, September 1, 1998, p. 1292.

Locus, February, 1989, p. 50.

Magpies, May, 1996, pp. 26-31.

New York Times Book Review, March 30, 1997, p. 18.

Reading Time, February, 1999, p. 26.

School Library Journal, April, 1991, p. 123; October, 1998, p. 146.*

Autobiography Feature

Lois Ruby

1942-

One Saturday at my local university, I was enjoying the free lunch that was our payment for judging History Day. Across the buffet table stood a striking woman, statuesque and sophisticated in both clothing and manner. Her classic high cheekbones were highlighted in just the right unnatural shade, and her eyebrows were plucked and shaped in perfect half-moons. She had prominent hip bones. She nibbled, whereas I *ate.* Naturally, I despised her on sight. So, I chanced a conversation. She told me she was working on her Ph.D. in history.

Well, I can talk history. After all, I write historical fiction, right? So I asked, "What are you doing your dissertation on?"

Peeking out from behind her cape of luxurious mink hair, she replied, "The History of Seventeenth-Century Ideas. You *know* how seventeenth-century ideas have influenced so much in our lives today."

"Oh, yes," I murmured, but for the life of me I couldn't think of one single seventeenth-century idea, and I defy you to come up with one now. What on *earth* could she have to write a whole thesis on? I wiped mustard off my nose, wondering what to say next. And then she asked, "And what are *you* in?"

"I write books for children and teenagers," I said proudly, to which she responded, "Well, there's nothing wrong with that."

Up until that moment I had never thought there *was,* but now I'm wondering if I should be searching for a normal job, because the truth is, there's nothing at all normal about writing books.

Think about it:

* Writing is a job you do in isolation, either in a library carrel with sides so high that you can't see another human being, or in a cluttered, silent room at home where even the people you love most are not welcome.

* Your coworkers are imaginary chess pieces you shuffle around in improbable ways until they play out their destinies to your satisfaction, months or years down the road.

* Your work uniform is baggy sweats and wool socks. On Casual Fridays you slum in a bathrobe and fuzzy slippers.

* On a bleak day you produce maybe ten minutes of survivable stuff in an eight-hour shift. On a bright day, you may work sixteen or eighteen hours and lose all sense of real time. *What's for dinner? Already? But I haven't taken anything out of the freezer yet.*

* You're fully alive and pulsating in worlds that do not exist for anyone else but you. Try to talk about them, and people's eyes glaze over. Refuse to talk about them, and people think you're standoffish.

* Every few days you rush to the mailbox up the block to drop your heart into it, and as soon as you hear the thud, you wish you could retrieve that manila envelope.

* You rush to your own mailbox and find (more often than not) a rejection letter that is masterful in its double-talk: we loved your story and wish we could offer you a contract, but it lacks a certain indefinable *something.* Good luck placing it elsewhere.

* There's no job security, no medical, dental, vacation, sick leave, maternity, or retirement benefits. And the pay is

Lois Ruby

rotten and slow in coming. It reminds me of the old joke: *the food at the banquet was terrible, and there was so little of it.*

Why would I subject myself to such intolerable working conditions? Simple, because I love the work.

*

At a recent school visit, people asked me if I wrote mysteries. No. Science fiction? Fantasy? No, no. Animal stories? Ghost stories? Love stories? No, no, no. Just as I was beginning to feel like a useless worm with no business masquerading as a writer, one girl asked, "Well, what *do* you write?" Ah, a chance to redeem myself. "I write stories about typical young people," I said, "contemporary and historical people, who are plucked from their ordinary lives and dropped down into extraordinary situations." There, that explained it. Still, she seemed puzzled, then blurted out, "But what are your stories *about?*" Well, that's as hard to capture as dandelion floss.

The thing is, I'm not interested in fantasy and ghosts. Real life is spooky enough and endlessly fascinating—families, relationships, daily life-and-death decisions, school dilemmas, dislocations, broken hearts, love and loss, human rights, civil rights, religious freedom, and personal victories. Each of us is made for quiet heroism. So, for example, the fireman who storms into a burning building to rescue a child is far less interesting to me than the child who heroically survives the ordeal.

I was not a particularly heroic child myself, although you might argue that it takes a certain amount of courage to survive as an only child in a world where everyone else has brothers and sisters to fight with. As an only child, you have two options—fight your battles internally, thereby making yourself miserable, or turn that indignation outward to public injustices. That's what I did, and that's why my books are filled with all sorts of moral and social justice dilemmas.

Nothing prepares you better for awareness of justice issues and appreciation for common heroes than living in a tropical, totalitarian country. I had my fifth birthday in the Dominican Republic in the days when a dictator, Rafael Trujillo, ruled the nation with two hands—one that gave food and money to illiterate peasants while the other slaughtered politically savvy dissidents without mercy. Our country constantly pulled against our Siamese-twin neighbor, Haiti, which occupied the other one-third of the island of Hispaniola. Suddenly, a small war would be declared, and mighty displays of armaments and tanks would parade through the streets of Ciudad Trujillo, led by a marching band. Soldiers would burst into our houses to make sure we had jumped to our feet with the first notes of the national anthem.

My father having died when I was three, and me being a very grown-up five-year-old, I became the translator and negotiator for my mother in this foreign country. I was the one bargaining with merchants for all our needs in the open-air market. I was the one hiring the maid who worked for fifty cents a day. I was the one buying fresh mangoes and pineapples each morning from the Pineapple Lady who worked and lived in a hut at the corner of our street.

I remember some pleasantries. I remember swimming in the bath-water-warm Caribbean Sea and washing our

"Me (Lois Fox) at age nine in my backyard in San Francisco," 1951.

backs with living sponges the length of a man's arm and the shade of our flesh, so pale compared to the black and mulatto natives we lived among. I remember some terrible things, also. A certain old gentleman used to take his daily constitutional past our house each morning at ten o'clock. There were rumors that he was something of a rebel, not in favor with Trujillo. And then one day, two days, three days passed, and he didn't come by. I chose the wrong time to ask my mother about this. We were sitting on a city bus. The only other passenger was a very dark-skinned man behind us. He seemed to be a native, but instead of the customary open-necked shirt and straw hat common to the tropics, this man wore a European suit, white shirt, tie, and a derby.

"Mommie," I said, "remember Mr. Alcedo who walks by our house every morning? I haven't seen him in a long time."

My mother always treated me as an adult and spared me no stark truths. "He spoke out against the government. Trujillo got him." I knew what this meant.

The man behind us leaned forward, and in a surprising, clipped Oxford accent, he said, "Madam, you must not say such things in public."

My mother was indignant. "Why, we're American citizens!" she cried. "We can say whatever we please!"

"Not in this country, Madam. In this country, no one is safe."

Images of that year are seared into my memory. Tempered by thousands of hours of research, they've been forged into an adult novel, *The Mercy Gate,* which I've rewritten a dozen times in an honest effort to capture life under such a cruel regime in such a lush, exotic setting. Maybe I'm closer to getting it right now, because, last winter, after fifty years, I returned to the Dominican Republic to stand in the shadow of the actual Mercy Gate in Santo Domingo.

Engagement picture, 1965.

*

Memories of my first ten years or so—other than the Dominican Republic sojourn—are sparse and anemic. They're more like murky, isolated impressions . . .

* Laundry freezing into ghostly mannequins on the clothesline one winter in New York.

* A consuming crush on a fellow third-grader, Barkley Massey, with the slicked-back hair.

* My father *not there*. I was only three when he died, and I have no memory of him, other than the pang of his absence.

* Being forced to give the only children's book I owned, *Black Beauty,* to a girl in my class who missed weeks and weeks of school because of cystic fibrosis, and then struggling to feel *good* about this sacrifice.

* Getting the pink-rare center of everybody's roast beef when we had dinner with my mother's childless friend, Helen.

* Sleeping under a mosquito net in a Quonset hut in Haiti, after an emergency landing when the plane ran out of fuel enroute to Ciudad Trujillo.

* Vicks Vap-O Rub and Musterole fumes rising from my chest and stinging my nose whenever I had a cold. I had a lot of colds.

* Growing graceless stalks from avocado pits suspended over a mayonnaise jar.

* Campfire Girls and the beads, the s'mores, the chocolate-covered mints we had to sell.

I do remember spending a lot of time with my Grandma Frieda, who wasn't a jolly lady to be around. She had come to America at the age of thirteen and had been married almost immediately to a man she didn't care much for. After her children were grown, she was widowed and eking by on Social Security. She never learned to read or write, either in English or her native tongue, Yiddish. Since I'd had lots of experience being responsible for my mother, it seemed like a natural step to appoint myself caretaker of my grandmother. I was her official secretary, and I handled all her personal correspondence and her battles with doctors, insurance, and Social Security. She would dictate letters with her colorful Yiddish accent, and I would write them down in proper English. She'd be angry and insulted by my editing, so when I read the letters back to her, I had to remember to read them just as she'd dictated.

I think this survival skill, designed to ward off my grandmother's wrath, may have influenced a writing style which comes very naturally to me today. I seem to be most comfortable telling my stories from two points of view simultaneously. Sometimes when I'm shifting from one point of view to another, I hear Grandma Frieda's voice in my head: "Dis isn't vhat I said. Write it de vay I mean."

As an only child, your most loyal companion is loneliness. You learn how to entertain yourself, especially if you grow up, as I did, without TV, computers, e-mail, interactive video games, CD changers, cellular phones, digital camcorders, and personal pagers. What do you *do* in such primitive times? One is, you listen to the radio and paint pictures in your mind of Lamont Cranston, the Shadow, and Tallulah Bankhead and Fibber McGee and Molly and all the incredible clutter in their famous closet. Then, when the radio clicks off, you read and you write. I re-created in my mind the worlds authors shaped for me, and I created for myself the worlds that most intrigued me.

When I was growing up, Mickey Spillane was the literature of choice in our house. His books were the only ones my mother ever read to escape the mundaneness of housewifery in the 1950s. The cheap paperbacks were strewn about our house like rose petals before the bride, with their colorful, mildly threatening macho detective covers luring readers into trashy pulp fiction before Quentin Tarantino snatched up that title for the movies. Yet, in spite of Mickey Spillane, I somehow found my way to good books. Follow me back to 1951 . . .

I'm nine years old. Every Saturday morning, my nose buried in a book, I make a twelve-block trek through the streets of San Francisco to an old Carnegie library, one of those buildings that harbored hidden treasure for those intrepid souls who dared to climb the marble steps and pass into the dark cavern where even whispers bounced off the walls. In this fortress I'd select my week's reading the way other '50s' girls might have chosen clear lipsticks or plastic barrettes at the five-and-ten.

The sentry is a librarian who sits just to the right of the front door on the raised platform of the circulation desk. She's eleven feet tall, including her salt-and-pepper topknot that pulls her eyes into an Eastern cast. A smile would bring her bun tumbling down, so she wisely flexes only those facial muscles that yield to frowns. Above her head are two signs: Children's Room and Adult Reading Room. Right away I'm faced with a dilemma: if I go to the Children's Room, I have to walk right in front of this frightening spectre.

From day one I sense that it's safer to head the other way. The librarian never leaves the circulation desk, of course, so I'm free to browse through the collection in the adult reading room and choose four or five books for the week. I'm transported to James Hilton's Shangri-La and Margaret Mitchell's Atlanta. I'm in medical school with A.J. Cronin's characters and at the left hand of God with Lloyd C. Douglas. I discover Pearl Buck and weep and gasp through *East Wind; West Wind* and *The Good Earth,* and I long to be Chinese.

*

Forty-six years later I followed the dream Pearl Buck awakened in me when my husband, Tom, and I traveled to China. At the Forbidden City, I relived my glamorous, yet circumscribed, lonely life as a courtesan of a great patriarch. On the banks of the Yangtze River, I once again labored with the leathery peasants, the coolies who coaxed measly sprigs of green life out of the dry earth and starved anyway. In the Li River valley I dragged bearded water

"As a bride with my uncle Harry," 1965.

buffalo into the rice paddies, and we stomped the young sprouts into mash, foot-to-foot.

After thirteen days, our tour group took a train from Guandong (Canton) to Hong Kong, which wasn't yet *China.* I cried through the whole two-hour train ride, grieving for my lost homeland. Call me fickle, but I had similar feelings in England, home of the poets I'd studied all my life, and in Israel, home of my ancient ancestors. But the pull of China exceeded them all.

*

As it turns out, bypassing the children's room and devouring adult novels when I was nine and ten and eleven was not just a reading decision. It was a career decision, as well, because, despite the forbidding librarian, I became a librarian myself. Through the years, I've wondered if I might have misjudged the old biddy, for while she never smiled, she also never stopped me from checking out anything I wanted to read, back in the days when children had restricted library cards. Maybe her silent approval molded me into an eclectic reader, and her stern bearing assured that I wouldn't stumble upon good children's literature until I was old enough to appreciate it—as a college sophomore.

That year a friend was shocked to hear that I'd reached nineteen and had never read *Winnie-the-Pooh* or *Charlotte's Web.* She assigned them to me, with a deadline for completion, and I was hooked. Eeyore, the world-weary, irritable donkey, became my alter ego when the public Lois was unrelentingly chirpy. Wilbur the pig enthralled me and projected me into life-long pig collecting, and Charlotte, the heroic spider, taught me what simple miracles can be performed by tirelessly plodding through the ordinary tasks to which we're called.

Now, let's slide from 1951 into 1953. It's my first day of seventh grade at a new school, among kids a year older than I. I know nothing about being a teenager, but suddenly I'm hot stuff. I've got a locker with a combination and a baggy, bloomer-style, one-piece, royal-blue gym suit with my name embroidered over my newly-sprouting bosom. No more all-day, mother-figure teachers for me; I'm going to be changing classes every fifty-two minutes!

I get my schedule, and in the little square for sixth period is the teacher's name—Mr. Ketuna, a *man*, and the name cracks me up. And the class is called Social Studies. Well, my heart leaps with joy. Here am I, an introverted girl of eleven, far more at ease among adults than among other children, but an exciting life awaits me, starting today at 1:40. Social studies! Mr. Ketuna is going to teach me how have a social life! I'll find out how to get along with boys, maybe learn to dance! And Mr. Ketuna, I discover, is so handsome; he's just the one to guide me on this breathtaking journey. Too good to be true?

Yes. Imagine my disappointment when Mr. Ketuna begins talking about continental drift. My joy flutters out the window and is quickly buried in the frozen wasteland of Antarctica. And I've never been much of a dancer since.

Of course, that particular deficiency may have more to do with the dance lessons I was subjected to in seventh grade. Our parents enrolled my best friend, Avra, and me in these truly awful classes. We girls had to wear nice dresses and white gloves. Remember, we're talking 1954, prejeans. We all lined up, girls on one side, boys facing us, and talked ourselves through these absurd steps in unison. On a signal, we'd have to *touch* each other. His hand at the small of my back, my hand on his shoulder, my glove in his sweaty palm, we'd grimly re-create the boxy steps we were taught, muttering "back-side-together; forward-side-together." We didn't know about hormones in 1954, but we knew something unwholesome was occurring, and it was horribly embarrassing, and as soon as the music stopped, we severed contact. When the six-week course was over, Avra and I vowed never to touch a boy again.

The only other thing I remember about junior high school, besides slogging through Hawthorne's *The House of the Seven Gables,* was entering an essay contest. The theme was "Use Your Garbage Can." I'm guessing maybe three people bothered to write on this spellbinding subject, and I was the only one who could spell garbage. Thus, I won and had to stand up in front of the whole school and read my essay. This piece of literature has mercifully been lost, along with the "novel" I wrote when I was ten, called "The Horse Who Never Ate." Of course, I was a city girl and had never seen a horse face to face and wouldn't have known what a horse ate if it actually *ate*, but the hero of my story didn't eat a bite, for about 250 loose-leaf notebook pages.

*

I'll slide past my high school years. They were punctuated by a less-than-ideal social life (Mr. Ketuna's magic didn't work); the realities of chemistry class, which convinced me that I wasn't cut out to be a doctor; my first publication in *Teen* magazine; and a modest brush with a radio talk show host who read a letter of mine on the air and was soon thereafter branded a Communist and brought before the rabid House Un-American Activities Committee.

Since I'd skipped a semester back in fifth grade, I graduated midterm. It was always my intention to go to college in the fall, but here I had seven months on my hands to earn some serious money—$235 a month—to pay for college. I went to work as a file clerk/typist at Crocker-Anglo Bank in downtown San Francisco. Up to that time, I'd pounded out all my term papers on a clunky manual typewriter, but here at my very own desk was a great big olive-green IBM Selectric typewriter. I was a perfect typist; the IBM made way too many mistakes because it went a whole lot faster than my fingers or even my brain.

At ten o'clock on my first day at the bank, a little bell tinkled, and everyone in the trust department got up for our fifteen-minute coffee break. At noon, we all filed back to the coffeepot for lunch. At three o'clock, coffee break again. By the time I got home that night, I was wired! My mother asked how the job was, and I replied, "I can handle the work okay. I just can't handle all that coffee." How liberating to find out that nowhere in my job description did it say that I had to guzzle caffeine.

I had not told the bank that I intended to quit after seven months to go to college, but as the summer was coming to an end, I couldn't avoid it any longer. I confess now: I lied. I told my boss, a fatherly type, that I'd been accepted at the University of California, Berkeley campus, and I'd suddenly decided that I needed to quit work and go to college while I had the opportunity. I expected him to shower his rage on me, because he'd trained me patiently

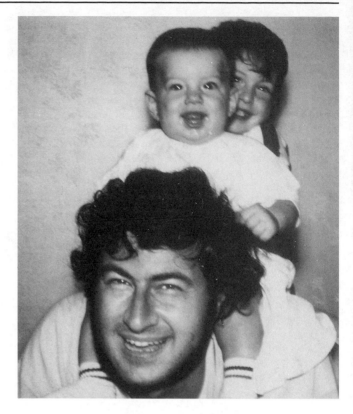

Ruby's husband, Tom, with first two sons, Kenn and David, 1971.

while I battled that IBM, and he'd entrusted me with more responsibility than my lowly position warranted. But that kind gentleman eased my guilt. He said, "You're too bright, Lois, to waste your life as a file clerk. If you were my daughter, I'd make sure you got to college. I'm glad it's going to work out for you." I don't remember the man's name, but I will always be grateful to him for his generosity.

Those first eighteen years were only the dress rehearsal for the play which opened on my first day of college when I met Tom, my future husband, and discovered real life beyond books. I stampeded into college starved for intellectual stimulation and determined to experience everything, everything. I was certain I'd never marry and never be bogged down with children. Instead, I would be a snobby intellectual and would travel the globe and have an exciting career of some vague sort and swoon over swarthy Mediterranean men who were mildly consumptive and not long for this world and therefore not interested in marriage. (As it turned out, the closest I came to *swarthy* was that my oldest son graduated from Swarthmore College.)

The first day of my college career, September 19, 1960, I walked into Spanish class, and there was this boy .... In the turbulent 60s of Berkeley, with its Free Speech Movement and People's Park and budding feminism and sit-ins and marches protesting everything from the war in Vietnam to DDT, I met a nice Jewish boy whom I would marry five years later. His name was—and still is—Tom Ruby, and he's the kindest gentleman I know. He's a clinical psychologist who cares deeply about the people who stream through his office with their woes and fears. But in 1960 he was a seventeen-year-old, skinny, fresh-scrubbed boy from a small town in Indiana. And the rest, as they say, is herstory.

College was all that I wanted it to be—fascinating subjects to study, new horizons every day, myriad world cultures swarming the campus, political passion, dances, soaring victories, plunging defeats—everything was intense. But money was a problem. My Crocker-Anglo savings were gone by the end of my freshman year, and so I worked at various jobs all through college. I was a waitress in the dorm cafeteria. I worked summers as a statistical typist, a soda jerk, a baby-sitter, a department store clerk. I thought I was incredibly lucky to land a job as assistant to a man who had a wine shop in downtown San Francisco. He hired me for my language skills, because he was writing a book on wine. But when I showed up for work, it was clear that it wasn't an editor that he wanted. He chased me around the counter twice, and I was out the door! So much for my first professional job as a writer. At that time, however, I had no intention of actually becoming a writer. I just had fun playing with words, the way other people played bridge or shot pool.

My college major was English, but I took nearly as much criminology and psychology as I did literature. Those courses that illuminated human and deviant behavior served me much better as a future writer than the analysis of Spenser's *Faerie Queene* or Joyce's *Ulysses.* Nor did I ever have a course in creative writing except for a ten-evening extension class long after I finished college. My teacher, Ben Santos, was a wonderful man, a superb writer, a Filipino exile who was author-in-residence at Wichita State University. I submitted one story for his gently critical appraisal, then waited with a lot of anxiety until my private conference with him. He handed me the story bleeding red ink, and my heart sank. "Is there any hope for me as a writer?" I asked, from the depths of my grief. And his reply? "If this is your first story, Lois, then there is a great deal of hope. But if this is your twentieth story, perhaps you should look for another line of work." A few months later I had my first book published, the short story collection, and I sent Professor Santos a copy. He was too kind to say so, but I think he was surprised that anyone would actually *pay* me for my work. I was, too.

*

There are various ways of choosing one's career path, and I disregarded all the sensible ones. The doctor thing, as I mentioned, dissolved in the caustic solution of high school chemistry. So then I decided I'd become a lawyer, because you can argue and prove points in a courtroom without balancing equations or erasing your fingerprints with acid. But by the time I graduated from Berkeley, that skinny boy I talked about earlier had evolved into a handsome man, one I wanted to marry who also wanted to marry me. Law school would take me three years, I reasoned, and at that rate I'd be an old woman of twenty-four before I could get married. To make matters worse, I'd be in law school in one state, and he'd be in graduate school eight hundred miles away. We talked and talked. Finally, Tom said, "You like books, you like children, and you love libraries. Why don't you become a children's librarian?" Well, that made sense to me, especially when I

found out that I could get a library science master's degree in half the time it would take to finish law school.

I stumbled into my first career.

And so, as bride and groom, Tom and I drove from San Francisco to our first home in Dallas, where I would support us while he worked on his graduate degree in psychology. I took a job with the Dallas Public Library. It wasn't in the children's department, where I had expected to surround myself with charming children who adored Eeyore and Wilbur as much as I did. Instead, I became a young adult librarian. I'd had no experience with teenagers and only sparse experience *being* one, and suddenly I was a young adult specialist! I knew teenagers were supposed to be aliens whom adults approached with kid gloves and dread. What if I hated them? What if they hated me?

That first day on the job was terrifying. My director ushered me into my little department of some two thousand books and said, in her pure Texas way, "Hun, y'all have two munts to read ever one uv 'em." I began with the A's on one side of the room and the nonfiction on the other, and worked my way toward the center. Happily, in those first few months, I discovered two things: (1) I *liked* teenagers a whole lot; and (2) the books that were written for and about them in the mid-60s were awful. I just knew I could do better. So, my second career was accidentally launched. I began writing young adult books and have had marvelous adventures ever since.

*

People ask why I write books for and about teenagers, and some people have been known to ask when I'm going to write a *real* book. Aside from the obvious point that books for teens are real books, in their bald-faced realism, I usually answer that I find teenagers more interesting than most adults I know. When we inch past thirty, our lives are pretty set in clay. The cast and scenery may differ a bit, but we are who we are for life.

Yet people between twelve and eighteen are in constant flux. The highs are higher than decently possible;

"Our three sons, Kenn, David, and Jeff," 1983.

the lows are the depths of despair, and the distance between the highs and lows isn't measured in miles or hours, but in inches and seconds. This is very fertile ground to sow for book material. It helps that I love and respect teenagers and feel a tremendous responsibility to avoid lying to them or patronizing them in any way. If you lie to or patronize adult readers, they just blow you off, but young people take everything to heart and they *wonder,* in every sense of that word.

The woman who never intended to land a husband has been married thirty-three years now, and the same woman who never intended to be "bogged down with children" has raised three outstanding sons, all born in four years during which their father was working on his Ph.D. I enjoyed the mixed blessing of being a stay-at-home mom. Those were the days of dragging one shopping cart full of squirmy little guys while pushing a second cart full of milk gallons and Cheerios and Campbell's Alphabet Soup. Those were the nights of putting the kids to bed and typing (on another IBM Selectric) dissertations for Tom and some of his colleagues.

And those were the days when I wrote my first book, my Sesame Street book. It had nothing whatsoever to do with the Children's Television Network program. It's just that *Sesame Street* was the only TV show we allowed our pre-kindergartners to watch. I'd park their little heads in front of the television at five o'clock each day, and they would be transfixed and battle-free for sixty glorious minutes. I'd be in the next room, which was the laundry room, and I'd write frantically, and when the tweedly music came up, signaling the end of our magic hour, I'd cap my pen, sigh deeply, turn off the TV, take my babies upstairs, and start dinner. That gave me twenty-three hours to think about what I was going to write the next day at five o'clock. I spent a full year of *Sesame Street* producing my first book, a collection of short stories called *Arriving at a Place You've Never Left.* Getting it published was a lot harder and took a lot longer than writing it, however.

I discovered a few valuable things in that experience, one being that you should never give a book such a complex and forgettable title. More important, I found that I could herd my writing passion into a discipline, and that it's pointless to sit around waiting for the muse to strike. Writers are people who *write.* Years later I discovered that I could work on stories in the crowded waiting room at the orthodontist's office or in the back row of a bustling meeting. Once I was stranded at New York's Kennedy Airport for fourteen hours during a blizzard. Hundreds of restless, hostile people milled around, chomping to fly home, and I found a corner and wrote, and the hours flew for me.

*

My favorite mother-time was when the boys were all teenagers, because they and their friends were great fun and a constant source of material for my stories. The luckiest thing for me is that I've had something very special to share with each of them. David, the oldest, was a spelling bee champ in his earlier years, and we spent scores of hours practicing weird words like jackanapes and jibboom and grosgrain. I have found a way to work a number of those words into stories, not to show off to my readers, but just as

a check on whether David is reading my books. In high school, he was a serious debater, and I got into debate with a vengeance. It appealed to the librarian/researcher in me and also to the right-brain aspect of my personality. We argued the annual debate topic and anything else that crossed our minds. He trained me so well as a debate mom that I taught debate in a private high school for a year.

Today David and his bright, beautiful wife, Lee Ann Merrill, live in Seattle. He's a lawyer and financial planner managing trust accounts at a bank. He has a lot more responsibility (and four more degrees) than I had in my Crocker-Anglo days, plus a computer in place of my IBM Selectric, but it still gives me a chuckle to think of him working in a trust department.

On December 2, 1998, Lee Ann gave birth to our first grandchild, a redheaded girl named Jocelyn. Her middle name happens to be the name of my favorite heroic spider, Charlotte. So, in a sense you could say I've come full circle, with David in the trust department and Jocelyn Charlotte in her crib. I suppose life would be truly sweet if one of my sons produced a curmudgeonly child named Eeyore.

Kenn is two years younger than David, and where he welcomed me into his life most warmly was in our synagogue youth group. I was the advisor of the group for fifteen years, including the year he was president. We shared terrific, deeply emotional experiences at regional conclaves where giddy girls flocked to me just *because* I was Kenn's mom. Kenn is an avid sports fan and knows more about baseball, basketball, and football than anyone on earth, and movies, as well. He actually earned a living as a football statistician for four years after graduating from Northwestern University. Now he's working as a technical writer for a computer consulting firm in the Washington, D.C., area.

When David was three and Kenn just a year old, we assaulted their sensitivity by bringing yet another child into the family. Jeff became everybody's pet, and today,

Author and husband dancing the hora at their son's wedding, 1995.

twenty-seven years later, he's the funniest person I've ever known. His humor pieces make your belly ache with laughter. He wrote a fine novel while he was in college, but he quickly figured out that a writer mustn't give up his day job. So, he earned a master's in journalism and is now the assistant dining editor for *Chicago* magazine. He gets to do features for the magazine on topics like the best pizza or best celebrity sports restaurant in Chicago.

It's marvelous having another professional writer in the family. Jeff is the only person I entrust to read and critique my unpublished manuscripts. Tom reads them, of course, but all I want from him is a smile and some sort of comment like, "This is the best thing you've done." I can't bear accepting his gentle criticism—which engenders my anger and defensiveness—but is usually on target. With Jeff, it's different, since as his mother, I've been his teacher, and now he is mine. Jeff has an eye for language. He can read a manuscript page and pick out *the* word which doesn't belong, which sounds discordant or is slovenly or too gassy. Very often it's a word I knew was wrong but thought I could slip past a sleepy reader. Not past him; he's always fully awake. I think he will end up as the *real* writer in the family.

Meanwhile, this one keeps plugging along. Despite those who think writing is a glamorous profession, I believe that most of writing is gratifyingly hard work. As the old adage goes, it's one part inspiration and nine parts perspiration. The inspiration part only kicks in after the blood, sweat, and tears soak through to your skin. I don't believe that creativity happens randomly but rather emerges when the soil is turned and tilled to make a bed for the seeds, when the foundation is poured and the house is framed to support the decorator's embellishments.

For me, the tilling and framing start with a character who interests me, who invades my quiet and compels me to listen to his voice. I let that person stumble around in my head for a few months until he takes on a bit more shape than the Pillsbury Dough Boy. I begin to ask questions and more questions, until I know the demographic layer of the character's life. Then I begin to explore the deeper emotional geography: what her small and large victories are, what makes him cry, or cry out in rage, whom he hates, whom she loves enough to lay down her life for. What I'm saying is, I scope the external and internal landscape of the character to see if this person is intriguing enough to explore for the next three years of my life, and to live with until the last library copy of the book falls to shreds.

Then come two or three years of research to pin down the location, the historical or technical details, and the social and political realities that inform the story. Even though I write fiction, I feel a burning responsibility to make my stories *true,* that is, as accurate and authentic as I can.

With the character and research clearly in my pocket, I start to glimpse what the conflicts are, and then the plot evolves, and the story begins to write itself. My husband, the psychologist who's always probing the secrets of the human psyche, says it's a deep mystery how a book works its way through the back roads of a writer's mind. I can tell you about the process, but I can't explain the magic when it takes flight, the sublime *creativity* part, because at that

"Our family today: Kenn, Jeff, David, and his wife, Lee Ann, mother of our first grandchild."

point, it's like watching a movie that is flickering across the small screen of my mind at breakneck speed, and my job is to write it down as quickly as I can before the movie clicks off and the lights come up to muddle the images on the screen. This was the way *Steal Away Home* told itself to me, in the ten-day marathon frenzy of the first draft. Ten days—after two years of wondering, researching, interviewing, reading, and thinking. And there followed several more months of revising and polishing, with the insight of a splendid editor, Judith Whipple.

Having said all this, I have to admit that *Skin Deep* was the exception to every one of my rules. It's the hardest thing I've ever done, and I think it's because it wasn't my idea in the first place. That is, I didn't start with a character who grabbed hold of me. Instead, Regina Griffen, then at Scholastic, asked me to write about a kid who is drawn into the neo-Nazi skinhead movement. The previous book Regina and I did together, *Miriam's Well,* convinced her that I could write about a controversial subject nonjudgmentally, in two opposing points of view (thank you, Grandma Frieda).

My first reaction to the topic was horror. How could I overcome my revulsion for these young, violent hatemongers, these anti-heroes, enough to spend three years with them moving around in my head, and *not* judge them? And how could I write compassionately about people who would hate me simply because I'm Jewish? I began with research, but after six months of reading white supremacist, racist propaganda, listening to hate music, and studying videos of skinhead concerts and rallies, I *really* started to sweat. What if I had tons of fascinating facts and ideas and theories and premises—but no story to tell?

Worse, after the research, I had to submit an outline of the entire book and a sample chapter. Not an easy thing to do when there's no story. And besides that, I'd never written a book whose outcome I knew. I've always let the

"Tom and me after thirty-three years of marriage," 1998.

ending naturally evolve from the beginning and middle, and sometimes when the ending is clear and irrefutable, I have to go back and *change* the beginning and the middle. What's this about knowing how the book will end before I know anything about the story? Not possible!

Then I had the bizarre opportunity to interview some skinheads in my town. I don't want to write about that experience here, because I enjoy telling it to students when I visit schools. But this meeting, at a Mexican fast-food restaurant, of all odd places to interview skinheads, turned me in the direction of the character I needed to make my story spring to life. I was sickened by the hate calmly, coldly spewing from the mouths of these young people. All through the writing I struggled against my own prejudices and my sadness and revulsion, but I'm pleased with the way the book came out, and doubly pleased with the reception it's had among thoughtful readers. One eighth-grade girl summed up the whole experience of the book perfectly for me. She said, "This is the worst book I ever loved."

*

Books like *Skin Deep* and *Miriam's Well* fall into the category of hard, contemporary fiction for mature teenage readers. It's what I love writing best of all. I discovered that I also love doing historical fiction, and that the historical

novels I'm writing now are read not only by teenagers, but by people as young as nine. Ironic, isn't it? As a nine-year-old I read adult books instead of children's books. Starting out in my professional life, I meant to be a children's librarian but was plunked down in the young adult department. And now I'm a young adult author who's unexpectedly writing children's books. This appears to be another career alley I staggered into.

My interest in historical fiction surprised me, since I wasn't a history fan in high school or college. Maybe it's that the older you get, the more recent history seems. I'm not interested in delving way back in time. You would never find me writing about seventeenth-century ideas, for example, like the lady with the prominent hip bones. It's the last 150 years that capture my imagination. Right now I'm working on the period right before and right after the Civil War, and I'm envisioning a series for middle-aged children highlighting the first quarter of this waning twentieth century.

Besides contemporary young adult fiction and historical juvenile fiction, I also write a lot about the American Jewish experience. I was raised in an ethnically Jewish, nonreligious family with strong pulls toward Yiddishisms and eastern European music, food, and idiom. I married into a religious, nonethnic Jewish family deeply rooted in assimilated American culture. I straddled the fence for a long time and finally made my peace with this dichotomy on the eve of my fortieth birthday when Tom and I became *b'nai mitzvah,* children of the Torah. We were pretty old children! Most people do this when they're thirteen, but not girls back in the 1950s, and somehow Tom escaped the call when he was a boy. So we taught ourselves Hebrew and studied intensively for a year and stood before our synagogue family, in the presence of our parents and our children, and read from the Torah for the first time. It was a frightening and exhilarating and deeply spiritual experience, and I can't imagine how a callow thirteen-year-old can manage it. And yet, all three of our sons did, before they were five feet tall.

When I was growing up, people said I should be a writer. "Not me!" I protested. People said I should be a teacher. Not a chance in the world would I do something so difficult. Yet, in the serendipitous way in which I've stumbled into my career moves, here I am writing and teaching.

My most fascinating job was teaching a summer writing workshop on an adolescent psychiatric unit. I can't forget Ray, a fifteen-year-old boy with fierce muscles, taut and sculpted. He stood at the door of my class that first day and said, "I don't read nuthin' and you ain't gonna make me write nuthin." I'd been warned about Ray. *He doesn't handle authority well,* the nurse had told me. Why, just the day before he'd yanked a toilet out of the wall and hurled it out the hospital window, so obviously I wasn't about to confront him. "Okay," I said with a shrug, trying to summon a modicum of dignity without sounding too authoritative.

Two days later, and every day all the rest of the summer, this kid wrote maudlin love poetry, more syrupy than baklava. No matter what the assignment, hearts and flowers and chaste, knightly courtship overtures flowed from his nubby pencil. The amazing thing was, the nurses

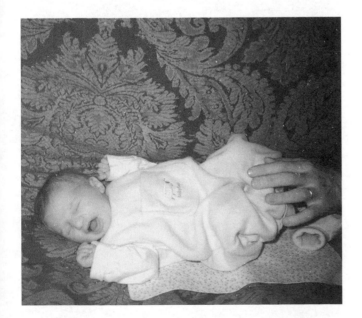

Granddaughter, Jocelyn Charlotte Ruby, two days old, 1998.

reported that his rage began to ebb. Such is the power of words, both the writing kind and the talk-therapy kind.

*

I visit some thirty schools each year. I'm always impressed by the enthusiasm of teachers and librarians who prepare students for my visit, and by the intelligence and ingenuity of the students who *think* about the ideas in my books and create projects through which they welcome my characters into their own generous hearts. I get to do lots of informal teaching in my creative writing workshops, sometimes among adults, but more often among kids spanning age nine to eighteen. Kids always work hard and well for a guest, but occasionally I encounter a young person who takes my breath away with the beauty of his or her imagery etched in precise language. For instance, when I asked students to think about old age and to project themselves into the body and mind of a person past eighty, a ten-year-old Kansas boy, Zach Kastens, wrote this poem:

IT SHOULD FEEL STRANGE
(WHEN I AM OLD)
IT SHOULD FEEL LIKE A MATTRESS WITH
　RUSTY SPRINGS
(WHEN I AM OLD)
IT SHOULD BE LIKE A BAD CLASH OF PANTS
　AND SHIRT
(WHEN I AM OLD)
IT SHOULD BE LIKE WATCHING A BRADY
　BUNCH MARATHON
(WHEN I AM OLD)
BUT I WILL ALWAYS BE YOUNG.

That kind of insight and respect for language and form in one so young renews my pride in the work writers do and the life experiences writers call upon to enable beautiful, funny, horrifying, enchanting images to link together into story and poem. It also reminds me that it takes courage to fill a pristine sheet of white paper with your own thoughts and words, then expose them to the critical eye of others. Which brings us back to those quiet, heroic acts that ennoble our ordinary days, the most amazing being that we bring new life into the world. My granddaughter, that sweet, redheaded Jocelyn Charlotte I mentioned earlier, was born three weeks ago today. It delights me as I look back over my first fifty-six years to project into her next fifty-six. I wonder, when she's asked to write a lengthy autobiographical essay, what will she select as the important happenings in her life?

The circle is complete.

*

By the way, in the seventeenth century Galileo proved the law of gravity and identified the Milky Way and the rings of Saturn, the King James version of the Bible was translated, the last heretics were burned at the stake in London, the first picture book for children was published, and bubonic plague broke out. I guess the lady with the prominent hip bones really *does* have something to write about.

Writings

FICTION; FOR YOUNG ADULTS

Arriving at a Place You've Never Left (short stories), Dial, 1977.
What Do You Do in Quicksand?, Viking, 1979.
Two Truths in My Pocket (short stories), Viking, 1982.
This Old Man, Houghton, 1984.
Pig-Out Inn, Houghton, 1987.

Miriam's Well, Scholastic, 1993.
Steal Away Home, Macmillan, 1994.
Skin Deep, Scholastic, 1994.

Contributor of young adult nonfiction to *VOYA Reader,* edited by Dorothy M. Broderick, Scarecrow Press, 1990; adult fiction to *Words on the Page, the World in Your Hands,* edited by Catherine Lipkin and Virginia Solotaroff, Harper, 1990; and short stories to *Writer's Digest.*

S

SCHOTTER, Roni

Personal

Married Richard Schotter (an English professor).

Career

Writer.

Awards, Honors

National Jewish Book Award for best children's picture book, 1991, for *Hanukkah!*

Writings

FOR YOUNG ADULTS

A Matter of Time, Collins, 1979.
Northern Fried Chicken, Philomel, 1983.
Rhoda, Straight and True, Lothrop, Lee, & Shepard, 1986.

FOR CHILDREN

Efan the Great, illustrated by Rodney Pate, Lothrop, Lee, & Shepard, 1986.
Bunny's Night Out, illustrated by Margot Apple, Joy Street Books (Boston, MA), 1989.
Captain Snap and the Children of Vinegar Lane, illustrated by Marcia Sewall, Orchard, 1989.
Hanukkah!, illustrated by Marylin Hafner, Joy Street Books, 1990.
A Fruit and Vegetable Man, illustrated by Jeanette Winter, Joy Street Books, 1993.
Warm at Home, illustrated by Dara Goldman, Maxwell, 1993.
When Crocodiles Clean Up, illustrated by Thor Wickstrom, Macmillan, 1993.
(With husband Richard Schotter) *There's a Dragon About: A Winter's Revel,* illustrated by R. W. Alley, Orchard, 1994.
That Extraordinary Pig of Paris, illustrated by Dominic Catalano, Philomel, 1994.

Passover Magic, illustrated by Marylin Hafner, Little, Brown (Boston), 1995.
Dreamland, illustrated by Kevin Hawkes, Orchard, 1996.
Nothing Ever Happens on 90th Street, illustrated by Kyrsten Brooker, Orchard, 1997.
Purim Play, illustrated by Marylin Hafner, Little, Brown, 1997.
They Saw the Future, illustrated by Kyrsten Brooker, Atheneum, in press.

Adaptations

A Matter of Time was made into a thirty-minute *ABC Afterschool Special,* written by Paul W. Cooper, directed by Arthur Allan Seidelman, and produced by Martin Tahse, Learning Corp. of America (New York), 1981.

Sidelights

A prolific writer of fiction and nonfiction for young people, Roni Schotter began her career with the successful young adult novel *A Matter of Time.* The novel is a "moving" story, according to a *Booklist* commentator, that has as its protagonist a high school senior, Lisl Gilbert, whose vivacious, artistic mother is dying of cancer. Lisl has always felt inferior to her mother; now she realizes that her mother is not only vulnerable, but has herself felt unloved and inferior at times. Lisl sorts out her tangled feelings with the help of sympathetic friends, relatives, and a social worker. The *Booklist* reviewer described Lisl as "believable and appealing," and commended Schotter for her "convincing" depiction of the girl's rapid maturation under tragic circumstances. *Horn Book* reviewer Ann A. Flowers lauded Schotter's "honest" and "straightforward" handling of the broad and difficult themes of life and death. The book was ultimately adapted for television as an *ABC Afterschool Special.*

Schotter's *Northern Fried Chicken* centers on heroine Betsy Bergman, a shy Jewish girl living in Providence, Rhode Island, in 1962. *Northern Fried Chicken* traces Betsy's involvement in civil rights protests, detailing the

Frannie expects her family's annual Purim play to be ruined when her cousins become ill, but her elderly neighbor proves to be an able actress. (From Purim Play, *written by Schotter and illustrated by Marylin Hafner.)*

personal growth that results from her participation in the movement. Zena Sutherland of the *Bulletin of the Center for Children's Books* applauded the story for providing "a touching picture of the way in which devotion to a cause can bring a reclusive individual to active participation." The characters and their relationships, Sutherland opined, are skillfully portrayed. A *Booklist* critic praised *Northern Fried Chicken* as an "effective and true" portrayal of the time and place in which it is set. Kate M. Flanagan, writing in *Horn Book,* similarly declared that the novel "evokes the era's feeling of hope and of change."

Another of Schotter's young adult novels, *Rhoda, Straight and True,* is set in Brooklyn in the summer of 1953. In this story, twelve-year-old title heroine Rhoda realizes that appearances—such as those of a huge family of scruffy-looking neighbors—are not reliable when assessing a person's character. A commentator for *Publishers Weekly* felt that "the sense of locale is nicely drawn, with original characters and humor rounding out a pleasant story." A critic for *Booklist* praised the "strong, sure characterizations," "careful plotting," and vivid setting in *Rhoda, Straight and True.*

Schotter made her picture-book debut with *Efan the Great,* a "touching and unusually substantial Christmas story," in the words of a *Bulletin of the Center for Children's Books* reviewer. Ten-year-old Efan, who lives in a poor neighborhood, wants to buy a Christmas tree with his life savings of $6.63. Finding the prices of trees too high, he agrees to work for a tree-seller, and to be paid with his pick of the trees at the end of the day. When the tree he picks is too big to fit into his apartment, Efan leaves it outside and decorates it for all to see. A *Publishers Weekly* contributor called the tale "heartwarming" and "jubilantly told."

The success of Schotter's initial effort in the picture book genre prompted more works for young readers, among them *Captain Snap and the Children of Vinegar Lane* and *Bunny's Night Out.* The former tells the simple story of a group of children who are initially afraid of an old man, but when they discover that he is ill they bring him food and blankets. In *Bunny's Night Out,* Bunny, who is afraid of bedtime, leaves his room to explore the world. Although Bunny finds the world is full of interesting creatures, he learns that he prefers his warm, safe home. A critic for *School Library Journal* dubbed *Bunny's Night Out* a "cheerful morality tale," while Ellen Mandel of *Booklist* applauded it as "perfect for settling restless youngsters into sweet dreams."

Bunny appears again in 1993's *Warm at Home.* In this story, Bunny has a cold and complains that there is nothing to do. By using his imagination, however, he eventually creates a long list of things to do (mostly involving vegetables). A *Publishers Weekly* critic called *Warm at Home* "a total charmer." Karen James, writing in *School Library Journal,* noted that Bunny is "the embodiment of any young child looking for amusement."

Schotter published two other well-received books for children in 1993, *A Fruit and Vegetable Man* and *When Crocodiles Clean Up. A Fruit and Vegetable Man* centers on longtime grocer Ruby Rubinstein, who has been tending his stand for fifty years. Ruby falls ill and is aided by young Asian immigrant Sun Ho and his family. *School Library Journal* contributor Cynthia K. Richey cheered this "satisfying story," while Hazel Rochman of *Booklist* praised the "unaffected" writing. *When Crocodiles Clean Up* is the story of a crocodile mother who gives her little crocodile children thirty minutes to clean up their room. They begin playing

Two dreamers in a family of tailors turn their imaginative designs into an amusement park. (From Dreamland, *written by Roni Schotter and illustrated by Kevin Hawkes.*)

instead, until they hear their mother returning. Frantically and successfully they start cleaning, gobbling down their very last toy before their mother appears. *School Library Journal* contributor Virginia E. Jeschelnig called *When Crocodiles Clean Up* a book "full of laughs," noting that "[c]hildren will recognize their own behavior as they enjoy the antics of the crocodile kids."

A vegetarian pig with a more-than-healthy appetite, especially for pastries, is the endearing swine in Schotter's *That Extraordinary Pig of Paris*. Schotter, along with her husband, Richard, also produced *There's a Dragon About: A Winter's Revel*. Written in verse and inspired by traditional St. George plays, the book features a cast of modern children performing a play in their neighbor's home. "The text could easily be adapted for live winter revels," noted Kathleen Whalin, writing in *School Library Journal*. "Great fun," maintained a *New York Times Book Review* commentator.

Schotter's *Dreamland* presents a family of tailors, some of whom possess an abundance of common sense and some of whom do not. Among the latter group are young Theo, who sketches plans for fantastic machines, and his uncle Gurney, who moves west to seek his fortune. At a time when the family business is failing, Gurney writes to Theo, asking him for exact instructions on how to build his machines. Gurney turns the machines into an amusement park. Constance Decker Thompson, writing in the *New York Times Book Review*, praised *Dreamland* as a "splendid" book, asserting that "Schotter deftly builds suspense to a wondrous climactic scene in which Theo's family sees Uncle Gurney's project." Pointing out, as well, that Schotter is the granddaughter of a tailor, Thompson observed that "her engaging phrases . . . spring from a tailor's world."

Another of Schotter's stories for children, *Nothing Ever Happens on 90th Street*, again focuses on the importance of imagination. Having to write a paper for school, Eva sits outside her house in the city watching people. She receives advice from several folks and witnesses some interesting events, including a bicycle accident. J. Patrick Lewis, writing in the *New York Times Book Review*, noted the "clever sprinkles" of characters that help to create a "spicy ethnic stewpot."

Schotter has also written a few picture books about Jewish holidays. *Hanukkah!* describes one family's celebration of the winter festival that commemorates the victory of the Maccabees against their Greek rulers. The book received the National Jewish Book Award in 1991 for best children's picture book on a Jewish theme. *Passover Magic*, a portrayal of one family's seder dinner, features colorful characters, such as amateur magician Uncle Harry, as well as holiday lore. A *Publishers Weekly* critic called the work a warm, original story filled with "intricate, often amusing details," engagingly recounted by its narrator, daughter Molly. *Purim Play* is Schotter's third book on Jewish holidays. With "warm, lively text," according to *School Library Journal* contributor Libby K. White, Schotter describes the story and traditions of the Purim holiday.

Like *Hanukkah!* and *Passover Magic, Purim Play* was illustrated by Marilyn Hafner, whose pictures for these and other Schotter stories have garnered considerable praise.

Works Cited

Review of *Bunny's Night Out, School Library Journal,* July, 1989, p. 76.

Review of *Efan the Great, Bulletin of the Center for Children's Books,* December, 1986, p. 75.

Review of *Efan the Great, Publishers Weekly,* September 26, 1986, pp. 75-76.

Flanagan, Kate M., review of *Northern Fried Chicken, Horn Book,* February, 1984, p. 65.

Flowers, Ann A., review of *A Matter of Time, Horn Book,* February, 1980, pp. 65-66.

James, Karen, review of *Warm at Home, School Library Journal,* June, 1993, p. 88.

Jeschelnig, Virginia E., review of *When Crocodiles Clean Up, School Library Journal,* December, 1993, p. 93.

Lewis, J. Patrick, review of *Nothing Ever Happens on 90th Street, New York Times Book Review,* August 3, 1997, p. 14.

Mandel, Ellen, review of *Bunny's Night Out, Booklist,* April 15, 1989, p. 1471.

Review of *A Matter of Time, Booklist,* November 15, 1979, p. 495.

Review of *Northern Fried Chicken, Booklist,* November 1, 1983, p. 404.

Review of *Passover Magic, Publishers Weekly,* March 20, 1995, pp. 60-61.

Review of *Rhoda, Straight and True, Booklist,* October 1, 1986, p. 275.

Review of *Rhoda, Straight and True, Publishers Weekly,* August 22, 1986, p. 99.

Richey, Cynthia K., review of *A Fruit and Vegetable Man, School Library Journal,* October, 1993, p. 112.

Rochman, Hazel, review of *A Fruit and Vegetable Man, Booklist,* September 1, 1993, p. 71.

Sutherland, Zena, review of *Northern Fried Chicken, Bulletin of the Center for Children's Books,* February, 1984, p. 117.

Review of *There's a Dragon About: A Winter's Revel, New York Times Book Review,* December 4, 1994, p. 76.

Thompson, Constance Decker, review of *Dreamland, New York Times Book Review,* April 13, 1997.

Review of *Warm at Home, Publishers Weekly,* March 8, 1993, p. 77.

Whalin, Kathleen, review of *There's a Dragon About: A Winter's Revel, School Library Journal,* September, 1994, p. 211.

White, Libby K., review of *Purim Play, School Library Journal,* April, 1998, p. 110.

For More Information See

PERIODICALS

Booklist, October 15, 1986, pp. 356-57; January 15, 1994, pp. 938-39; November 1, 1994, p. 509; March 1, 1995, pp. 1249-50; April 1, 1996, p. 1374.

Bulletin of the Center for Children's Books, November, 1990, pp. 69-70.
Horn Book, January, 1991, p. 95.
Kirkus Reviews, April 1, 1989, p. 554; February 1, 1997, p. 228.
New York Times Book Review, September 17, 1989, p. 39; December 9, 1990, p. 31.
Publishers Weekly, September 20, 1993, p. 71; April 11, 1994, p. 64; September 12, 1994, p. 90; February 3, 1997, p. 106; February 23, 1998, p. 67.
School Library Journal, December, 1979, p. 92; July, 1994, pp. 88-89; March, 1997, pp. 166-67.*

*   *   *

SCHULMAN, Arlene 1961-

Personal

Born August 13, 1961, in Bronx, NY; daughter of Alan and Dorothy Schulman. *Politics:* "Sporadic." *Religion:* "Diverse." *Hobbies and other interests:* "Writing, reading, shopping for thrift shop bargains."

Addresses

Home and office—P.O. Box 460, Inwood Station, New York, NY 10034. *Electronic mail*—Aeschulman@ aol.com.

Career

Freelance journalist and photojournalist for publications including *New York Times, New York Post, New York Daily News, El Diario-La Prensa, Village Voice, Newsday, Inside Sports, Cosmo,* and others, 1985—. Ohio State University, School of Journalism, visiting professor, 1996; James Thurber House Writing Camp, instructor, 1996; *Columbus Dispatch,* writing coach, 1996; New York City Public Schools, artist/writer-in residence, 1997—; Inwood West Neighborhood Association, President, 1998—. *Exhibitions:* Photographs included in the collections of The National Baseball Hall of Fame, The International Boxing Hall of Fame, The Museum of the City of New York, and The New York Public Library, as well as in private collections. *Member:* Association of Women in Sports Media, Boxing Writers Association of America, Professional Women Photographer's Association, Newswomen's Club of New York.

Awards, Honors

Award for Exclusive and Outstanding Reporting, Gannett, Inc., 1987; Front Page Award for Sports Reporting, Newspaper Guild of New York, 1990; Miller Lite Women's Sports Journalism Award, 1992; Yaddo Fellowship, 1994; Sporting News Award, 1994, for "Photograph of Young Boxer"; William Hill Sports Book of the Year finalist, 1995, for *The Prizefighters;* Best Books, New York Public Library, 1995, for *The Prizefighters,* and 1997, for *Muhammad Ali: Champion;* A. J. Liebling Award for Outstanding Boxing Writing, Boxing Writers Association of America, 1996; fellowship, James Thurber House, Columbus, Ohio, 1996.

Writings

SELF-ILLUSTRATED WITH PHOTOGRAPHS

The Prizefighters: An Intimate Look at Champions and Contenders, Lyons, 1994.
Carmine's Story: A Book about a Boy Living with AIDS, Lerner (Minneapolis), 1997.
T. J.'s Story: A Book about a Boy Who Is Blind, Lerner, 1998.

OTHER

Muhammad Ali: Champion, Lerner (Minneapolis), 1996.
Robert F. Kennedy: Promise for the Future, Facts on File, 1998.

Sidelights

An accomplished sportswriter and photojournalist, Arlene Schulman has been branching out to embrace new formats and new subjects in her work. Her comments to *SATA* identify an underlying motivation that connects all of her creative efforts: "I'd like to bring a new awareness of different people to a diverse audience and show just how much people really do have in common. Carmine Buete, a ten-year-old boy living with AIDS, enjoyed the same video games and pizza that other kids his age enjoyed. Boxers in *The Prizefighters* considered

From Arlene Schulman's **The Prizefighters,** *a compilation of interviews with famous boxers accompanied by the author's black-and-white photo portraits.*

themselves the same as other men, except they box for a living. T. J. Olsen, a ten-year-old boy who is blind, said, 'this is the way that I am.'"

About her craft, Schulman told *SATA:* "I've always loved words, ever since I learned how to write. When we were required to put spelling words into stories in the third grade, I would turn in not just one story, but three, sometimes four. My father was a fantastic amateur photographer who documented our lives and took us to museums on the weekends. The writers and illustrators who have influenced my work include John Steinbeck, Carl Sandburg, Langston Hughes, Margaret Bourke-White, and Dorothea Lange."

Schulman put her photojournalistic and sportswriting skills to work in her first book, *The Prizefighters: An Intimate Look at Champions and Contenders.* The book is a compilation of interviews with famous boxers accompanied by black-and-white portraits. *Booklist* critic Wes Lukowsky wrote that *The Prizefighters* "succeeds on the merits of both its visuals and its text." With sincere admiration for boxers and their strenuous careers, Schulman elicits from her subjects a sense of "humility," wrote Lukowsky, "induced by a sport in which all the posturing and bravado can disappear in an instant." A *Publishers Weekly* reviewer especially appreciated Schulman's "engrossing text" and "most effective shots ... [of] youngsters who dream of fame and money in the ring," and deemed the entire book "outstanding."

After writing another book about boxing, *Muhammad Ali: Champion,* Schulman was presented with an opportunity to write a book about a child with Acquired Immunodeficiency Syndrome (AIDS). According to Schulman's comments to *New York Daily News* writer Vic Ziegel, she let the idea "rattle around" for about a month; "I was apprehensive," Schulman admitted. Through a social worker recommended by a pediatric AIDS foundation, Schulman was introduced to 10-year-old Carmine. Born with the AIDS virus and having developed full-blown AIDS at age two, Carmine lived with his very loving grandmother Kay Beute. Carmine's mother had died of AIDS just three months after giving birth to her son. Visiting with Carmine in his Queens, New York home, Schulman began taking notes. In the *New York Daily News* article, she described her visits with Carmine: "His mood would change depending on nothing. He was kind of quiet, very introspective. Sometimes he just wanted to sit on the couch and watch TV. Sometimes he wanted to be held by his grandmother. But once he found out he could beat me at video games, I became accepted." The story that Schulman has helped Carmine tell is a very real and very lonely one: "My best friends are my cousins," the boy relates in *Carmine's Story.* "They're the only friends I have. My favorite holiday is Halloween because my cousins and I go trick-or-treating. I just wish I had more energy to play. I'm used to spending a lot of time by myself, so I kind of like my peace and quiet after they leave." Schulman told Ziegel, "The book is geared to Carmine's peers. So I wanted to show him as somebody who is interested in the same things all kids are. Pizza, video games, Kentucky Fried Chicken." A *Kirkus Reviews* critic noted that Carmine "tried to have an outwardly normal life," but admitted that Schulman's photographs told a "haunting story—of an exhausted 34-pound child who knew he was dying." Carmine, according to the book's epilogue, died two months after his tenth birthday.

Works Cited

Review of *Carmine's Story: A Book about a Boy Living with AIDS, Kirkus Reviews,* November 15, 1997, p. 1713.

Lukowsky, Wes, review of *Prizefighters: An Intimate Look at Champions and Contenders, Booklist,* October 1, 1994, p. 228.

Review of *Prizefighters: An Intimate Look at Champions and Contenders, Publishers Weekly,* August 15, 1994, p. 83.

Schulman, Arlene, *Carmine's Story: A Book about a Boy Living with AIDS,* 1997.

Ziegel, Vic, "AIDS Kid's Fight for His Life," *New York Daily News,* November 18, 1997, p. 18.

For More Information See

PERIODICALS

Booklist, March 15, 1998, p. 1236.
Children's Bookwatch, May, 1996, p. 6.
School Library Journal, June, 1996, p. 164.

*   *   *

SCIESZKA, Jon 1954-

Personal

Last name rhymes with "Fresca"; born September 8, 1954, in Flint, MI; son of Louis (an elementary school principal) and Shirley (a nurse) Scieszka; married Jerilyn Hansen (an art director); children: Casey (a daughter), Jake. *Education:* Attended Culver Military Academy; Albion College, B.A., 1976; Columbia University, M.F.A., 1980. *Hobbies and other interests:* "For me to know, and you to find out."

Addresses

Agent—c/o Children's Marketing, Penguin USA, 345 Hudson St., New York, NY 10014.

Career

Writer. Has also worked as an elementary school teacher, a painter, a lifeguard, and a magazine writer, among other jobs.

Awards, Honors

New York Times Best Books of the Year citation, ALA Notable Children's Book citation, Maryland Black-Eyed Susan Picture Book Award, and *Parenting's* Reading Magic Award, all 1989, all for *The True Story of the*

Three Little Pigs!; New York Times Best Illustrated Books of the Year citation, *School Library Journal* Best Books of the Year citation, *Booklist* Children's Editors' "Top of the List" citation, and ALA Notable Children's Book citation, all 1992, Caldecott Honor Book, 1993, all for *The Stinky Cheese Man and Other Fairly Stupid Tales;* Best Children's Book citation, *Publishers Weekly,* Blue Ribbon citation, *Bulletin of the Center for Children's Books,* Top of the List and Editors' Choice citations, *Booklist,* all 1995, Best Book for Young Adults citation, ALA, 1996, all for *Math Curse.*

Writings

The True Story of the Three Little Pigs!, illustrated by Lane Smith, Viking, 1989.
The Frog Prince, Continued, illustrated by Steve Johnson, Viking, 1991.
(With Lane Smith) *The Stinky Cheese Man and Other Fairly Stupid Tales,* Viking, 1992.
The Book That Jack Wrote, illustrated by Daniel Adel, Viking, 1994.
(With Lane Smith) *Math Curse,* Viking, 1995.
Squids Will Be Squids: Fresh Morals, Beastly Fables, illustrated by Lane Smith, Viking, 1998.

"THE TIME WARP TRIO" SERIES

Knights of the Kitchen Table, illustrated by Lane Smith, Viking, 1991.
The Not-So-Jolly Roger, illustrated by Lane Smith, Viking, 1991.
The Good, the Bad, and the Goofy, illustrated by Lane Smith, Viking, 1992.
Your Mother Was a Neanderthal, illustrated by Lane Smith, Viking, 1993.
2095, illustrated by Lane Smith, Viking, 1995.
Tut, Tut, illustrated by Lane Smith, Viking, 1996.
Summer Reading Is Killing Me, illustrated by Lane Smith, Viking, 1998.
It's All Greek to Me, illustrated by Lane Smith, Viking, 1999.

Several of Scieszka's works have been recorded on audio cassette and have been translated into other languages, including Spanish.

Adaptations

Knights of the Kitchen Table and *The Not-So-Jolly Roger* were adapted for video by PBS Video, 1994.

Work in Progress

The Stinky Cheese Man is being adapted into an animated feature-length movie, and "The Time Warp Trio" books are being developed into an animated television series for the Public Broadcasting System (PBS).

Sidelights

"Jon Scieszka," writes a critic in *Children's Books and Their Creators,* "enters classic fairy tales, turns them

Jon Scieszka

upside down, and exits with a smirk." In works such as *The True Story of the Three Little Pigs!, The Frog Prince, Continued, The Stinky Cheese Man and Other Fairly Stupid Tales,* and *Math Curse,* Scieszka and his collaborator/artist friend Lane Smith bring a postmodern sense of absurdity and a satiric edge to a classic category of writing. They take away the sense of easy familiarity and boredom that sometimes surrounds modern perceptions of the fairy tale genre. "What remains," the *Children's Books and Their Creators* contributor concludes, "is hilarious buffoonery within these energetic, yet sophisticated parodies."

The fact that Scieszka's parody plays to a more mature audience has astounded some critics. His works—sold as picture books intended for beginning readers—are equally funny to older children and young adults who have grown beyond the picture-book stage and are used to sophisticated humor. In appealing to a number of age groups, he follows the pioneering examples of other great writers in children's literature, such as L. Frank Baum, E. Nesbit, and Dr. Seuss. "What Scieszka has done," wrote Patrick Jones and Christine Miller in *Twentieth-Century Children's Writers,* "is make a book equivalent of a happy meal—taking the things that most kids like in books like humor, adventure, fairy tales, and plain old silliness, and combining them into easy to read tomes which will indeed appeal to an audience of all ages." "Our audience is hardcore silly kids," Scieszka told Amanda Smith in a *Publishers Weekly* interview. "And there are a lot of 'em out there."

Jon Scieszka attended Columbia University and studied writing there. He intended, said Smith in the same *Publishers Weekly* interview, to "write the Great American novel." The author reported, "Then I taught first and second grade and got sidetracked." Later he realized that a children's book is a condensed short story, and since he enjoyed writing short stories, he decided to try writing children's books. He remarked that it was surprising he hadn't thought of writing for children sooner, since he came from a large family, had always loved children, was the son of an elementary school teacher, and had enjoyed being a teacher himself.

Scieszka left teaching for a year to develop book ideas. After having stories rejected for months, he met Lane Smith. They started working together. Regina Hayes at Viking Press saw the early drawings and text for *The True Story of the Three Little Pigs!* and decided to take a risk and publish the story. "Lane and I got turned down in a lot of places," Scieszka told Amanda Smith, "because people thought the manuscript of *The Three Little Pigs* was too sophisticated. That became a curse word—the 'S' word." "People don't give kids enough credit for knowing the fairy tales and being able to get what parody is," the author continues. "When I taught second-graders, that's the age when they first discover parody. They're just getting those reading skills and nothing cracks them up like a joke that turns stuff upside down." Teachers confirm this idea at book signings, saying how useful the book is in teaching point-of-view as an important facet of any story.

In The True Story of the Three Little Pigs, *Scieszka presents a familiar children's tale from a different perspective, as narrator A. Wolf asserts that he has been framed for the deaths of two of the three little pigs. (Illustration by Lane Smith.)*

The True Story of the Three Little Pigs! is the story of Alexander T. Wolf ("Call me Al"). A. Wolf has, he believes, been framed for the deaths of two of the three little pigs. This "revisionist 'autobiography,'" as Stephanie Zvirin called it in her *Booklist* interview with Lane and Scieszka, presents the familiar story from a different aspect. "It turns out that Alexander ... only wanted to borrow a cup of sugar for a birthday cake for his granny," wrote Roger Sutton in the *Bulletin of the Center for Children's Books.* "After knocking politely on the first pig's door, Al's nose started to itch. 'I felt a sneeze coming on. Well I huffed. And I snuffed. And I sneezed a great sneeze. And do you know what? That whole darn straw house fell down.'" The scene is repeated at the wooden home of the second pig, and Al continues to the home of the third pig, where he is finally arrested, tried, and confined in the "Pig Penn."

Al maintains his innocence, stated Kimberly Olson Fakih and Diane Roback in *Publishers Weekly,* by implying "that had the first two [pigs] happened to build more durable homes and the third kept a civil tongue in his head, the wolf's helpless sneezes wouldn't have toppled them." "He ably points out that wolves just naturally eat cute little animals like bunnies and sheep and pigs. It's just their normal dietary practice," explained Frank Gannon in the *New York Times Book Review.* "'If cheeseburgers were cute,' says A. Wolf, 'folks would probably think you were Big and Bad, too.' It's hard to argue with him on that point."

One of the factors making *The True Story of the Three Little Pigs!* intriguing to readers is its dark humor. There is a sly contrast between Scieszka's "innocent wolf" narrator and Lane Smith's sometimes morally ambiguous pictures. Alexander's grandmother, noted Sutton, "looks a bit all-the-better-to-*eat*-you-with herself, and is that a pair of bunny ears poking out of the cake batter?" "At one strategic point the letter 'N' appears as a string of sausages," declared Marilyn Fain Apseloff in the *Children's Literature Association Quarterly.* "After the destruction of their homes, the first two pigs are shown bottom-up in the midst of the rubble; it is hard to tell if they are really dead or are just trying to hide. We have to take the wolf's word for their demise." One view of the second little pig frames his backside between a knife and fork. The reader's final view of Alexander shows him, older, behind bars, and dressed in a convict's uniform, still trying to borrow that cup of sugar.

Scieszka's second fairy tale, *The Frog Prince, Continued,* was illustrated by Steve Johnson rather than Smith. As the title indicates, it takes up the story of *The Frog Prince* and traces it through its traditional happily ever after ending. It seems that the disenchanted prince and his princess are not well matched. "In fact," wrote Linda Boyles in *School Library Journal,* "they're downright miserable. He misses the pond; she's tired of him sticking out his tongue and hopping on the furniture." The prince decides to rectify his unhappy home life by finding a witch to change him back to a frog. He encounters several witches and magic makers from other fairy tales, but none of them have the power to remedy

Eighteen fractured contemporary fables have twisted and amusing morals. *(From* Squids Will Be Squids: Fresh Morals, Beastly Fables, *written by Scieszka and illustrated by Lane Smith.)*

From the humorous "Time Warp Trio" series, Scieszka's book takes his three heroes back to the Wild West. (From The Good, the Bad, and the Goofy, *illustrated by Lane Smith.)*

the situation. "At the end, tired and bedraggled and ready to re-count his old blessings," explained *New York Times Book Review* contributor Peggy Noonan, "he returns home to a by now anxious and rueful Princess, who is eager to kiss his moist amphibian mouth."

Several reviewers commented on Scieszka's continued use of a witty, mature outlook in *The Frog Prince, Continued.* "Like Sondheim's *Into the Woods*," declared Mary M. Burns in *Horn Book*, "Scieszka's tale is a sophisticated variant on traditional themes; it has a wry, adult perspective and yet is accessible to younger readers who enjoy—and understand—the art of parody and lampoon." Noonan also expressed the opinion that the book speaks best to older readers. "To fully appreciate *The Frog Prince, Continued*," she stated, "you have to have a highly developed sense of irony and a sharp sense of the absurd, which most children don't develop before they can read, despite exposure to random television programming."

Scieszka and Lane Smith have also produced a series of books for younger readers called "The Time Warp Trio." The books are, according to Amanda Smith, "an introduction for children to other genres of literature." The creators tend to downplay the satire and parody of their picture books in favor of fast-moving plots and contemporary comedy. "I saw a need for something between a picture book and a chapter book," Scieszka told Amanda Smith. "Kids get stuck in that lull there. When I taught third and fourth grades, I couldn't find cool-looking books to hand to boys, who, for the most part, were reluctant readers and didn't want to be seen as dummies." Scieszka and Smith wanted to make the

books attractive to those readers, he continues, "so they'd pick 'em up and not feel bad about walkin' around with 'em. But still make 'em short enough, action-packed enough, disgusting enough." The titles take the three boys, Joe, Fred, and Sam, to the court of King Arthur in *Knights of the Kitchen Table*, to face the pirate Blackbeard in *The Not-So-Jolly Roger*, and into the distant future to meet their own descendants in *2095*. The books, declared a reviewer for *Publishers Weekly*, "demonstrate Scieszka's perfect ear for schoolyard dialogue and humor—most notably of the bodily function variety." In their seventh adventure in this popular series (soon to be an animated series on PBS), The Time Warp Trio gets mixed up with a host of literary figures in *Summer Reading Is Killing Me*.

Scieszka and Smith teamed up again for *The Stinky Cheese Man and Other Fairly Stupid Tales*, which takes on still more classic fairy tales. "With a relentless application of the sarcasm that tickled readers of *The True Story of the Three Little Pigs*," declared Diane Roback and Richard Donahue in *Publishers Weekly*, "Scieszka and Smith skewer a host of juvenile favorites." "Blend 'Saturday Night Live' with 'Monty Python,' add a dash of *Mad* magazine with maybe a touch of 'Fractured Fairy Tales' from the old 'Rocky and Bullwinkle' show," stated *Horn Book* contributor Mary M. Burns, "and you have an eclectic, frenetic mix of text and pictures with a kinetic display of typefaces." The stories range from "The Little Red Hen" and "Jack and the Beanstalk" to "Cinderumplestiltskin," "Little Red Running Shorts," and "The Tortoise and the Hair." Not only does Cinderella fail to win the prince, but Little Red Running Shorts out paces the wolf to Grandma's house, the Ugly Duckling grows into an ugly duck, and the Frog Prince turns out to be ... a frog. Even the title character has a twist; unlike the more famous Gingerbread Man, the Stinky Cheese Man is avoided by everyone. "What marvelous liberties Scieszka and Smith take here," enthused *Bulletin of the Center for Children's Books* contributor Roger Sutton, "playing around with the entire cast of *Into the Woods*, but managing to be twice as funny as Stephen Sondheim."

One of the most noticeable aspects of *The Stinky Cheese Man and Other Fairly Stupid Tales* is its unconventional arrangement of pages and its anarchic approach to storytelling. Jack and the Hen serve as commentators and narrators in the text. "The little reddish hen on the back makes fun of the ISBN, and one blurb from the flap brags that there are seventy-three percent more pages than 'those old thirty-two-page "Brand X" books,'" observed Signe Wilkinson in the *New York Times Book Review*. "The title page reads 'Title Page' in blaring $2\frac{1}{2}$-inch-tall generic black type." The table of contents appears in the middle of the book instead of the front. Jack complains when the first story begins on the endpapers of the book instead of the first leaf. Later he avoids being eaten by the giant by distracting him with a never ending story. The Hen—"a kvetch if ever there was one," declared Burns—appears at odd points in the volume, complaining about the position of her story in the book. In a dark moment, after one of these appearances she is apparently eaten by the giant. "For those that are studying fairy tales at the college level," Wilkinson states, *"The Stinky Cheese Man* would be the perfect key to the genre, but no one would mistake it for the old-fashioned originals."

Although *The Book That Jack Wrote* was not a Scieszka-Smith collaboration—the illustrations are by Daniel Adel—it continues Scieszka's theme of taking traditional fairy tales and nursery rhymes, including the works of Lewis Carroll, and turning them upside down. Its pictures are more realistic but fully as surreal as any of the collaborations between Scieszka and Lane Smith. "The characters are borrowed largely from children's literature—a grinning Cheshiresque cat, a cow jumping over the moon, a pie man at the fair, Humpty Dumpty, and the Mad Hatter—but they bear only a passing resemblance to their traditional forms," stated Nancy Menaldi-Scanlan in *School Library Journal.* "Readers who require logic will be stymied," declared Elizabeth Devereaux and Diane Roback in *Publishers Weekly;* "those who appreciate near-Victorian oddities and Escher-like conundrums will tumble right in." "This one," said a *Kirkus Reviews* contributor, "will wow even the most sophisticated."

Like *The Stinky Cheese Man and Other Fairly Stupid Tales, The Book That Jack Wrote* operates on several different levels, according to the sophistication of the reader. The original rhyme, "The House That Jack Built," is very old—perhaps dating back to 1590, according to William S. and Ceil Baring-Gould in *The Annotated Mother Goose*—and belongs to a class of poems known to scholars as "accumulative rhymes." It builds on a single statement and adds more and more detail with each line, like the Christmas carol "The Twelve Days of Christmas." In *The Book That Jack Wrote,* however, Scieszka and Adel turn this structure on its head by looping the last page to the first page—the title character appears on both pages crushed under a fallen portrait. So what appears to be a straight-line story is in fact a never-ending circle.

Math Curse, another Smith-Scieszka collaboration, "is one of the great books of the decade, if not of the century," averred Dorothy M. Broderick in *Voice of Youth Advocates.* The narrator, a little girl, is caught up in a remark made by her math teacher, Mrs. Fibonacci: "You know, you can turn almost anything into a math problem." "The result," according to Deborah Stevenson in *Bulletin of the Center for Children's Books,* "is a story problem gone exponentially berserk." Soon the anonymous narrator can think of nothing except math problems. "It's a math curse: for the next twenty-four hours no activity remains uncontaminated by this compulsive perspective," explained Amy Edith Johnson in the *New York Times Book Review.* The narrator finally "breaks out of her prison," Stevenson continued, "by using two halves of chalk to make a (w)hole."

As in Scieszka and Smith's earlier works, *Math Curse* slyly introduces mature elements of humor. Mrs. Fibonacci likes to count using the Fibonacci series of numbers. The author and illustrator credits are contained within a Venn diagram, and the price is written in binary rather than Arabic numerals. Like a traditional math textbook, the answers to the questions are printed in the book. In this case, they appear upside-down on the back cover. "This isn't coating math with fun to make it palatable," said Stevenson, "it's genuine math as genuine fun." Scieszka and Smith, Johnson concluded, "capture a genuine intellectual phenomenon: possession . . . that can swallow up a student, generally in junior high school, as systems of thought spring into three dimensions and ideas become worlds—for a time."

Some of the author's most recent works include *Summer Reading Is Killing Me* and *Squids Will Be Squids: Fresh Morals, Beastly Fables,* both of which are illustrated by Smith. The latter work is a collection of eighteen fractured fables, each possessing its own twisted moral and, according to Deborah Stevenson in her *Bulletin of the Center for Children's Books* review, "dopey kid-appealing humor." Beastly characters featured range from a grasshopper to bacteria to the title's featured creature, a squid. "A funny collection of warped fables," deemed *New York Times Book Review* contributor Patricia Marx. Similarly, Julie Cummins, writing in *School Library Journal,* noted that while "warped humor and offbeat bits of wisdom often overstretch to the bizarre and stupid," children will still appreciate "most of the jejune logic."

"I think that turning something upside down or doing something wrong is the peak of what's funny to second graders," Scieszka told *Booklist* interviewer Stephanie Zvirin. "Catching adults or the world at large doing

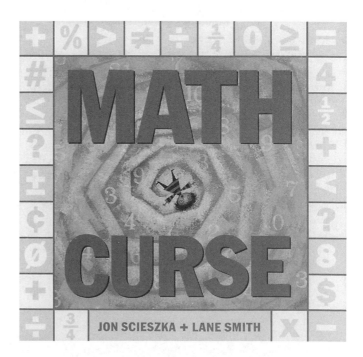

A little girl, caught up in her math teacher's remark that everything can be turned into a math problem, spends twenty-four hellish hours possessed by this view of her life. (Cover illustration by Lane Smith.)

something wrong empowers kids because they know the right thing—like brushing your hair with your toothbrush. If they get a gag like that, they know they're in the real world." Scieszka believes that kids are smarter than anyone knows. He told *SATA:* "They learn by playing. They know they can learn by playing. The serious-minded adult protectors of 'children's education' could learn a lot from them."

Works Cited

Apseloff, Marilyn Fain, "The Big, Bad Wolf: New Approaches to an Old Folk Tale," *Children's Literature Association Quarterly,* fall, 1990, pp. 135-37.

Baring-Gould, William S., and Ceil Baring-Gould, *The Annotated Mother Goose,* Bramball House (New York City), 1962, pp. 43-45.

Review of *The Book That Jack Wrote, Kirkus Reviews,* August 15, 1994, p. 1139.

Boyles, Linda, review of *The Frog Prince, Continued, School Library Journal,* May, 1991, pp. 83-84.

Broderick, Dorothy M., review of *Math Curse, Voice of Youth Advocates,* February, 1996, p. 376.

Burns, Mary M., review of *The Frog Prince, Continued, Horn Book,* July-August, 1991, pp. 451-52.

Burns, Mary M., review of *The Stinky Cheese Man and Other Fairly Stupid Tales, Horn Book,* November-December, 1992, p. 720.

Cummins, Julie, review of *Squids Will Be Squids: Fresh Morals, Beastly Fables, School Library Journal,* October, 1998, p. 113.

Devereaux, Elizabeth, and Diane Roback, review of *The Book That Jack Wrote, Publishers Weekly,* July 4, 1994, p. 63.

Fakih, Kimberly Olson, and Diane Roback, review of *The True Story of the Three Little Pigs!, Publishers Weekly,* July 28, 1989, p. 218.

Gannon, Frank, "Everybody's Favorite Swine," *New York Times Book Review,* November 12, 1989, p. 27.

Hepperman, Christine, essay on Scieszka in *Children's Books and Their Creators,* edited by Anita Silvey, Houghton, 1995, pp. 581-82.

Johnson, Amy Edith, "Your Days Are Numbered," *New York Times Book Review,* November 12, 1995, p. 31.

Jones, Patrick, and Christine Miller, "Jon Scieszka," *Twentieth-Century Children's Writers,* 4th edition, St. James, 1995, pp. 851-52.

Review of *Knights of the Kitchen Table* and *The Not-So-Jolly Roger, Publishers Weekly,* May 17, 1991, p. 64.

Marx, Patricia, review of *Squids Will Be Squids: Fresh Morals, Beastly Fables, New York Times Book Review,* November 15, 1998, p. 30.

Menaldi-Scanlan, Nancy, review of *The Book That Jack Wrote, School Library Journal,* September, 1994, pp. 193, 199.

Noonan, Peggy, "Those Moist Amphibian Lips," *New York Times Book Review,* May 19, 1991, p. 25.

Roback, Diane, and Richard Donahue, review of *The Stinky Cheese Man and Other Fairly Stupid Tales, Publishers Weekly,* September 28, 1992, pp. 79-80.

Smith, Amanda, "Jon Scieszka and Lane Smith," *Publishers Weekly,* July 26, 1991, pp. 220-21.

Stevenson, Deborah, review of *Math Curse, Bulletin of the Center for Children's Books,* October, 1995, pp. 68-69.

Stevenson, Deborah, review of *Squids Will Be Squids: Fresh Morals, Beastly Fables, Bulletin of the Center for Children's Books,* November, 1998, p. 112.

Sutton, Roger, review of *The True Story of the Three Little Pigs!, Bulletin of the Center for Children's Books,* September, 1989, p. 19.

Sutton, Roger, review of *The Stinky Cheese Man and Other Fairly Stupid Tales, Bulletin of the Center for Children's Books,* October, 1992, pp. 33-34.

Wilkinson, Signe, "No Princes, No White Horses, No Happy Endings," *New York Times Book Review,* November 8, 1992, p. 29, 59.

Zvirin, Stephanie, "Jon Scieszka and Lane Smith," *Booklist,* September 1, 1992, p. 57.

For More Information See

BOOKS

Children's Literature Review, Volume 27, Gale, 1992, pp. 152-57.

Seventh Book of Junior Authors and Illustrators, Wilson, 1996, pp. 289-90.

PERIODICALS

Booklist, September 1, 1992, p. 57; October 1, 1993, p. 344; June 1, 1995; November 1, 1995, p. 472; October 1, 1996, p. 352.

Horn Book, November-December, 1995, p. 738; November-December, 1996, pp. 713-17; November-December, 1998, p. 718.

Los Angeles Times Book Review, January 7, 1996, p. 15.

New Advocate, spring, 1999, p. 201.

New York Times Book Review, November 12, 1989, p. 27; October 6, 1991, p. 23; November 8, 1992, pp. 29, 59.

People, November 28, 1994, p. 42.

Publishers Weekly, September 11, 1995, p. 86.

Riverbank Review, winter, 1998-1999, p. 27.

School Library Journal, May, 1991, pp. 83-84; August, 1991, p. 169; December, 1993, p. 27; July, 1995, p. 81; September, 1995, p. 215.

Time, December 21, 1992, pp. 69-70.

OTHER

http://www.Chucklebait.com.

*   *   *

SHARP, Luke
See ALKIVIADES, Alkis

*   *   *

SMYTH, Iain 1959-

Personal

Born October 6, 1959, in Harpenden, England; son of Owen (a silver polish manufacturer) and Brenda (Blakemore) Smyth; married Alison Cook (an editor), April 1,

1989; children: Samuel, Joshua. *Education:* Received honors degree from Bristol Polytechnic University.

Addresses

Home—11 Southfield Rd., Cotham, Bristol BS6 6AX, United Kingdom. *Agent*—Rosemary Canter, Peters Fraser & Dunlop, Chelsea Harbour, London, United Kingdom.

Career

Writer. Formerly worked as a graphic designer. *Member:* Society of Authors (London).

Writings

SELF-ILLUSTRATED; AND PAPER ENGINEER

The Mystery of the Russian Ruby: A Pop-Up Whodunit, Orchard (London), 1994, Dutton (New York), 1996.

(With Jacqueline Crawford) *The Eye of the Pharaoh: A Pop-Up Whodunit,* Orchard, 1995, Dutton, 1995.

Pirate Plunder's Treasure Hunt: A Pop-Up Whodunit, Dutton (New York), 1996.

Dug the Digger, Orchard, 1997, published in the United States as *Dig, Dig, Dig It,* Crown (New York), 1997.

Ruby the Fire Engine, Orchard, 1997, published in the United States as *Zoom, Zoom, Fire Engine!,* Crown (New York), 1997.

The Quest for the Aztec Gold, Collins (London), 1997.

Professor Screwloose, Orchard, 1998.

Work in Progress

Two pop-up whodunits, *Lifeboat/Helicopter* and *Don't Open the Box.*

Sidelights

Former graphic artist Iain Smyth writes and designs pop-up books for young readers that are all the more unique for their multiple endings. The father of two boys, Smyth approached the pop-up form as a learning experience in itself, a sort of interactive work that could help children solve a mystery or puzzle though a series of hidden clues. One of his first titles was *The Eye of the Pharaoh: A Pop-Up Whodunit,* for which Jacqueline Crawford served as assistant writer and assistant illustrator. The 1995 comic mystery about a jewel that disappears from an Egyptian excavation site is rich with puns—"Doug Sands" is the archeologist and one of the suspects, for instance—and clues are hidden in elaborate tomb walls and mummy cases.

Smyth soon embarked upon a successful solo career as writer, illustrator, and paper engineer in the pop-up genre. For his book *Pirate Plunder's Treasure Hunt,* an entire three-dimensional ship can be explored by readers looking for the mysterious lost treasure, while a last-page wheel offers three separate conclusions. A *Kirkus Reviews* critic found Smyth's story lacking in verve, but "as a pop-up, pull-out, flip-open extravaganza, it's awesome!" Another of Smyth's books published that same year in the United States was *The Mystery of the Russian Ruby: A Pop-Up Whodunit.* Here Smyth writes of a country house party in England at the Countess Wilby's estate, a snowstorm that strands all guests, and a missing gem. Little dossiers, or file packets, slide out of the pages to help young readers draw their own conclusions about the possible criminal motives of each guest and staff member. As for the Wilby Court mansion itself, Smyth constructs hidden rooms and other foils; again, a rotating wheel at the end allows readers to choose a trio of endings. "The paper engineering, not the cast, takes center stage here," noted a *Publishers Weekly* reviewer, who likened some elements of Smyth's mystery novel style to those of Agatha Christie and Sir Arthur Conan Doyle.

Works Cited

Review of *The Mystery of the Russian Ruby, Publishers Weekly,* October 3, 1994, p. 67.

Review of *Pirate Plunder's Treasure Hunt, Kirkus Reviews,* September 1, 1996, p. 1332.

Iain Smyth's self-illustrated pop-up book offers young readers a host of humorous inventions and ideas for science experiments.

For More Information See

PERIODICALS

New York Times Book Review, November 12, 1995, p. 18.
Publishers Weekly, September 23, 1996, p. 78.

*   *   *

STAPLES, Suzanne Fisher 1945-
(Suzanne Fisher)

Personal

Born August 27, 1945, in Philadelphia, PA; daughter of Robert Charles (an engineer) and Helen Brittain (a manager) Fisher. *Education:* Cedar Crest College, B.A., 1967. *Politics:* Independent. *Religion:* Episcopalian. *Hobbies and other interests:* Running, tennis, music, theater.

Addresses

Home—Chattanooga, TN. *Agent*—Jeanne Drewsen, 250 Mercer, New York, NY 10012.

Career

Asian marketing director, Business International Corp., 1974-76; United Press International, Washington, DC, news editor and correspondent in New York, Washington, DC, Hong Kong, and India, 1975-83; *Washington Post,* part-time editor for foreign desk, 1983-85; consultant, U.S. Agency for International Development, 1986-87; fiction writer, 1988—. Lecturer on the status of women in the Islamic Republic of Pakistan. Citizens for a Better Eastern Shore, board member. *Member:* Asia Society, Authors Guild.

Awards, Honors

Newbery Honor citation, American Library Association, 1990, and IBBY Honor List, International Board on Books for Young People, 1992, both for *Shabanu: Daughter of the Wind;* Best Books, *Publishers Weekly,* 1996, Best Books for Young Adults: 1996, American Library Association, 1997, and Books for the Teen Age, New York Public Library, 1997, all for *Dangerous Skies.*

Writings

Shabanu: Daughter of the Wind, Knopf, 1989.
Haveli, Knopf, 1993.
Dangerous Skies, Farrar, Straus, 1996.

Contributor, sometimes under name Suzanne Fisher, to periodicals, including *Smithsonian.*

Work in Progress

Shiva's Fire, a novel, publication by Farrar, Straus expected in 2000.

Sidelights

Staples's novel for young adults, *Shabanu: Daughter of the Wind,* tells the story of a spirited young nomadic girl who lives in the Cholistan desert in Pakistan. Though she is perfectly happy to tend to her beloved band of camels, twelve-year-old Shabanu soon finds herself unwillingly betrothed to an older man of her parents' choosing. A series of unfortunate occurrences present her with the opportunity to choose between this arranged marriage to a wealthy landowner—who already has three wives—and her independence. Echoing the praises of numerous reviewers, *Horn Book* reviewer Hanna B. Zeiger claimed that the "vivid portrayal of life and death in this desert world is stunning in its honesty." Staples's first book earned her a Newbery Honor citation.

Staples, who worked for many years as a journalist, wrote her book out of her need to express what she describes as "the essential human-ness of us all." She once commented, "Most cultures have fiction writers who portray their worlds vividly for Western readers. But the Islamic world is different. Thanks in part to terrorism ... most of us have a fairly monolithic view of many Islamic societies that reflects fear and revulsion but little or nothing of the poetry and the intellectual, emotional, and general universality we all share with Muslims."

Suzanne Fisher Staples

Shabanu: Daughter of the Wind offers the reader many vivid pictures of everyday life in a nomadic community, in addition to descriptions of the more colorful marriage preparations and rituals. Maurya Simon, writing in the *New York Times Book Review,* said, "Some of the most affecting and lyrical passages of the book detail the austere beauty of the Cholistan, as seen through the young narrator's eyes." Simon added: "It is a pleasure to read a book that explores a way of life so profoundly different from our own, and that does so with such sensitivity, admiration, and verisimilitude." *Voice of Youth Advocates* reviewer Marijo Grimes simply stated: "More multi-cultural [young adult] novels of this caliber are needed in today's market."

Staples continues Shabanu's story in *Haveli,* a novel that takes its name from the home where Shabanu finds shelter from her tumultuous life. Continuing Shabanu's story six years after the earlier novel ended, Staples explores the intrigues among the four wives of the aging Rahim. The youngest, the most beautiful, and the least-cultured of the women, Shabanu falls prey to the scheming of the elder wives and must use all her wits to protect herself and her young daughter, Mumtaz. Ever the idealist, Shabanu also seeks to protect her best friend from an arranged marriage to her husband's mentally-deficient son. As the intricate plot unwinds, Shabanu loses both her husband and her friend to violent deaths, and falls in love with Omar, a relative of her husband who has returned from the United States.

"While the intricate cast and unfamiliar terms will send readers scuttling to the list of characters and glossary from time to time," wrote Betsy Hearne of the *Bulletin of the Center for Children's Books,* "the dramatic plot will bring them breathlessly back to the story." Although there is sex and violence, the critic added, "it's never sensationalized and yet will draw YA readers like a magnet." As with *Shabanu,* reviewers praised Staples's vivid characterization and her skill in communicating the essence of an unfamiliar culture. Ellen Fader of *Horn Book,* for instance, observed that "Staples shows considerable talent in crafting a taut, suspenseful narrative with strong female characters and a terrific sense of place." *Booklist* reviewer Ilene Cooper maintained: "Staples brews a potent mix here: the issue of a woman's role in a traditional society, page-turning intrigue, tough women characters, and a fluidity of writing that blends it all together."

In her third novel, *Dangerous Skies,* Staples turns her attention to the racism that continues to pervade a small town on the shore of Virginia's Chesapeake Bay. Two twelve-year-old friends, white male Buck and black female Tunes, find the body of their older friend Jorge Rodrigues floating in a creek. The friends suspect Jumbo Rawlins, a respected white landowner, but when Jumbo implicates Tunes in the murder, the friends are brought face-to-face with the different worlds they inhabit. Fearing that her word won't be trusted against the word of a white man, Tunes flees, and Buck comes to question whom he should trust, his longtime friend or the family who advises him to stay clear of Tunes. "Buck's loss of

When twelve-year-old Buck finds his black friend Tunes implicated in a murder, he comes to question whom he should trust: his longtime friend or the family who advises him to stay clear of her? (Cover illustration by Paul Lee.)

innocence is played out with anguished energy," noted *Horn Book* reviewer Nancy Vasilakis, and though Tunes is not convicted she leaves the town forever, her reputation ruined. While some critics complained that *Dangerous Skies* did not quite equal the standards of *Shabanu* and *Haveli,* virtually all applauded Staples nuanced treatment of the perils of racism. Several made comparisons between *Dangerous Skies* and Harper Lee's classic *To Kill a Mockingbird.* A *Publishers Weekly* reviewer, for instance, called *Dangerous Skies* a "masterfully crafted story" which "boldly conveys uncomfortable truths about society while expressing the innocence of children."

Works Cited

Cooper, Ilene, review of *Haveli, Booklist,* June 1-15, 1993, p. 1813.

Review of *Dangerous Skies, Publishers Weekly,* July 1, 1996, p. 61.

Fader, Ellen, review of *Haveli, Horn Book,* January-February, 1994, pp. 75-76.

Grimes, Marijo, review of *Shabanu: Daughter of the Wind, Voice of Youth Advocates,* April, 1990, pp. 34-35.

Hearne, Betsy, review of *Haveli, Bulletin of the Center for Children's Books,* November, 1993, pp. 73-74.

Simon, Maurya, review of *Shabanu: Daughter of the Wind, New York Times Book Review,* November 12, 1989, p. 32.

Vasilakis, Nancy, review of *Dangerous Skies, Horn Book,* January-February, 1997, pp. 67-68.

Zeiger, Hanna B., review of *Shabanu: Daughter of the Wind, Horn Book,* January-February, 1990, p. 72.

For More Information See

BOOKS

Children's Books and Their Creators, edited by Anita Silvey, Houghton Mifflin, 1995, p. 624.

St. James Guide to Young Adult Writers, Second Edition, edited by Tom and Sara Pendergast, St. James Press, 1999, pp. 785-86.

PERIODICALS

Bulletin of the Center for Children's Books, October, 1996, p. 77.

New York Times Book Review, November 14, 1993, p. 59.

School Library Journal, August, 1993, pp. 189-90; October, 1996, pp. 149-50.

Voice of Youth Advocates, December, 1993, p. 302; December, 1996, p. 274.

* * *

STRONG, J. J.
See STRONG, Jeremy

* * *

STRONG, Jeremy 1949-
(J. J. Strong)

Personal

Born November 18, 1949, in London, England; son of Charles (a pharmacist) and Una (a teacher; maiden name, Shaw-Kyd) Strong; married Susan Noot (a child behaviorist), August 31, 1973; children: Daniel, Jessica. *Education:* University of York, B.A., 1972; St. John's College, York, certificate of education, 1975.

Addresses

Home—White Flags, Battlefields, Wrotham, Kent, England. *Agent*—David Higham Associates Ltd., 5-8 Lower John St., Golden Square, London W1R 4HA, England.

Career

Author of children's books. Teacher, 1975-1992. Freelance writer, 1992—.

Awards, Honors

Overall honors, Children's Book Awards, 1997; category winner, Sheffield Children's Book Award, 1998.

Writings

(Under name J. J. Strong) *Smith's Tail,* illustrated by Ross, Evans Bros.(London), 1978.

(Under name J. J. Strong) *Emily's a Guzzleguts,* illustrated by Catherine Brighton, Evans Bros., 1979.

(Under name J. J. Strong) *Smith Takes a Bath,* illustrated by Ross, Evans Bros., 1980.

Trouble with Animals, illustrated by Jonathan Allen, Crowell (London), 1980.

Lightning Lucy, illustrated by Toni Goffe, A. & C. Black (London), 1981, Puffin, 1993.

Travels with an Atlas, Edward Arnold (London), 1983.

The Woff, A. & C. Black, 1983.

Fatbag, illustrated by John Shelley, A. & C. Black, 1983.

Fox on the Roof, illustrated by Doffy Weir, A. & C. Black, 1984.

Money Doesn't Grow on Trees, A. & C. Black, 1984.

Lucky Dip, Edward Arnold, 1984.

I Didn't Mean to Do It, Bell & Hyam (London), 1984.

(Under name J. J. Strong) *I Was Only Trying to Help,* Evans, 1984.

Lightning Lucy Strikes Again, illustrated by Toni Goffe, A. & C. Black, 1985, Chivers North America, 1997.

Jeremy Strong

Fanny Witch and the Boosnatch, illustrated by Annabel Spenceley, Hodder & Stoughton (London), 1985.

The Princess and Bungle, illustrated by Peter Stevenson, Hodder & Stoughton, 1985, Silver Burdett, 1986.

The Air Raid Shelter, illustrated by Doffy Weir, A. & C. Black, 1986.

The Karate Princess, illustrated by Simone Abel, A. & C. Black, 1986.

Look Twice, E. Arnold, 1986.

Starbiker, illustrated by Jim Ranson, A. & C. Black, 1986.

Dogs Are Different, illustrated by Robert Bartelt, A. & C. Black, 1987.

Lightning Lucy Storms Ahead, illustrated by Toni Goffe, A. & C. Black, 1987.

Bungle's Ghost, illustrated by Peter Stevenson, Hodder & Stoughton, 1987.

Fanny Witch and the Thunder Lizard, illustrated by Annabel Spenceley, Hodder & Stoughton, 1987.

Liar, Liar, Pants on Fire!, illustrated by Colin Payne, A. & C. Black, 1988.

Little Pig's Party, illustrated by Tony Morris, Hodder & Stoughton, 1988.

The Everything Machine, illustrated by Robert Geary, Hodder & Stoughton, 1989.

It's a Tough Life, illustrated by Caroline Crossland, A. & C. Black, 1989.

The Karate Princess and the Cut-throat Robbers, illustrated by Simone Abel, A. & C. Black, 1989.

Bungle to the Rescue, Hodder & Stoughton, 1990.

Pandemonium at School, illustrated by Judy Brown, A. & C. Black, 1990.

There's a Viking in My Bed, illustrated by John Levers, A. & C. Black, 1990.

The Karate Princess to the Rescue, illustrated by Simone Abel, A. & C. Black, 1991.

Little Pig Goes to School, illustrated by Tony Morris, Hodder & Stoughton, 1992.

Viking in Trouble, illustrated by John Levers, A. & C. Black, 1992.

My Dad's Got an Alligator, illustrated by Nick Sharratt, Viking, 1994.

Fanny Witch Goes Spikky Spoo! illustrated by Annabel Spenceley, Puffin, 1994, Chivers North America, 1997, as *Fanny Witch and the Wicked Wizard,* Puffin, 1995.

There's a Pharaoh in Our Bath, illustrated by Nick Sharratt, Dutton, 1995.

The Pirate Bed, Ginn (Aylesbury, Scotland), 1995.

The Desperate Adventures of Sir Rupert and Rosie Gussett, illustrated by Chris Mould, A. & C. Black, 1995.

The Karate Princess and the Last Griffin, illustrated by Simone Abel, A. & C. Black, 1995.

The Indoor Pirates, illustrated by Nick Sharratt, Dutton, 1995.

The Dinosaur Robbers, illustrated by David Mostyn, Macdonald, 1996.

The Hundred-Mile-an-Hour Dog, illustrated by Nick Sharratt, Viking, 1996.

Aliens in School, illustrated by David Mostyn, Macdonald, 1997.

Giant Jim and the Hurricane, illustrated by Nick Sharratt, Viking, 1997.

Viking at School, illustrated by John Levers, A. & C. Black, 1997.

My Granny's Great Escape, illustrated by Nick Sharratt, Viking, 1997.

Otherworld (graphic novel), illustrated by Anthony Morris, A. & C. Black, 1997.

Pirate Pandemonium, illustrated by Judy Brown, A. & C. Black, 1997.

The Indoor Pirates on Treasure Island, illustrated by Nick Sharratt, Puffin, 1998.

Max and the Petnappers, illustrated by David Mostyn, 1998.

Dinosaur Pox, illustrated by Nick Sharratt, Puffin, 1999.

Contributor to periodicals, including *Junior Education* and *Child Education.*

Sidelights

British author Jeremy Strong combines elements of fantasy and humor in his off-beat stories for elementary school-aged readers. With an admitted love of making others laugh, he creates short novels with titles like *There's a Pharaoh in Our Bath, Fatbag,* and *Fanny Witch and the Thunder Lizard* that are guaranteed to attract beginning bookworms. Winner of the Children's Book Award's overall honor for *The Hundred-Mile-an-Hour Dog,* Strong's lighthearted approach was described by *Books for Keeps* contributor Clive Barnes as full of "humour, invention, and [a] grasp of human nature," making them excellent read-aloud choices.

Born in London, England, in 1949, Strong began writing in 1966, composing poetry and experimental prose. He wrote his first story for children four years later, and he gradually discontinued his other work in favor of writing for young people. Meanwhile, he completed his college education, first at the University of York, where he received his bachelor's degree in 1972, and then at St. John's College, York, where he was granted a certificate of education in 1975. While teaching full-time at a school in Sevenoaks, England, Strong published *Smith's Tail.* Published under the name J. J. Strong, *Smith's Tail* would be first among a mountain of books that Strong has authored since.

"Although I have tried one or two more serious children's stories, I prefer writing humorous tales," Strong once told *SATA.* Many of these stories have been inspired by things that happened to Strong, either at home or at school. *Trouble with Animals,* the story of a young boy's search for the perfect pet, has a classic portrayal of a disapproving older sister, and "family relationships [that are] typical," according to *School Library Journal* contributor Dorcas Hand, who went on to say that "the story is alive with the humor second and third graders love." *Emily's a Guzzleguts* was also based on Strong's son, Daniel, at a young age, and his reactions to his sister, Jessica.

Children between the ages of eight and ten often pop up in Strong's stories. In *Lightning Lucy,* which a *Junior Bookshelf* contributor called "a bright little story told with humour and deft characterisation," an eight-year-old girl with the ability to fly causes no end of difficulty for her parents, while *My Dad's Got an Alligator* finds a young lad perplexed over his father's choice of pet: an alligator appropriately named "Crunchbag" disrupts the home life of the boy's slightly eccentric family in a tale that showcases Strong's "feel for the funny throwaway line," according to a *Books for Keeps* contributor.

Sometimes Strong features unusual protagonists in his comic tales. In *Fatbag,* a lumbering vacuum cleaner decides to take over the world, beginning with an elementary school where it starts sucking up all sorts of things before the janitor puts an end to its escapades. Science-fiction elements are combined with humor in stories like *The Woff,* as a creature from outer space accidentally collides with Earth and ends up in a small grade school. To return to orbit, the tiny Woff needs a diamond, which sends the schoolchildren scurrying to assist it, in a tale that a *Junior Bookshelf* reviewer praised as "full of delightful twists of imagination" and containing "humour, slapstick, suspense and pleasure in plenty."

In addition to unusual characters, Strong enjoys weaving elements of fantasy into his novels for beginning readers. Giants walk the earth in *Giant Jim and the Hurricane,* wherein a giant who loves to play the saxophone ends up causing no end of trouble for a tiny village due to his enormous size. However, when a hurricane hits the village and tosses whole buildings around, the giant puts his size to good use in returning things to normal, thus winning the regard of all involved. *Bungle's Ghost* features a young princess who dreads the visit of her Aunt Moldred and her perfectly horrid cousin, Prince Conrad. When the pair arrive at the royal palace, Conrad torments everyone and everything in his path, including the princess's pet cat, Bungle. Fortunately, after a night spent hiding in the royal flour bin, Bungle emerges to set things right in a story that a *Junior Bookshelf* contributor described as having "a satisfying amount of lively text." The spirited princess and her pampered puss Bungle are reunited in several other books, including *Bungle to the Rescue.*

Animals also star in other Strong titles. In *The Hundred-Mile-an-Hour Dog,* a wild-mannered pooch named Streaker is the subject of a bet between two young boys: Can the dog be trained to behave in two weeks? Trevor decides to take on the challenge in a story that *School Librarian* contributor Lucinda Fox maintained would appeal "to any children with a recalcitrant dog in the family, and to any who like zany pets." Rambunctious dogs also refuse to stay still in *Dogs are Different,* as young Martin's puppy, Geronimo, trashes the family garden and does horrible things to Martin's stepfather's car interior. After Geronimo is expelled from dog obedience school, the word comes down that the dog must go. Martin contemplates running away with his

pup, but fortunately a better solution to the family's problem is found, in a tale that a *Junior Bookshelf* contributor praised as containing "pace and purpose, challenge and coherence."

While Strong has occasionally written for an adult readership, he keeps returning to children's fiction. "I find working for adults far more exacting and as yet have not discovered a line of humor that will help me to enjoy such work," he explained. "I've got to laugh or I get bored." Strong told *SATA* that as a teacher he enjoyed his interactions with the children, finding the company of eight-to-nine year olds stimulating. "I think my level of humor must have stuck at that age," he said. Strong has since left teaching and now writes freelance and is much in demand as a speaker at schools.

In an essay for *Carousel* magazine, Strong explained that "writing has rarely, if ever, seemed like labour. Each time I write a story I hope it will be better than the last one I wrote, and I try to make it so. I am conscious that I don't always succeed, but that is part of the fun (and toil)."

Works Cited

Barnes, Clive, review of *Giant Jim and the Hurricane, Books for Keeps,* November, 1997, pp. 24-25.

Review of *Bungle's Ghost, Junior Bookshelf,* February, 1988, p. 26.

Review of *Dogs Are Different, Junior Bookshelf,* February, 1988, p. 36.

Fox, Lucinda, review of *The Hundred-Mile-an-Hour Dog, School Librarian,* February, 1997, p. 34.

Hand, Dorcas, review of *Trouble with Animals, School Library Journal,* February, 1982, p. 71.

Review of *Lightning Lucy, Junior Bookshelf,* June, 1982, p. 101.

Review of *My Dad's Got an Alligator, Books for Keeps,* May, 1996, p. 13.

Strong, Jeremy, "Meet Jeremy Strong," *Carousel,* summer, 1998, p. 22.

Review of *The Woff, Junior Bookshelf,* February, 1984, p. 29.

For More Information See

PERIODICALS

Booklist, January 1, 1989, p. 797.

Books for Keeps, March, 1988, p. 19; March, 1997, p. 23; September, 1997, p. 25.

Bulletin of the Center for Children's Books, July-August, 1981, p. 220.

Kirkus Reviews, March 15, 1981, p. 358.

School Librarian, March, 1983, p. 249; March, 1984, p. 41; June, 1986, p. 155; February, 1996, p. 20; August, 1997, p. 135; November, 1997, p. 202.

School Library Journal, October, 1984, p. 163.

V

Van ALLSBURG, Chris 1949-

Personal

Born June 18, 1949, in Grand Rapids, MI; son of Richard (a dairy owner) and Chris Van Allsburg; married Lisa Morrison (a self-employed consultant); children: Sophia, Anna. *Education:* University of Michigan, B.F.A., 1972; Rhode Island School of Design, M.F.A., 1975. *Religion:* Jewish. *Hobbies and other interests:* "When I'm not drawing, I enjoy taking walks and going to museums. I play tennis a few times a week, like to sail—although I have fewer opportunities to do it now (I used to have more friends with boats). I read quite a lot."

Career

Artist; author and illustrator of children's books. Rhode Island School of Design, Providence, RI, teacher of illustration, 1977—. Exhibitions include Whitney Museum of American Art, New York, NY; Museum of Modern Art, New York, NY; Alan Stone Gallery, New York, NY; Grand Rapids Art Museum, Grand Rapids, MI; and Port Washington Public Library, NY.

Awards, Honors

Best Illustrated Children's Books citations, *New York Times,* 1979, for *The Garden of Abdul Gasazi,* 1981, for *Jumanji,* 1982, for *Ben's Dream,* 1983, for *The Wreck of the Zephyr,* 1984, for *The Mysteries of Harris Burdick,* 1985, for *The Polar Express,* and 1986, for *The Stranger;* Caldecott Honor Book citation, American Library Association (ALA), and *Boston Globe-Horn Book* Award for illustration, both 1980, and International Board on Books for Young People citation for illustration, 1982, all for *The Garden of Abdul Gasazi;* Irma Simonton Black Award, Bank Street College of Education, 1980, for *The Garden of Abdul Gasazi,* and 1985, for *The Mysteries of Harris Burdick; New York Times* Outstanding Books citations, 1981, for *Jumanji,* and 1983, for *The Wreck of the Zephyr;* Caldecott Medal,

ALA, 1982, for *Jumanji,* and 1986, for *The Polar Express; Boston Globe-Horn Book* Award for illustration, 1982, for *Jumanji,* 1985, for *The Mysteries of Harris Burdick,* and 1986, for *The Polar Express;* Children's Choice Award, International Reading Association, and American Book Award for illustration, Association of American Publishers, both 1982, Kentucky Bluegrass Award, Northern Kentucky University, and Buckeye Children's Book Award, Ohio State Library, both 1983, Washington Children's Choice Picture Book Award, Washington Library Media Association, 1984, and West Virginia Children's Book Award, 1985, all for *Jumanji;* Parents' Choice Award for Illustration, Parents' Choice Foundation, 1982, for *Ben's Dream,* 1984, for *The Mysteries of Harris Burdick,* 1985, for *The Polar Express,* 1986, for *The Stranger,* 1987, for *The Z Was Zapped: A Play in Twenty-Six Acts,* and 1992, for *The Widow's Broom;* Kentucky Bluegrass Award, Northern Kentucky University, 1987, for *The Polar Express.*

Ben's Dream was included in the American Institute of Graphic Arts Book Show in 1983, *The Wreck of the Zephyr* was included in 1984, and *The Mysteries of Harris Burdick* in 1985; One Hundred Titles for Reading and Sharing, New York Public Library, 1983, for *The Wreck of the Zephyr,* and 1985, for *The Polar Express;* Ten Best Picture Books for Kids, *Redbook Magazine,* and Children's Books of the Year, Child Study Association, both 1985, both for *The Polar Express;* Hans Christian Andersen Award nomination, 1985; Children's Books of the Year, Child Study Association, 1987, for *The Stranger;* runner-up, Colorado's Children's book Award, 1990, Virginia Young Readers Award, and Washington Children's Choice Award, 1991, and Georgia Children's Picture Storybook Award, 1992, all for *Two Bad Ants.*

Writings

FOR CHILDREN; SELF-ILLUSTRATED

The Garden of Abdul Gasazi, Houghton, 1979.
Jumanji, Houghton, 1981.

Ben's Dream, Houghton, 1982.
The Wreck of the Zephyr, Houghton, 1983.
The Mysteries of Harris Burdick, Houghton, 1984.
The Polar Express, Houghton, 1985.
The Stranger, Houghton, 1986.
The Z Was Zapped: A Play in Twenty-Six Acts, Houghton, 1987.
Two Bad Ants, Houghton, 1988.
Just a Dream, Houghton, 1990.
The Wretched Stone, Houghton, 1991.
The Widow's Broom, Houghton, 1992.
The Sweetest Fig, Houghton, 1993.
Bad Day at Riverbend, Houghton, 1995.

ILLUSTRATOR; ALL WRITTEN BY MARK HELPRIN

Swan Lake, Houghton, 1989.
A City in Winter, Viking, 1996.
The Veil of Snows, Viking, 1997.

A selection of Van Allsburg's work is held in the Kerlan Collection at the University of Minnesota.

Adaptations

Several of Van Allsburg's books have been adapted for audio cassette; his *Jumanji* was adapted for a movie of the same title starring Robin Williams, 1995; *The Polar Express* is available on CD-ROM.

Sidelights

Two-time Caldecott Medal-winner Chris Van Allsburg has created a magical, even surreal, world with his picture books such as *Jumanji* and *The Polar Express,* helping to revolutionize the field of children's literature. "While most children's literature remains steeped in saccharin morality tales," Linnea Lannon noted in a 1995 profile of the author and illustrator in the *Detroit Free Press,* "Chris Van Allsburg has found critical acclaim and commercial success with children's books that embrace the mystery and randomness of life." Lannon was not dealing in hyperbole: in addition to the great number and variety of awards Van Allsburg has garnered for his unique if not quirky tales, he has also made illustrating and writing children's books a distinctly profitable profession. *The Polar Express* was reissued on its tenth anniversary and has sold over ten million copies worldwide, assuring that this Christmas fable will be a children's classic for generations to come. His first Caldecott Medal book, *Jumanji,* was turned into a feature film starring the irascible Robin Williams, and his $800,000 advance for the illustrations of *Swan Lake* in 1989 set records in the world of children's publishing. Van Allsburg's picture books "offer a glimpse into a world—and a mind—far more imaginative than those found in most adult fiction," according to Lannon. The dominant message in Van Allsburg's books is not that either good or bad things can happen in life, but that strange things occur; Van Allsburg sees his books as challenging rather than comforting. As Stephanie Loer recounted in *Children's Books and Their Creators,* "Van Allsburg's illustrations never fail to fascinate the intel-

lect, pique the senses, and emphasize the power of imagination."

Born in Grand Rapids, Michigan, in 1949, Van Allsburg "liked to do the normal kid things like playing baseball and building model cars, trucks, and planes," as he once told *SATA*. Raised in the suburbs, Van Allsburg had access to open fields and dirt roads, riding his bike to school and catching tadpoles in the nearby creeks. Early reading included the Dick, Jane, and Spot books, and he was also an avid fan of comic books—which had an influence that can be seen in some of his later work. Drawing provided early diversion for Van Allsburg, but as he got older, and more masculine activities were expected of young boys, art took a back seat to athletics. "I had no idea what I wanted to be when I grew up," Van Allsburg told *SATA*. "I thought I'd be a lawyer, mostly because I couldn't think of anything else." But as high-school graduation approached, he once again began to focus on art and was accepted to the University of Michigan School of Art & Design.

"The enthusiasm I had for art as a child was once again rekindled," Van Allsburg noted. He was particularly taken with sculpture, and upon graduating from Michigan he entered the Rhode Island School of Design, where he earned a masters degree in fine art. For several years afterward he made his living as an artist, with well-received shows in New York, and also taught illustration at the School of Design. Slowly his interest in art broadened to include drawing as well as sculpture. "A friend of mine who illustrated books saw my drawings and encouraged me to consider illustration," Van Allsburg told *SATA*. His wife, then an elementary school teacher, also encouraged him to consider illustrating, introducing him to children's picture books. Van Allsburg began to find his own expression in both illustration, opting initially for black and white, and in text, choosing prose over verse.

Van Allsburg's first book, *The Garden of Abdul Gasazi,* tells the story of a young boy whose dog runs away into the bizarre garden of a magician, a garden filled with topiary creatures. Created with black and white illustrations, this first picture book "gained [Van Allsburg] almost instantaneous recognition in the field of illustration," according to *Dictionary of Literary Biography* essayist Laura Ingram. Van Allsburg himself thought the book would perhaps sell a few copies, and then he would have the remaining copies left to give away as Christmas presents. In actuality, *The Garden of Abdul Gasazi* started a new career for him. Critics immediately responded to the eerie, dreamlike quality of Van Allsburg's work. *Booklist* contributor Barbara Elleman noted Van Allsburg's ability to "provide an underlying quality of hushed surrealism, seemingly poised at the brink of expectancy," while Paul Heins, a reviewer for *Horn Book,* compared the illustrator's "stippled tones of gray and the precisely outlined figures" to the pointillist technique of the painter Georges Seurat. A Caldecott Honor Book, *The Garden of Abdul Gasazi* displays the edgy, challenging nature of story and illustration that would become Van Allsburg's trademark. The puzzle motif that informs much of his work is also introduced here: the reader is left to contemplate the possibility that the runaway dog was changed into a fowl by the magician.

Puzzles and magic also feature prominently in Van Allsburg's second book, *Jumanji,* intruding into the domesticity of a suburban home when bored siblings Judy and Peter suddenly get more action than they bargained for playing a board game. The two-dimensional jungle adventures of the game become real, with lions materializing in the living room and monkeys in the kitchen. The surreal game only comes to an end when Judy finally reaches the Golden City—the goal of the game. Again illustrated in black and white, this second book won the Caldecott Medal. "Van Allsburg's

pictures," commented Ingram, "which at first glance could be mistaken for photographs, are impressive not only for their realism but for the skill with which he manipulates light and shadow to create a vaguely unsettling mood, and for the odd angles which present disconcerting views of common scenes." This cinematic effect, a tip of the hat to the films of Orson Welles, has been noted by more than one reviewer.

Another early title that most critics consider to be a classic example of the Van Allsburg style, *The Wreck of the Zephyr,* was the author's first full-color book. Employing selected pastel over paint, Van Allsburg consciously sought a Rembrandt resonance in color; his sculpted figures stand out in the muted tones like sentinels, echoing the fantastic tale related by an old

When the two-dimensional jungle adventures of their board game become real, bored siblings Judy and Peter get more action than they bargained for. (From Jumanji, *written and illustrated by Chris Van Allsburg.*)

Litterbug Walter dreams about a frightening future of ecological devastation in Van Allsburg's self-illustrated cautionary tale. (*From* Just a Dream.)

When he woke up the next morning, Bibot was confused. He was not in his bed. He was beneath it. Suddenly a face appeared in front of him—his own face!

"Time for your walk," it said. "Come to Marcel." A hand reached down and grabbed him. Bibot tried to yell, but all he could do was bark.

A Parisian dentist faces a dilemma when he is paid for his work with two magical figs that can make his dreams come true. (From The Sweetest Fig, *written and illustrated by Van Allsburg.)*

man. In this story-within-a-story, the narrator tells of a boy who was the best sailor in his town. Stranded on an island during a storm, he uses magical powers to fly his ship home. In the end, the reader is left to wonder if the aged narrator is, in fact, the boy-sailor of the tale. John Russell, reviewing the book in the *New York Times Book Review,* compared Van Allsburg's illustrations to the work of the painter Magritte, while noting that the "text is as spare, as sober and telling as ever." Russell concluded that "It would be difficult to imagine a better book of its kind." Margery Fisher, writing in *Growing Point,* dubbed Van Allsburg's fourth book a "joyous celebration of change and mystery."

Van Allsburg returned to black and white illustration with *The Mysteries of Harris Burdick,* a wordless book of illustrations for which the viewer is prompted to build stories by means of suggestive captions. Ingram noted that these series of drawings were designed "to challenge even those who claim to have no imagination." But it was Van Allsburg's fifth title that has remained his best known. *The Polar Express,* another full-color production, presents a first-person narrative of a little boy who sets off on a mysterious train for the North Pole. He meets Santa Claus and is presented with a reindeer bell from Santa's sleigh. "When I started *The Polar Express,*" Van Allsburg remarked in his Caldecott Medal acceptance speech for the book, "I thought I was writing about a train trip, but the story was actually about faith and the desire to believe in something."

Denise M. Wilms, writing in *Booklist,* noted that "Darkened colors, soft edges, and the glow of illuminated snow flurries create a dreamlike adventure that is haunting even as it entertains." Wilms concluded that the book is an "imaginative, engrossing tale of Christmas magic." Children around the world have agreed, making *The Polar Express* the most popular of all of Van Allsburg's books.

Fantastic tales and subtle magic continue in further Van Allsburg's titles, including *The Stranger,* an allegory of winter, and *The Z Was Zapped,* an alphabet book with attitude. In the former title, Farmer Bailey injures a man on the road, takes the stranger home to recuperate, and there learns he is mute and without memory. The stranger becomes part of the family, and a few weeks into his stay, the weather turns as warm as summer—though when he abruptly leaves, winter sets in. Every year thereafter, winter comes late to the Bailey farm. Patricia Dooley, writing in *School Library Journal,* called *The Stranger* "a down-homey modern myth." Anne Rice praised the book in the *New York Times Book Review,* noting that it is "marvelous that this master painter and storyteller has added a new dimension to his consistently original and enchanting body of work."

Van Allsburg has continued his high level of both productivity and artistic resolve. Among his other self-illustrated stories are *Just a Dream, The Wretched Stone, The Widow's Broom, The Sweetest Fig,* and *Bad Day at*

Then they saw the mysterious light shine brightly just over the next hill. The men crawled up the hill, but the light faded away as they peeked over the top. Looking down, the brave cowboys saw something that made them gasp. There was a man standing perfectly still at the bottom of the hill. He was as tall as a cottonwood tree and as skinny as a broomstick. And he looked like he was made entirely of the greasy stuff that now covered the countryside.

When greasy strings of slime cover the town of Riverbend, Sheriff Ned Hardy gathers a posse and hunts down the villain— a child scribbling crayon marks in the coloring book which the town inhabits. *(From* Bad Day at Riverbend, *written and illustrated by Van Allsburg.)*

Riverbend. "Walter will *never* throw his jelly doughnut wrapper on the street again," declared Roger Sutton in a *Bulletin of the Center for Children's Books* review of *Just a Dream.* In this book, a frightening dream takes an environmentally insensitive ten-year-old into a techno-nightmare future where smog chokes the atmosphere and the forests have been reduced to toothpicks. Most reviewers found the message a bit didactic in this title, but they also found Van Allsburg's artwork at its best. "If Van Allsburg's story is less than scintillating, his artwork, as always, is striking," commented *Booklist's* Ilene Cooper. "The message," concluded Sutton, "is worthy if sentimentalized."

A better critical response greeted *The Wretched Stone,* a sea tale involving the sailors of the *Rita Ann* and their adventures and misadventures under the spell of a magic stone they discover on an uncharted island. The glowing stone turns the crew into monkeys when they stare at it, making them swing through the ship's riggings, and only the captain's violin playing and reading aloud can bring the crew back to their normal selves. Lee Lorenz, writing in the *New York Times,* remarked that throughout "his distinguished career, Chris Van Allsburg has challenged, expanded and redefined our notions of what a book for children can be.... He continues to break new ground with *The Wretched Stone,* which is in some ways his most ambitious work." In his *Bulletin of the Center for Children's Books* review, Sutton interpreted

the book as a parable on the dumbing-down influences of television, and noted in particular the sea setting which provides Van Allsburg "plenty of space for his moody pastels, which add a menacing tone to the plain spoken narrative."

Van Allsburg continued to serve up magical flights of fancy in several other titles. *The Widow's Broom* relates the story of a broom abandoned after it has lost the power of flight; *The Sweetest Fig* deals with a Parisian dentist, Bibot, who is paid in figs for his work—a magical payment, as the fruit will make his dreams come true; *Bad Day at Riverbend* takes the reader into the life of a coloring book bedecked with the squiggles and marks of a child's scribbles. In a starred *Booklist* review, Cooper noted that "Van Allsburg explores the nature of good and evil" in *The Widow's Broom,* concluding that his artwork in the book is some of his "finest: oversize, sepia-tone drawings, with precise linework that has both visual clarity and intriguing nuance." A folktale in format, *The Sweetest Fig* "is a sophisticated picture book," according to Betsy Hearne in *Bulletin of the Center for Children's Books,* "but not at the expense of its audience." Hearne concluded that "Van Allsburg has become a veteran at showing how imagination controlled by art unleashes magic." When greasy strings of slime cover the town of Riverbend in *Bad Day at Riverbend,* Sheriff Ned Hardy gathers a posse and hunts down the villain—a child scribbling crayon marks in the coloring book which the town inhabits. Reviewing the book in the *New York Times,* Robin Tzannes commented on the fact that Van Allsburg's sculpting also affects his illustrations by giving them "a depth and a sculptural quality that is literally arresting, prompting readers of all ages to just stop for a moment, spellbound, and stare at the pictures." Tzannes called *Bad Day at Riverbend* "clever and entertaining," and "a good introduction to his work for the younger readers."

"A book is a four-and-a-half month commitment," Van Allsburg told *SATA,* "and the challenge is to actually finish it. My problem is maintaining self-motivation after the tenth drawing. There are fourteen to fifteen drawings in a conventionally laid-out book and by the tenth drawing I'm ready to start another project." Starting with text and then moving to illustrations, Van Allsburg works from crude thumbnail sketches all the way to fine, museum-quality drawings. "I like the idea of withholding something, both in drawings and writing." It is this sense of the missing part, the unfinished business, that appeals to many young readers.

Van Allsburg told Lannon in *The Detroit Free Press* that he enjoys having a large audience for his work. As a sculptor, his work is perhaps seen by only a few hundred people. But as a successful author, "every time the book is read, the book happens," Van Allsburg said. "I feel, not a sense of power, but a sense of connectedness, I guess. Just to be able to make those books and have them out there, and to know kids are going to take them out and actually have an experience, not identical with the one I had … but they're going to be in a way, captives of my mind and their imagination. That's a stimulation."

Works Cited

Cooper, Ilene, review of *Just a Dream, Booklist,* October 15, 1990, p. 452.
Cooper, Ilene, review of *The Widow's Broom, Booklist,* September 15, 1992, p. 147.
Dooley, Patricia, review of *The Stranger, School Library Journal,* November, 1986, p. 84.
Elleman, Barbara, review of *The Garden of Abdul Gasazi, Booklist,* November 15, 1979.
Fisher, Margery, review of *The Wreck of the Zephyr, Growing Point,* July, 1984, p. 4292.
Hearne, Betsy, review of *The Sweetest Fig, Bulletin of the Center for Children's Books,* November, 1993, p. 104.
Heins, Paul, review of *The Garden of Abdul Gasazi, Horn Book,* February, 1980.
Ingram, Laura, "Chris Van Allsburg," *Dictionary of Literary Biography,* Volume 61: *American Writers for Children since 1960: Poets, Illustrators, and Nonfiction Authors,* Gale, 1987, pp. 306-13.
Lannon, Linnea, "The Van Allsburg Express," *Sunday Magazine, Detroit Free Press,* October 22, 1995, pp. 7-9, 12-13, 17.
Loer, Stephanie, essay on Van Allsburg in *Children's Books and Their Creators,* edited by Anita Silvey, Houghton, 1995, pp. 660-62.

Lorenz, Lee, review of *The Wretched Stone, New York Times,* November 10, 1991, p. 36.
Rice, Anne, "Jack Frost's Amnesia," *New York Times Book Review,* November 9, 1986, p. 58.
Russell, John, review of *The Wreck of the Zephyr, New York Times Book Review,* June 5, 1983, p. 34.
Sutton, Roger, review of *Just a Dream, Bulletin of the Center for Children's Books,* November, 1990, p. 72.
Sutton, Roger, review of *The Wretched Stone, Bulletin of the Center for Children's Books,* November, 1991, p. 78.
Tzannes, Robin, review of *Bad Day at Riverbend, New York Times,* March 24, 1996, p. 23.
Van Allsburg, Chris, "Caldecott Medal Acceptance," *Horn Book,* July-August, 1986, pp. 420-24.
Wilms, Denise M., review of *The Polar Express, Booklist,* October 1, 1985, pp. 271-72.

For More Information See

BOOKS

Berger, Laura Standley, editor, *Twentieth-Century Children's Writers,* St. James Press, 1995, pp. 980-81.
Children's Literature Review, Gale, Volume 5, 1983, pp. 231-42; Volume 13, 1987, pp. 201-14.
Holtze, Sally Holmes, editor, *Fifth Book of Junior Authors and Illustrators,* H. W. Wilson, 1983, pp. 316-17.

PERIODICALS

Booklist, October 1, 1991, p. 338; October 15, 1995, p. 413; October 15, 1996, p. 421; November 15, 1997, p. 560.
Horn Book, January-February, 1991, p. 61; January-February, 1992, pp. 62-64; January-February, 1997, p. 57.
Publishers Weekly, September 9, 1996, p. 84; September 29, 1997, p. 90.
School Library Journal, February, 1995, p. 18; October, 1995, pp. 121-22; January, 1996, p. 18; November, 1997, pp. 118-19.*

—*Sketch by J. Sydney Jones*

*   *   *

Van LAAN, Nancy 1939-

Personal

Born November 18, 1939, in Baton Rouge, LA; daughter of Philip Johannes (a colonel, U.S. Air Force) and Sarah (Hawkins) Greven; twice divorced; children: Jennifer, David, Anna. *Education:* Sullins College, Bristol, VA, A.A. in dance, 1959; University of Alabama, B.A. in radio and television, 1961; Rutgers University, M.F.A. in theater, 1979. *Politics:* Democrat. *Religion:* Protestant. *Hobbies and other interests:* Biking, kayaking.

Addresses

Electronic mail—nvanlaan@aol.com. *Agent*—Gail Hochman, Brandt and Brandt, 1501 Broadway, New York, NY 10036.

Nancy Van Laan

Career

Writer, 1987—. J. Walter Thompson Advertising Agency, New York, assistant, 1961-62; ABC-TV, New York, network censor, 1962-66; Solebury School, New Hope, PA, English teacher, 1984-89; Rutgers University, New Brunswick, NJ, creative writing instructor, 1986-89. *Member:* Society of Children's Book Writers and Illustrators; National Storytelling Association.

Awards, Honors

Notable Book, American Library Association (ALA), 1990, Parents' Choice Picture Book Award, 1990, Honor Book, Florida Reading Association, 1991, all for *Possum Come A-Knockin'*; Reading Rainbow Selection, Keystone State Reading Book Award, and Alabama Library Association Author's Award, all 1991, all for *Rainbow Crow: A Lenape Tale;* Notable Book, ALA, and ABC Choice Award, both 1996, both for *In a Circle Long Ago: A Treasury of Native Lore from North America;* Notable Book, ALA, 1997, and Carolyn Field Honor Award, Pennsylvania Library Association, 1998, both for *Shingebiss: An Ojibwe Legend;* Editors' Choice, *Booklist,* 1998, and Notable Book, ALA, 1999, both for *With a Whoop and a Holler: A Bushel of Lore from Way Down South;* Blue Ribbon designation, *Bulletin of the Center for Children's Books,* Best Books, *School Library Journal,* and Pick of the Lists, American Booksellers Association, all 1998, all for *So Say the Little Monkeys.*

Writings

The Big Fat Worm, illustrated by Marisabina Russo, Knopf, 1987.
(Reteller) *Rainbow Crow: A Lenape Tale,* illustrated by Beatriz Vidal, Knopf, 1989.
Possum Come A-Knockin', illustrated by George Booth, Knopf, 1990.
A Mouse in My House, illustrated by Marjorie Priceman, Knopf, 1990.
(Adaptor) *The Legend of El Dorado: A Latin American Tale,* illustrated by Beatriz Vidal, Knopf, 1991.
People, People Everywhere, illustrated by Nadine Bernard Westcott, Knopf, 1992.
This Is the Hat: A Story in Rhyme, illustrated by Holly Meade, Joy Street Books, 1992.
The Tiny, Tiny Boy and the Big, Big Cow, illustrated by Marjorie Priceman, Knopf, 1993.
(Reteller) *Buffalo Dance: A Blackfoot Legend,* foreword by Bill Moyers, illustrated by Beatriz Vidal, Little, Brown, 1993.
Round and Round Again, illustrated by Natalie Bernard Westcott, Hyperion, 1994.
Sleep, Sleep, Sleep: A Lullaby for Little Ones Around the World, illustrated by Holly Meade, Little, Brown, 1995.
Mama Rocks, Papa Sings, illustrated by Roberta Smith, Knopf, 1995.
In a Circle Long Ago: A Treasury of Native Lore from North America, illustrated by Lisa Desimini, Apple Soup Books, 1995.
La Boda: A Mexican Wedding Celebration, illustrated by Andrea Arroyo, Little, Brown, 1996.
(Reteller) *Shingebiss: An Ojibwe Legend,* illustrated by Betsy Bowen, Houghton Mifflin, 1997.
Little Baby Bobby, illustrated by Laura Cornell, Knopf, 1997.
With a Whoop and a Holler: A Bushel of Lore from Way Down South, illustrated by Scott Cook, Atheneum, 1998.
Little Fish, Lost, illustrated by Jane Conteh-Morgan, Simon and Schuster, 1998.
(Reteller) *The Magic Bean Tree: A Legend from Argentina,* illustrated by Beatriz Vidal, Houghton Mifflin, 1998.
So Say the Little Monkeys, illustrated by Yumi Heo, Atheneum, 1998.
Moose Tales, illustrated by Amy Rusch, Houghton Mifflin, 1999.

Also author of two plays, *Park Place* and *The Disintegration of Daphne.*

Work in Progress

When Winter Comes: A Lullaby, illustrated by Susan Gaber, for Atheneum; *The Laughing Man,* illustrated by Lisa Desimini, for Simon and Schuster; *Teeny Tiny Tingly Tales,* illustrated by Victoria Chess, for Atheneum; *Busy Busy Moose,* for Houghton Mifflin; *A Tree for Me,* for Knopf.

Sidelights

Nancy Van Laan is the author of numerous picture books for young readers, including the popular and award-winning *Possum Come A-Knockin'* and *Rainbow Crow.* Many of her read-aloud books feature animal protagonists and utilize rhythm and rhyme to introduce young listeners and readers to the world of words. Additionally, Van Laan often uses folktales and legends from around the world as the story line for her books.

"As soon as I was able to hold a pencil, I scribbled poetry and drew," Van Laan told *SATA.* "I still have poems and plays that I wrote when I was in elementary school. It was my favorite thing to do besides read. I loved books, especially those with lots of illustrations." Yet Van Laan would ultimately come to professional writing in a roundabout way—through dance, television, theater, and teaching—publishing her first book at age forty-eight.

The daughter of an Air Force colonel, Van Laan travelled a great deal when she was a child; in the eighth grade she attended schools in Canada, England, and the United States. Her avid reading continued throughout these years, her favorite books coming from the "My Book House" series originally published in the 1930s. "To this day I can quote most of the poetry found in those wonderful books which, unfortunately, are long out of print," Van Laan told *SATA.* But as a teenager, dance took priority over books, and by age seventeen she had her own dance company and later choreographed *The Wizard of Oz* ballet for the Alabama Public Television network. Her dance career came to an abrupt end, however, when she sledded down a snowy hill on a cafeteria tray and broke the base of her spine. Subsequently she studied television and radio production at the University of Alabama, and after graduation worked for a time in New York as a censor for ABC-TV.

In 1965 and 1966 she had the first two of her three children, and domestic affairs occupied her time for several years thereafter. She also began painting, eventually doing murals for schools and private homes. Returning to college in 1976, she studied theater and playwriting; two of her plays were produced in regional productions in New Jersey and won "Best Play of the Year" awards. Her third child was born in 1980, and throughout much of the 1980s Van Laan headed the English department at a private boarding school in Pennsylvania. Then came publication of her first children's book in 1987, *The Big Fat Worm,* and two years later she was able to give up teaching to write full time.

With her initial title, much of Van Laan's style and content were already in place. A circular tale, featuring repetitive and easy-to-read text, *The Big Fat Worm* features the first of her familiar animals as protagonist. A *School Library Journal* reviewer noted that the simplicity of text and pictures "makes it extremely versatile, for it may be read as part of a program on animals, farms, or funny stories," or even for inventive dramatics. An earlier review by Lee Bock from that same journal declared that Van Laan's first book "provides an almost textbook example of what a good book for the very young can look like." Bock also drew attention to the rhythm and repetition of the tale and the bold colors employed for illustrations.

"Most of my picture books are full of rhythm and sometimes rhyme," Van Laan told *SATA.* "This is because each story is like music to me. Sometimes I hear a certain beat before I actually put words to it." Additionally, Van Laan's years of teaching came in handy when she turned to writing children's books. "I taught for many years, so I usually try to incorporate hidden lesson plans in many of my books for young children.... Books for young children should teach as well as entertain, I think."

More animal protagonists were featured in Van Laan's next three books, *Rainbow Crow, Possum Come A-Knockin',* and *A Mouse in My House.* These three books also set the tone for her future output: books of legend, folktales, and simple rhythm and rhyme. Her *Rainbow Crow* retells a Lenape Indian legend and was the result of a lifelong interest in Native-American folklore. She consulted with a Lenape elder for the book and gathered tales from many tribes. The result was "a fine read-aloud because of the smooth text and songs with repetitive chants," according to Kathleen Riley in *School Library Journal.* Rainbow Crow brings fire to the woodland creatures; his voice turns to a "caw" because of the smoke. Other woodland animals are also featured in this

Various trickster tales, African folktales, and Appalachian tall tales are brought together in Van Laan's compilation of Southern lore.

book that a contributor to *Kirkus Reviews* called "A good story for all ages."

Rhyming and animals are at the center of both *Possum Come A-Knockin'* and *A Mouse in My House,* as well. Possum, dressed in a top hat and vest, comes knocking at Granny's house, setting the house in a tizzy. "Practically begging to be read aloud, Van Laan's cumulative rhyme is a real toe-tapper," commented a reviewer for *Publishers Weekly,* while *Horn Book* contributor Elizabeth S. Watson dubbed the book a "raucous romp." With *A Mouse in My House,* Van Laan created the more traditional, cuddly-animal style of picture book, featuring a cookie-nibbling mouse and a rather greedy pig, among other animals. In this story, a little boy compares his own behavior to several such animals. The "text's rollicking rhythm, rhyme, and repetition will encourage young listeners to join in," remarked Danita Nichols writing in *School Library Journal.* Leone McDermott concluded in *Booklist* that "Bouncy rhymes are quick and fun to read aloud, and children will enjoy knowing that others share their difficulty with self-restraint."

With the success of these first titles, Van Laan was able to give up full-time teaching for full-time writing, but she had to allow for her own "undisciplined" work habits. "I do not sit down each day and write," she told

SATA. "In fact, I might stew for months about an idea before actually writing it down in a notebook. I always create my stories in longhand first, then, much later, transfer the final draft to computer. If I get what I think is a really good idea, then I work and work until it is finished. I write very quickly, so sometimes a story is finished in a few days. Not always, though. I once spent several months trying to think of how to write the last line of one tale, so it really depends on my muse, I suppose." One of her books, *In a Circle Long Ago,* took her three years to complete; another was written on the tablecloth in a restaurant where she was dining.

Van Laan's writing has followed the three directions set out in her earliest books: retellings of legends from Native American and other cultures, folktales, and contemporary stories that employ rhyme and rhythm to entice young listeners and readers. Van Laan recreated the Mayan legend of the Gold Man in her *The Legend of El Dorado,* a book that a contributor to *Booklist* found to be "moving." Blackfoot legend was mined for *Buffalo Dance,* the story of the capture of a buffalo for winter food. "The universal themes of courage, love, self-sacrifice, and loyalty are movingly conveyed," commented Carolyn Polese in *School Library Journal.* Maeve Visser Knoth, writing in *Horn Book,* called *Buffalo Dance* "a graceful and attractive retelling of a

In Van Laan's retelling of an Ojibwe Indian legend, a defiant duck holds out against Winter Maker by refusing to be cold during the bleak months. (Cover illustration by Betsy Bowen.)

Native-American myth." An Ojibwe legend was retold in *Shingebiss,* in which the eponymous duck defies Winter Maker and will not be cold during the bleak months. Janice M. Del Negro noted in *Bulletin of the Center for Children's Books* that Van Laan "communicates the irreverent joy of Shingebiss as he happily overcomes winter's cold." With *In a Circle Long Ago,* Van Laan collected native lore from across North America in twenty-five legends and poems. In another *Horn Book* review, Knoth dubbed the collection "a true smorgasbord" and noted that "readers will get a taste of the richness of Native-American folklore and will be tempted to search other books for a closer look at individual peoples." Wedding rituals of Mexico take center stage in Van Laan's *La Boda,* and the author has ranged as far afield as South America to gather other legends in her *The Magic Bean Tree,* from Argentina, and *So Say the Little Monkeys,* a Brazilian folktale that pokes fun at procrastinators.

Van Laan also employs folktales from closer to home to create focus for her rhythmic tales. Adapting a Scottish folktale for *The Tiny, Tiny Boy and the Big, Big Cow,* Van Laan told about the difficulties a little boy has trying to milk a large cow. Patricia Pearl Dole, writing in *School Library Journal,* called the book a "pleasing, culturally neutral romp," while *Horn Book* reviewer Knoth concluded that the "story begs to be shared aloud and will have children chanting" along with the text. Van Laan rummaged through the cultural history of her native South for various trickster tales, African folktales, and Appalachian tall tales for her compilation, *With a Whoop and a Holler,* a book that was, according to a *Publishers Weekly* reviewer, "presented ... in the kind of slide-off-the-tongue colloquialisms guaranteed to make a sure-fire storyteller of the most shrinking violets." A critic for *Kirkus Reviews* concurred, noting that the book "crackles with vernacular humor."

More cumulative rhyming and rhythmic fun is presented in Van Laan's books about everyday objects, faces, sleep time, and even ecology. For the latter, Van Laan created a recycling mother in *Round and Round Again* who is such an ardent recycler that she has built a house from other people's discarded objects. Lullabies come in *Sleep, Sleep, Sleep* and the world of a Haitian family is presented in *Mama Rocks, Papa Sings,* a story told partly in Creole. The adventures of a hat, blown away on a rainy day, are recounted in more cumulative rhyme in *This Is the Hat,* which *Booklist's* Jim Jaske called "clever" and a "fine book to use with preschoolers." A *Kirkus Reviews* contributor noted that *This Is the Hat* "tells another story with a rambunctious lilt."

Lilting rhymes and shoe-tapping rhythms are Van Laan's stock in trade, one that she was a long time in coming to, but one in which she is very much at home with now. "Today, writing is as much a part of me as going to sleep, waking up, singing laughing, dancing, talking, baking pies, listening to music, and taking long walks down country roads," Van Laan told *SATA.* "I could not imagine *not* writing. It would make me sad and grumpy if I was told never to do it again.... The nicest part of writing is that I can take it with me wherever I go. I can also continue to do it for as long as I would like. And, my goal is to do it for a long, long time!"

Works Cited

Review of *The Big Fat Worm, School Library Journal,* February, 1992, p. 41.

Bock, Lee, review of *The Big Fat Worm, School Library Journal,* December, 1987, p. 78.

Del Negro, Janice, M., review of *Shingebiss: An Ojibwe Legend, Bulletin of the Center for Children's Books,* September, 1997, p. 29.

Dole, Patricia Pearl, review of *The Tiny, Tiny Boy and the Big, Big Cow, School Library Journal,* September, 1993, p. 221.

Jaske, Jim, review of *This Is the Hat: A Story in Rhyme, Booklist,* November 15, 1992, p. 611.

Knoth, Maeve Visser, review of *Buffalo Dance: A Blackfoot Legend, Horn Book,* September-October, 1993, pp. 612-13.

Knoth, Maeve Visser, review of *In a Circle Long Ago: A Treasury of Native Lore from North America, Horn Book,* January-February, 1996, p. 84.

Knoth, Maeve Visser, review of *The Tiny, Tiny Boy and the Big, Big Cow, Horn Book,* May-June, 1993, pp. 325-26.

Review of *The Legend of El Dorado: A Latin American Tale, Booklist,* October 15, 1991, p. 378.

McDermott, Leone, review of *A Mouse in My House, Booklist,* October 1, 1990, p. 342.

Nichols, Danita, review of *A Mouse in My House, School Library Journal,* December, 1990, p. 89.

Polese, Carolyn, review of *Buffalo Dance: A Blackfoot Legend, School Library Journal,* September, 1993, p. 227.

Review of *Possum Come A-Knockin', Publishers Weekly,* March 30, 1990, p. 61.

Review of *Rainbow Crow: A Lenape Tale, Kirkus Reviews,* April 1, 1989, p. 555.

Riley, Kathleen, review of *Rainbow Crow: A Lenape Tale, School Library Journal,* July, 1989, p. 81.

Review of *This Is the Hat: A Story in Rhyme, Kirkus Reviews,* October, 1992, p. 1261.

Watson, Elizabeth S., review of *Possum Come A-Knockin', Horn Book,* July-August, 1990, pp. 448-49.

Review of *With a Whoop and a Holler: A Bushel of Lore from Way Down South, Kirkus Reviews,* January 15, 1998, pp. 119-20.

Review of *With a Whoop and a Holler: A Bushel of Lore from Way Down South, Publishers Weekly,* January 26, 1998, p. 92.

For More Information See

PERIODICALS

Booklist, October 1, 1994, p. 225; January 15, 1995, p. 940; November 15, 1995, p. 558; December 15, 1995, p. 718; October 1, 1997, p. 339; April, 1998, p. 1328.

Bulletin of the Center for Children's Books, February, 1995, p. 217; January, 1998, p. 103.

Horn Book, November-December, 1990, p. 734; November-December, 1995, p. 739; November-December, 1997, pp. 691-92.

Kirkus Reviews, March 15, 1993, p. 381; August 15, 1995, p. 1195; April 15, 1996, p. 608; January 15, 1998, p. 119.

Publishers Weekly, November 6, 1995, p. 93; January 5, 1998, p. 66; August 17, 1998, p. 70.

School Library Journal, July, 1990, pp. 64-65; October, 1992, p. 98; December, 1994, p. 103; May, 1996, p. 101; April, 1998, p. 111; June, 1998, p. 136; September, 1998, pp. 198-99.

—*Sketch by J. Sydney Jones*

*   *   *

VOGEL, Carole Garbuny 1951-

Personal

Born April 9, 1951, in Pittsburgh, PA; daughter of Max (a physicist) and Melitta (a math teacher) Garbuny; married Mark A. Vogel (an electrical engineer), June 17, 1973; children: Joshua, Kate. *Education:* Kenyon College, B.A., 1972; University of Pittsburgh, M.A.T., 1973. *Hobbies and other interests:* Hiking, camping, traveling.

Addresses

Office—P.O. Box 122, Bedford, MA 01730-0122. *Agent*—Tracey Adams, McIntosh & Otis, Inc., 353 Lexington Avenue, New York, NY 10016. *E-mail*—cvogel@World.std.com.

Carole Garbuny Vogel

Career

Writer, freelance science editor, public speaker, 1978—. Works extensively in the field of science education, developing trade books, textbooks, activities, and teacher's guides for grades 3-12. *Member:* Authors Guild, Society of Children's Book Writers and Illustrators, National League of American PEN Women, National Writers Union.

Awards, Honors

Outstanding Science Trade Book for Children, National Science Teachers Association, 1990, and Children's Choice, International Reading Association-Children's Book Council, 1991, for *The Great Yellowstone Fire,* written with Kathryn Allen Goldner; Anna Cross Giblin nonfiction Work-in-Progress grant, Society of Children's Book Writers and Illustrators, 1994, for *The Legends of Landforms: Native American Lore and the Geology of the Land;* Joan Fassler Memorial Book Award, Association for the Care of Children's Health, 1996, Honor Book in the science category, Society of School Librarians Book Award, 1996, and Outstanding Nonfiction for newly literate adults, PLA/ALLS Top Titles for Adult New Readers, Publishers Liaison Committee of PLA's Adult Lifelong Learning Section, 1996, all for *Will I Get Breast Cancer? Questions and Answers for Teenage Girls;* Book of Excellence, Children's Literature Choice List, 1997, for *Shock Waves through Los Angeles: The Northridge Earthquake; Horn Book* list of recommended books on natural disasters, 1997, for *Shock Waves through Los Angeles: The Northridge Earthquake* and *The Great Midwest Flood.*

Writings

NONFICTION

The Great Midwest Flood, Little, Brown, 1995.

Will I Get Breast Cancer: Questions and Answers for Teenage Girls, Silver Burdett, 1995.

Shock Waves through Los Angeles: The 1994 Northridge Earthquake, Little, Brown, 1996.

Inside Earth ("Science Explorer" series textbook for middle graders), Prentice Hall, 1999.

Legends of Landforms: Native American Lore and the Geology of the Land, Millbrook Press, 1999.

NONFICTION; WITH KATHRYN ALLEN GOLDNER

Why Mount St. Helens Blew Its Top, illustrated by Roberta Aggarwal, Dillon Press (Minneapolis, MN), 1981.

The Dangers of Strangers, illustrated by Lynette Schmidt, Dillon Press, 1983.

HBJ Science - Activity Workbooks for Levels 3-6, Harcourt, 1984.

Humphrey, the Wrong-Way Whale, Dillon Press, 1987.

The Great Yellowstone Fire, Sierra Club/Little, Brown, 1990.

CONTRIBUTOR

(With Kathryn Allen Goldner) *Hidden Worlds,* National Geographic Society, 1981.

(With Goldner) *3-2-1 Contact Activity Book,* Silver Burdett, 1983.

(With Goldner) *Facts on File Scientific Yearbook 1985,* Facts on File, 1985.

(With Goldner) *The New Golden Book Encyclopedia,* Macmillan, 1988.

Earth Explorer, Sonic Images, 1995.

(With Goldner) *Invitations to Literacy: Level 4,* Houghton Mifflin, 1996.

Newfangled Fairy Tales, Meadowbrook Press (Minnetonka, MN), 1997.

A 2nd Chicken Soup for the Woman's Soul, Health Communications, 1998.

OTHER

(Editor) *We Shall Not Forget! Memories of the Holocaust,* Temple Isaiah (Lexington, MA), 1994.

Contributor to periodicals, including *Working Mother, 3-2-1 Contact, Good Housekeeping, Ladies' Home Journal,* and *The Writer.*

Sidelights

Carole Garbuny Vogel is fascinated by science, and she shares her enthusiasm with young readers in many works of nonfiction, including the well-received *Shock Waves through Los Angeles: The 1994 Northridge Earthquake* and *The Great Midwest Flood.* "My friends and colleagues have dubbed me the 'Queen of Natural Disasters,'" Vogel explained to *SATA.* "I hardly look the part but it certainly describes my passion for writing about Mother Nature's wrath. Volcanoes, hurricanes, tornadoes, and other natural disasters have always fascinated me." Vogel's books have been praised by reviewers for describing events in terms that children can comprehend, while also adding terms and explanations that help to increase their knowledge and interest in the field of science.

Vogel recalls one childhood occurrence in particular: an unusually violent thunderstorm that took place when she was about two years old. "My older sister and I watched the lightning display from my parents' bedroom window while my father tried to soothe us with scientific explanations," the author recalled to *SATA.* "I didn't understand a word, but I knew I needn't be afraid." In school, a lesson about the volcanic eruption that buried the ancient city of Pompeii further fueled Vogel's interest in the power of nature: "I was fascinated by the images of people frozen in motion by Vesuvius's fury. From that point on I was hooked."

Written as an outgrowth of this childhood interest, Vogel's books have included discussions of the eruption of Washington State's Mount St. Helens in 1980, the Yellowstone fire of 1988, the Midwest flood of 1993, and the Northridge, California earthquake of 1994. "I don't experience first-hand the disasters I write about," Vogel assured her readers. "Instead, I pore over newspaper clippings, magazine articles, and videotapes. I surf the web, and conduct extensive telephone interviews with eyewitnesses, scientists, and other experts. My

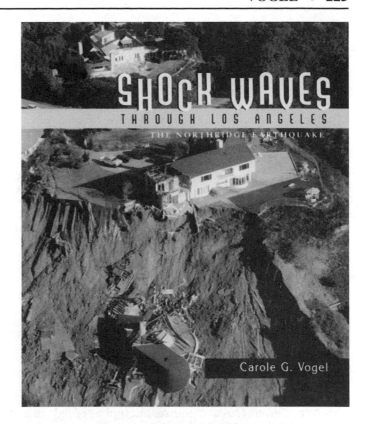

In her account, illustrated with photographs, maps, and diagrams, Vogel describes the cause and impact of the 1994 Los Angeles quake. (Cover photo by Al Seib.)

telephone bills are humongous. However, I do need to feel the impact of nature's wrath emotionally. My writing contains strong action verbs, and getting into the subject helps me get into the spirit."

In 1980, near the beginning of her writing career, Vogel teamed with Kathryn Allen Goldner, a science editor, to create a number of books and essays. Their partnership, which lasted nine years, enabled both women to establish viable writing careers and still have time to devote to their families. Among their most notable co-written efforts are *The Great Yellowstone Fire, Why Mount St. Helens Blew Its Top, Humphrey the Wrong-Way Whale,* and *The Dangers of Strangers.*

In *The Great Yellowstone Fire,* Vogel and Goldner explain the events surrounding the huge blaze that destroyed much of Yellowstone National Park in 1988. Not only the fire, but the forestry policies that contributed to its severity and its impact on area wildlife are discussed in descriptive text that "vividly conveys events and their significance as history," according to *Horn Book* reviewer Margaret A. Bush. A *Kirkus Reviews* critic proclaimed *The Great Yellowstone Fire* "well organized, gracefully written, and beautifully produced," and an *Appraisal* contributor declared the book a "model of good science writing."

In *The Great Midwest Flood,* the deluge that laid waste to many Midwestern states in 1993 is played out for young readers. Beginning with the history of the

Mississippi River that bursts its banks, Vogel goes on to explain the mechanisms created to control river flow, as well as the costs of the flood cleanup, in both human misery and money. Calling Vogel's analysis of the causes and effects of the 1993 disaster "insightful and well founded," *School Library Journal* contributor Charlyn Lyons dubbed *The Great Midwest Flood* "clear and concise," while in *Appraisal,* reviewer Ellen Rappaport maintained that the book contains "scientific, historical, and human interest [elements that] involve the reader in the power of nature to transform the environment."

Shock Waves through Los Angeles: The Northridge Earthquake describes the cause and impact of the 1994 Los Angeles quake that destroyed 112,000 buildings and caused the deaths of fifty-eight people. In reporting the earthquake and its aftermath, Vogel concentrates on "acts of heroism and the tragedies that followed the natural disaster," according to *School Library Journal* contributor Anne Connor, who praised Vogel for her "clear prose" and her avoidance of sensationalism. The inclusion of full-color photographs and maps provide young readers the opportunity to "see for themselves" what happened during the quake, "without the inclusion of any grisly images," in the opinion of *Booklist* reviewer Susan Dove Lempke. Lempke added that Vogel "adeptly walks the line between scientific information and the irresistible fascination with disasters ... and she puts it all at child level."

In one of her more recent efforts, *The Legends of Landforms: Native American Lore and the Geology of the Land,* Vogel describes the exploits of fearsome dragons, bloodthirsty serpents, mighty giants, and other spirit beings that Native Americans of long ago attributed to the creation of spectacular landforms, such as the Grand Canyon and Niagara Falls. Juxtaposed with the legends is the dynamic scientific explanation of the earth-shaping forces responsible for the formations. Stories of colliding continents, simmering volcanoes, earth-rattling quakes, and colossal floods take their place within the context of earth-building and earth-demolishing forces. Together, the legends and science contribute to a well-rounded and thought-provoking examination of landforms.

In contrast to much of her writing, which features natural disasters, Vogel's most personal work is *Will I Get Breast Cancer? Questions and Answers for Teenage Girls.* The book was written in memory of Vogel's best friend, who died of the disease while in her early thirties. "I wanted to show my friend's daughter that her mother's fate did not have to be her own," Vogel explained. Using a question-and-answer-approach, Vogel imparts up-to-date information on a topic of concern for many young women. *Will I Get Breast Cancer?* drew

praise from *Booklist* commentator Stephanie Zvirin, who called it "a fine book on the subject ... that not only always keeps its teenage audience in mind, but also presents the facts without patronizing or pretending."

When choosing a subject to write about Vogel always keeps her readers in mind. "Kids don't think of my books as science books even though my writing is laced with scientific explanations. I feel a great obligation to make my text as accurate as possible, so I always have a series of experts review my manuscripts," she said. Now that her children are nearly grown, Vogel keeps in touch with her readers by giving author presentations in schools and libraries. Her next book, to be published by Scholastic, will offer eyewitness accounts of some of America's worst natural disasters, such as the 1900 Galveston Hurricane, the 1925 Tri-State Tornado, and the 1964 Alaskan Earthquake.

The subject of Vogel's next book? "Just watch the headlines," replied the author.

Works Cited

Bush, Margaret A., review of *The Great Yellowstone Fire, Horn Book,* May-June, 1990, p. 351.

Connor, Anne, review of *Shock Waves through Los Angeles: The Northridge Earthquake, School Library Journal,* October, 1996, p. 119.

Review of *The Great Yellowstone Fire, Appraisal,* winter, 1991, p. 55.

Review of *The Great Yellowstone Fire, Kirkus Reviews,* May 15, 1990, p. 735.

Lempke, Susan Dove, review of *Shock Waves through Los Angeles: The Northridge Earthquake, Booklist,* October 1, 1996, p. 346.

Lyons, Charlyn, review of *The Great Midwest Flood, School Library Journal,* January, 1996, pp. 126-27.

Rappaport, Ellen, review of *The Great Midwest Flood, Appraisal,* summer, 1996, p. 38.

Zvirin, Stephanie, review of *Will I Get Breast Cancer? Questions and Answers for Teenage Girls, Booklist,* August, 1995, p. 1940.

For More Information See

PERIODICALS

Booklist, March 1, 1990, p. 1340; December 15, 1995, p. 702.

Bulletin of the Center for Children's Books, April, 1984, p. 157; December, 1995, pp. 143-44.

Publishers Weekly, November 25, 1983, p. 65; October 7, 1996, p. 78.

School Library Journal, January, 1984, p. 69; October, 1987, pp. 132-33; July, 1995, p. 103.

W

WALLACE, John 1966-

Personal

Born August 23, 1966, in Felixstowe, England; son of Graham (a teacher) and Iris (a nurse; maiden name, Ward) Wallace; married Sarah Beattie (a lawyer), August 29, 1991; children: William John, Samuel Robert. *Education:* St. Catharine's College, Cambridge, degree in religious studies. *Religion:* Church of England. *Hobbies and other interests:* "I love my work, so the division between work and play is not always clear. In particular, I enjoy going out into the country and painting water colours. I also go to galleries and exhibitions whenever I have the chance. I play football (soccer) on a mixed team. At home I share in the hobbies and enjoyments of our two boys. My other real love is the garden—always a good place to escape to. We have about half an acre of derelict market garden, upon which we engage in battle with the nettles and brambles."

Addresses

Home—11 to 13 De Montfort Rd., Brighton BN1 4HN, United Kingdom. *Office*—The Annexe, Belmont St., Brighton BN1 4HN, United Kingdom.

Career

Writer and illustrator.

Writings

SELF-ILLUSTRATED; FOR CHILDREN

Little Bean, Collins (London, England), 1996.
Little Bean's Friend, Collins, 1996; HarperFestival, 1997.
Little Bean's Holiday, Collins, 1997.
Building a House with Mr. Bumble, Walker (London, England), 1997.
Dressing up with Mr. Bumble, Walker, 1997.
The Twins, Collins, 1998.

ILLUSTRATOR; FOR CHILDREN

Lois Rock, *Little Chick's Easter Surprise,* Lion (Oxford, England), 1997.
John Foster, *Bouncing Ben* (poetry), Oxford University Press, 1998.
John Foster, *Doctor Proctor,* (poetry), Oxford University Press, 1998.

Sidelights

John Wallace told *SATA,* "I write and illustrate books for pre-school children. What motivates me is producing work that children will find fun. I don't believe we can

John Wallace

In Wallace's second self-illustrated picture book about Little Bean, the spunky pigtailed girl meets her next-door neighbor and experiences the joy of friendship. (From Little Bean's Friend.*)*

ever match a child's imagination. We can only hope to fuel it."

Fueling imaginations of children in England and the United States is Little Bean, the title character of three books by Wallace, including *Little Bean's Friend*. In this, the second of Little Bean's adventures, the spunky pigtailed girl meets her next-door neighbor. The story begins with Little Bean happily playing with pots, pans, and other banging things, when her father suggests she take her exuberant play out into the garden. Outside, Little Bean and her dog Bouncer get a bit carried away with their fun, sending Little Bean's favorite bear sailing over the garden wall. The neighbor brings her son Paul over to return the bear, and Little Bean's father invites Paul to play. Playing together, Little Bean and Nice Paul have double the fun that Little Bean had experienced playing by herself. Claiming the book is "sure to win hearts," *Booklist* critic GraceAnne A. DeCandido found "Little Bean's roundheaded, pigtailed charm [and] the

freshness of the watercolors ... warm and inviting." Also recognizing the character as endearing, a *Junior Bookshelf* critic wrote that Little Bean, "easily recognisable [in her] unusual plaits," could potentially "establish herself as an enduring picture book character." In *Horn Book,* reviewer Martha V. Parravano, praised Wallace's ability "to capture, seemingly effortlessly, the essence of being a toddler."

Works Cited

DeCandido, GraceAnne A., review of *Little Bean's Friend, Booklist,* June 1, 1997, p. 1723.

Review of *Little Bean's Friend, Junior Bookshelf,* December, 1996, p. 243.

Parravano, Martha V., review of *Little Bean's Friend, Horn Book,* September-October, 1997, p. 566.

For More Information See

PERIODICALS

Kirkus Reviews, January 1, 1997, pp. 66-67.
Times Educational Supplement, March 21, 1997, p. 9; March 28, 1997, p. 11.

* * *

WESTERDUIN, Anne 1945-

Personal

Born September 19, 1945; daughter of Cor and Ansele (Vanryckeshem) Westerduin; married Luc Tas (an engineer), May 7, 1969; children: Sander, Jasper, Wouter. *Education:* Attended Bruges art school.

Addresses

Office—Abdijstraat, 105 B-1050, Brussels, Belgium.

Awards, Honors

First Prize for illustrations, Boekenpauw, 1996.

The other barnyard animals join mother duck and her ducklings in their efforts to bring about rain for swimming. (From Ducks Like to Swim, *written by Agnes Verboven and illustrated by Anne Westerduin.)*

Writings

FOR CHILDREN

A Cookie for Blekkie, Clavis (Belguim), 1995.
(Illustrator) Agnes Verboven, *Ducks Like to Swim,* Clavis, 1997, translated by Dominic Barth, Orchard Books (New York), 1997.
The Pencil Princess, Clavis, 1998.
Peter's Little Secret, Clavis, 1998.
The Candy-Box, Clavis, 1999.

Also contributor to reading and educational books for children, ages eight to twelve.

Sidelights

Flemish artist Anne Westerduin makes her American debut as an illustrator of children's picture books with *Ducks Like to Swim,* written by Agnes Verboven. In this story, a mother and her baby ducks would like to swim but there is no water to accommodate them. Mother begins quacking for rain and her barnyard friends join her with rounds of barks and cock-a-doodle-doos. Their noisy efforts are rewarded with rain and the ducks happily swim away. Susan M. Moore, writing in *School Library Journal,* found Westerduin's illustrations "rich with color." Writing in *Booklist,* reviewer Julie Corsaro described Westerduin's "big colorful paintings" as "show-stealing pictures" and recommended the picture book for "lap-sitting story times."

Works Cited

Corsaro, Julie, review of *Ducks Like to Swim, Booklist,* September 1, 1997, p. 136.
Moore, Susan M., review of *Ducks Like to Swim, School Library Journal,* September, 1997, pp. 197-98.*

* * *

WIDENER, Terry 1950-

Personal

Born December 15, 1950 in Tulsa, OK; son of Floyd Widener and Jean Hutchinson Edwards; married Leslie Stall (an art director), October 1, 1977; children: Kate, Kellee, Michael. *Education:* University of Tulsa, B.F.A., 1974. *Hobbies and other interests:* Golf, soccer (coaching), and travel.

Addresses

Home and Office—808 Cedar St., McKinney, TX 75069. *Agent*—Michele Manasse, 200 Aquetong Rd, New Hope, PA.

Career

Phillips Knight Walsh, Inc., Tulsa, OK, designer, 1975-79; Richards, Sullivan, Brock & Associates, Dallas, TX, designer, 1980-81; Terry Widener Studio, McKinney, TX, illustrator, 1981—. Texas A & M University at

Widener's solid and expressive paintings for David A. Adler's **Lou Gehrig: The Luckiest Man** *complement the story of the indomitable baseball player, his outstanding career, and the tragedy of his fatal illness.*

Terry Widener

Commerce, adjunct professor. *Exhibitions:* Artwork has been exhibited at the Galerie St. Michel, Lambertville, NJ, at the permanent collection of Harvard University, and in New York Society of Illustrators Travelling Exhibitions to Japan and to various universities across the United States. *Member:* Society of Children's Book Writers and Illustrators.

Awards, Honors

Honor Book, *Boston Globe-Horn Book,* Golden Kite Award Finalist, Notable Book, American Library Association, 100 Titles for Reading and Sharing, New York Public Library, Best Books, San Francisco *Chronicle,* and New York Society of Illustrators Original Art Show, all 1997, all for *Lou Gehrig: The Luckiest Man.*

Illustrator

FOR CHILDREN

David A. Adler, *Lou Gehrig: The Luckiest Man,* Harcourt Brace, 1997.
David A. Adler, *The Babe and I,* Harcourt Brace, 1999.
Joy Jones, *Tambourine Moon,* Simon & Schuster, 1999.

Work in Progress

Illustrations for *Peg and the Whale,* by Kenneth Oppel, for Simon & Schuster, and for *Trudy,* by David A. Adler, for Harcourt Brace.

Sidelights

Terry Widener told *SATA:* "Early in my career I almost always included illustration in my graphic design work, so my decision to become an illustrator was easy.

"Although I have been an illustrator since 1981, my first picture book didn't happen until 1995. When I'm in the children's section of book stores I notice that more and more of my contemporaries are also illustrating picture books. Just a few years ago this wasn't happening— most books were illustrated by artists who specialized in picture books. But, more artists means a greater variety of styles can now be found in picture books. This makes books more exciting for children.

"When I illustrate, my hope is to create a beautiful book. My part of the book is to make the author's words come alive visually. My aim is to show the emotions and events that authors write about in their stories. Artists N. C. Wyeth and Paul Davis have been my most important influences. Over all, my primary goal is to provide fun and exciting entertainment for children. The best advice I can give to young illustrators is to be patient. It's very hard to wait, but I have found that if you work towards your goal, things seem to happen."

Illustrated by Terry Widener, *Lou Gehrig: The Luckiest Man,* written by David A. Adler, recalls Gehrig's childhood and successful career in baseball. Portrayed as a genuine hero on and off the field, the talented athlete left college early to help his family financially by playing ball for the New York Yankees. He brought to the game of baseball a disciplined behavior from his early school days, playing 2,130 consecutive games—a perfect attendance record for fourteen seasons. A critic in *Publishers Weekly* called Widener's illustrations "memorable paintings ... [which] vividly recreate the look and feel of major league baseball in the '20s and '30s." *School Library Journal* contributor Tom S. Hurlburt asserted: "Widener's acrylic paintings sweep across the pages, melding comfortably with Adler's spare writing style while adeptly portraying Gehrig and the era." Ilene Cooper of *Booklist* praised Widener's "impressive" art, and noted that "the last spread, showing Yankee Stadium on the day of Gehrig's funeral, awash in rain, provides a silent but powerful ending to Gehrig's story."

Works Cited

Cooper, Ilene, review of *Lou Gehrig: The Luckiest Man, Booklist,* May 15, 1997, p. 1575.
Hurlburt, Tom S., review of *Lou Gehrig: The Luckiest Man, School Library Journal,* May, 1997, p. 118.
Review of *Lou Gehrig: The Luckiest Man, Publishers Weekly,* February 24, 1997, p. 91.

For More Information See

PERIODICALS

Horn Book, July-August, 1997, pp. 471-72.
Instructor, October, 1997, p. 24.
Kirkus Reviews, February 1, 1997.

Cumulative Indexes

Illustrations Index

(In the following index, the number of the *volume* in which an illustrator's work appears is given *before* the colon, and the *page number* on which it appears is given *after* the colon. For example, a drawing by Adams, Adrienne appears in Volume 2 on page 6, another drawing by her appears in Volume 3 on page 80, another drawing in Volume 8 on page 1, and so on and so on....)

YABC

Index references to *YABC* refer to listings appearing in the two-volume *Yesterday's Authors of Books for Children,* also published by The Gale Group. *YABC* covers prominent authors and illustrators who died prior to 1960.

Illustrations Index

Illustrations Index

Author Index

The following index gives the number of the volume in which an author's biographical sketch, Autobiography Feature, Brief Entry, or Obituary appears.

This index includes references to all entries in the following series, which are also published by Gale Research Inc.

YABC—*Yesterday's Authors of Books for Children: Facts and Pictures about Authors and Illustrators of Books for Young People from Early Times to 1960*

CLR—*Children's Literature Review: Excerpts from Reviews, Criticism, and Commentary on Books for Children*

SAAS—*Something about the Author Autobiography Series*

C

Author Index

Author Index